THE ARTFUL DICKENS

THE ARTFUL DICKENS

DICKENS

Tricks and Ploys of the
Great Novelist

JOHN MULLAN

BLOOMSBURY PUBLISHING
LONDON · OXFORD · NEW YORK · NEW DELHI · SYDNEY

BLOOMSBURY PUBLISHING
Bloomsbury Publishing Plc
50 Bedford Square, London, WC1B 3DP, UK

BLOOMSBURY, BLOOMSBURY PUBLISHING and the Diana logo are
trademarks of Bloomsbury Publishing Plc

First published in Great Britain 2020

A catalogue record for this book is available from the British Library

ISBN: HB: 978-1-4088-6681-8; EBOOK: 978-1-4088-6683-2

4 6 8 10 9 7 5 3

Typeset by Newgen Knowledgeworks Pvt. Ltd., Chennai, India
Printed and bound in Great Britain by CPI Group (UK) Ltd, Croydon CR0 4YY

For John Sutherland

Contents

A Note on References ix

1 Introduction 1
2 Fantasising 15
3 Smelling 41
4 Changing tenses 71
5 Haunting 95
6 Laughing 127
7 Naming 155
8 Using coincidences 189
9 Enjoying clichés 217
10 Speaking 245
11 Foreseeing 281
12 Drowning 309
13 Knowing about sex 337
14 Breaking the rules 363

Acknowledgements 393
Notes 395
Bibliography 412
Index 421

A Note on References

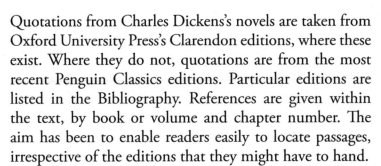

Quotations from Charles Dickens's novels are taken from Oxford University Press's Clarendon editions, where these exist. Where they do not, quotations are from the most recent Penguin Classics editions. Particular editions are listed in the Bibliography. References are given within the text, by book or volume and chapter number. The aim has been to enable readers easily to locate passages, irrespective of the editions that they might have to hand.

Quotations from Dickens's journalism are, where possible, taken from *The Dent Uniform Edition of Dickens' Journalism*, ed. Michael Slater and John Drew, 4 vols (London: J. M. Dent, 1994–2000), abbreviated to *Dickens' Journalism* in the notes.

Quotations from Dickens's letters are taken from *The Letters of Charles Dickens*, ed. Madeline House, Graham Storey, et al., 12 vols. (Oxford: Clarendon Press, 1965–2002), abbreviated to *Letters* in the notes.

Quotations from Forster's *Life* of Dickens, first published 1872–4, are taken from John Forster, *The Life of Charles Dickens*, ed. A. J. Hoppé, 2 vols (London: J. M. Dent, 1966) abbreviated to 'Forster' in the notes.

I

Introduction

... such conjurings ... never took place in these parts before
Letter to C. C. Felton, 2 January 1844[1]

What is so good about Dickens's novels? This book tries to answer that question, oddly evaded by many who have written about him. While it is common to hear Dickens called 'our greatest novelist', it is easy to find even those who acknowledge his status telling us what is bad about his novels. They are sentimental, melodramatic, sermonising. His characters are grotesque, or monstrous, or two-dimensional. And it has been like this since his own lifetime. Nobody could gainsay his popularity, but this meant that he was a great entertainer rather than a great writer. The author satirised as 'Mr Popular Sentiment' in Anthony Trollope's 1855 novel *The Warden* was 'a very powerful man' because of this popularity.[2] Trollope went on to observe, 'The artist who paints for the million must use glaring colours'.[3] Mass appeal was only achieved by simplification. Contemporaries were always wondering at Dickens's mass appeal, often as a prelude to regretting some deficiency of his newest work. G. H. Lewes, writing just after Dickens's death, declared that 'there probably never was a writer of so vast a popularity who was so little *appreciated* by the critics.'[4]

With Dickens, supposed faults can often be virtues. Take one small example from *Great Expectations*. It is Pip's second visit to Miss Havisham's gloomy home, Satis House, and his first encounter with her relations, the Pockets, who haunt the place in the hope of securing an inheritance.

> There were three ladies in the room and one gentleman. Before I had been standing at the window five minutes, they somehow conveyed to me that they were all toadies and humbugs, but that each of them pretended not to know that the others were toadies and humbugs: because the admission that he or she did know it, would have made him or her out to be a toady and humbug.
>
> (Ch. XI)

Many are the protests against the supposed shallowness of Dickens's characterisations, his pleasure in summing a person up in a sentence or two. Yet sometimes this readiness immediately to appraise a character is just what is truthful. Pip is about eight years old at the time remembered, and the narration recaptures his childish perceptiveness. The certainty of his judgement is there in the repetition of that irreverent phrase 'toadies and humbugs'. It serves these people right, that the child sees through them. (It soon becomes clear that, while the Pockets behave obsequiously to the rich old woman, they are entirely self-interested and predatory.) The repetition sounds ludicrous and it is: each of these hangers-on is trapped in an absurd deception that fools no one, but must be kept up.

The passage is based on a set-up that Dickens had recorded in the notebook of 'Memoranda', where, from January 1855 until the late 1860s, he jotted down ideas for future novels. Here, perhaps only a few months before he began *Great Expectations*, he had written,

> The House-full of Toadies and Humbugs. They all know and despise one another; but—partly to keep their hands in, and partly to make out their own individual cases—pretend not to detect one another.[5]

When he raided this, Dickens characteristically seized on the colloquial insult – 'Toadies and Humbugs' – that he had used in his note to himself. A more refined novelist would not pass judgement so readily (these characters have not even spoken yet) or use three times in a row such an idiomatic slur, but Dickens's unpolite English brilliantly gets the clarity of a child's perception. 'They somehow conveyed to me' is audaciously convincing: the requirement for a novelist to provide some grounds for his psychological judgement is waved away. Somehow, Pip immediately *knew* what these people were like, the way a child sometimes does. The passage exemplifies Dickens's special mix of unliterariness and formal daring. This book tries to do justice to those qualities, sometimes unappreciated by critics even when relished by readers. Dickens's very popularity seems to have made it hard to recognise his technical boldness and his experimental verve. It is strange that it needs saying, but our enjoyment of Dickens does not come despite our better judgement, but because of his extraordinary skills as a novelist.

He was always trying something new. As one of the best, because most appreciative, critics of Dickens has put it, 'every novel was an experiment in form, every sentence an exploration into what it meant to write as himself.'[6] 'Exploration' in a special way, because every single one of his novels was written for serialisation: not written and then divided into serialised parts, like earlier serialised novels, but composed with the monthly or weekly template already in the novelist's (and therefore the eventual reader's) mind. With *Pickwick Papers*, Dickens more or less invented the novel of monthly parts. Later, as the 'conductor' of the weekly magazines *Household Words* and *All the Year Round*, he fed the public appetite for weekly serial narratives. Out of commercial necessity he made new creative opportunities. His novels had to live in the imaginations of his readers over long periods, varying from just over four months for *Hard Times*, the shortest of his weekly serialisations, to more than a year and a half for each of his eight novels originally published in twenty monthly parts. An anxious monitor of the sales figures for succeeding instalments of each novel, Dickens was always feeling for the public's responses. This sensitivity produced extraordinary results. It is now not difficult to believe that *Pickwick Papers* and *The Old Curiosity Shop* were bestsellers; it is harder to stretch to the fact that *Bleak House* was too.[7] Dickens's commercial success allowed him to evolve increasingly complex and formally ambitious fiction. His publishers could hardly object. For him, popularity and literary ambition were twinned. 'Complexity was a luxury earlier success had entitled him to.'[8]

Dickens had a minimal education: aged about nine, he spent perhaps a year at a small school in Chatham run by William Giles, a Baptist minister; from the age of thirteen, he was granted two years at Wellington House Academy, run by William Jones, 'by far the most ignorant man I have ever had the pleasure to know'.[9] There are some memorably terrible schools and teachers in Dickens's novels. Supposedly educated men and women are often shown up in his fiction. In *Great Expectations*, Mr Pocket, father of Pip's friend Herbert, has been to Harrow and Cambridge, but this has given him an air of bewilderment and the qualifications merely to follow 'the calling of a Grinder' (Ch. XXV). That is to say, he is doomed to be a private tutor, cramming students for exams. Those indolent young gentlemen in the novels (James Harthouse, Sydney Carton, Eugene Wrayburn) have had a good education, and look what it has done for them! Like one of his alter egos, David Copperfield, Dickens was a self-made man of literature. Lewes recalled being shocked when he visited the young author in Doughty Street and saw that his book collection consisted entirely of three-volume novels and books of travels, all of them, he believed, presentation copies from authors or publishers.

Yet Dickens had always been a hungry reader. While he might have ignored literary decorum, his novels are densely allusive. They are saturated in Shakespeare, for one thing.[10] From a young age, he appears to have known lengthy passages of Shakespeare off by heart and many witnesses testify to his ability exactly to recall appropriate lines of Shakespeare on the spur of any moment.[11] It is true that the novelist whose most memorable Shakespearean performer is the sublimely incompetent Mr Wopsle does often like his Shakespeare allusions to be incongruous, but in Dickens's hands incongruity can be a complex literary affect. In *David Copperfield*, Mr Micawber, reading from his letter explaining how he was drawn into Uriah Heep's machinations, cannot resist flourishing a line from *Macbeth*.

> 'Then it was that – HEEP – began to favour me with just so much of his confidence, as was necessary to the discharge of his infernal business. Then it was that I began, if I may so Shakespearianly express myself, to dwindle, peak, and pine.'
>
> (Ch. LII)

'Shakespearianly': it is a word that Mr Micawber audibly enjoys coining. The *Oxford English Dictionary* records the earliest use of *Shakespearianly* as being in a review article of 1861, some eleven years later than Mr Micawber's neologism. He takes 'dwindle, peak, and pine' from the First Witch, who is describing the fate of a sailor whom she curses. The quote is wittily appropriate (Mr Micawber must have been bewitched to fall for the schemes of 'HEEP') and comically superfluous. With his Shakepearian flourish, Mr Micawber, a character whose love of words was inspired by Dickens's father, John Dickens, rises above Heep's low designs.

It is telling that, Shakespeare apart, the English literary work to which Dickens refers most often is Daniel Defoe's *Robinson Crusoe*, a novel that, in the mid-nineteenth century, was on the dubious border between literature and popular entertainment.[12] It is one of the books that, under the grim Murdstone regime, saves the young David Copperfield from despair, keeping alive 'my fancy, and my hope of something beyond that place and time' (Ch. IV).

In *Hard Times*, the inhabitants of Coketown who use the Library 'took De Foe to their bosoms', much to Mr Gradgrind's dismay (I Ch. VIII). When Scrooge is returned to his childhood by the Ghost of Christmas Past in *A Christmas Carol*, he sees the fictions that he once loved come to life.

> 'There's the Parrot!' cried Scrooge. 'Green body and yellow tail, with a thing like a lettuce growing out of the top of his head; there he is! Poor Robin Crusoe, he called him, when he came home again after sailing round the island. "Poor Robin Crusoe, where have you been, Robin Crusoe?"'
>
> (Stave II)

The sour old miser briefly recaptures the life of imagination that he had as a boy. Along with the fables and fairy tales of childhood, *Robinson Crusoe* was the work that ignited it. Dickens's Uncommercial Traveller, the narrator of a series of articles in *All the Year Round* that were based on the author's own experiences, thinks of those places of the imagination that it is 'agreeable to revisit when I am in an idle mood ... I never was in Robinson Crusoe's island, yet I frequently return there'.[13] He goes on to give a close description of what he finds when, in his daydreams, he revisits. Crusoe's island was a place that Dickens never forgot.

He fancied himself the Robinson Crusoe of English letters, triumphing by dint of his resourcefulness with only the materials he found to hand. He always liked to emphasise his self-sufficiency. In a speech at a dinner in his honour before he left for America in October 1867, he spoke feelingly of treading the path of a writing career as a young man 'without influence, without money, without

companion, introducer, or adviser'.[14] He had benefited
from an unconventional kind of tuition. In his early work
as a journalist and parliamentary reporter, he learned to
write at speed for a specified space. His had been a life
of copious scribbling and endless deadlines. So it would
continue to be, when he became the most famous writer
in the English-speaking world. His early working life
helped make him speedy and improvisational, but along
with the speed and improvisation there were qualities that
rarely get sufficiently valued, or even noticed. These were
qualities of formal ingenuity.

As the title of this book suggests, Dickens's artfulness is
often an almost impudent trickery. We might remember
Oliver Twist watching and laughing in delight at the 'very
curious and uncommon game' played after breakfast in
their lodgings by Fagin, the Dodger and Charley Bates (Ch.
IX). 'The merry old gentleman', kitted out with valuables,
pretends to be an elderly window shopper, while the two
young thieves, variously distracting him, practise relieving
him of his possessions 'with the most extraordinary
rapidity'. They are honing their criminal techniques, of
course, but Oliver notices only the gusto and deftness of
the performance. Oliver's innocence allows Fagin to be
seen, briefly, as a resourceful entertainer, while the Artful
Dodger comes alive through his sleights of hand and
sleights of language. Dickens always admired a resourceful
performer. It is not surprising to find that, in his thirties,
he himself became an accomplished amateur conjuror.[15] In
the early 1840s, inspired by popular magicians of the day,
he purchased elaborate props and developed a conjuring
routine for children's parties. His tricks, which included
putting the raw ingredients for a plum pudding into a
top hat and then producing a steaming pudding out of

it, were performed for adults too: Jane Carlyle called him
'the best conjurer I ever saw – (and I have paid money
to see several)'.[16] Dickens came to pride himself on what
he called his 'feats of legerdemain', a self-description that
might equally well apply to his writing. Ingenuity was a
performance. What some have thought his carelessness is
often his technical audacity, his gift for trying things out,
his willingness to take risks unimagined by other novelists.

You can see it in the extraordinary original manuscripts
of his novels. Spend any time poring over these in the
lofty reading room of the V&A's National Art Gallery,
where most of them are held, and you will gain a strong
impression of Dickens's peculiar blend of improvisational
rapidity and stylistic scruple. Harry Stone, whose
wonderful edition of *Dickens' Working Notes for His Novels*
is a trove for any Dickens critic, accurately describes
'their bewildering tangles of additions, cancellations, and
rewritings', which are the 'tessellated, in-progress record'
of Dickens's creative rigour.[17] Almost always, the novelist's
first thoughts set the pattern for the sentence, which is
then corrected and supplemented. Words and phrases
are heavily crossed out, and new words and phrases are
written in above the line. It is often hard to read even the
finished sentences, but Dickens has made sure that it is
usually impossible to see the words and phrases that he
has excised. His deletions, as Helen Small puts it well,
take the form of 'overwriting in close circling patterns,
rather like old-fashioned telephone cable, rather than a
single strikethrough that would permit the underlying
text to be detected'.[18] It almost seems that Dickens wanted
to blot out his earlier thoughts even from himself.

Certainly he wanted to blot out any rejected wordings
from the gaze of the compositor in the printshop.

Remarkably, the first draft, with all its tiny inky alterations, was what went to the printer. Dickens often had to write fast because he was keeping up with the demands of monthly or weekly serialisation. Yet even when he was beginning a new novel and had time to spare, his habits of composition and correction were the same. Now and then he directed the printers to look at the back of a sheet, where he had added sentences that needed to be interpolated. Very occasionally he appears to have made a fair copy of a page that had, presumably, been so heavily corrected as to be indecipherable, but essentially the compositors at his printers had to work from his first drafts.[19] He never employed a copyist. 'Never make a fair copy of a much-corrected manuscript,' he told Marcus Stone, the illustrator of *Our Mutual Friend*. A clearly written manuscript with few or no corrections 'is always given to the boy beginner to set up, and you will get a proof full of errors'.[20] However, a manuscript that is 'difficult to decipher' (as the pages of Dickens's novels certainly were) 'is put into the hands of a first rate compositor whose proof will give very little trouble'. The manuscripts may have presented, as his son Charley put it, 'all kinds of traps for compositors', but that was how he wanted it.[21] Late in his career, in a speech to the Printers' Pension Society, he paid a public tribute to compositors, based on his own experience.[22] 'For quickness of perception, amount of endurance, and willingness to oblige, I have ever found the compositor pre-eminent'.[23] Anyone working through his manuscript pages would have to agree.

It is tantalising that we are only rarely able to make out the wordings that Dickens has rejected, for it is hard to think of any other literary manuscripts where the activity of invention is so dynamically visible.[24] You can see just how he writes. He composes on the wings of inspiration, yet meticulously adjusts his diction and phrasing. Occasionally, the first words of a sentence are excised, indicating a false start, but very rarely is a whole sentence erased. Sometimes he might go back from one sentence to the previous one to adjust a wording, but mostly he gets one sentence right – and then, satisfied, moves on to the next. Now and then you can discern from the changed colour of his ink that he has gone back over a section after a break, but when he does this the alterations are always light and slight. Essentially, he is revising as he writes – not after he has written. Here is a small example. At the end of Chapter X of *Bleak House*, Mr Tulkinghorn, the lawyer, has been taken by Mr Snagsby to the squalid lodgings of Nemo, the impoverished law writer, whose handwriting in a legal document has mysteriously perturbed Lady Dedlock. It is night. He makes out a man on a low bed, but as he calls to him and rattles on the door, his candle goes out and the chapter ends. For the opening of the next chapter, Dickens first writes, 'Mr Tulkinghorn stands in the death room, irresolute.' But then he quickly changes his mind for a better beginning: 'A touch on the lawyer's wrinkled hand as he stands in the death room, irresolute, makes him start ...'[25] The new opening phrase is as immediate and electric as the touch itself.

'Death room' will be changed to 'dark room' in proof. Improvisational he may have been, but at proof stage Dickens was still minutely adjusting wordings. This too was a process of rapid improvement and invention, probably undertaken without any reference to the original manuscript: often Dickens appeared in the printing house to correct the proofs as they were run off.[26] Explaining in the same chapter of *Bleak House* why

Mr Snagsby's partner Peffer no longer appears in Cook's Court, where the premises of 'Peffer and Snagsby' are located, the manuscript tells us, 'he has lain this quarter of a century in the churchyard of Saint Andrew's, Holborn'. In the proof, Dickens changed 'has lain' to 'has been recumbent'.[27] An even more pleasingly periphrastic wording for 'he has been dead'. A few paragraphs later, we find Mr Tulkinghorn in his chambers, withdrawn and retentive. 'Like as he is to look at, so is his apartment,' wrote Dickens in manuscript. At proof stage he inserted, after 'apartment', 'in the dusk of this present afternoon'. The sense of mystery and foreboding is sharpened with the sharpening of the present tense, the last light of a winter's day almost bled away.

We are able to study the manuscripts of his novels because, from *The Old Curiosity Shop* onwards, he took such good care to preserve them. He knew that they would be valuable to later generations. He also preserved his working notes for those novels that were published in monthly parts, allowing us an unparalleled picture of the planning that went into each of them. He deliberately left us the evidence of his intentions and his ambitions. Clearly, he wanted posterity to be able to see him in the business of composing and to recognise that, however improvisational his prose might seem, his fiction was carefully and elaborately contrived. What we should now recognise is a writer who tested out some of the tricks and ploys much later adopted by the literary fiction of the late twentieth century. In a career that spanned some thirty-five years, he moved from one experiment to the next, always trying new things.

Dickens was a pioneer, inventing new shapes for narrative fiction. He alternated between past-tense and present-tense narration, or interleaved a story told in

the first person with a story told in the third person. He
jumped ahead of himself to tell us about what would
happen in the future. He combined supernatural plots
with anatomies of social ills: he extracted farcical comedy
from episodes of pathos. He gave prose new dramatic
powers. When David Copperfield recalls being drunk,
the narration adopts the mixed self-importance and
unawareness of a drunk.

> We went downstairs, one behind another. Near the
> bottom, somebody fell, and rolled down. Somebody
> else said it was Copperfield. I was angry at that
> false report, until, finding myself on my back in
> the passage, I began to think there might be some
> foundation for it.
>
> (Ch. XXIV)

When John Jasper at the opening of *The Mystery of Edwin
Drood* is in an opium trance, the narration becomes
drugged.

> Ten thousand scimitars flash in the sunlight, and thrice
> ten thousand dancing-girls strew flowers. Then, follow
> white elephants caparisoned in countless gorgeous
> colours, and infinite in number and attendants. Still
> the Cathedral Tower rises in the background, where it
> cannot be ...
>
> (Ch. I)

No other novelist before the twentieth century dared
write like this. Dickens offended against literary decorum,
savouring clichés and highlighting coincidences. He
invented an unmatched host of characters – we all know

that – but then got each one to speak in a strange and singular voice. Making the rules as he went along, he was full of tricks and ploys. From one artful sentence to the next, he was, and is, the most exciting novelist writing in English.

2

Fantasising

I think it is my infirmity to fancy or perceive relations
in things which are not apparent generally.
Letter to Bulwer Lytton, 28 November 1865[1]

This is almost the first dinosaur in fiction.

London. Michaelmas term lately over, and the Lord
Chancellor sitting in Lincoln's Inn Hall. Implacable
November weather. As much mud in the streets as
if the waters had but newly retired from the face of
the earth, and it would not be wonderful to meet a
Megalosaurus, forty feet long or so, waddling like an
elephantine lizard up Holborn Hill.
Bleak House, Ch. I

Almost the first dinosaur, because a Megalosaurus had
already appeared in Dickens's weekly journal *Household
Words*, in a piece of short fiction by the young staff writer

Henry Morley. In August 1851, just over six months before
the first instalment of *Bleak House*, Morley wrote an article
for that journal in which he imagined voyaging to 'some
part of South America' where he could go back in time to
find that dinosaurs roamed. This Victorian Jurassic Park
included an inaccurately conceived Megalosaurus.

> Here is a land reptile, before which we take the liberty
> of running. His teeth look too decidedly carnivorous.
> A sort of crocodile, thirty feet long, with a big body,
> mounted on high thick legs, is not likely to be friendly
> with our legs and bodies. Megalosaurus is his name,
> and, doubtless, greedy is his nature.[2]

Dickens, as editor, certainly read the article. Perhaps it
was in his head when he came to imagine a contemporary
London, swallowed in mud, for his next novel.

Morley and Dickens were at the beginnings of a
craze: *Bleak House* began appearing in the year that
Benjamin Hawkins was commissioned to create concrete
dinosaurs for the grounds of the re-erected Crystal Palace
in Sydenham. These duly included a Megalosaurus,
wrongly made into a quadruped and given a hump on its
back. It is still there in south London. Dickens's primeval
beast was about to find a ready place in the popular
imagination. But what is it doing in a novel about the
absurd and ruinous machinery of the law in Victorian
England? Dickens, thinking of mud in the London
streets, decided on the hyperbole of a slimy post-deluvian
world (as muddy as you can ever get), and then, his
imagination seized, animated it with that Megalosaurus.
It is a flight of fantasy, yet 'waddling like an elephantine
lizard', the monstrous creature is comically substantial.

In the manuscript of *Bleak House*, you can see Dickens setting down his fantastic speculation before adding, as an afterthought above the line, that phrase 'as if'.[3]

In all its gigantic absurdity, the gargantuan reptile making its way through central London epitomises Dickens's gift for the outlandish. No respectably literary novelist would ever have imagined it. The Dickensian *as if* is the phrase, more than any other, that unlocks the novelist's fantastic vision of the sheer strangeness of reality. 'As if' is everywhere in his novels. In his early fiction, it often seems deployed just for the pleasure of it, as a flight of comic self-delight. In *Martin Chuzzlewit*, when Mrs Gamp, who partly earns her living watching over recently dead bodies, enters the premises of Mr Mould, the undertaker, 'a peculiar fragrance was borne upon the breeze, as if a passing fairy had hiccoughed, and had previously been to a wine-vaults' (Ch. XXV). The fantasy creatively participates in Mrs Gamp's endless fictionalising of herself. To be plain, she is an alcohol-saturated fraud, but Dickens would like to make something better of the evidence for this.

'In all Mr Dickens's works the fantastic has been his great resource', wrote the young Henry James in a largely dismissive review of *Our Mutual Friend*.[4] He was right. Dickens saw the gift in himself. When he told his friend and fellow novelist Bulwer-Lytton that it was his 'infirmity' to see 'relations in things' that were not 'apparent generally', he sounded proud of himself. He was replying to a letter in which Lytton had evidently praised *Our Mutual Friend*, shortly after its completion, while remarking upon the extravagance of its figurative language. In fact, Dickens replied, 'I work slowly and with great care, and never give way to my invention recklessly, but constantly restrain it.'[5]

Yet he confessed that he had 'such an inexpressible enjoyment of what I see in a droll light' that he could not help but 'pet it as if it were a spoilt child'. It is not only 'as if' that allows for such visions of things 'in a droll light': it can also be 'as though' or 'one might have thought' or 'one might imagine'. The last of these allows the meteorological fantasy in the opening of *Bleak House*, where we see flakes of soot falling in a 'soft black drizzle', 'gone into mourning, one might imagine, for the death of the sun'. Conjuring the gloom and filthiness of this urban November day, Dickens envisages solar extinction. Again, in manuscript, that 'one might imagine' is an afterthought, inserted above the line, Dickens marking out the flight of his fantasy.

His fiction is full of *as ifs*, from the beginning. In the first instalment of his earliest novel, *The Pickwick Papers*, Mr Pickwick and the reader encounter a waterman, whose job is to water the horses at a coach stand and notify the driver when he has a fare (in this instance, fetching him from the nearest pub). ' "Here you are, sir," shouted a strange specimen of the human race, in a sackcloth coat, and apron of the same, who, with a brass label and number round his neck, looked as if he were catalogued in some collection of rarities' (Ch. II). The label that turns the man into an exhibit is in fact an anachronism: the novel is set in 1827, but it was only by the London Hackney Carriage Act of 1831 that every waterman had to be licensed and wear a badge with his number 'conspicuously upon his breast'.[6] No matter, this first example from Dickens's first novel is suitably Dickensian. Everyone met in Pickwick's peregrinations will be one in 'a collection of rarities'.

The 'as if' construction tickled Dickens's imagination from his earliest writings. In *Sketches by Boz* he had already visited this scene of 'a hackney coach stand under the very window at which we are writing', with the coachman again in the nearby pub and the waterman trying to keep warm as he waits for a customer. This time, the horses divert Dickens's fancy.

> The horses, with drooping heads, and each with a mane and tail as scanty and straggling as those of a worn-out rocking-horse, are standing patiently on some damp straw, occasionally wincing, and rattling the harness; and now and then, one of them lifts his mouth to the ear of his companion, as if he were saying, in a whisper, that he should like to assassinate the coachman.[7]

Solicitude for the ill-used animals turns into a daydream about the horses' secret vengefulness. Well before Orwell's *Animal Farm*, Dickens imagined animals as the conspiring enemies of humanity.

When applied to humans, Dickens's device insists on imputing to characters thoughts that might well not be theirs. In *Nicholas Nickleby*, our hero walks through Portsmouth with the thespian couple Mr and Mrs Crummles, for both of whom perambulation is a performance. 'Mrs Crummles trod the pavement as if she were going to immediate execution with an animating consciousness of innocence, and that heroic fortitude which virtue alone inspires.' Her husband, meanwhile, 'assumed the look of a hardened despot' (Ch. XXIII). Is this what is going through each of their minds? Who knows. It expresses as well as an observer can the histrionic self-importance with which the theatrical pair attract attention from the awed pedestrians of Portsmouth. In *Barnaby Rudge*, John Willett is stunned

to meet his son Joe again, after many years. Joe Willett,
sick of his father's ill-treatment, left to become a soldier
and now has returned from the American wars without
an arm. The bullying father is reduced to chastened
befuddlement:

> he wandered out again, in a perfect bog of uncertainty
> and mental confusion, and in that state took the
> strangest means of resolving his doubts: such as feeling
> the sleeve of his son's greatcoat as deeming it possible
> that his arm might be there; looking at his own arms
> and those of everybody else, as if to assure himself
> that two and not one was the usual allowance; sitting
> by the hour together in a brown study, as if he were
> endeavouring to recall Joe's image in his younger days,
> and to remember whether he really had in those times
> one arm or a pair; and employing himself in many
> other speculations of the same kind.
>
> (Ch. LXXII)

Comically as well as poignantly, the *as if*s give the
impression of the character's behaviour, the unlikeliness
of the suppositions matching the character's shock.

A few critics have noted Dickens's liking for the *as if*
construction.[8] Yet none seem to distinguish his use of
it from that of many other novelists. George Eliot and
Henry James, for instance, use *as if* almost as frequently
as Dickens, yet never in his special way. In the opening
chapter of Eliot's *Middlemarch*, we are invited to see
Dorothea through the jaundiced eyes of those who
disapprove of her moral intensity. 'A young lady of some
birth and fortune, who knelt suddenly down on a brick

floor by the side of a sick labourer and prayed fervidly as if she thought herself living in the time of the Apostles.'⁹

This *as if* renders the sense of impropriety felt by her neighbours, but also accurately depicts Dorothea's enthusiastic Puritan Christianity. In the next chapter she meets Mr Casaubon for the first time and he speaks of his obscure scholarly researches. 'He delivered himself with precision, as if he had been called upon to make a public statement.'¹⁰ The incongruity of Eliot's simile is satirical, but only just removed from the literal. Or take this moment from a conversation in Henry James's *The Portrait of a Lady* between Isabel Archer and her unwanted suitor, Caspar Goodwood.

> 'I displease you very much,' said Caspar Goodwood gloomily; not as if to provoke her to compassion for a man conscious of this blighting fact, but as if to set it well before himself, so that he might endeavour to act with his eyes upon it.¹¹

James's *as ifs* track Isabel's thoughts, as she tries to interpret Goodwood's words and tone. Like Eliot, James uses *as if* for a simile that allows us to see a plausible implication in a character's behaviour. Dickens, in contrast, uses *as if* to discover analogies that are so far-fetched they can hardly be called similes at all.

The device developed through Dickens's career. Each of his later novels has its own distinctive sense of fantasy – its own special *as if*-ness. That of *Great Expectations* is captured in the novel's use of the phrase in its first chapter, fusing childhood terror with an adult's sense of the ludicrous. At the end of that chapter, after his encounter with the escaped convict in the lonely graveyard, Pip watches the

man return to the marshes, 'picking his way' between the
graves: 'he looked in my young eyes as if he were eluding
the hands of the dead people, stretching up cautiously out
of their graves, to get a twist upon his ankle and pull him
in' (Ch. I). In manuscript, the mingled horror and comedy
of this – unmatched before horror films of the twentieth
century – is arrived at only after much revision: 'eluding
the hands of the dead people' is an inserted afterthought,
as is the brilliantly comic adverb 'cautiously' (in the
child's imagination, the dead people cannot actually leave
the graves that are their resting places). In Dickens's first
wording, the dead 'try to get hold of his ankle' to 'pull
him down'. He then has the better ideas of 'get a twist
upon' (a nicer turn of supernatural malice) and 'pull
him in' (not just trip him up but haul him down into
the underworld). [12] In *Great Expectations*, horror is always
tinged with absurdity.

> On the edge of the river I could faintly make out the
> only two black things in all the prospect that seemed
> to be standing upright; one of these was the beacon
> by which the sailors steered,—like an unhooped cask
> upon a pole,—an ugly thing when you were near it;
> the other, a gibbet, with some chains hanging to it
> which had once held a pirate. The man was limping
> on towards this latter, as if he were the pirate come to
> life, and come down, and going back to hook himself
> up again.

It is a childish thought, haunted and ridiculous. Adult
retrospect colours the fear with comedy. That childishness,
and its comic aspect, are confirmed by what follows. 'It
gave me a terrible turn when I thought so; and as I saw the

cattle lifting up their heads to gaze after him, I wondered
whether they thought so too'.

Fantastic suppositions are essential to this narrative.
A couple of chapters later, when Pip brings food to the
convict he notices something peculiar about him. This
desperate man, gobbling and shivering, says that he cannot
believe that any boy would help others 'hunt a wretched
warmint hunted as near death and dunghill as this poor
wretched warmint is!' His expression of vulnerability has
a strange effect. 'Something clicked in his throat, as if he
had works in him like a clock, and was going to strike'
(Ch. III). No one but Dickens could have written that
sentence, so perplexingly reliving a child's perception. It
makes the convict utterly individual, even as the young
Pip's idea of him as a clockwork machine shows the
limitation of his sympathy. The sound is repeated two
chapters later. As the re-arrested convict is taken away, Joe
tells him that he is welcome to the pie that Pip stole for
him. 'The something that I had noticed before, clicked in
the man's throat again, and he turned his back' (Ch. V).
Much later in the novel, we hear the sound a third time,
when the convict comes to the adult Pip in his London
chambers to reveal that it is he who has 'made a gentleman
on you'. '"Don't you mind talking, Pip," said he, after
again drawing his sleeve over his eyes and forehead, as
the click came in his throat which I well remembered'
(Ch. XXXIX). The noise, we infer, is a sign of Magwitch's
heightened emotions (the opposite of mere machinery),
the glitch of his inexpressible feelings. Pip does not tell us
this; he hears but does not understand.

Pip draws fantastic analogies to escape subjection to the
wills of others. Take our first sight of one of the petty
tyrants who bully him, Uncle Pumblechook. 'A large

hard-breathing middle-aged slow man, with a mouth like a fish, dull staring eyes, and sandy hair standing upright on his head, so that he looked as if he had just been all but choked, and had that moment come to' (Ch. IV).

Again, this seemingly inspired analogy was arrived at after much rewriting. In manuscript, the fish-like mouth was there from the beginning, but the adjectives 'hard-breathing middle-aged slow' (expressively unseparated by commas – they all belong together) were inserted after the first drafting of the sentence. The 'dull staring eyes' were also a second thought, while Dickens only arrived at the phrasing of 'as if he had just been all but choked, and had that moment come to' after excising a now illegible earlier idea. At the proof stage, he was still honing the wording, inserting 'all but' before 'choked'. After all these adjustments, there he is, this small-town charlatan, identified and undermined for ever. A fish drowning in air, Pumblechook belongs to Dickens's gallery of beings recently brought back to life. Something akin is Jeremiah Flintwinch in *Little Dorrit*, in whom 'natural acerbity and energy' contend with 'a second nature of habitual repression', giving his features 'a swollen and suffused look … a weird appearance of having hanged himself at one time or other, and having gone about ever since halter and all, exactly as some timely hand had cut him down' (I Ch. III). Dickens had seen a man hanged, and so, he would know, had some proportion of his readers.[13] The analogy is as disturbing as it is absurd, for this disturbing and absurd character, the wife-bullying servant who is in fact Mrs Clennam's co-conspirator.

The *as if*s in *Great Expectations* (there are 266 of them) are often both perceptive and baffled.[14] They recapture Pip's sense of the mysterious – apparently providential,

but in fact threatening or punishing – world in which he
must make his way.

> Mr Jaggers never laughed; but he wore great bright
> creaking boots, and, in poising himself on these boots,
> with his large head bent down and his eyebrows joined
> together, awaiting an answer, he sometimes caused
> the boots to creak, as if *they* laughed in a dry and
> suspicious way.
>
> (Ch. XXIV)

Jaggers, a man who 'seemed to bully his very sandwich
as he ate it', is always exerting his power over others,
including Pip (Ch. XIX). But Pip feels that he is
somehow being laughed at, as well as bullied. Jaggers is a
daunting generator of *as if*s. When we first meet him as
a stranger in the Three Jolly Bargemen, he bests the self-
important Mr Wopsle, throwing his forefinger and then
'taking possession of Mr Wopsle, as if he had a right to
him' (Ch. XVIII). He intimidates those who work for
him. His clerk Wemmick has acquired occupationally
hardened features, including 'such a post-office of a
mouth that he had a mechanical appearance of smiling'.
When Pip revisits Jaggers's office, the metaphor returns.
'Wemmick was at his desk, lunching—and crunching—
on a dry hard biscuit; pieces of which he threw from
time to time into his slit of a mouth, as if he were
posting them.' Another novelist would imagine the grim
influence of Wemmick's master, but Dickens's fancy sees
the comedy of it too.

Pip is bamboozled by his own hopes of gentility. From
the first, his aspirations and his bewilderment are projected
onto others. When, at Miss Havisham's command, he

plays the card game Beggar my Neighbour with Estella
on his initial visit to Satis House, she, of course, beggars
him. 'She threw the cards down on the table when she
had won them all, as if she despised them for having been
won of me.' When he is released from the house Estella
tells him to wait. As he explores the brewery yard, and
then the derelict building itself, he keeps catching sight
of her, apparently (but only apparently) ignorant of this
gaze, walking into his view then out of it. He is being
tormented and fascinated: 'she seemed to be everywhere'.
Finally, she ascends some stairs in the brewery in order
to 'go out by a gallery high overhead, as if she were
going out into the sky.' The optical illusion is unerringly
recalled by the adult narrator, a memory of yearning in
which the girl becomes an unearthly being, beyond him,
and irresistible.

The illusions of youth, so much the subject of this novel,
contain weird insights. Pip recalls that, immediately after
his vision of Estella 'going out into the sky', 'a strange
thing happened to my fancy. I thought it a strange thing
then, and I thought it a stranger thing long afterwards.'
(The second sentence here is not in Dickens's manuscript;
he must have inserted it at the proof stage, making the
strangeness reverberate down the years.) Pip thinks for a
moment that he sees a figure hanging by the neck from a
great wooden beam.

> A figure all in yellow white, with but one shoe to the
> feet; and it hung so, that I could see that the faded
> trimmings of the dress were like earthy paper, and that
> the face was Miss Havisham's, with a movement going
> over the whole countenance as if she were trying to
> call to me.

FANTASISING 27

In terror he runs first away from and then towards the figure. 'And my terror was greatest of all, when I found no figure there' (Ch. VIII). The greatest terror because he knows the illusion is his own creation. But the sight is not only born of fear. It is 'as if' Pip is being summoned or implored by this deadly being. On his last visit to Satis House, years later, the vision returns to him when he turns to look into the brewery yard.

> A childish association revived with wonderful force in the moment of the slight action, and I fancied that I saw Miss Havisham hanging to the beam. So strong was the impression, that I stood under the beam shuddering from head to foot before I knew it was a fancy.
>
> (Ch. XLIX)

The presentiment is complete; a few moments later Miss Havisham is in flames, destroyed by her ghastly marital costume.

Dickens makes Pip use that word 'childish' with perfect ambiguity. Perhaps the revived memory is infantile and foolish – or perhaps, frighteningly, it is a buried remnant of the childhood that has shaped him. Every 'fancy' in this novel combines the absurd with the truly fearful. Pip recalls being sent by Miss Havisham to wait in a dimly lit, dusty room where a cobwebbed feast covers a long table. Abandoned to his own thoughts, his fanciful *as ifs* take over.

> I saw speckle-legged spiders with blotchy bodies running home to it, and running out from it, as if some circumstances of the greatest public importance had just transpired in the spider community.

> I heard the mice too, rattling behind the panels, as if
> the same occurrence were important to their interests.
> But the black beetles took no notice of the agitation,
> and groped about the hearth in a ponderous elderly
> way, as if they were short-sighted and hard of hearing,
> and not on terms with one another.
>
> (Ch. XI)

Childish fantasy in adult diction makes what is horrible
become comical. Pip, fascinated, is suddenly roused by
Miss Havisham's hand on his shoulder; she tells him that
under the cobwebs is her bride-cake. The childish *as ifs*
get at the truth. When Pip recalls Joe's helper at the forge,
the taciturn and baleful Orlick, he re-animates a fearful
fantasy,

> Orlick plunged at the furnace, drew out a red-hot bar,
> made at me with it as if he were going to run it through
> my body, whisked it round my head, laid it on the
> anvil, hammered it out—as if it were I, I thought, and
> the sparks were my spirting blood.
>
> (Ch. XV)

Orlick *is* murderous and malevolent; those *as if*s tell us
how the child already knew what the narrator now knows.
His laughable horror-story fancy is prophetic.

In his brilliant and obsessive study of Dickens's fearful
obsessions, *The Night Side of Dickens*, Harry Stone outlines
cannibalistic fantasies at work in *Great Expectations* and
Bleak House. Miss Havisham, he tells us, is 'a passionate,
obsessive, aggressive devourer'.[15] Certainly, Pip tells us so.
'She hung upon Estella's beauty, hung upon her words,
hung upon her gestures, and sat mumbling her own

trembling fingers while she looked at her, as though she were devouring the beautiful creature she had reared' (Ch. XXXVIII).

As though does the trick for Dickens, admitting us to a ghoulish reality of what Stone calls 'profane feeding'. Yet eating people is also funny. When Miss Havisham herself talks of being feasted on by her greedy relatives after her death, one of them, Camilla Pocket, bridles at the far-fetched thought. 'I am determined not to make a display of my feelings, but it's very hard to be told one wants to feast on one's relations,—as if one was a Giant' (Ch. XI). Miss Havisham's complicity in this cannibalistic idea confirms Pip's vision of her. Dickens was not afraid to let us see monsters. One such is the vampiric lawyer Mr Vholes in *Bleak House*, who will suck the life (and money) out of Richard Carstone by abetting his pursuit of the hopeless chancery case. The little phrase, 'as if', reveals his predation. According to Esther, he gazes at Richard 'as if he were looking at his prey and charming it' (Ch. XXXVII), or, another time, 'as if he were making a lingering meal of him with his eyes' (Ch. XXXIX). When Vholes departs, with all the money from the estate eaten up in costs, Esther observes how 'he gave one gasp as if he had swallowed the last morsel of his client' (Ch. LXV). She thinks like Dickens. A different novelist might go so far as this, in the spirit of metaphor, but Dickens has the nerve to make Vholes utterly monstrous: returning from court to his office, accompanied by Richard, 'Mr Vholes takes off his close black gloves as if he were skinning his hands, lifts off his tight hat as if he were scalping himself' (Ch. XXXIX). This ghoul seems to emerge from a kind of horror fiction (H. P. Lovecraft? Stephen King?) that has not yet been invented.

Dickens teases the absurdity out of horror, knowing that cannibals and vampires are excellent subjects for humour. His flights of fancy discover what is laughable about truly dedicated nastiness. In *Our Mutual Friend*, Alfred Lammle, embarked with his wife on the project of tricking Georgiana Podsnap into marrying the mercenary Fascination Fledgeby, is full of angry resentment after a hard evening of making conversation with the two young people, both of whom he secretly despises. By now we are used to the cynicism of the Lammles' exchanges when they find themselves alone together, but this time we have something angrier. Sophronia sits, 'moody and weary', 'looking at her dark lord engaged in a deed of violence with a bottle of soda-water as though he were wringing the neck of some unlucky creature and pouring its blood down his throat'(II Ch. IV).

The hardly suppressed violence is real enough, but the fantastic transfer to the soda-water bottle is suitably comic. Her husband, wiping his 'dripping whiskers' in 'an ogreish way', is, to the seeing eye, not a Victorian gentleman whetting his whistle, but a man-like monster, drinking hot blood.

Another kind of monster is Uriah Heep in *David Copperfield*, who generates his own special *as if*s, with his twisting body and his clammy hands. 'He frequently ground the palms against each other as if to squeeze them dry and warm, besides often wiping them, in a stealthy way, on his pocket-handkerchief' (Ch. XVI).

David is haunted by him, the charity schoolboy educated in the show of humility. Invited to a dinner party in London with Agnes, he inevitably encounters him: 'his shadowless red eyes, which looked as if they had scorched their lashes off, turned towards me without looking at me'. Uriah is set on taking hold of Mr Wickfield's legal business and obtaining his daughter Agnes as his wife. David's knowledge of this provokes physical disgust. 'The image of Agnes, outraged by so much as a thought of this red-headed animal's, remained in my mind when I looked at him, sitting all awry as if his mean soul griped his body, and made me giddy' (Ch. XXV).

David is tormented by the thought of Uriah Heep obtaining Agnes into candid demonisation. He watches the coach containing both of them leave, 'she waving her hand and smiling farewell from the coach window; her evil genius writhing on the roof, as if he had her in his clutches and triumphed' (Ch. XXVI).

His analogies impart to him a touch of the supernatural, as when Uriah balefully stays the night in David's London rooms. 'When I saw him going downstairs early in the morning (for, thank Heaven! he would not stay to breakfast), it appeared to me as if the night was going away in his person' (Ch. XXV).

His powers are all foreseen by the young David's fancy on their first meeting. Soon after arriving at Mr Wickfield's house in Canterbury, David looks out of a window and sees him 'breathing into the pony's nostrils, and then immediately covering them with his hand, as if he were putting some spell upon him' (Ch. XV). Heep, who repels his fellow humans, might well know how to make animals obey his black magic.

In the realm of Dickens's fantasy, animals are infected by humanity. In *Martin Chuzzlewit*, the gruesome funeral of the predatory miser Anthony Chuzzlewit spurs the undertaker's horses to what the novelist discerns as delight.

The four hearse-horses, especially, reared and pranced, and showed their highest action, as if they knew a man was dead, and triumphed in it. 'They break us, drive us, ride us; ill-treat, abuse, and maim us for their pleasure—But they die; Hurrah, they die!'

(Ch. XIX)

Even dead animals can be human, like the fish being offered by the fishmonger to the newly enriched Boffins in *Our Mutual Friend*, 'the gaping salmon and the golden mullet lying on the slab seem to turn up their eyes sideways, as they would turn up their hands if they had any, in worshipping admiration' (I Ch. XVII).

Alive or dead, the animals that serve people, in Dickens's eyes, mock them. In *Little Dorrit*, the proud yet toadying Mrs Gowan visits Mrs Merdle at her opulent Harley Street home, finding her 'in her nest of crimson and gold, with the parrot on a neighbouring stem watching her with his head on one side, as if he took her for another splendid parrot of a larger species' (I Ch. XXXIII). The parrot's fantastically perceived error is, we are to see, quite understandable.

In Dickens's world, animals and humans easily exchange places. In *A Tale of Two Cities*, Mr Lorry, the agent of Telson's Bank, has time to kill in Dover as he waits for Lucie Manette, whom he will take to Paris to meet her long-imprisoned father. He takes a morning stroll through the town and we are allowed to see how odd a place it is. 'The air among the houses was of so strong a piscatory flavour that one might have supposed sick fish went up to be dipped in it, as sick people went down to be dipped in the sea' (Ch. IV).

The effect relies on the fact that Mr Lorry is a man of utter reliability, distracted briefly, as we are, by Dickens's conceit. Only this author 'might have supposed' something so peculiar. It is a formula that he uses occasionally, invariably with a sense of the ludicrous. When David Copperfield encounters Mr Micawber on the eve of sailing for Australia, he finds that he has already, in his histrionic way, taken on a new part.

> Mr Micawber, I must observe, in his adaptation of himself to a new state of society, had acquired a bold buccaneering air, not absolutely lawless, but defensive and prompt. One might have supposed him a child of the wilderness, long accustomed to live out of the confines of civilization, and about to return to his native wilds.
>
> (Ch. LVII)

The absurdity of the notion that comes into the narrator's head is just its point. The plump and loquacious spendthrift becomes a noble savage; Mr Micawber is capable of acting up even to this incongruous part.

There is often mockery in fantastic analogies. In *Bleak House* Mr Tulkinghorn, lawyer to aristocratic houses, takes care of all those cast-iron boxes with the Dedlock family name upon them, 'as if the present baronet were the coin of the conjurer's trick, and were constantly being juggled through the whole set' (Ch. II). Dickens refers the Victorian reader to the trick familiar from many a street magician where a coin was apparently made to 'move' from one sealed box to another.[16] We look with the novelist at all those boxes embossed with that self-important name and we glimpse the lawyer's dizzying, disrespectful dexterity. By the Dickensian alchemy of 'as if …', all circumstantial detail becomes metaphorical, the material world the reflector of human attributes. We are told that Tulkinghorn, this master of secrecy, likes to sip his old port, retrieved from 'some artful cellar' under Lincoln's Inn Fields. 'As if it whispered to him of its fifty years of silence and seclusion, it shuts him up the closer' (Ch. XXII). We remember that fearlessly mixed metaphor used much earlier of the Dedlock lawyer. 'An Oyster of the old school, whom nobody can open' (Ch. X).

Dickens brings alive the material world. In *A Christmas Carol*, the church bell near Scrooge's premises strikes the hours and quarters 'with tremulous vibrations afterwards as if its teeth were chattering in its frozen head up there'. Scrooge is opposed to all fantasy. 'Scrooge had as little of what is called fancy about him as any man in the City of London, even including—which is a bold word—the corporation, aldermen, and livery.' His fate is to be confronted by those fantastic beings, ghosts, and in a narrative prose that is constantly animated by fancy. 'The bells ceased as they had begun, together. They were succeeded by a clanking noise, deep down below; as if some person were dragging a heavy chain over the casks in the wine-merchant's cellar.' The *as if*s are comic as much as frightening. Scrooge cannot escape his ghosts, but he cannot escape fancy either, even at home. The building where he has his rooms is 'up a yard, where it had so little business to be, that one could scarcely help fancying it must have run there when it was a young house, playing at hide-and-seek with other houses, and forgotten the way out again' (Stave I).

There is nothing like buildings for getting Dickens's fancy going. They will insist on taking on the qualities of their inmates, like Tellson's Bank in *A Tale of Two Cities*. 'Mr Lorry sat at great books ruled for figures, with perpendicular iron bars to his window as if that were ruled for figures too, and everything under the clouds were a sum' (II Ch. XII).

In *American Notes*, Dickens visits the old French quarter of St Louis where the 'crazy old tenements' seem to have 'a kind of French shrug about them; and being lop-sided with age, appear to hold their heads askew, besides, as if they were grimacing in astonishment at the American Improvements.'[17] *Our Mutual Friend*, a novel in which every character and every story seems drawn to the river, features a tavern that shares the inclination. The Six Jolly Fellowship Porters is very close to the Thames, 'impending over the water'. Dickens imagines that it once wanted to immerse itself, 'but seemed to have got into the condition of a faint-hearted diver who has paused so long on the brink that he will never go in at all' (I Ch. VI).

Looking at a place, Dickens's fantastic eye supercharges it with meaning. When Bradley Headstone, doomed to disappointment, declares himself to Lizzie in *Our Mutual Friend*, it is next to a graveyard, with some of the tombstones 'droopingly inclined from the perpendicular, as if they were ashamed of the lies they told' (II Ch. XV). He could have chosen a more promising location, you might think. Describing the poor lodgings near the Marshalsea in *Little Dorrit*, Dickens tells us that the backs of the houses have 'poles and lines thrust out of them, on which unsightly linen hung: as if the inhabitants were angling for clothes' (I Ch. IX). That odd fancy converts poverty into desperate hopefulness. Barnard's Inn in *Great Expectations* is a place depressing enough to inspire an amusing supposition: the number of To Let signs makes it seem 'as if no new wretches ever came there, and the vengeance of the soul of Barnard were being slowly appeased by the gradual suicide of the present occupants and their unholy interment under the gravel' (Ch. XXI).

Above all, fantastic analogy is the ploy developed by Dickens to match people's strangeness and self-contradiction. When we first see Mr Squeers in *Nicholas Nickleby*, he is wearing a suit of 'scholastic black' appropriate for his profession, 'but his coat sleeves being a great deal too long, and his trousers a great deal too short, he appeared ill at ease in his clothes, and as if he were in a perpetual state of astonishment at finding himself so respectable'. He is, of course, an ignorant and sadistic rogue, but Dickens's speculation catches something comic, his own seeming surprise at the role he is playing – and somehow getting away with. His wife is a less funny tormentor of children ('the enemy') than him because she lacks his instinct for self-confutation.

> The only difference between them was, that Mrs Squeers waged war against the enemy openly and fearlessly, and that Squeers covered his rascality, even at home, with a spice of his habitual deceit; as if he really had a notion of someday or other being able to take himself in, and persuade his own mind that he was a very good fellow.
> (Ch. IV)

His 'deceit' is unnecessary – there is no one to save his pupils from his cruelty – but is a fiction oddly vital to himself.

Dickens's supposings detect the comic awkwardness of even more subtle villains, when the parts they play become surprisingly demanding. Ralph Nickleby, drawn almost against his will to say something well-intentioned to his niece Kate, for whom he has a certain *tendresse*, says, 'Good night – a – a – God bless you': 'The blessing seemed to stick in Mr Ralph Nickleby's throat, as if it were not use to the thoroughfare, and didn't know the way out' (Ch. XIX). We recollect Macbeth, the murderer of Duncan.

But wherefore could not I pronounce 'Amen'?
I had most need of blessing, and 'Amen'
Stuck in my throat.

Macbeth, II.ii. 31–3

The mock-Shakespeare emphasises the absurdity of Dickens's fancy, as Ralph Nickleby finds that his own badness has made the uttering of good words physiognomically taxing.

The body betrays the character. Such awkwardness does not have to be grotesque; it can be endearing. When we first meet the benevolent Kit in *The Old Curiosity Shop*, we find that he 'had a remarkable manner of standing sideways as he spoke, and thrusting his head forward over his shoulder, as if he could not get at his voice without that accompanying action' (Ch. I). Or there is the schoolmaster Mr Sharp in *David Copperfield*, who had 'a way of carrying his head on one side, as if it were a little too heavy for him' (Ch. VI). Such characters are puzzled by life, and their bodies know it. In *Great Expectations*, Pip first encounters Startop, his fellow lodger and tutee at the house of Mr Pocket, and finds him 'reading and holding his head, as if he thought himself in danger of exploding it with too strong a charge of knowledge' (Ch. XXIII). We know that this supposition is Pip's, but it is impossible not to see Startop having the thought too. Dickens is alive to the strange features of physique or habits of deportment by

which a person tries to get away from him- or herself, like
Twemlow in the second chapter of *Our Mutual Friend*,
with 'cheeks drawn in as if he had made a great effort to
retire into himself some years ago, and had got so far and
had never got any farther'. Ever the ignored guest, valued
only because he is the cousin of Lord Snigsworth, poor
Twemlow is condemned to self-nullification.

Hypocrites, in contrast, do not so much deny themselves
as transcend themselves. Think of Mr Pecksniff, the pious
fraud of *Martin Chuzzlewit*, affecting moral loftiness in
order to impress the wealthy, disillusioned old Martin
Chuzzlewit, and 'towering on tiptoe among the curtains, as
if he were literally rising above all worldly considerations,
and were fain to hold on tight, to keep himself from
darting skyward like a rocket'. 'Literally', that over-used
word, turns a cliché into a figurative flourish as ridiculous
as Pecksniff's self-display. This character's show of moral
consciousness is allowed to shape his every gesture. When
he warms his hands before the fire in the village inn, he
does so 'as benevolently as if they were somebody else's'.
He goes on to warm his back 'as if it were a widow's back,
or an orphan's back, or an enemy's back, or a back that any
less excellent man would have suffered to be cold' (Ch.
III). Dickens follows the logic of Pecksniff's performance,
as he turns himself into somebody else. Similarly, in
Bleak House, when Esther describes Skimpole's cheerful
irresponsibility, she catches the way in which he seems to
escape himself.

> All this and a great deal more he told us, not only
> with the utmost brilliancy and enjoyment, but with
> a certain vivacious candour—speaking of himself as if
> he were not at all his own affair, as if Skimpole were

a third person, as if he knew that Skimpole had his
singularities but still had his claims too, which were
the general business of the community and must not
be slighted.

(Ch. VI)

The three *as if*s in rapid succession express her perplexity
and enact the consummate illogicality of his performance.

A different kind of pretender is the financier Mr
Merdle in *Little Dorrit*. Dickens's language pictures
what the novel's characters ignore. Everyone talks of
Merdle's wealth and power, but the man himself seems
unconfident, hamstrung, self-reprehending, and thus a
visible absurdity. There is 'a somewhat uneasy expression
about his coat-cuffs as if they were in his confidence, and
had reasons for being anxious to hide his hands' (I Ch.
XXI). Merdle hugs walls and retreats from the Society
for which he has such great respect. The self-abnegating
plutocrat provokes the narrator to *as if*s. When Mr Dorrit
offers him his hand, 'Mr Merdle looked at the hand for
a little while, took it on his for a moment as if his were
a yellow salver or fish-slice, and then returned it to Mr
Dorrit' (II Ch. XVI).

There is something strange to him about himself. When
he visits his stepson and his stepson's wife, he converses
with his usual awkwardness, pausing in a sentence: 'here
he looked all over the palms of both his hands as if he
were telling his own fortune' (I Ch. XXIV). He knows –
as no one else does – that he is succeeding in a kind of
fraud on everyone, and his manners concede it. We see
him in his mansion amidst all his wealth, 'looking out at
a distant window, with his hands crossed under his uneasy
coat-cuffs, clasping his wrists as if he were taking himself

into custody' (I Ch. XXXIII). Before the narrative ever condemns him, he appears to condemn himself, as when he greets Mrs Sparkler (the erstwhile Fanny Dorrit) on her arrival in London:

> When he put his lips to hers, besides, he took himself into custody by the wrists, and backed himself among the ottomans and chairs and tables as if he were his own Police officer, saying to himself, 'Now, none of that! Come! I've got you, you know, and you go quietly along with me!'
>
> (II Ch. XVI)

Another kind of novelist might tell you Merdle's thoughts, or at least the symptoms of his anxieties. Dickens insists on seeing this character only from the outside and spinning a fantasy. Like so many of his tricks, it goes against all the rules of literary description, and thereby adds new powers to fiction.

3

Smelling

… the smell seizes hold of the bridge of my nose
exactly half way up, and won't let it go again.
Letter to Wilkie Collins, 13 April 1856[1]

Sometimes, what we remember about a person is a
distinctive smell. In *Great Expectations*, during Pip's
second visit to Miss Havisham at Satis House, he is being
led upstairs by Estella when he encounters 'a gentleman
groping his way down'. ('Groping' because it is a house
where light is always kept out.) This burly man stops to
examine Pip. 'He took my chin in his large hand and
turned up my face to have a look at me by the light of the
candle'. His peremptory questions elicit the information
that Pip is a 'boy of the neighbourhood' whom Miss
Havisham has summoned.

'Well! Behave yourself. I have a pretty large experience
of boys, and you're a bad set of fellows. Now mind!'

said he, biting the side of his great forefinger as he
frowned at me, 'you behave yourself!'

With those words, he released me – which I was
glad of, for his hand smelt of scented soap – and went
his way downstairs. I wondered whether he could be a
doctor; but no, I thought; he couldn't be a doctor, or
he would have a quieter and more persuasive manner.

(Ch. XI)

Odd and memorable, that the smell of soap should be
what is peculiarly unpleasant for the boy – what puzzles
him too. Who, apart from a doctor, would smell like this?

That smell of soap stays in his mind and his senses.
Some ten years later (four weeks later for those who first
read the novel as serialised in *All the Year Round*) Pip is
with Joe in the Three Jolly Bargemen, listening to the
absurd Mr Wopsle read aloud an account of a murder
trial from the newspaper, when he becomes aware of 'a
strange gentleman' looking on. Wearing an expression of
contempt, 'he bit the side of a great forefinger as he watched
the group of faces.' He is the same man whom Pip met
on the stairs: we recognise that weirdly aggressive habit
of biting his finger. After interrogating the unfortunate
Wopsle as to his understanding of the case that he has
been narrating, and thoroughly crushing him, the man
announces that he has come to find 'an apprentice ...
commonly known as Pip'. 'The stranger did not recognize
me, but I recognized him'. Pip checks off the visual details
that he remembers from that first meeting – 'his large
head, his dark complexion, his deep-set eyes, his bushy
black eyebrows, his large watch-chain, his strong black
dots of beard and whisker' – and something else: 'the smell
of scented soap on his great hand.' The man is Mr Jaggers,

the lawyer who comes with the momentous news that Pip is 'a young fellow of great expectations'(Ch. XVIII). We, like Pip, should notice the scent he brings with him, on his hands.

Eventually, in the sixteenth instalment, nine weeks after that initial meeting for the first readers, we find out why this sweet, discomfiting smell always accompanies Jaggers. Pip has moved to London and has met him in his legal premises, near Smithfield and not far from Newgate Prison. Summoned there once more, he finds him cleaning up after some bit of business. 'My guardian was in his room, washing his hands with his scented soap'. Washing his hands is his habit because of the dirty work that he does amongst criminals or those accused of crimes.

> I embrace this opportunity of remarking that he washed his clients off, as if he were a surgeon or a dentist. He had a closet in his room, fitted up for the purpose, which smelt of the scented soap like a perfumer's shop. It had an unusually large jack-towel on a roller inside the door, and he would wash his hands, and wipe them and dry them all over this towel, whenever he came in from a police court or dismissed a client from his room.

The washing means that his job is done and is a kind of acknowledgement of what he is up to in his legal work. A little soap clears him of his deeds. Pip is invited to dinner the next day and meets Jaggers at his office once more, at six o'clock, before accompanying him to his Soho home. Again, he is washing – not just his hands this time, but also 'laving his face and gargling his throat.' The smell after his ablution is sufficiently menacing. 'There were some people slinking about as usual when we passed out

into the street, who were evidently anxious to speak with
him; but there was something so conclusive in the halo of
scented soap which encircled his presence, that they gave
it up for that day' (Ch. XXVI).

Jaggers's smell goes before him. When Pip meets him
once more at Satis House, it is that scent that again
announces him. Miss Havisham is speaking with mad
passion of her self-humiliating love for the man who
betrayed her years earlier; she rises from her chair and
strikes at the air. She seems about to do herself some
harm, so Pip steps forward. 'As I drew her down into
her chair, I was conscious of a scent I knew, and turning,
saw my guardian in the room' (Ch. XXIX). It is Jaggers,
as self-contained and intimidating as ever. Even Miss
Havisham seems afraid of him. Pip knows he is there
before he even sees him. Smell, that animal sense, is what
cannot be forgotten, what brings back one's original
impressions of a person. This particular smell is disturbing
for being used to cloak the actions of the man who thus
perfumes himself. Jaggers does not just move amongst
criminals: he specialises in finding ways of getting them
off. The smell – incontrovertible and insistent – tells you
all this. The perfume is made even more incongruous by
the brutal strength in those huge hands: we remember
this extraordinary moment at his dinner table, when his
housekeeper is clearing away the meal. 'Suddenly, he
clapped his large hand on the housekeeper's, like a trap,
as she stretched it across the table.' He wants to show the
power of her wrists and hands. (We will later find that she
killed a woman with those hands.) 'I have had occasion
to notice many hands; but I never saw stronger in that
respect, man's or woman's, than these,' Jaggers tells his

puzzled dinner guests (Ch. XXVI). But his manual power
can match hers.

That soap fragrance is pure Dickens. Partly it is a matter
of the author's sheer sensory inclusiveness. Dickens's
former office boy, William Edrupt, interviewed when
he was eighty, had one particularly sharp memory of the
novelist.

> I think Mr Dickens was a man who lived a lot by his
> nose. He seemed to be always smelling things. When
> we walked down by the Thames he would sniff and
> sniff – 'I love the smell of this,' he used to say.[2]

Indeed, Dickens sometimes wrote as if his nose were a
sensitive instrument. Here he is in Genoa, in his *Pictures
from Italy*.

> In the streets of shops, the houses are much smaller,
> but of great size notwithstanding, and extremely high.
> They are very dirty: quite undrained, if my nose be at
> all reliable: and emit a peculiar fragrance, like the smell
> of very bad cheese, kept in very hot blankets.[3]

The smell that Dickens told his friend Wilkie Collins
'seizes hold of the bridge of my nose exactly half way up,
and won't let it go again' was the smell of vomit, vividly
imagined when Dickens heard that Collins had had a
stormy passage by boat from England to France.

> We checked you off at the various points of your
> journey all day, but never dreamed of the half gale.
> You must have had an abominable passage with that
> convivial club! My soul sickens at the thought of it.[4]

Dickens, who had crossed the Atlantic as well as the Channel, knew from his nose's memory what a ship full of sea-sick passengers smelt like. He was a connoisseur of smells good and bad. Yet it is more than this. In their original serial form, his novels had to find ways of helping their readers remember characters whom they might not have encountered for weeks, or even months. That persistent scent on Jaggers's hands does this, and is a memory trigger for Pip. He cannot get away from it. The scent alerts him and us to the persistent, mysterious role that Jaggers is playing in his life. Dickens was the first novelist to make smell a narrative device.

Pip's acute sense of smell forces his memories on him. Near the end of the extraordinary episode that opens the novel and that will shape his future, he recalls accompanying the soldiers who have recaptured the two escaped convicts in their march across the marshes. In the hut they enter by the landing place, he cannot help remembering the 'smell of tobacco and whitewash' (Ch. V). He has returned so completely to the past that this distinctive smell comes back to him. Dickens treats smells as the very stuff of experience. Later, Pip, now in his late teens and about to depart for a gentlemanly life in London, is superciliously informing Biddy that Joe 'is rather backward ... in his learning and his manners.' As Biddy listens, she plucks a blackcurrant leaf and rubs it to pieces in her hand, the gesture telling us something of her pained feelings at his foolish haughtiness, feelings not sensed by the young Pip. The older narrator knows better and is condemned by Biddy's rubbing of that leaf not to be able to escape the memory: 'and the smell of a black currant bush has ever since recalled to me that evening in the little garden by the side of the lane'

(Ch. XIX). The smell will never stop taking him back to his own arrogance and folly.

Smells are so irresistible that Pip seems to think that everyone else will know them too. He recalls how, travelling from London back to Kent, he encounters the convict who, years earlier, had mysteriously accosted him in the Three Jolly Bargemen and given him money. Now, there he is again, in the coach-yard of the Cross Keys, in the company of another convict. Pip finds that he must share the coach with the two of them and their 'keeper', and that they bring with them 'that curious flavour of bread-poultice, baize, rope-yarn, and hearthstone, which attends the convict presence' (Ch. XXVIII). ('Flavour' is as frequently a synonym for smell as for taste in Dickens.) Charlotte Mitchell's notes to the Penguin Classics edition of the novel work away at explaining each element of this olfactory list (convicts had to break stones and unpick old ropes, baize might have been used for convicts' clothes, prison bread might have been so stale as to need soaking in hot water).[5] Yet what is remarkable is Pip's phrasing: '*that* curious flavour'. He knows the smell so well that he presumes others know it too. It is another aspect of the 'taint of crime' that he cannot escape.

The Dickens novel with the most smells is the most autobiographical, and the one most dedicated to the strange operations of memory: *David Copperfield*. In the second chapter of this novel the narrator looks back into 'the blank of my infancy' and finds that 'the first objects I can remember' are his mother and Peggotty. 'What else do I remember? Let me see.' There is his childhood home, Peggotty's kitchen, the yard with a frightening cock and the geese that follow him. And, inevitably, a particular smell.

Here is a long passage—what an enormous perspective I make of it!—leading from Peggotty's kitchen to the front door. A dark store-room opens out of it, and that is a place to be run past at night; for I don't know what may be among those tubs and jars and old tea-chests, when there is nobody in there with a dimly-burning light, letting a mouldy air come out of the door, in which there is the smell of soap, pickles, pepper, candles, and coffee, all at one whiff.

Everything in a 'whiff'. The child's sense of smell is discerning. When he is taken out for the day by Mr Murdstone and meets his two friends Quinion and Passnidge, he smells them as well as listening to them. 'All the time we were out, the two gentlemen smoked incessantly—which, I thought, if I might judge from the smell of their rough coats, they must have been doing, ever since the coats had first come home from the tailor's' (Ch. II). The smell tells us of the conspiratorial male comradeship that the young David scarcely comprehends (the cigar-loving men are in fact joking about Murdstone's scheme to marry David's mother). Smells yank the narrator right back to his past. He recalls arriving in London as a boy and waiting at an inn to be picked up to be taken to school. He sits in the booking-office, 'inhaling the smell of stables (ever since associated with that morning)'. When he places himself back in the schoolroom at Salem House, a distinctive odour returns. 'There is a strange unwholesome smell upon the room, like mildewed corduroys, sweet apples wanting air, and rotten books' (Ch. V).

Often, outside his novels, when Dickens seems to be writing about his own past, you find that spots of time from childhood are remembered by particular smells. In an autobiographical fragment that he wrote in the mid-1840s, he recalled how, on his way back home from working at Warren's blacking factory, on Saturday nights, he would wander the streets near Blackfriars, gazing in at shops and street entertainments.

> There were two or three hat-manufactories there then (I think they are there still); and among the things which, encountered anywhere or under any circumstances, will instantly recall that time, is the smell of hat-making.[6]

This was a time of such hopelessness for the young Dickens that, as an adult, he had to avoid not only the place where he had once worked, but the smell that might take him back there in his memory.

> For many years, when I came near to Robert Warren's in the Strand, I crossed over to the opposite side of the way, to avoid a certain smell of the cement they put upon the blacking-corks, which reminded me of what I was once.[7]

A 'certain smell' is overpowering. Writing one of his columns as the Uncommercial Traveller in *All the Year Round*, he described his return to 'the scenes among which my earliest days were passed; scenes from which I departed when I was a child'. The place is Dullborough, a thinly disguised version of Chatham.

> As I left Dullborough in the days when there were no railroads in the land, I left it in a stage-coach. Through all the years that have since passed, have I ever lost the

> smell of the damp straw in which I was packed—like
> game—and forwarded, carriage paid, to the Cross
> Keys, Wood-street, Cheapside, London?[8]

Forster confirmed that this was indeed the smell that
Dickens always remembered from his own departure
from Chatham.[9] Remembering birthdays in another of
the Uncommercial Traveller columns, Dickens latches
onto the special combination of smells that is the key to
his memories.

> When shall I disconnect the combined smells of
> oranges, brown paper, and straw, from those other
> birthdays at school, when the coming hamper casts its
> shadow before, and when a week of social harmony—
> shall I add of admiring and affectionate popularity—
> led up to that Institution?'[10]

Memory survives through the sense of smell. In an
anonymous article in *Household Words* published on
1 January 1859, Dickens interrupted an account of the
New Year's memories he shared with his younger sister
with this curious parenthesis.

> (A day or so before her death, that little sister
> told me that, in the night, the smell of the fallen leaves
> in the woods where we had habitually walked as very
> young children, had come upon her with such strength
> of reality, that she had moved her weak head to look for
> strewn leaves on the floor of her bedside).[11]

This is evidently recalled from the deathbed of his beloved sister Fanny, who had died of consumption more than ten years earlier. He would never forget what she told him about that smell, so redolent of their shared childhood.

A few months after her death, Dickens began writing *David Copperfield*, in which a child's experience of death lives on through particular smells. Remembering the day when he was told of his mother's death, David naturally begins with the smell of it. 'How well I recollect the kind of day it was! I smell the fog that hung about the place; I see the hoar frost, ghostly, through it; I feel my rimy hair fall clammy on my cheek'. He travels back from boarding school to his Suffolk home town for the funeral. He can still remember a special smell at Mr Omer's the haberdasher's, where he goes to be fitted for mourning clothes. 'There was a good fire in the room, and a breathless smell of warm black crape – I did not know what the smell was then, but I do now'. Smells are the elemental stuff of experience, singular, sometimes puzzling, undeniable. The day of his mother's funeral, seared on his memory, is full of smells.

> If the funeral had been yesterday, I could not recollect it better. The very air of the best parlour, when I went in at the door, the bright condition of the fire, the shining of the wine in the decanters, the patterns of the glasses and plates, the faint sweet smell of cake, the odour of Miss Murdstone's dress, and our black clothes.
>
> (Ch. IX)

This sweet cake smell was clearly a distinctive scent of funeral preparation for Dickens, because it recurs in *Great Expectations*, when Pip goes back to his childhood home for the funeral of his sister, Mrs Joe. Pip recalls 'the air of the parlour being faint with the smell of sweet cake' (Ch. XXXV).

In *David Copperfield*, Dickens stirs memories with smells: the smell of the leaves in the garden of his childhood home that comes with an 'old, unhappy feeling' (Ch. XLV); the solace, for the newly orphaned David, of taking refuge for an afternoon with the kindly doctor, Mr Chillip, where he reads in his surgery 'with the smell of the whole Pharmacopoeia coming up my nose' (Ch. X); 'The earthy smell, the sunless air, the sensation of the world being shut out' of Sunday services in the Cathedral during his years at school in Canterbury, which take him back and hold him 'hovering above those days, in a half-sleeping and half-waking dream' (Ch. XVIII). David recalls his first conversation alone with Dora and her smelling the geraniums in her father's greenhouse. He confesses, 'The scent of a geranium leaf, to this day, strikes me with a half comical half serious wonder as to what change has come over me in a moment' (Ch. XXVI). It is the present tense because he is re-experiencing the smell and the excitement of that moment. Near the end of the novel, he has returned to Canterbury after three years abroad; he gazes from a window as he used to do, many years earlier.

> The feeling with which I used to watch the tramps, as they came into the town on those wet evenings, at dusk, and limped past, with their bundles drooping over their shoulders at the ends of sticks, came freshly back to me; fraught, as then, with the smell of damp earth, and wet leaves and briar, and the sensation of

the very airs that blew upon me in my own toilsome
journey.

(Ch. LX).

Smell is both memory and fresh sensation. With the
freshness of what has gone, it invariably opens the narrator
to some kind of melancholy.

Where Dickens's narratives explore the present-
ness of what is lost, they exploit smell with peculiar
brilliance. When Scrooge in *A Christmas Carol* is returned
wonderingly to his own childhood, it is to a sense of smell.
'He was conscious of a thousand odours floating in the
air, each one connected with a thousand thoughts, and
hopes, and joys, and cares long, long, forgotten!' These are
indeterminate smells, without the energising specificity of
the Cratchits' Christmas pudding, as sniffed by Scrooge
the invisible spectator.

> Hallo! A great deal of steam! The pudding was out of
> the copper. A smell like a washing-day! That was the
> cloth. A smell like an eating-house and a pastrycook's
> next door to each other, with a laundress's next door to
> that! That was the pudding!
>
> (Stave III)

The author knows this aroma from personal experience;
knowing from experience is what smell confirms. In *Little
Dorrit*, Arthur Clennam returns, after many years, to the
family home of Flora Casby, whom he loved as a young
man. Approaching the front door, he already knows the
smell of the house from memory, before he knows it again,
in fact. 'I know its staid repose within. The smell of its
jars of old rose-leaves and lavender seems to come upon

me even here'. In a strange way, the memory of a smell becomes the thing itself. Reality confirms it: as soon as a servant opens the door, 'those faded scents in truth saluted him like wintry breath that had a faint remembrance in it of the bygone spring' (I Ch. XIII). It is the faded life of what he once felt.

Smell for Dickens is the most visceral sense. The most extraordinary, and perhaps the most horrible, event in all his fiction makes itself known by a smell – a smell so strong and so nasty that it is almost a taste. In *Bleak House* Mr Snagsby, the law stationer, meeting Tony Jobling in Cook's Court, remarks on something 'greasy' in the air. Burnt chops in the kitchen of the adjacent tavern? If so, they cannot have been 'quite fresh' when cooking began. Mr Snagsby leaves and Tony (aka 'Mr Weevle') is joined by his friend and fellow conspirator Mr Guppy. The two of them have arranged for Tony, under a pseudonym, to rent a room from Krook in order to spy on him. They retire to Tony's room, but are disturbed by the soot and some oily deposit on the window-sill, 'offensive to the touch and sight, and more offensive to the smell'. Guppy asks for water and 'so washes, and rubs, and scrubs, and smells, and washes'; he seems to be smelling himself to be sure that nothing clings to him.

The smell reaches and disgusts these characters before they have any notion of its source. They go down to Krook's lodging and get more of 'the burning smell'; 'he is not there', but 'there is a smouldering suffocating vapour in the room, and a dark greasy coating on the walls and ceiling'. 'O Horror, he IS here!' Krook, permeating himself with gin, has perished by 'Spontaneous Combustion' (Ch. XXXII). His fate is incredible, and famously provoked even some of Dickens's former admirers to say so. G. H.

Lewes, a critical partisan for Dickens's writing, irked the novelist by pointing out, in two published open letters, the scientific impossibility of this eventuality.[12] He did so while the novel was still unfolding in its monthly parts. Dickens would include a paragraph in his preface to the eventual one-volume edition of *Bleak House* referring to his dispute with 'my good friend Mr Lewes' and insisting that Lewes was 'quite mistaken'. The swiftly convened Coroner's Inquest is told how 'a very peculiar smell was observed by the inhabitants of the court' (Ch. XXXIII). As if to insist on the factuality of this form of self-destruction by 'the corrupted humours of the vicious body itself', he makes Krook's nasty fate evident through the nose.

The cause of the very first death in this death-filled novel had already made itself known by a special smell that reaches into the mouth as well as the nose. Mr Tulkinghorn, seeking out the law scrivener whose handwriting has so inexplicably discomposed Lady Dedlock, enters the second-floor room above Krook's shop where Nemo lives. It is night and, in the very dim light of one candle, the olfactory sense is sharpened.

> Foul and filthy as the room is, foul and filthy as the air is, it is not easy to perceive what fumes those are which most oppress the senses in it; but through the general sickliness and faintness, and the odour of stale tobacco, there comes into the lawyer's mouth the bitter, vapid taste of opium.
>
> (Ch. X)

It seems that Tulkinghorn, a man of the world, after all, knows this smell, so palpable as to become a taste. Dickens knew it – his friend Wilkie Collins was a

frequent consumer of laudanum – and so would not a
few of his readers. The man who occupies the squalid
room is recently dead and the smell tells its own story.
The surgeon who is called has no doubts. ' "He has died
… of an over-dose of opium, there is no doubt. The room
is strongly flavoured with it." ' The next day the coroner's
court sits in a first-floor room in the adjacent Sol's Arms.
Death brings more irresistible olfactory associations. The
coroner is used to conducting inquests in rooms in public
houses. 'The smell of sawdust, beer, tobacco-smoke, and
spirits, is inseparable in his vocation from death in its
most awful shapes'.

And where is Nemo's body taken, once the semi-farcical
inquest has reached its verdict of 'accidental death'? To 'a
hemmed-in churchyard, pestiferous and obscene, whence
malignant diseases are communicated to the bodies of our
dear brothers and sisters who have not departed', which
is reached down 'a reeking little tunnel of a court' (Ch.
XI). Like most of his contemporaries in the 1850s, Dickens
believed that cholera and other contagious diseases were
spread by 'miasma' in the air; smell and disease are intimately
connected in this novel.[13] Death spreads outwards from
the slums of Tom-all-Alone's and its 'pestiferous' burial
ground. When he accompanies Inspector Bucket in search
of Jo, Mr Snagsby 'sickens in body and mind'.

> Mr Snagsby passes along the middle of a villainous
> street, undrained, unventilated, deep in black mud and
> corrupt water—though the roads are dry elsewhere—
> and reeking with such smells and sights that he, who
> has lived in London all his life, can scarce believe his
> senses.
>
> (Ch. XXII)

The bad smells of *Bleak House* can be lethal. In a speech to the Metropolitan Sanitary Association in May 1851, a few months before he began *Bleak House*, Dickens warned his well-heeled fellow diners of the dangers spawned by the capital's filth, for 'if you once have a vigorous pestilence raging furiously in Saint Giles's, no mortal list of Lady Patronesses can keep it out of Almack's'.[14] (Saint Giles was an area of notorious slums; Almack's was the most fashionable club in the wealthy West End.)

> I can honestly declare tonight, that all the use I have since made of my eyes – or nose [*laughter*] – that all the information I have since been able to acquire through any of my senses, has strengthened me in the conviction that searching sanitary Reform must precede all other social remedies [*cheers*].

Since the late 1840s, he had been taking part in public arguments about the best way in which to dispose of London's sewage. He was almost certainly co-author of an article in the *Examiner* in July 1849, 'Drainage and Health of the Metropolis', calling for some 'system of works, that, by distributing the miasma-breeding filth of the metropolis, would minimise or extinguish its pestilential quality'.[15]

In *Bleak House*, what you smell is grim reality. 'He gloats over mould, damp, rottenness, and smells' observed one contemporary reviewer, with distaste.[16] The impoverished brickmaker confronts the heartless philanthropist Mrs Pardiggle with what he and his family have to consume. 'Look at the water. Smell it! That's wot we drinks. How do you like it, and what do you think of gin instead!' (Ch. VIII). You can just about fend off noisome odours if you are the Lord Chancellor, who presides with, just in front of him, 'an immense flat nosegay, like a little garden, which scented the whole court' (Ch. XXIX). Elsewhere in *Bleak House*, the bad smells are unmistakable. In Mr Vholes's chambers we encounter a unique odour. 'A smell as of unwholesome sheep blending with the smell of must and dust is referable to the nightly (and often daily) consumption of mutton fat in candles and to the fretting of parchment forms and skins in greasy drawers' (Ch. XLIV). Later, when the odious Vholes visits John Jarndyce's home at Bleak House, Esther notices that his black clothes steam before the fire, 'diffusing a very unpleasant perfume' (Ch. XLV). Even attempts to improve the smell of the world can seem revolting. When Esther finds that the lawyer's clerk Mr Guppy is going up in the world, she notes that he has a 'new suit of glossy clothes' and that he has 'quite scented the dining-room with bear's-grease and other perfumery'. No wonder that good smells come to her only in moments of release – and escape from London. When she visits Boythorn's house in Lincolnshire, 'the smell of sweet herbs and all kinds of wholesome growth (to say nothing of the neighbouring meadows where the hay was carrying) made the whole air a great nosegay' (Ch. XVIII). But how much less distinct this is than the noxious fumes elsewhere in the novel.

Only a few novelists are drawn to smells as Dickens was. John Sutherland has pointed out how one such writer, George Orwell, relied in his fiction on his 'singularly diagnostic sense of smell'.[17] For Orwell, smell was base reality, and his gift was 'to particularize and separate out the ingredients that go into any aroma'. One of Dickens's favourite novelists was another smell-sensitive writer, Tobias Smollett, whose fiction David Copperfield reads with the author's own enthusiasm. David mentions *Roderick Random*, *Peregrine Pickle* and *Humphrey* (sic) *Clinker* as amongst the 'glorious host' that 'kept alive my fancy' during the grim reign of the Murdstones (Ch. IV). Perhaps this is where Dickens learnt the literary power of smells; when the eponymous narrator of *Roderick Random* wishes to convey the true horrors of a situation he will often do it through the nose. Press-ganged into a naval ship, he descends to the hold of the ship to be 'saluted with an intolerable stench of putrified cheese, and rancid butter'.[18] Reality is what you can smell. He suddenly realises that the genteel young lady he meets at the theatre is really a courtesan when, as he kisses her, he smells the gin on her breath. 'I was almost suffocated with the steams of Geneva!'[19] Matthew Bramble, the central character in Smollett's final novel, *The Expedition of Humphry Clinker*, is always describing the 'fetid effluvia' he encounters in London or Bath. Here he is explaining in a letter to his doctor why he fainted at a ball.

> Imagine to yourself a high exalted essence of mingled odours, arising from putrid gums, imposthumated lungs, sour flatulencies, rank armpits, sweating feet, running sores and issues, plasters, ointments, and embrocations, hungary-water, spirit of lavender, assafoetida drops, musk, hartshorn, and sal volatile; besides a thousand frowzy steams, which I could not analyse. Such, O Dick! is the fragrant aether we breathe in the polite assemblies of Bath.[20]

Not for nothing did Smollett's contemporary, Laurence Sterne, re-name him Smelfungus in his comic novel *A Sentimental Journey*.

We might think that Dickens's novels are smelly because Victorian London was smelly (though Smollett's writing shows that urban odours did not begin with the nineteenth century). Social historians often invite us to imagine the stench of Victorian London. 'Think of the worst smell that you have ever met. Now imagine what it was like to have that in your nostrils all day and all night, all over London.'[21] The worst of it would have been the stink of human excrement, about which Dickens's novels are notably inexplicit. 'The stench of human excrement in London was so pervasive that it only became noticeable in its worst manifestations'.[22] This particular bad smell is invariably unspecified in Dickens's fiction. In *A Tale of Two Cities*, the slum is a 'great foul nest', full of 'spoilt and sickly vapours'. We are left to imagine what might be behind the smell of 'decomposition' and other 'intangible impurities' (Ch. V). Even when Dickens was away from London, he thought of its smells. Writing to John Forster from his seaside retreat in Broadstairs in October 1847, Dickens referred to Forster's Lincoln's Inn Fields address as 'the fragrant neighbourhood of Clare-market and the Portugal-street burying-ground': the adjacent Clare Market was where sheep were slaughtered, while the local burial ground, noted in the *Morning Chronicle* for its 'stench', had been closed down.[23] Here is perhaps an original for the pestilence-breeding burial ground in *Bleak House*. The smell of London was at its worst in the summer of 1858. The whole city near the Thames was enveloped in what came to be called 'The Great Stink'.[24] Dickens experienced it first-hand.

You will have read in the papers that the Thames at London is most horrible. I have to cross Waterloo or London Bridge to get to the Railroad when I come down there, and I can certify that the offensive smells, even in that short whiff, have been of a most head-and-stomach distracting nature. Nobody knows what is to be done; at least, everybody knows a plan, and everybody else knows it won't do; in the meantime cart-loads of chloride of Lime are shot into the filthy stream, and do something—I hope.[25]

It was this crisis that finally persuaded parliament to authorise Joseph Bazalgette's plan for intercepting sewers, pumping stations and treatment works.

For nineteenth-century city dwellers, the other ubiquitous odour was that of horses and their dung. In November 1839, when Dickens was looking for a house to rent, smell was a consideration. He told his close friend and solicitor Thomas Mitton that he had considered a house in Kent Terrace, a fashionable address near Regent's Park, but had been put off by the problems that another friend, the actor William Macready, had encountered when living in the same street.

Macready tells me that when they lived in Kent Terrace (2 doors from No. 10) the stench from the stables at certain periods of the wind was so great that they could scarcely breathe—and this circumstance alone was the cause of their not retaining the house constantly, as, liking it very much, they would otherwise have done. He holds it to be a decided and insurmountable objection, and, when *he* speaks so strongly, I—alas!— am compelled to do the same.[26]

The smell of horses and stables is everywhere in Dickens's fiction. London mews, nowadays highly desirable

residential cul-de-sacs, were once where the wealthy kept
their horses. This meant that grand residences were often
adjacent to the sources of a distinctive aroma. In *Little
Dorrit*, Arthur Clennam and Mr Meagles are wandering
through the less alluring streets of Mayfair, London's
grandest district, in search of Miss Wade and Tattycoram.
'Parasite little tenements, with the cramp in their whole
frame, from the dwarf hall-door on the giant model of
His Grace's in the Square to the squeezed window of the
boudoir commanding the dunghills in the Mews, made
the evening doleful' (I Ch. XXVII). Concentrations of
wealth mean concentrations of horse dung.

The Barnacles, determined to live in this same area, rent
a 'squeezed' residence in a mews just off Grosvenor Square,
'a hideous little street of dead wall, stables, and dunghills,
with lofts over coach-houses inhabited by coachmen's
families'. It is immediately known to the visiting Arthur
Clennam by its odour. 'To the sense of smell, the house
was like a sort of bottle filled with a strong distillation
of Mews; and when the footman opened the door, he
seemed to take the stopper out' (Ch. X).

Later in the same novel, after Fanny Dorrit has become
Mrs Sparkler, she returns with her new husband to 'a
little mansion, rather of the Tite Barnacle class'. Their
London house is 'quite a triumph of inconvenience, with
a perpetual smell in it of the day before yesterday's soup
and coach-horses, but extremely dear, as being exactly
in the centre of the habitable globe' (II Ch. XXIV).
Presumably it too is shoved up against a mews and with
the poorly ventilated kitchen close to every other room.
Because there is no getting away from this smell, Dickens
repeats his description of it nine chapters later. It tells
you of the torment that Fanny will share with her hated

antagonist, Mrs Merdle, who comes to live with them after her husband's suicide, in this 'genteel little temple of inconvenience to which the smell of the day before yesterday's soup and coachhorses was as constant as Death to man' (II Ch. XXXIII). The comparably vainglorious Mr Turveydrop in *Bleak House* lives in a once fine house in a 'great room … which was built out into a mews at the back … It was a bare, resounding room smelling of stables' (Ch. XIV). You had to pay to avoid this odour.

Every reader could be presumed to know this smell, which often mingles with other scents in Dickens's novels. When David Copperfield goes to meet Micawber, who has mysteriously summoned him and Traddles to Canterbury, he finds himself staying in a hotel whose narrow passages 'smelt as if they had been steeped, for ages, in a solution of soup and stables' (Ch. LII). It was evidently the prevailing aroma of many a hostelry. In *Great Expectations*, when Pip recalls his tea at a coaching inn with Estella, he says,

> I was, and I am, sensible that the air of this chamber, in its strong combination of stable with soup-stock, might have led one to infer that the coaching department was not doing well, and that the enterprising proprietor was boiling down the horses for the refreshment department. Yet the room was all in all to me, Estella being in it.
>
> (Ch. XXXIII)

The narrator can still sniff that special combination of smells, comically undermining his younger self's romantic yearning.

So, even when smells are bad, in Dickens's narratives they can be intriguing compounds that distinguish a place or person. In *Martin Chuzzlewit*, we arrive with the Pecksniffs at Todgers' boarding house, an especially dark place most vividly sensed through the nose.

> There was an odd smell in the passage, as if the concentrated essence of all the dinners that had been cooked in the kitchen since the house was built, lingered at the top of the kitchen stairs to that hour, and like the Black Friar in Don Juan, 'wouldn't be driven away.' In particular, there was a sensation of cabbage; as if all the greens that had ever been boiled there, were evergreens, and flourished in immortal strength.
>
> (Ch. VIII)

The smell is so 'odd' that the narrator forgets that it might be disgusting. Here is Poll Sweedlepipe's barber's shop in the same novel.

> The staircase was sacred to rabbits. There in hutches of all shapes and kinds, made from old packing-cases, boxes, drawers, and tea-chests, they increased in a prodigious degree, and contributed their share towards that complicated whiff which, quite impartially, and without distinction of persons, saluted every nose that was put into Sweedlepipe's easy shaving-shop.
>
> (Ch. XXVI)

Those rabbits, along with the birds with which he fills his shop, merge their smells, no doubt, with the barber's soaps and pomades to produce a uniquely 'complicated whiff'. Earlier in *Martin Chuzzlewit*, Pecksniff tries to look through the keyhole of old Martin Chuzzlewit's room in a dark corridor, but bangs heads with someone else doing the same thing. As he recoils from the pain, 'Mr Pecksniff found himself immediately collared by something which smelt like several damp umbrellas, a barrel of beer, a cask of warm brandy-and-water, and a small parlour-full of stale tobacco smoke, mixed' (Ch. IV). These are the blended olfactory aspects of Montague Tigg, with the 'several' umbrellas the mysterious yet magical ingredient.

A Dickens character might be introduced by his or her smell. Mr E. W. B. Childers, the circus horseman in *Hard Times*, is given a physical description, a summary of his clothing and the information that he 'smelt of lamp-oil, straw, orange-peel, horses' provender and sawdust' (Ch. VI). And there he is, in all his quiddity. In this novel, where the stink of industrial waste predominates, there is something heady in the smells that this showman brings with him. They are what Dickens smelt when he went to circus entertainments at Astley's Amphitheatre in Lambeth, celebrated in one of his *Sketches by Boz*.[27] Kit visits it with his sweetheart Barbara in *The Old Curiosity Shop*, experiencing before the show begins 'the vague smell of horses suggestive of coming wonders' (Ch. XXXIX). Dickens knew these wonders first-hand. When his friend Clarkson Stanfield wrote to him in Italy telling him that he had recently been to Astley's, Dickens in reply readily imagined the banter and foolery of the resident clown, Barry.

> I see him run away after this;—not on his feet, but on his knees and the calves of his legs alternately—and that smell of sawdusty horses, which was never in any

other place in the world, salutes my nose with painful distinctness.[28]

The liberating smells of the circus performer in *Hard Times* are something similar to the smells that greet the protagonist of *Nicholas Nickleby*, when he is first ushered into the world of the theatre, 'turning at length into an entry, in which was a strong smell of orange-peel and lamp-oil, with an under-current of sawdust' (Ch. XXIII). Having escaped the horrors of Dotheboys Hall and joined the Crummles's travelling troupe, he too has been freed into this dizzy new world of smells. The smells of the theatre were always thus for Dickens. Here he is writing to his actor friend Macready and imagining coming round to his dressing room at the Drury Lane Theatre.

Well a day!—I see it all, and smell that extraordinary compound of odd scents peculiar to a theatre, which bursts upon me when I swing open the little door in the hall; accompanies me, as I meet perspiring supers in the narrow passage; goes with me, up the two steps; crosses the stage; winds round the third entrance P.S. as I wind; and escorts me safely into your presence ...[29]

To imagine it is to smell it and be intoxicated. Though there was also the nightmare of an evening at the theatre in Paris with Wilkie Collins, as described to his sister-in-law:

we were obliged to leave, at the end of the first act, by the intolerable stench of the place. The whole theatre must be standing over some vast cesspool. It was so alarming that I instantly rushed into a café and had brandy.[30]

There were some smells that Dickens could not get away from. He was peculiarly possessed by the smells of churches. When Paul Dombey is christened in *Dombey and Son*, it is in a 'chill and earthy' church that makes the narrator think of graves and funerals: 'the strange, unusual, uncomfortable smell, and the cadaverous light; were all in unison. It was a cold and dismal scene' (Ch. V). The earthiness is the smell of death. Given the scene, 'Little Paul might have asked with Hamlet "into my grave?"' And it will be to this place that he will be brought, only a few years later, for his funeral. 'Earthy' is the common word for what you might sniff in a church. In *Pickwick Papers*, Jingle includes amongst the architectural delights of Rochester, 'old cathedral too—earthy smell' (Ch. II). In an article in *Household Words* in September 1850, Dickens counted amongst the distinguishing characteristics of an English cathedral, 'the earthy smell, preaching more eloquently than deans and chapters, of the common doom'.[31] It is the smell of death in the nostrils of the living.

This smell returns in *Bleak House*, where the ancestor-worship of the Dedlocks can be sensed in the nostrils. 'On Sundays the little church in the park is mouldy; the oaken pulpit breaks out into a cold sweat; and there is a general smell and taste as of the ancient Dedlocks in their graves' (Ch. II).

Smell and taste are very close to each other, as ever in Dickens. This makes it all the more discomfiting when we are invited to imagine the aromatic impression as Chesney Wold is briefly filled with fashionable guests, invited down to the country for a winter's week or two. 'On Sunday the chill little church is almost warmed by so much gallant company, and the general flavour of the Dedlock dust is quenched in delicate perfumes' (Ch. XII).

And what about when the great house is empty? 'On all
the house there is a cold, blank smell like the smell of a
little church, though something dryer, suggesting that the
dead and buried Dedlocks walk there in the long nights
and leave the flavour of their graves behind them' (Ch.
XXIX). The Dedlock story will end with death and the
novel's final visit to the family mausoleum in Lincolnshire.

Dickens readily sensed this earthy, churchy smell.
Working in the offices of *All the Year Round* in Covent
Garden in the summer of 1869, he complained of 'a
mouldy smell from some forgotten crypt—an extra
mouldy smell, mouldier than of yore'.[32] In an essay in
this very periodical, his Uncommercial Traveller visits
unfrequented London churches on a Sunday and finds in
one of these that he is breathing 'a strong kind of invisible
snuff' which is composed of 'the decay of matting, wood,
cloth, stone, iron, earth, and something else.'[33] He is
smelling and even tasting the dead. 'Is the something
else, the decay of dead citizens in the vaults below? As
sure as Death it is!' Yet though, in this reporter's tour of
City churches, 'rot and mildew and dead citizens formed
the uppermost scent', there was also, 'infused into it in a
dreamy way not at all displeasing', a smell that denoted
'the staple character of the neighbourhood'. He goes on
to enumerate the smells of whatever is being sold nearby.

> In the churches about Mark-lane, for example, there was
> a dry whiff of wheat; and I accidentally struck an airy
> sample of barley out of an aged hassock in one of them.
> From Rood-lane to Tower-street, and thereabouts,
> there was often a subtle flavour of wine: sometimes,
> of tea. One church near Mincing-lane smelt like a
> druggist's drawer. Behind the Monument the service

had a flavour of damaged oranges, which, a little further
down towards the river, tempered into herrings, and
gradually toned into a cosmopolitan blast of fish. In
one church, the exact counterpart of the church in the
Rake's Progress where the hero is being married to the
horrible old lady, there was no speciality of atmosphere,
until the organ shook a perfume of hides all over us
from some adjacent warehouse.[34]

The smells of life mingle fascinatingly with those of death.

We could just say, what a nose Dickens had! Except
that he also made extraordinary fictional use of it. Those
accounts of church smells seem to have laid the ground
for his representation of Cloisterham and its Cathedral in
The Mystery of Edwin Drood. The setting is a place built
on the dead.

A monotonous, silent city, deriving an earthy flavour
throughout from its Cathedral crypt, and so abounding
in vestiges of monastic graves, that the Cloisterham
children grow small salad in the dust of abbots and
abbesses, and make dirt-pies of nuns and friars.

(Ch. III)

That 'earthy flavour' again. In Cloisterham, everyone has
death in the nostrils; the dead fertilise vegetables and
are in the dirt in children's fingernails. On a glorious
summer's day, the sun's warmth might 'penetrate into
the Cathedral, subdue its earthy odour, and preach the
Resurrection and the Life' (Ch. XXIII). But only for a
little while. Cloisterham is closely based on Rochester,
which Dickens knew so well (we might recall Jingle's
recollection of the 'earthy smell' of Rochester Cathedral

in *Pickwick Papers*). *The Mystery of Edwin Drood* centres on a possible murder and therefore perhaps the disposal of a body. With the novel only half-completed when the author died, the mystery remains; one unwitting agent in its unravelling was clearly to have been the alcoholic stonemason, Durdles, who possesses the keys to every part of the Cathedral. He spends much time, as he himself says, 'down in the crypt among the earthy damps there, and the dead breath of the old 'uns' (Ch. IV). The choirmaster, John Jasper, engages Durdles in conversation, telling him, 'my lot is cast in the same old earthy, chilly, never-changing place'. Why does Jasper ask Durdles 'to let me go about with you sometimes, and see some of these odd nooks in which you pass your days' (Ch. V)? We know that he is obsessed with Rosa, the young woman to whom his nephew Edwin is engaged. In an extraordinary episode he accompanies Durdles by night into the crypt and plies him with drink. Durdles falls asleep and dreams 'that something touches him, and that something falls from his hand. Then something clinks' (Ch. XII). A key has been taken from him, we infer. Jasper is exploring.

The 'dead breath of the old 'uns' – the many who are buried in often unmarked places under the Cathedral – is in Jasper's nostrils too. Surely, he is looking for a place to bury a body, a place where it might easily be lost amongst all those 'old 'uns'. The very smell of the crypt, which is the smell of the Cathedral, which is the smell of the old city itself, is surely preparing us for another burial. Earth to earthiness.

4

Changing tenses

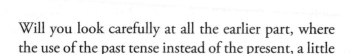

> Will you look carefully at all the earlier part, where
> the use of the past tense instead of the present, a little
> hurts the picturesque effect?
>
> Letter to Charles Knight, 27 July 1851[1]

Here is the last paragraph of Dickens's last, unfinished novel.

> Mrs Tope's care has spread a very neat, clean breakfast
> ready for her lodger. Before sitting down to it, he opens
> his corner-cupboard door; takes his bit of chalk from
> its shelf; adds one thick line to the score, extending
> from the top of the cupboard door to the bottom; and
> then falls to with an appetite.

It is the end of Chapter XXIII of *The Mystery of Edwin
Drood*, concluding the sixth monthly instalment of the
novel. It was published from Dickens's manuscript by
John Forster after the author's death. The 'lodger' is the
mysterious Mr Datchery, who arrived in Cloisterham

in the middle of the previous month's instalment. Mr Datchery, whose true identity has been a rich topic of speculation for critics, poses as an elderly 'buffer ... living idly on his means', but has evidently come to Cloisterham with a purpose connected to the disappearance of Edwin Drood, and with some knowledge of the sinister John Jasper, Drood's uncle (Ch. XVIII). He has just been in the Cathedral observing Princess Puffer, the opium woman, as she watches Jasper from behind a pillar, 'carefully withdrawn from the Choir Master's view' (Ch. XXIII). Seeing her shake her fist at Jasper leads him to add another line to that chalked score, which must, we infer, be some kind of tally of testimonies against Jasper.

There is much to tease us in this premature close to the novelist's *oeuvre*, but one thing above all: Dickens ends his career in the present tense. His story is still unspooling before us. *The Mystery of Edwin Drood* is one of three late novels (along with *Bleak House* and *Our Mutual Friend*) that are divided up between chapters in the past tense and chapters in the present tense. None of Dickens's narrative tricks is stranger or more audacious than this. It is as if each of these novels is composed of two separate stories, providing two separate experiences for the reader. Dickens seems to have said nothing about this narrative method. The number plans that survive for all three novels remain silent about their tense switches. Tantalisingly, a letter to Charles Knight, a contributor to his journal *Household Words*, advising him to switch an article from the past to the present tense shows Dickens to be highly conscious of the powers of present-tense narrative. He is advising Knight on his series of 'Shadows', short narratives of the lives of lesser-known historical figures. He advocates the use of the present tense. 'I understand each phase of the thing to be *always a thing present, before the mind's eye*—a shadow passing before it. Whatever is done, must be *doing*. Is it not so?'

Yet he never comments on his own reasons for making 'a thing present' in his novels. Even more surprisingly, contemporary readers and critics appear not to have remarked upon on his trick of dividing a novel between tenses, as if it were so odd that they just had to ignore it.

When Dickens first used this method in *Bleak House*, published in monthly instalments between March 1852 and September 1853, there had been nothing like it in the English novel before. The compositors working for Dickens's printers were so unused to the technique that they sometimes turned present-tense verbs into the past tense.[2] Yet the first reviewers, disagreeing sharply about the quality of the new work, failed to notice its most unusual characteristic.[3] While the opening paragraph is a list without a single main verb, when we reach the second paragraph, where the fog 'flows among green aits and meadows' and 'rolls defiled among the tiers of shipping', it becomes evident that we are in the present tense. There we stay as we are introduced to the High Court of Chancery, where 'Jarndyce and Jarndyce drones on'. There we stay for Chapter II, in which we see the Dedlock estate in Lincolnshire, where 'the waters are out', and then Sir Leicester and Lady Dedlock at their house in town, where the family lawyer calls. 'Sir Leicester Dedlock is with my Lady, and is happy to see Mr Tulkinghorn'. A jolt for Dickens's first readers came when, at the beginning of Chapter III, the narrative suddenly shifted to the first person and the past tense. This is the moment when you begin to see that the novel is composed of two separate narrative strands, braided together.

Thirty-four of the sixty-seven chapters of *Bleak House* are in the present tense; thirty-three are in the past tense. Each of the first six monthly instalments of the novel consisted of a mixture of past-tense and present-tense chapters. Four follow the same pattern: two chapters of Esther's narrative in the past tense, followed by a third chapter of third-person, present-tense narrative. The effect is unsettling: we keep abandoning our protagonist for a larger, stranger world that she cannot comprehend. This pattern of an instalment beginning with chapters of Esther's narrative, but then ending with a single chapter in the third person and present tense, is followed in four more of the novel's monthly parts. Yet the patterns of the other parts are unpredictable. Five consist entirely of chapters in the present tense, while the final two-part concluding instalment is dominated by Esther's past-tense narrative (six chapters out of eight). It is Esther's final account, looking back in fond contentment over what is past, that concludes, we might say stabilises, the novel.

Events in these two narratives in their different tenses unfold alongside each other, matching each other chronologically. Most characters move from one to the other, but a few do not. Esther herself never appears in the present-tense narrative, even though she is sometimes mentioned there. In Ch. XIX Mrs Chadband tells Mr Guppy that she once, in her previous guise as Miss Barbary's servant, was 'left in charge of a child named Esther Summerson'. In Ch. XXIX Mr Guppy approaches Lady Dedlock with the information that the daughter she presumed dead is very much alive, that Esther Summerson is in fact Esther Hawdon. Yet Esther never enters the time zone in which these exchanges take place. She cannot. Near the novel's climax, Dickens brings his reader hard up

against the barrier that Esther must not cross. At the end
of the seventeenth number of the novel, which appeared
in July 1853, Inspector Bucket waits at the door of Mr
Jarndyce's house for Miss Summerson to come downstairs
to join him in his search for Lady Dedlock. We are in
the present tense: she is on her way. But then the chapter
and the instalment end; after a month's wait for the first
readers, came a new chapter, now in 'Esther's Narrative', in
the past tense. It begins a few minutes before the previous
chapter ended. We have crossed between two tenses, two
different ways of knowing the world.

The other important character who cannot inhabit
both the novel's time zones is the calculating, inexpressive
lawyer Mr Tulkinghorn, a man who appears to serve the
aristocrats who employ him, but in fact preys upon them.
He is confined to the present tense. He is mentioned
within Esther's narrative, but never turns up in it. Esther
is part of his plot – he discovers that Lady Dedlock has
had an illegitimate child before she met and married
Sir Leicester – but she never meets him. He is the arch-
schemer in a narrative in which she is innocent. Esther's
sections of the novel have her moral authority; when we
step outside her narrative we are plunged into tumultuous
events, with no moral arbiter. Mr Tulkinghorn tries to
exert control over people and events, but, clever as he is, he
cannot. Knowing the tense to which his part of the story
is bound, we might have understood that his self-masking
mastery was an illusion. In the present tense plots unfold
with a momentum of their own, to the bewilderment of
most of those involved.

Mr Snagsby cannot make out what it is that he has had
to do with. Something is wrong somewhere, but what

something, what may come of it, to whom, when, and from which unthought of and unheard of quarter is the puzzle of his life.

(Ch. XXV)

Mr Snagsby, the law-stationer who lives near Krook's shop, who has employed Hawdon as a scrivener, who works for Mr Tulkinghorn, who meets everyone, is at the very centre of the novel, but his encounters with Tulkinghorn and Bucket persuade him that 'he is a party to some dangerous secret, without knowing what it is'. He is trapped in the present tense.

Impelled by the mystery of which he is a partaker and yet in which he is not a sharer, Mr Snagsby haunts what seems to be its fountain-head—the rag and bottle shop in the court. It has an irresistible attraction for him. Even now, coming round by the Sol's Arms with the intention of passing down the court, and out at the Chancery Lane end, and so terminating his unpremeditated after-supper stroll of ten minutes' long from his own door and back again, Mr Snagsby approaches.

(Ch. XXXII)

Something is indeed wrong somewhere. Some try to understand the unfolding mystery, like Mr Guppy, laying out before Lady Dedlock his investigations into Esther's true identity. 'It's going on, and I shall gather it up closer and closer as it goes on' (Ch. XXIX). In these present-tense chapters, everything is 'going on'. This is what gives the reader of *Bleak House*, for all the novel's connectedness and the intricacy of its plotting, an experience of a world

beyond control or comprehension. 'Mrs Snagsby Sees It
All' is the title and the refrain of one chapter, in which
we follow Mrs Snagsby's watchful discovery of every sign
in her husband's behaviour that he is in fact the father
of Jo, the crossing sweeper. But it is all utter delusion,
unspooling on the page as it confirms itself in her
thoughts. No wonder the characters are befuddled when
the narrator sometimes seems so too. The present tense
of the third-person narrative in *Bleak House* makes that
narrator into an amazed or amused or appalled witness to
what is taking place in front of him. The novel's present
tense is a permanent condition as well as a developing
narration.

> It is night in Lincoln's Inn—perplexed and troublous
> valley of the shadow of the law, where suitors find but
> little day—and fat candles are snuffed out in offices,
> and clerks have rattled down the crazy wooden stairs
> and dispersed. The bell that rings at nine o'clock has
> ceased its doleful clangour about nothing; the gates
> are shut; and the night-porter, a solemn warder with a
> mighty power of sleep, keeps guard in his lodge.
>
> Ch. XXXII

This is how it always happens – not just the historic
present that tells us a story, but the present tense of an
unchangeable state of things.

From early in his career, Dickens had used present-tense
narration in short bursts, to dramatise heady episodes. In
The Old Curiosity Shop it is used for the passing comedy of
Kit's trial, where the absurdity of the prosecuting counsel
is staged and his act takes place and is gone before he
can be caught out (Ch. LXIII). In *Martin Chuzzlewit*, the

present tense briefly takes over for the ebullience of the increasingly drunken dinner at Todger's: 'The enthusiasm is tremendous. The gentleman of a debating turn rises in the midst, and suddenly lets loose a tide of eloquence which bears down everything before it' (Ch. IX). Later we step into the present tense for the pleasure of a winter walk. 'And, lo! the towers of the Old Cathedral rise before them, even now! and by-and-bye they come into the sheltered streets, made strangely silent by their white carpet' (Ch. XII). Dickens experimented with the present tense in his journalism and travel writing. In *American Notes* (1842), for instance, he uses the present tense to turn narrative into enactment. See the opening of the sixth chapter, 'New York', where two introductory paragraphs lead to, 'Warm weather! The sun strikes upon our heads at this open window ...'[4] Most of the rest of the chapter is in the present tense. Or his first observations of Washington. 'Arrived at the hotel, I saw no more of the place that night ... Breakfast over next morning, I walk about the streets for an hour or two, and, coming home, throw up the window in the front and back, and look out. Here is Washington, fresh in my mind and under my eye ...'[5]

These are flickerings. The novel in which he first extensively tested the powers of the present tense was *Dombey and Son*. In its sixth monthly instalment, at the opening of Chapter XVIII, it suddenly switches into the present tense for the aftermath of Paul Dombey's death. The present tense pauses the narrative ('There is a hush through Mr Dombey's house') and strangely depersonalises events. 'After dark there come some visitors—noiseless visitors, with shoes of felt' (these are the undertakers, professionals in their quietness). 'At the offices in the City, the ground-glass windows are made more dim by shutters' (with the son dead, Dombey and Son goes into a kind of corporate mourning). 'And now, among the knot of servants dressed in mourning, and the weeping women, Mr Dombey passes through the hall to the other carriage that is waiting to receive him' (utterly self-isolated, Mr Dombey sets off for the funeral).

> The service over, and the clergyman withdrawn, Mr Dombey looks round, demanding in a low voice, whether the person who has been requested to attend to receive instructions for the tablet, is there?

Someone comes forward and says 'Yes.' Things are done and things are said: nothing of what Mr Dombey feels is to be told. We have to infer his state of mind when that 'someone', who is to carve the memorial tablet, corrects the proposed wording: ' … beloved and only child'. 'It should be, "son," I think, Sir?' Of course, he has forgotten Florence, his daughter.

Once the novel turns back to Florence, we return to the past tense. But it is as if Dickens has discovered a new resource, and from now on the narrative will readily switch into the present tense. It does so as Mr Dombey travels by train to Leamington Spa for his arranged match with the widowed Edith, and the speed and noise of the locomotive warn him of his doom. 'Louder and louder yet, it shrieks and cries as it comes tearing on resistless to the goal: and now its way, still like the way of Death, is strewn with ashes thickly' (Ch. XX).[6] The present tense reminds us of death again in Ch. XLI, where Florence returns to Brighton and her dead brother's school and where, in the same town, Mrs Skewton is dying. 'Night after night, the lights burn in the window, and the figure lies upon the bed, and Edith sits beside it, and the restless waves are calling to them both the whole night long'. Even when Florence marries Walter, in a chapter narrated entirely in the present tense, we end with thoughts of her brother and those death-betokening waves. So it seems inevitable that the novel ends in the present tense – happily, we might say, but with 'the voices in the waves' speaking low to the scarred, penitent Mr Dombey.

A few critics have tried to explain Dickens's tense shifts. 'The present-tense chapters in *Dombey and Son* mark the crises of the action,' observes one.[7] This is right as far as it goes, but does not catch the effect on the reader, who is suddenly cut loose from his or her narrative moorings. The present tense is used for the stages of Mr Dombey's journey to self-destruction. First, there is the wedding to Edith (Ch. XXXI), then the return of Mr and Mrs Dombey from honeymoon (Ch. XXXV), then Mr Dombey's situation after his wife's elopement and his daughter's disappearance (Ch. LI), and finally his ruin (Ch. LIX). The first of these mirrors the funeral chapter; the marriage takes place, after all, in the same church as the funeral. Edith has accepted her grim fate and events are taking over. This is what the present tense can do: erase any retrospective wisdom, any moral sense. 'In a firm, free hand, the Bride subscribes her name in the register'. The end of the previous chapter gave us Edith's inner turmoil; now, seen only externally, she has become 'the Bride'. The narrator has abandoned her. When the novel switches again to the present tense for the evening of Mr Dombey's return with Edith from their honeymoon: 'the happy pair are looked for every minute' (Ch. XXXV). The present tense merely reports, for bitterly ironical purposes. Dickens uses the present tense to suspend his narrative. After Edith has left Dombey, he is abandoned to silent pride and the lapping gossip of servants and men in the city.

> What the world thinks of him, how it looks at him, what it sees in him, and what it says—this is the haunting demon of his mind. It is everywhere where he is; and, worse than that, it is everywhere where he is not.
>
> (Ch. LI)

When financial ruin has come, Dombey's home is opened to new visitors. 'After a few days, strange people begin to call at the house, and to make appointments with one another in the dining-room, as if they lived there' (Ch. LIX). The new reality is something over which the house's owner is powerless. 'The callers and appointments in the dining-room become more numerous every day, and every gentleman seems to have pen and ink in his pocket, and to have some occasion to use it. At last it is said that there is going to be a Sale' (Ch. LIX). This is the state of things.

Dickens was not the only Victorian novelist to experiment with the present tense. Charlotte Brontë's *Jane Eyre* switches into the present tense in order to dramatise particular episodes, making them seem to live again in the memory with special vividness.

> When I draw up the curtain this time, reader, you must fancy you see a room in the George Inn at Millcote … I am warming away the numbness and chill contracted by sixteen hours' exposure to the rawness of

an October day ... Reader, though I look comfortably accommodated, I am not very tranquil in my mind.[8]

Brontë uses the present tense sparingly for intensely dramatised episodes. These include the evening when Jane returns to Thornfield from her visit to the dying Mrs Reed and meets Mr Rochester in his garden, an encounter leading to his proposal of marriage to her.

Sweet-briar and southernwood, jasmine, pink, and rose have long been yielding their evening sacrifice of incense: this new scent is neither of shrub nor flower; it is—I know it well—it is Mr Rochester's cigar. I look round and I listen. I see trees laden with ripening fruit. I hear a nightingale warbling in a wood half a mile off; no moving form is visible, no coming step audible; but that perfume increases: I must flee. I make for the wicket leading to the shrubbery, and I see Mr Rochester entering. I step aside into the ivy recess; he will not stay long: he will soon return whence he came, and if I sit still he will never see me.[9]

The smells are so intoxicating that the narrator is there again, reliving her experience.

Such passages in *Jane Eyre* are brief and rare, powerful because they surprise the reader. Brontë's technique is comparable to the use of the present tense in *David Copperfield*, a work composed soon after the appearance of Brontë's novel. Dickens intensifies the moments when his narrator returns to his past, compelled to re-experience it. 'And now I see the outside of our house ... Now I am in the garden at the back ... A great wind rises, and the summer is gone in a moment' (Ch. II). The present tense dramatises David's discovery that the distant past is still vividly present to him. As he moves into the present tense he succumbs to his memories. We feel the events of his childhood exerting their power, often revivifying pain, as in the torment of life with the Murdstones after his mother has remarried.

> Again, the dreaded Sunday comes round, and I file into the old pew first, like a guarded captive brought to a condemned service. Again, Miss Murdstone, in a black velvet gown, that looks as if it had been made out of a pall, follows close upon me; then my mother; then her husband. There is no Peggotty now, as in the old time.
>
> (Ch. IV)

How suited this is to the experience of a child, for whom there seems no escape from the present. Dickens makes audacious use of the present tense for David's memories of his schooldays. Here is the 'forlorn and desolate' schoolroom at Salem House. 'I see it now ... Scraps of old copybooks and exercises, litter the dirty floor'. The present tense re-animates the painful routines of the past. 'Here I sit at the desk again, watching his eye ... Here I sit at the desk again, on a drowsy summer afternoon ... Here I am in the playground ...' (Ch. VII). Yet it also makes us feel the presence of the older David, viewing his younger self.

Present-tense narration asks us to share the sharpness of childhood memory, erupting into the narrative rather than forming part of it. This tense is for the day David was told about his mother's death, and his recollection of just what kind of day it was.

I smell the fog that hung about the place; I see the
hoar frost, ghostly, through it; I feel my rimy hair fall
clammy on my cheek; I look along the dim perspective
of the schoolroom, with a sputtering candle here and
there to light up the foggy morning, and the breath
of the boys wreathing and smoking in the raw cold as
they blow upon their fingers, and tap their feet upon
the floor.

He returns to the past tense to tell us how he was told,
how he grieved, and then how he returned home for the
funeral. 'If the funeral had been yesterday, I could not
recollect it better'. Where the past is clearest and most
insistent, he changes back to the present tense.

Mr Chillip is in the room, and comes to speak to me
… And now the bell begins to sound, and Mr Omer
and another come to make us ready … When we go
out to the door, the Bearers and their load are in the
garden; and they move before us down the path, and
past the elms … We stand around the grave. The day
seems different to me from every other day, and the
light not of the same colour—of a sadder colour …
It is over, and the earth is filled in, and we turn to
come away …

Some things get forgotten, but some things remain clear.
'All this, I say, is yesterday's event' (Ch. IX).
     Strange things happen to time in *David Copperfield*, and
Dickens's tense shifts brilliantly enact this. The present
tense is not only for the sudden power of a memory, but
also for the rapid passing of time, conjured in the business
of recollection. Chapter XVIII of *David Copperfield* takes

the reader right through David's schooldays and out the other side, 'from childhood up to youth'. 'Weeks, months, seasons, pass along.' The chapter is entitled 'A Retrospect'; three further chapters have 'Retrospect' in their titles, and all move into the present tense.[10] Later, the present tense takes us through the months of his courtship and of his apprenticeship in his new trade of writing, and then to the 'incoherent dream' of the wedding day itself. Finally, abstracting him from the reality of narrative time, the present tense is used for the routine of his wife's illness, the inescapable present of her dwindling, 'a strange rest and pause in my life'. 'I am again with Dora, in our cottage. I do not know how long she has been ill. I am so used to it in feeling, that I cannot count the time.' We stay in the present for her final moments. 'It is over. Darkness comes before my eyes; and, for a time, all things are blotted out of my remembrance' (Ch. LIII). Dickens is still in touch with the conventions of Victorian fiction, but in *David Copperfield* he is stretching those conventions to do justice to the power of memory. It is a preparation for the radically unconventional use of the present tense in his next novel, *Bleak House*.

The use of present-tense narration is no longer rare in novels. Literary history commonly associates the sustained use of the present tense with innovative, experimental fiction. Citing present-tense narration in Jean-Paul Sartre's *La Nausée* (*Nausea*) (1938) and Samuel Beckett's *L'Innomable* (*The Unnamable*) (1952), John Harvey tells us that 'the remarkable technical departure of writing whole narratives in the present tense was first introduced in works that were artistically and philosophically demanding – in *avant garde* novels written in Paris'.[11] He adds Joyce's *Ulysses* and *Finnegans Wake*, Woolf's

The Waves and Burroughs' *The Naked Lunch* as examples of 'innovative fiction' displaying 'significant use of the present tense'. The regulated movement between past-tense and present-tense narration, however, is rarer. *Ulysses* used this movement in new ways, letting us experience event and consciousness alongside each other. Here is Bloom at Dignam's funeral.

> They halted by the bier and the priest began to read out of his book with a fluent croak.
> Father Coffey. I knew his name was like a coffin. *Domine-namine.* Bully about the muzzle he looks. Bosses the show.[12]

We move from a narrative of events into Bloom's consciousness, and thence into the present tense of his thoughts and associations.

In fiction from the late twentieth century onwards, the alternation of past and present tense has become one of the markers of 'literary' fiction. *Waterland* by Graham Swift (1983), for instance, has a narrator, Tom Crick, who takes us back in time, sometimes to his own childhood and adolescence in the Cambridgeshire fens, and sometimes into the more distant past (he is a History teacher), to tell us the history of the fens. As he does this, he usually narrates at first in the past tense and then, as the narrative becomes vivid to him, switches into the present tense. It is a technique distantly learnt from *David Copperfield*. Margaret Atwood, a novelist wedded to the use of the historic present tense, divides *The Handmaid's Tale* (1985) between a dominant present tense of the narrator's experience in a politically and sexually repressive state, and a past tense used for her recollections of the world before religious fundamentalism took over – our world. We feel the difference between a narrative in which Offred (as she has been renamed) can look back with the wisdom of retrospect, and the narrative in which she is forced to live in the endless present tense of subjugation.

The formal division of a book into alternating sections in different tenses became a feature of literary fiction in the 1980s and 1990s. Penelope Lively's *Moon Tiger* and Michael Ondaatje's *The English Patient*, winners of the Booker Prize in, respectively, 1987 and 1992, were notable examples. *Moon Tiger* moves between passages in the past tense, narrated in the first person by Claudia Hampton, looking back on her life in her old age, and passages in the present tense, narrated in the third person, in which Claudia is always one of the actors. You might say that *Bleak House* made this narrative structure possible, though Lively's tense alternation has an effect all of its own. As the first-person, past-tense narrative – sorting, commenting, making sense of things – gives way to the present tense, 'I' becomes 'she', and we experience the painful distance between the dying woman whose story it is, and her younger self. In *The English Patient*, Ondaatje uses the present tense for most of the scenes at the Tuscan villa where, in the last year of the Second World War, the novel's leading characters – Hana, a Canadian nurse; the English patient, the badly burned man she tends; Caravaggio, a mysterious fellow Canadian who knows her; and Kip, the young Sikh British Army sapper who becomes her lover – meet. Ondaatje uses the past tense for each of their back stories, inserted in fragments, building to an explanation of what has brought each of them to the present place. It is tense shift alone that gives the novel its narrative coherence.

That sharp division of a novel into chapters in the present tense and chapters in the past tense that was invented in *Bleak House* is to be found in turn-of-the-century novels like Kate Atkinson's *Behind the Scenes at the Museum* (1995) and Sarah Waters's *Fingersmith* (2002). Margaret Atwood uses it again in *The Blind Assassin* (2000). Dickens's method is inherited by Don DeLillo's *Underworld* (1997), which begins in the present tense for a lengthy Prologue, narrating the events surrounding a famous baseball game in 1951, before changing to the past tense for the story, in reverse chronology, of its protagonist Nick Shay. DeLillo goes on to use what, in an Afterword, he calls the 'flipped switch' of tense change for three more sections in the present tense, following the history of the ball that Bobby Thomson hit into the crowd for the winning home run in that Prologue.[13] Finally, a substantial Epilogue returns us to the present tense, this time taking the novel's protagonist, Nick Shay, into something like the 'now' of 1997, when the book was published. Tense shift is how we feel the novelist's power of arrangement, as he brings American history and the story of one American together.

It might seem strange to suggest that Dickens anticipated the narrative experiments of the modernists, or the structural games of the post-modernists, but so it is. In his two last novels, *Our Mutual Friend* and *The Mystery of Edwin Drood*, Dickens returned to the innovative method of *Bleak House*. Switching between past and present had become essential to his fiction, though rarely noted by critics (none of the introductions to the Penguin Classics or Oxford World's Classics editions of either novel mentions the fact). *Our Mutual Friend* first turns to the present tense in its second chapter. Having introduced us to the nouveau riche Veneerings and their shabby but almost-aristocratic acquaintance Twemlow, a feeble soul who makes up the numbers at dinner parties, the narrative adopts the present tense for a special event: 'This evening the Veneerings give a banquet ...' The present tense is to be used for the novel's cameos of 'Society', unchangingly hypocritical – just as it *is*. 'It is always noticeable at the table of the Veneerings, that no man troubles himself much about the Veneerings themselves, and that anyone who has anything to tell, generally tells it to anybody else in preference' (Ch. II).

Some of the guests at the Veneerings' gruesome gatherings, like Eugene and Mortimer, have the power to move across into the past-tense narrative, where the central plot unfolds. They attend that first dinner party but leave when news of the drowned man breaks into the evening. As soon as they do so a new chapter begins and the narrative returns to the past tense. The present tense is where the Veneerings remain – their very *milieu*, drawing in those impecunious confidence tricksters the Lammles (who have deceived each other into marriage) and that embodiment of monied self-satisfaction, Podsnap. Every single one of the seven chapters in which the Veneerings appear is narrated in this tense. It is used for the gathering of acquaintances to ease Veneering into Parliament. 'Veneering feels that his friends are rallying round him' (II Ch. III). It is used for the maimed rites of the breakfast celebrating the Lammles's first wedding anniversary, with Veneering as guest of honour. 'Who so fit to discourse of the happiness of Mr and Mrs Lammle, they being the dearest and oldest friends he has in the world' (II Ch. XVI). It recurs in the novel's last chapter, 'The Voice of Society', where characters gather once more *chez* Veneering

'to dine with one another and not with them', and where
Twemlow, after a lifetime of submissiveness, finally asserts
himself to approve the love match of Eugene Wrayburn
and the low-born Lizzie Hexam, to general amazement.
'Somehow, a canopy of wet blanket seems to descend
upon the company' (II Ch. XVII).

It is not just for satire that the present tense is used.
The second present-tense chapter of the novel is the
seventh, where Silas Wegg calls on Mr Venus, taxidermist
and articulator of skeletons. It ended the second
monthly number. Dickens had miscalculated the length
of the chapter he had originally intended to place here,
describing the hellish nuptials of Alfred and Sophronia
Lammle, presided over by Veneering. As this chapter was
in the present tense, perhaps its substitute had to be. To fill
his space Dickens improvised Wegg's visit to Mr Venus's
spooky premises after accompanying his illustrator,
Marcus Stone, to Mr Willis's shop near Holborn Circus.[14]
The present tense is suitable for our first encounter in
his dark workplace with this skilled artisan, the nature
of whose vocation is at first unclear. 'His eyes are like
the over-tried eyes of an engraver, but he is not that; his
expression and stoop are like those of a shoemaker, but he
is not that' (I Ch. VII).

What is he? The tense of uncertainty clings to Mr
Venus, and Dickens adopts it again when he reappears,
a whole book later, to visit Silas Wegg: 'here is Mr Venus
come, and ringing at the Bower-gate'. Wegg intends to
make Mr Venus his collaborator in his ill-motived search
of the dust heaps. By his next appearance in Book III,
Ch. VI, Dickens had decided that Mr Venus would be
not Wegg's ally but his nemesis. We get a hint when he
responds to Wegg's greeting him as 'Brother in arms' with

'a rather dry good evening' (II Ch. VII). We should also
know by the fact that we are in the past tense. Mr Venus
has taken his place in the grander narrative.

It is the very transition between tenses that unsettles
our assumptions. At the end of Book III Chapter II,
narrated in the past tense, a body, recovered from the river,
is brought in on a stretcher to the Six Jolly Fellowship
Porters. 'Miss Abbey started back at sight of it.' She has
recognised Rogue Riderhood. And then we begin a new
chapter. 'In sooth, it is Riderhood and no other, or it is
the outer husk and shell of Riderhood and no other, that
is borne into Miss Abbey's first-floor bedroom.' This short
chapter, in which the apparently drowned Riderhood is
brought back from near death, is narrated in the present
tense. The narrator becomes one of those anxiously
gathered around the nearly dead, nearly living man: 'Stay!
Did that eyelid tremble?' Riderhood's destiny has become
provisional: 'He is struggling to come back'. The outcome
really is unknown. Dickens has established our antipathy
to this cunning predator, but now he imagines everyone –
including himself – wanting him to be brought back from
'that inexplicable journey'. He is 'like all of us', waking
from sleep, or a swoon, and even his abused daughter can
briefly enjoy the 'sweet delusion' of seeing her brutish
father 'an object of sympathy'. Then 'he begins to breathe
naturally'. He lives – and returns to his brutish self. He
walks out of the chapter and back into the past tense.

There is a submerged pattern to the disposition of the
ten present-tense chapters (out of forty-seven) of *Our
Mutual Friend*. The novel was, from the first, divided into
four Books, and Dickens fitted his present-tense chapters
to this structure: Book the First has four such chapters,
Book the Second three of them, Book the Third has

two, and Book the Fourth has just one (the last chapter of the novel). Dickens slowly diminishes the intensity of present-tense narration. Yet each of the four Books ends in the present tense. The effect is to disturb our confidence in the shaping, finishing work of the plot. Dickens may have arranged for happy endings and just outcomes, yet, at every stage, we find ourselves returning to the troubling present of what the novel's first sentence has identified as 'these times of ours'.

The first readers of Dickens's next novel, *The Mystery of Edwin Drood*, might have supposed that the present tense was now the norm, for the whole of the first monthly number of the new work, in four chapters, was in the historic present. The first paragraph is as weird as anything in nineteenth-century fiction, featuring the tower of an ancient English cathedral, a Sultan going to his palace 'in long procession', flashing scimitars and white elephants, and a fearsome-looking spike, maybe set up 'for the impaling of a horde of Turkish robbers'. What is happening? 'Stay! Is the spike so low a thing as the rusty spike on the top of a post of an old bedstead that has tumbled all awry?' Yes, it is, and we have been in an opium reverie. The person who experiences it is not named – though when, at the end of the chapter, he hurries into a Cathedral for vespers and the choir intones verses about 'THE WICKED MAN' we infer that his hidden life betokens his evil intentions.

He is choirmaster John Jasper. Four of the five opening present-tense chapters follow Jasper's hidden purposes, the narrative intensifying the dark forces of his desires. The only present-tense chapter that does not involve Jasper is Chapter III, where Edwin Drood and Rosa, promised in marriage to each other by their now dead parents, meet and unhappily discuss their prospective life together. This has its own kind of mystery. 'Can't you see a happy Future?' Rosa asks at the end of the chapter. 'For certain, neither of them sees a happy Present, as the gate opens and closes, and one goes in, and the other goes away.' The present is where they are trapped, without narrative resolution, quite as mystified as the reader (can they really marry each other, having been commanded that they must do so?). Jasper is present even here. They have come 'very near to the Cathedral windows' and hear the organ and choir, making Edwin think of the previous evening, when Jasper has told him 'as a warning' of his hidden 'ambition, aspiration, restlessness, dissatisfaction'. ' "I fancy I can distinguish Jack's voice," is his remark in a low tone in connection with the train of thought.' Dark, unspecified feelings ripple through the narration.

The first chapter of the second monthly number is also in the present tense, but then, something shifts. In the novel's sixth chapter we at last find ourselves in the past tense. Now events are narrated from the viewpoint of the Reverend Septimus Crisparkle, Minor Canon of Cloisterham Cathedral and tender son to his widowed mother. The past tense at last gives the narrative moral purchase; we can be sure that Mr Crisparkle will be an agent for good. From now on, we move, apparently unpredictably, between past-tense chapters and present-tense chapters, with every one of the monthly numbers after the first having at least one switch of tenses. The switching shows us that this Trollopian cathedral city harbours dangerous or corrosive passions. Whenever we have access to John Jasper's consciousness we are in the present tense; where he is seen only from the outside, we go to the past. So we pass from the end of Chapter XIX, in which Jasper terrifyingly declares to Rosa his passion for her, to the beginning of Chapter XX, where Rosa, now on her own, 'came to herself'. The present tense is for sexual obsession as well as opiated reverie. Perhaps half-consciously, the reader realises that the present tense is for all those chapters where the consciousness of one of the book's tormented men is dominant. It exerts its influence, to use a phrase that Dickens liked to use in his working notes, 'almost imperceptibly'. The repressed feelings of the two 'kinsmen' – Jasper and Drood – generate a narrative of restive provisionality. The present is the tense, you might say, of perturbed masculinity.

While the last chapter of Dickens's last novel may begin in the past tense, describing the mutual wariness of Mr Crisparkle and John Jasper, 'more than half a year' after Edwin Drood's unaccountable disappearance, it soon switches to the present tense as it narrates Jasper's departure from Cloisterham and arrival in London. 'Eastward and still eastward through the stale streets he takes his way, until he reaches his destination.' That destination is the opium den, where we first encountered him in the novel's opening chapter. The present tense serves to represent addiction and obsession. In *The Mystery of Edwin Drood*, it trembles with passion. Dickens has a reputation for moral certainty, even moral simplicity. Yet in his narrative experiments he managed to let the reader sense what the loss of moral security would feel like.

5

Haunting

I don't seem to be able to get rid of my spectres unless
I can lose them in crowds
                        To John Forster, 20 September 1846[1]

Dickens did not restrict his flights of fancy to the natural
world; they reached into the realms of the supernatural.
He often had ghosts on his mind. When we are introduced
to Mr Snagsby, the law stationer in *Bleak House*, we find
him in gloomy Cook's Court, Cursitor Street, 'on the
eastern borders of Chancery Lane', in premises honoured
by the notice PEFFER AND SNAGSBY.

> Peffer is never seen in Cook's Court now. He is not
> expected there, for he has been recumbent this quarter
> of a century in the churchyard of St Andrews, Holborn,
> with the waggons and hackney-coaches roaring past
> him all the day and half the night, like one great
> dragon. If he ever steal forth when the dragon is at rest,
> to air himself again in Cook's Court, until admonished

to return by the crowing of the sanguine cock in the
cellar at the little dairy in Cursitor Street, whose ideas
of daylight it would be curious to ascertain, since he
knows from his personal observation next to nothing
about it—if Peffer ever do revisit the pale glimpses of
Cook's Court, which no law-stationer in the trade can
positively deny, he comes invisibly, and no one is the
worse or wiser.

(Ch. X)

Only Dickens would write such a paragraph merely to
tell us that Snagsby's erstwhile business partner died
many years ago. You can hear him being caught up in
his own fancies about that hopeful London cockerel,
heralding the daylight that he never sees (he is the urban
descendant of the cock, 'trumpet to the morn', that sent
Hamlet's father's ghost back to his unearthly 'confine').
Dickens has to stop himself in mid-speculation, in order
to go back to imagining Peffer's ghost returning to his
old haunts. Peffer's thin afterlife as a faded name on a
sign tempts the novelist to summon up his ghost, but it
is a revenant so unimpressive that no one has ever seen it.
Poor Peffer! With a name like that he could hardly linger
on after death as anything but a joke.

The comedy of Dickens's flight of fancy relies on the
notion that no one 'can positively deny' the existence of
a ghost. For a moment, we imagine any number of law
stationers wondering whether their bit of town might not
indeed be haunted by Peffer. It is a grim joke, for the next
paragraph tells us that a piece of Peffer has indeed outlived
him, balefully enough. His acid niece once dwelt with
him and, courted by her uncle's then young partner, Mr
Snagsby, duly became Mrs Snagsby (or, as Dickens has it,

with frightening emphasis, 'Mr Snagsby and the niece are one'). Mrs Snagsby is a self-pitying bully with a peculiarly piercing voice. As Mr Snagsby presides in his shop, from the basement, 'as from a shrill ghost unquiet in its grave, there frequently arise complainings and lamentations in the voice already mentioned'. It is Mrs Snagsby, berating and persecuting the hapless maid servant, Guster. Dickens cannot help still thinking of ghosts, but this spirit is as loud and keening as Peffer's was reticent. Mrs Snagsby is a ghost who haunts her husband. Later in the novel, she becomes suspicious of his interest in Jo and takes to following him secretly, 'a ghostly shade'.

It is not surprising that a novelist who loved the fantastic should be willing to summon up ghosts. *Bleak House* is full of glimpses or half-glimpses of them. The comic fantasy of Peffer as a very retiring spirit – and his niece as a very assertive one – is characteristic of a fictional world where we are invited to laugh at legends of the supernatural, only to find that characters who take them seriously are vindicated. Dickens brings elements of the supernatural to *Bleak House*, but does not let us brush them all off as mere metaphors. Indeed, this novel has a ghost that seems to shape the plot. In the first instalment of *Bleak House*, in Chapter II, readers are shown Chesney Wold, the Dedlock ancestral home in Lincolnshire, where the November rain falls and 'the heavy drops fall—drip, drip, drip—upon the broad flagged pavement, called from old time the Ghost's Walk, all night'. Why does the terrace have this name? In the final chapter of the next monthly instalment, readers were to find out. The lawyer's clerk Mr Guppy gets a tour of Chesney Wold and is told, by Rosa the maid, what the terrace is called. She does not know why, but when Mr Guppy has left, the housekeeper, Mrs

Rouncewell, who has lived in the house for many years, tells Rosa and her grandson, Watt, the story. She seems almost pleased to do so:

> she considers that a family of such antiquity and importance has a right to a ghost. She regards a ghost as one of the privileges of the upper classes, a genteel distinction to which the common people have no claim.

So, we start with a joke about ownership of a haunted house being an aristocratic prerogative. The Ghost's Walk, Mrs Rouncewell explains, is a terrace where, in the seventeenth century, a former Lady Dedlock had liked to walk. She quarrelled violently with her husband during the Civil War. One day he found her laming his horses when he was going to ride out in support of the King. They struggled and she was herself 'lamed in the hip'. Afterwards, she would limp up and down the terrace, 'with greater difficulty every day'. One day, she dropped to the ground and died there. But before she died, she swore, 'I will walk here, though I am in my grave'. When 'calamity' or 'disgrace' is coming to the house, 'let the Dedlocks listen for my step!' This step will be heard whenever there is 'sickness or death in the family', says Mrs Rouncewell. Her grandson, understanding the story better, adds, '—And disgrace, grandmother—'. 'Disgrace never comes to Chesney Wold,' she retorts. Yet she goes on to declare that the ghostly sound is inescapable. 'My Lady, who is afraid of nothing, admits that when it is there, it must be heard. You cannot shut it out.' The chapter ends, as dusk falls, with a strange experiment. The housekeeper tells her grandson to set going the tall

French clock that has a loud beat and plays music. Then she asks Rosa,

> 'Can you hear the sound upon the terrace, through the music, and the beat, and everything?'
> 'I certainly can!'
> 'So my Lady says.'
>
> (Ch. VII)

Perhaps there is some natural cause of this acoustic phenomenon – something to do with the falling of rain on stone? Perhaps. But Dickens was determined that belief in the ghostly sound be more than superstition. 'Foreshadowing Legend of the country house' he wrote in his notes.[2] The supposedly quaint aristocratic legend alerts us to an impending catastrophe. Lady Dedlock can hear the ominous sound, naturally. It recurs. At the end of the chapter, Jo shows a veiled lady the foul burial ground where the man calling himself Nemo is interred and the narrative flits back to Chesney Wold. There, Sir Leicester is irked by the monotonous pattering of the rain on the terrace, and Mrs Rouncewell tells Rosa, 'in all these years I never heard the step upon the Ghost's Walk more distinct than it is to-night!' (Ch. XVI). The legend crosses into Esther's narrative. After Mr Boythorn has told her the story of the Chesney Wold haunting, she sits on a bench in her favourite spot in the woods overlooking the house, 'wondering how the rooms ranged and whether any echo like a footstep really did resound at times, as the story said, upon the lonely Ghost's Walk' (Ch. XXXVI). One day she is looking at the Ghost's Walk and 'picturing to myself the female shape that was said to haunt it' when she sees Lady Dedlock approaching her. The thought of the ghost is a prelude to Lady Dedlock's revelation that she is Esther's mother. The next day, in the aftershock, Esther wanders to the great house and finds herself on the Ghost's Walk.

> I was passing quickly on, and in a few moments should have passed the lighted window, when my echoing footsteps brought it suddenly into my mind that there was a dreadful truth in the legend of the Ghost's Walk, that it was I who was to bring calamity upon the stately house and that my warning feet were haunting it even then. Seized with an augmented terror of myself which turned me cold, I ran from myself and everything ...
>
> (Ch. XXXVI)

Dickens, who always gave precise instructions to his illustrators, ensured that on the page facing this passage was Hablot Browne's suitably spectral illustration of the Ghost's Walk, touched by the last streaks of dying evening light. It is like a visual endorsement of the 'legend', a ghost story that cannot be gainsaid.

Characters come to believe in the ghostly sounds because they share the reader's sense of impending disaster. As Lady Dedlock paces her room, fearful that the secret of her pre-marital affair is to be revealed, she is 'followed by the faithful step upon the Ghost's Walk' (Ch. XLI). She is dogged by the ghost: sometimes she hears it, sometimes the narrator hears it for her. After the murder of Mr Tulkinghorn, Mrs Rouncewell approaches Lady Dedlock with a letter that she has received, accusing her mistress of being the 'murderess'. She also tells her that she has heard what seem to be just the ghostly sounds that family tradition predicts.

'My Lady, I came away last night from Chesney Wold
to find my son in my old age, and the step upon the
Ghost's Walk was so constant and so solemn that I never
heard the like in all these years. Night after night, as
it has fallen dark, the sound has echoed through your
rooms, but last night it was awfullest. And as it fell
dark last night, my Lady, I got this letter.'

(Ch. LV)

The step on the Ghost's Walk is apparently there for all to
hear, but, as Mrs Rouncewell tells her son, it follows and
haunts Lady Dedlock. 'When I saw my Lady yesterday,
George, she looked to me—and I may say at me too—as
if the step on the Ghost's Walk had almost walked her
down'. He tries to say that her belief is foolish. 'Come,
come! You alarm yourself with old-story fears, mother.'
She knows that she is right. The ghost is implacable, as
ghosts are: 'the step on the Ghost's Walk will walk my
Lady down, George; it has been many a day behind her,
and now it will pass her and go on' (Ch. LVIII).

Whatever her son says, her fears will come true. Who
but Dickens would allow a supernatural explanation to
infiltrate what many a critic has insisted is a novel about
the condition of mid-nineteenth-century England. Into
this anatomy of contemporary society, the novelist brings
the fabulous elements of the ghost story, blithely offending
against codes of rational explanation. Other Victorian
novelists toyed with the supernatural, but invariably to
allow us to explain it away. Near the opening of Emily
Brontë's *Wuthering Heights*, Lockwood, the narrator, has
been forced by a sudden snowstorm to stay the night at
Wuthering Heights. In the bedroom that he is given he
finds a pile of mildewed books on a ledge, which is itself

'covered with writing scratched on the paint'. There is a name, repeated in different variants: '*Catherine Earnshaw*, here and there varied to *Catherine Heathcliff*, and then again to *Catherine Linton*'. In the books, he finds that the person who scratched her name has written diary entries. Reading them, he falls asleep and begins to dream. His fingers close on a little, ice-cold hand and a voice sobs to be let in.

> 'Who are you?' I asked, struggling, meanwhile, to disengage myself. 'Catherine Linton,' it replied, shiveringly (why did I think of *Linton*? I had read *Earnshaw* twenty times for Linton)—'I'm come home: I'd lost my way on the moor!' As it spoke, I discerned, obscurely, a child's face looking through the window. Terror made me cruel; and, finding it useless to attempt shaking the creature off, I pulled its wrist on to the broken pane, and rubbed it to and fro till the blood ran down and soaked the bedclothes: still it wailed, 'Let me in!' and maintained its tenacious grip, almost maddening me with fear.[3]

He yells aloud and Heathcliff bursts into the room. When Lockwood tells him of his nightmare, Heathcliff reacts as though Lockwood has indeed been visited by a spirit. Throwing open the window, he calls the spectre in.

The novel ends with a parallel intimation of the supernatural. After Heathcliff has died and been buried next to Cathy in the local churchyard, Lockwood meets a boy with some sheep out on the moor. He is crying and says that he has seen 'Heathcliff and a woman yonder' and dares not pass that way.[4] Lockwood tells him to go by a different route and offers the rational explanation for what the boy, a child after all, thinks that he has seen. 'He probably raised the phantoms from thinking, as he traversed the moors alone, on the nonsense he had heard his parents and companions repeat' – though the narrator adds that he himself does not like being out in the dark now.

In Charlotte Brontë's final novel *Villette*, the narrator, Lucy Snowe, tells us that the superstitious schoolgirls at the *pensionnat* where she teaches in the city of 'Villette', a fictionalised version of Brussels, believe that the school is haunted by the ghost of a nun. The legend, tremblingly relished by these teenage girls, is that she was a young nun who, centuries earlier, when the building was a convent, had been 'buried alive for some sin against her vow'.[5] Lucy is suitably scornful, until one day she retreats to the garret of the school building to read a letter from a young English doctor whom she admires – perhaps loves. She is disturbed in 'that ghostly chamber' by a stealthy footfall and turns to see a veiled figure.

> Say what you will, reader—tell me I was nervous or mad; affirm that I was unsettled by the excitement of that letter; declare that I dreamed; this I vow—I saw there—in that room—on that night—an image like—a NUN.
>
> I cried out; I sickened.[6]

There are two more manifestations of the ghostly nun, before all is explained. The most spoilt and sophisticated of the pupils, the glamorous and worldly Ginevra Fanshawe, eventually elopes with her aristocratic young lover, Hamal. She leaves Lucy a letter that sardonically explains how he would dress up as a nun for his clandestine visits to her.

'Nearly a year ago I chanced to tell him our legend of the nun; that suggested his romantic idea of the spectral disguise, which I think you must allow he has very cleverly carried out.'[7]

These are audacious versions of what is sometimes called the 'explained supernatural', pioneered by Anne Radcliffe, the doyenne of Gothic fiction during its first heyday, in the 1790s. Forbidding surroundings or old tales lead characters into apprehensiveness. Mysterious phenomena confirm their fears. Eventually, the protagonist comes to understand the natural causes of what appeared supernatural. Dickens preferred what we might call 'the unexplained supernatural'. His experiments with ghost stories began with his first novel, *Pickwick Papers*. Its fifth monthly number ended with the interpolated tale 'The Bagman's Story', narrated to Pickwick's companions one evening by a one-eyed man in a Suffolk inn. The story is itself set in an inn, where a traveller, Tom Smart, stops on a wild night. After he has gone to bed the old chair in his room metamorphoses into an old man, who tells him that the man courting the attractive female innkeeper below is a fraud, with six children already. The spectre tells him where to find the letter that incriminates Jinkins. Tom finds the letter and shows it to the innkeeper. She duly rejects Jinkins and marries Tom instead. Dickens was following the precedent of Sir Walter Scott, who had included the ghost story 'Wandering Willie's Tale', also told in an inn, by a blind fiddler, in his novel *Redgauntlet* (1824). It was supposedly repeated from popular legend. There are other supernatural tales in *Pickwick*. Two of them, 'The Goblins Who Stole a Sexton' and 'The Story of the Bagman's Uncle', are fabular and playful. A couple of others, about haunted legal chambers, told to Pickwick in a public house near the Inns of Court, are darker. Like Scott's, all are detached from the novel that surrounds them.

Soon, however, ghosts began to get into the fabric of Dickens's novels and to come alive in the minds of his characters. In *Barnaby Rudge*, one hectically stormy night, Solomon Daisy, who is responsible for winding up the church clock, arrives at the Maypole Inn in a state of abject terror. He tells the ill-natured landlord, John Willet, and his two fellow topers, Mr Cobb and Mr Parkes, that he has had a supernatural visitation. He was in the church when he suddenly realised that it was the nineteenth of March, the anniversary of Reuben Haredale's murder, some twenty-seven years earlier. 'I have heard it said that as we keep our birthdays when we are alive, so the ghosts of dead people, who are not easy in their graves, keep the day they died upon.' He tells the drinkers that he heard a voice and, as he came out of the church, saw 'something in the likeness of a man'. 'It was a ghost – a spirit'. Who was it? Mr Willet answers the question for him. 'Gentlemen … you needn't ask. The likeness of a murdered man.' Solemnly they discuss the conditions under which a ghost is likely to appear, with Mr Parkes, 'who had a ghost in his family, by the mother's side', appearing to speak with some authority (Ch. XXXIII). These public-house cronies, exciting themselves with supernatural speculations, are comical. Yet there is something in it. Later in the novel Solomon Daisy sees the same figure again by night, in the smouldering ruins of the Warren. 'The horror-stricken clerk uttered a scream that pierced the air, and cried, "The ghost! The ghost!"' (Ch. LVI). It is a revenant, certainly, but in fact a living figure from the past: the elder Barnaby Rudge, a murderer who has faked his own murder and thereby become a kind of spectre. When he secretly visits his wife, he tells her that he is 'in the body … a spirit, a ghost upon the earth, a thing from which all creatures shrink, save those curst beings of another world, who will not leave me' (Ch. XVII).

Dickens's characters see ghosts when they are frightened of the past, and especially when they would rather not think of what they have done. Dickens was fascinated by the psychology of those who see ghosts. On his first trip to America, he wrote to John Forster about a visit to a Pittsburgh prison where a 'horrible thought' had occurred to him. *What if ghosts be one of the terrors of these jails?*[8] He had been brooding on the thought of a prisoner in solitary confinement, 'sometimes an evil conscience very busy', possessed at night by the thought of 'some inexplicable silent figure'. 'The more I think of it, the more certain I feel that not a few of these men (during a portion of their imprisonment a least) are nightly visited by spectres.' Such visitation by spectres conjured by a solitary, self-tormented soul takes place in the novel that Dickens wrote after his return, *Martin Chuzzlewit*. Here the guilt-racked Jonas Chuzzlewit, who has wished for the death of his father, old Anthony Chuzzlewit, and planned to hurry it on, has to inhabit the same chambers as the corpse, 'stretched out, stiff and stark, in the awful chamber above-stairs' (Ch. XIX). Jonas wrongly believes that his father has died from poison administered by himself.

> During the whole long seven days and nights, he was always oppressed and haunted by a dreadful sense of its presence in the house. Did the door move, he looked towards it with a livid face and starting eye, as if he fully

believed that ghostly fingers clutched the handle. Did
the fire flicker in a draught of air, he glanced over his
shoulder, as almost dreading to behold some shrouded
figure fanning and flapping at it with its fearful dress.
The lightest noise disturbed him; and once, in the
night, at the sound of a footstep overhead, he cried
out that the dead man was walking—tramp, tramp,
tramp—about his coffin.

(Ch. XIV)

A belief in ghosts is readily animated. Much later, Jonas
does commit a murder, the killing of Montague Tigg,
and, like the older Barnaby Rudge before him, becomes a
kind of ghost himself.

Dread and fear were upon him, to an extent he had
never counted on, and could not manage in the least
degree. He was so horribly afraid of that infernal room
at home. This made him, in a gloomy murderous,
mad way, not only fearful *for* himself, but *of* himself;
for being, as it were, a part of the room: a something
supposed to be there, yet missing from it: he invested
himself with its mysterious terrors; and when he
pictured in his mind the ugly chamber, false and
quiet, false and quiet, through the dark hours of two
nights; and the tumbled bed, and he not in it, though
believed to be; he became in a manner his own ghost
and phantom, and was at once the haunting spirit and
the haunted man.

Jonas is the most brutally materialistic of men but becomes
a confirmed and helpless believer in the supernatural. 'He
knew it must come. And his present punishment, and

torture and distraction, were, to listen for its coming. Hush!'
(Ch. XLVII). That 'Hush!' is the theatrical interjection of
a narrator who is used to telling frightening stories to an
assembled company. He asks us to listen alongside the
murderer for the retributive spirit that must be pursuing
him. In the chapter in his *Life* on Dickens's personal
characteristics, Forster remarked, 'Among his good things
should not be omitted his telling of a ghost story.'[9] Forster
seems to be thinking of Dickens's skill at telling a story
out loud. The narrator of his next work of fiction and
the most famous of all ghost stories, *A Christmas Carol*,
sometimes seems to be Dickens, performing in person.
Here he is telling the reader of Scrooge's confrontation
with the first of the three Christmas ghosts.

> The curtains of his bed were drawn aside, I tell you, by
> a hand. Not the curtains at his feet, nor the curtains
> at his back, but those to which his face was addressed.
> The curtains of his bed were drawn aside; and Scrooge,
> starting up into a half-recumbent attitude, found
> himself face to face with the unearthly visitor who
> drew them: as close to it as I am now to you, and I am
> standing in the spirit at your elbow.
>
> (Stave II)

With its insistent repetitions and redundancies ('I
tell you'), this is like a speaking voice. The storyteller's
comparison of the ghost's proximity to his own is half-
joke, half-threat. In contrast with the Gothic terrors
of old, the Dickensian ghost is nearby – almost within
touching distance. The person who tells ghost stories is
really someone who summons up spirits into our midst.

It is difficult to recapture the initial novelty, the once startling originality, of *A Christmas Carol*. Perhaps the most frequently adapted of all literary works – for stage, for radio, for television, for film – and the most frequently imitated or parodied, it is now like a mythical tale that has always been there. Yet it was once a kind of challenge to those who, like its protagonist, would only believe in what was empirical and palpable. Comical scepticism about the supernatural is Scrooge's self-deception in *A Christmas Carol*. Convinced that his vision of Marley's ghost is an illusion brought on by poor digestion, he manages the novella's best quip: 'There's more of gravy than of grave about you, whatever you are!' But Scrooge's waggishness is for keeping down his terror. At first, it seems that it might all be a joke. When Scrooge's door knocker turns into Marley's face, it has 'a dismal light about it, like a bad lobster in a dark cellar.' Yet even now, as Dickens tries to do justice to the strangeness of something never exactly described in literature before, there is something of horror in it.

> The hair was curiously stirred, as if by breath or hot air; and, though the eyes were wide open, they were perfectly motionless. That, and its livid colour, made it horrible; but its horror seemed to be in spite of the face and beyond its control, rather than a part of its own expression.
>
> (Stave I)

After *A Christmas Carol*, ghosts were in the mainstream of Victorian fiction, yet no other writer invoking the supernatural was to tinge the terrifying with the ludicrous as daringly as Dickens.

When Dickens embarked on his career as a novelist, the ghost story was an undeveloped genre. While he himself became an accomplished writer of ghost stories, he was an even more important promoter of them. As editor first of *Household Words*, then of *All the Year Round*, he commissioned many ghost stories and established the convention of publishing them at Christmas. The genre flourished with the huge growth of magazines (including Dickens's) from the 1850s. These periodicals usually sold themselves on their fiction, both serialised novels and short stories. The ghost story became one of their favoured commodities. Dickens was an epicure of its special effects, always on the lookout for new ways in which a supernatural tale could unsettle its reader. When Elizabeth Gaskell submitted her ghost story, 'The Old Nurse's Story', to *Household Words* (it was the first true ghost story to appear in one of Dickens's special Christmas numbers) Dickens wrote to her rightly praising it. 'A very fine ghost-story indeed. Nobly told, and wonderfully managed.'[10] But he added a suggestion about changing its ending in a way that would make it 'very new and very awful'. His idea was a good one: instead of the nurse (who narrates the story in old age) and all the other members of the household in the remote mansion in the Cumberland hills seeing the phantoms of long-dead family members, would it not be better if '*only the child* saw the spectral figures'? Despite his repeating the suggestion in another letter three days later, Mrs Gaskell did not comply.[11]

As editor (or 'conductor', as he preferred to have it) of *All the Year Round*, Dickens also commissioned and published Sheridan Le Fanu's classic 'Green Tea', the tale of a clergyman, the Rev Jennings, who drinks large quantities of green tea and finds himself haunted by an evil spirit in the shape of a small black monkey.[12] His torment is real (eventually leading him to cut his own throat), but is the malign spirit also real? Our uncertainty is increased by the fact that the narrator is a doctor who knows Jennings, but has no direct knowledge of the supernatural phenomenon that tortures its victim. In a letter to Le Fanu expressing his admiration for the tale, Dickens invoked the case of a woman he had known for many years, Augusta De La Rue, who suffered, he believed, from physiological or nervous disorders that produced illusions of ghostly apparitions.[13] She was the English wife of the Swiss banker, Emile De La Rue; Dickens had first met her and her husband when living in Genoa in 1844–5. She suffered from of 'phantoms' and often saw 'spectres'. Notoriously, he became involved in her case and mesmerised her, apparently with therapeutic consequences.[14]

On one occasion, Dickens wrote to her husband after a 'phantom' had appeared to Madame De La Rue, warning that she should not join him on a planned trip to Rome. 'I have told her that she must set no store whatever, by anything this creature says. That it is in its Nature a false thing—an unreal creation; a lie of her eyes and Ears—and cannot speak the Truth.'[15]

Another member of the household who had heard voices must have 'received the impression magnetically from Madame De la Rue'. 'It is a philosophical explanation of many Ghost Stories. Though it is hardly less chilling than a Ghost-Story itself.' Twenty-five years later, Dickens was still preoccupied with her case. He described it to Le Fanu, enclosing a letter from Madame De La Rue in which she detailed her visions. Only his own powers of 'Animal Magnetism' had kept them at bay, he claimed:

wheresoever I travelled in Italy, she and her husband
travelled with me, and every day I magnetized her;
sometimes under olive trees, sometimes in Vineyards,
sometimes in the travelling carriage, sometimes at
wayside Inns during the mid-day halt.[16]

But in the years during which she and Dickens had been
apart, she had been haunted once more. 'When I left Italy
that time, the spectres had departed. They returned by
degrees as time went on, and have ever since been as bad
as ever.'

Dickens recognised that 'Green Tea' was something
singular: a story that could be taken as either a case study
of mental disorder or a tale of the supernatural. If it were
the first of these, it described something like what he had
himself observed. In most cases, however, Dickens was
drawn to ghost stories because they exemplified the power
of narrative, even when – especially when – it contradicted
reason or 'philosophy'.

That power is invoked in a jesting analogy in *A Tale
of Two Cities*. Dickens is describing Jerry Cruncher's
consistently suspicious treatment of his wife. 'The
devoutest person could have rendered no greater homage
to the efficacy of an honest prayer than he did in this
distrust of his wife. It was as if a professed unbeliever in
ghosts should be frightened by a ghost story' (II Ch. XIV).
As such an unbeliever often is. Frightening even a sceptical
reader was an incontrovertible proof of narrative power.
Dickens wrote to Mary Boyle in January 1866 expressing
his pleasure at her response to his ghost story 'To Be
Taken with a Grain of Salt'. 'I am charmed to learn that
you have had a freeze out of my Ghost story. It rather gave
me a shiver up the back, in the writing.'[17] The writer who

can give himself 'a shiver' is truly accomplished. Dickens was fascinated by ghost stories because he was devoted to the powers of narrative manipulation. The 'shiver' of 'To Be Taken with a Grain of Salt', first published in the Christmas number of *All the Year Round* in December 1865, might remind us of Esther's vision of herself as a haunting spirit in *Bleak House*. It is narrated by a man who has visions of a murderer and his victim before he is asked to be a juror at the murderer's trial. The twist is the murderer's revelation, after he is convicted, that he has been haunted, in the night, by the narrator, now Foreman of the Jury, whom he has seen putting a rope round his neck.[18]

When it came to ghost stories, Dickens was always after a new variation on expected patterns. Thus, his praise, in a letter to Angela Burdett-Coutts, of a tale recently supplied to his journal by Dinah Mulock. 'I think I have just got the best Ghost story (sent by a lady for Household Words) that ever was written, and with an idea in it remarkably new.'[19] (The novelty is that the ghost is visible to everyone except those it haunts.)[20] His relish for new supernatural thrills reached beyond the fictional. That 'hankering' after ghost stories that Forster identified ran to supposedly 'true' stories of hauntings. The journalist George Augustus Sala, who wrote regularly for Dickens's periodicals, recalled,

> What he liked to talk about was the latest new piece at the theatres, the latest exciting trial or police case, the latest social craze or social swindle, and especially the latest murder and the newest thing in ghosts.[21]

'The newest thing in ghosts'. This went for both fictional and documentary accounts. As editor first of *Household*

Words and then of *All the Year Round*, he solicited and published many 'true' accounts of apparently supernatural events. It is clear from Dickens's correspondence with those who supplied such narratives that, as Sala suggests, their novelty was the essential thing. When Frances Elliot send him some accounts of ghostly phenomena, he objected to one story on the grounds that 'It is an old one, perfectly well known *as* a story'. He wanted whatever she recounted to be narratively convincing, because distinctive. He assured her that he did not doubt her own faith in these accounts, just the qualities that would make them credible to readers.

> My state of mind on the general subject is yours exactly. I do not set myself up to pretend to know what the Almighty's laws are, as to disembodied spirits. I do not profess to be free from disagreeable impressions and apprehensions, even. But these are no reasons for calling that, evidence, which is no evidence at all, or for taking for granted what cannot be taken for granted.[22]

Mental disorders produced supernatural impressions, he believed, so that many people had their ghost stories. As he told Elizabeth Gaskell, what made any of these interesting was the narration. 'Ghost-stories, illustrating particular states of mind and processes of the imagination, are common-property, I always think—except in the manner of relating them, and O who can rob some people of *that*!'[23]

Forster observed that 'such was his interest generally in things supernatural that, but for the strong restraining power of his common sense, he might have fallen into the follies of spiritualism.'[24] In fact, he became known as an energetic foe of contemporary Spiritualists – those who claimed to be able to communicate with the dead. He began something of a campaign against them in *Household Words* in 1852, when he set about exposing the trickery of the renowned American medium Mrs W. R. Hayden, who had recently arrived in London.[25] He deputed Wills and Morley to investigate one of her seances incognito, and Morley's mocking article 'The Ghost of the Cock Lane Ghost', describing 'our visit to the London ghosts established in genteel apartments in Upper Seymour Street, Portman Square', appeared in *Household Words* on 20 November 1852.[26] The title referred to an infamous fraud of the eighteenth century and was devised by Dickens.

> I think a good name for the paper would be *The Ghost of the Cock Lane Ghost*. If Morley looks to that precious business, in the Annual Register, he will find (if I understand your account) that the two spirits are greatly alike. I was thinking that *Spirits far above proof* would be a good title. But it is a great thing in such a case to shew that the imposition is an old and exploded one.[27]

Sitting at a table with Mrs Hayden, Morley and Wills (attending under the pseudonyms Brown and Thompson) are put in touch with the latter's dead mother, who communicates by means of raps on the table but gets every factual question about herself wrong. She is followed by the spirit of Wills's sister. 'His only sister being in vigorous health, he did not expect her ghost; but it was there, and very prompt to answer him.' The article led to some controversy, with Dickens being accused of attending the seance himself. He retorted in his journal a few weeks later:

> Mr Dickens was never at the intensely exciting house and never beheld any of its intensely exciting inhabitants. Two trustworthy gentlemen attached to this Journal tested the spirit rappers at his request, and found them to be the egregious absurdity described.[28]

His scorn did not prevent Mrs Hayden acquiring many genteel devotees. Her popularity was trumpeted, and Dickens's scepticism assailed, in the New York-based journal *The Spiritual Telegraph*, which circulated in London. Dickens was being given more reasons to assail the Spiritualists.

He was amazed that his friend Bulwer Lytton credited the claims of some to be able to communicate with the dead. In a letter to *Household Words* contributor the Rev. James White in 1854, he reported attending a party of Lytton's at which spirits were to be raised. 'I stayed till the ghostly hour, but the rumour was unfounded.' In the same letter he reported the case of novelist and renowned writer on the supernatural Catherine Crowe, an erstwhile *Household Words* contributor. Dickens told White that she 'has gone stark mad—and stark naked—on the spirit-rapping imposition'. [29] Apparently she was found naked in the street, having been informed by spirits that she would be invisible. The case was reported in *The Times*. Six years earlier, Dickens had anonymously and satirically reviewed her *The Night Side of Nature* in the *Examiner*. Crowe's book, subtitled 'Ghosts and Ghost-Seers', was a compendium of attested examples of apparently supernatural occurrences. 'If I could only induce a few capable persons, instead of laughing at these things, to look at them, my object would be attained, and I should consider my time well spent.'[30]

Dickens detected that she wrote 'apparently with an implicit belief in everything she narrates'. Having covered 'a few obvious heads of objection that may be ranged against the ghosts', he proposed, the following week, 'to sum in what may be said in their favour'.[31] This follow-up article never appeared.

His goading of the Spiritualists continued with further articles in *Household Words*. In 'The Spirit Business', in May 1853, Dickens satirised the enthusiasm for spiritualism in America, and paraded a series of 'important communications ... received from spirits', all notable for their banality. The article ridiculed, in particular, that 'branch of the spiritual proceedings' known as 'Tippings'. This 'denotes the spiritual movements of the tables and chairs, and of a mysterious piece of furniture called a "stand", which appears to be in every apartment.'[32] There followed a collection of delectably absurd instances of supernatural visitation, ending with mockery of the social reformer Robert Owen for claiming communication with his dead wife and daughter, in which they revealed continuing support for his political causes.[33] In one later article written by Dickens, on 'Well-Authenticated Rappings', published on 20 February 1858, 'the writer' purported to have been the recipient of communications 'of spiritual origin' via 'rappings on the forehead'.[34] On another occasion, messages come through 'a hurried succession of angry raps in the stomach' from a spirit calling itself 'Pork Pie'. (Though the article was anonymous, the

Dickens-alert reader might have recalled Scrooge's theory about ghostly visitations arising from dyspepsia.) The article ended with a slapstick account of a family seance at a household in Bungay, Suffolk, where a spiritual force causes the table around which the participants are sitting to tip and revolve, bumping and bruising them. 'Was this, or was it not a case of Tipping? Will the sceptic and the scoffer reply?'

In a letter of 1859 to the *Household Words* contributor William Howitt, who had become a keen Spiritualist, Dickens offered to moderate his scepticism.

> My own mind is perfectly unprejudiced and impressible on the subject. I do not in the least pretend that such things are not. But I positively object, on most matters, to be thought for, or—if I may use the odd expression—asserted down. And I have not yet met with any Ghost Story that was proved to me, or that had not the noticeable peculiarity in it—that the alteration of some slight circumstance would bring it within the range of common natural probabilities. I have always had a strong interest in the subject, and never knowingly lost an opportunity of pursuing it.

He went on to refer to his theory that those who believed themselves visited by spectres were often suffering from some 'nervous' disorder.

> I think the testimony which I cannot cross-examine, sufficiently loose, to justify me in requiring to see and hear the modern witnesses with my own senses, and then to be reasonably sure that they were not suffering under a disordered condition of the nerves or senses,

which is known to be a common disease of many phases.[35]

Dogged in his desire to puncture Howitt's confidence, Dickens went with Wilkie Collins, W. H. Wills and John Hollingshead to investigate a house in Cheshunt, Hertfordshire that, according to Howitt, was haunted and had therefore been abandoned by its owner. On his return to London, Dickens wrote to Howitt to inform him,

> I have been to Cheshunt, and have found myself no nearer to a haunted house than I was before. Not a locally well-informed person in the place knows of any haunted stories there. The house in which Mr Chapman lived, has been greatly enlarged and commands a high rent, and is no more deserted than this house of mine is.[36]

Howitt, a Quaker, had admired Dickens for his commitment to social reform, but the two men now fell out over spiritualism. Howitt's credulous *History of the Supernatural* provoked Dickens to write 'Rather a Strong Dose', published in *All the Year Round* in March 1863. This catalogues the absurdities that Howitt's book ('the gospel according to Howitt') required its readers to believe.[37] It ends with all that his readers are asked to disbelieve, including the fact that

> One of the best accredited chapters in the history of mankind is the chapter that records the astonishing deceits continually practised, with no object or purpose but the distorted pleasure of deceiving.[38]

Two weeks later he followed this with another article, 'The Martyr Medium', which attacked Howitt in passing, but focused on the recently published memoir of the Scottish medium Daniel Dunglas Home. Renowned for his seances and his supposed powers of levitation, Home attracted audiences of the rich and famous, and considerable financial patronage.[39] As its title suggested, Dickens highlighted Home's complaints about his sufferings at the hands of 'men of Science', apparently determined to expose his trickery.[40] Pouring scorn on Home's 'odious book', Dickens was evidently unafraid for his journal to declare a man lauded by many to be a fraud.

Dickens's very disputes with the Spiritualists gave him material for supernatural tales. His argument with Howitt seems to have prompted him to organise a group of ghost stories for the extra Christmas number of *All the Year Round* in 1859. He had the idea of a humorous frame narrative, involving the narrator renting a supposedly haunted house. In the introductory chapter the narrator travels by night from the north of England to view the house, sharing a railway carriage with a man who mysteriously makes notes and sometimes enunciates letters of the alphabet for no apparent reason. The narrator surmises that 'the gentleman might be what is popularly called a rapper'. His suspicion is well founded, for the man soon tells him, 'I have passed the night – as indeed I pass the whole of my time now – in spiritual intercourse.' 'There are 17,479 spirits here', he explains, including Socrates, Galileo and John Milton.[41] The narrator is hugely relieved to get out at the next station. It is as if Dickens has to establish the difference between the Spiritualists' self-delusions and absorbing ghost stories. The narrator goes on to fill the house with friends for the Christmas season.

Each character stays in a different room (the timorous and eventually hysterical servants are all dismissed) and they all tell each other their stories on Twelfth Night. Wilkie Collins and Elizabeth Gaskell were among those who supplied tales. Dickens's contribution was 'The Ghost in Master B's Room'. The seven tales in fact have little to do with the house, whose supposed ghostliness is comical.

In his novels, Dickens frequently associated the frightening with the comical in his intimations of the supernatural, especially when he credited the fears that take possession of children. In *Great Expectations*, Pip revisits the dread and alarm of childhood. His fears come from his strange acquaintance with death. When he is first summoned to Miss Havisham, still garbed in the wedding dress that she wore many years earlier, when her husband-to-be abandoned her on the day of their wedding, her grotesque appearance triggers terrifying recollections.

> I saw that the bride within the bridal dress had withered like the dress, and like the flowers, and had no brightness left but the brightness of her sunken eyes. I saw that the dress had been put upon the rounded figure of a young woman, and that the figure upon which it now hung loose had shrunk to skin and bone. Once, I had been taken to see some ghastly waxwork at the Fair, representing I know not what impossible personage lying in state. Once, I had been taken to one of our old marsh churches to see a skeleton in the ashes of a rich dress that had been dug out of a vault under the church pavement. Now, waxwork and skeleton seemed to have dark eyes that moved and looked at me. I should have cried out, if I could.
>
> (Ch. VIII)

The child's memories of waxwork and skeleton, disturbingly fused in this deathly living woman, make this an experience of near-supernatural horror.

A novel about the unwanted claims of the past is receptive to the appearance of ghosts. Being haunted is the narrator's metaphor for his half-recognition, half-repression, of the submerged patterns in his story. Here Pip, now a young man, has been summoned back from London by Miss Havisham to meet Estella, who is now a beautiful young woman. The two of them walk out into the grounds of Satis House.

> In another moment we were in the brewery so long disused, and she pointed to the high gallery where I had seen her going out on that same first day, and told me she remembered to have been up there, and to have seen me standing scared below. As my eyes followed her white hand, again the same dim suggestion that I could not possibly grasp, crossed me. My involuntary start occasioned her to lay her hand upon my arm. Instantly the ghost passed once more, and was gone.
>
> What *was* it?
>
> (Ch. XXIX)

What ghost? Estella's hand reminds him of something, or somebody. The ghost is a dim recollection, retrieved only much later. When Pip finally realises that Molly, Jaggers's housekeeper, is Estella's mother, her hands come before anything else: 'her hands were Estella's hands, and her eyes were Estella's eyes' (Ch. XLVIII). They are the hands with which Molly almost certainly killed a woman.

Sometimes it seems that only the language of haunting and apparitions can do justice to the terrible shape that Pip's life is taking in his eyes. After Magwitch has returned to him, Pip becomes oppressed by disillusion and apprehension. He and Herbert plan some means of spiriting 'Provis', as he has been renamed, down the river and away from England. In the midst of their schemes, Pip distracts himself with a visit to a play followed by a pantomime, where he finds Mr Wopsle performing. As he does so, Mr Wopsle stares in his direction, 'as if he were lost in amazement'. Afterwards, Pip finds him waiting for him at the theatre door. Mr Wopsle had noticed Pip in the audience, but that was not what amazed him. 'Yes, of course I saw you. But who else was there?' He talks at first obscurely of recognising another person in the theatre. 'It is the strangest thing … and yet I could swear to him'. His 'mysterious words' give Pip 'a chill'. 'I had a ridiculous fancy that he must be with you, Mr Pip, till I saw that you were quite unconscious of him, sitting behind you there like a ghost.' Slowly it becomes clear that the 'ghost' that Mr Wopsle has seen was one of the convicts that he vividly remembers, caught on the marshes all those years ago – the one whom Magwitch fought in the ditch. 'The more I think of him, the more certain I am of him.'

> I cannot exaggerate the enhanced disquiet into which this conversation threw me, or the special and peculiar terror I felt at Compeyson's having been behind me 'like a ghost.'
>
> (Ch. XLVII)

What Mr Wopsle has noticed is not in fact supernatural: Compeyson is evidently tracking Pip because he is after

Magwitch. Yet he is right to think that he has seen a ghost. To Pip's fearful imagination, a spirit is coming from the past to claim him.

Pip keeps thinking that he is in a ghost story. As in *Bleak House*, or that strange little tale 'To Be Taken with a Grain of Salt', his insight is that he himself might be the ghost. Thinking back to his self-tormenting visits to the house where Estella was lodging, where she made use of him 'to tease other admirers', while inflicting on him 'every kind and degree of torture', he imagines himself unable to escape the pain of it even after death. If the house should come to be haunted, 'when I am dead, it will be haunted, surely, by my ghost' (Ch. XXXVIII). Near the novel's end, lured by night to the lonely old sluice house out on the marshes, Pip finds himself tied up by the monstrous, vengeful Orlick, who tells him, 'I'm a going to have your life!' Orlick is drinking slugs of strong spirits from a tin bottle hung around his neck.

> I distinctly understood that he was working himself up with its contents, to make an end of me. I knew that every drop it held, was a drop of my life. I knew that when I was changed into a part of the vapour that had crept towards me but a little while before, like my own warning ghost, he would do as he had done in my sister's case – make all haste to the town, and be seen slouching about there, drinking at the ale-houses.
>
> (Ch. LIII)

Fearfully now, Pip sees the story of all his 'great expectations' ending with him as a ghost condemned to warn his living self about his doom.

Like no other novelist, Dickens interleaved the natural and the supernatural. In his last, uncompleted novel, *The Mystery of Edwin Drood*, he was still doing so. Has Edwin Drood been murdered? If so, where is his body? The alcohol-befuddled stonemason Durdles knows the Cathedral and all its burying places, its underground tunnels and hidden spaces, better than anyone. He is giving John Jasper 'a moonlight hole-and-corner exploration' of the Cathedral, when he asks Jasper whether he believes there may be 'Ghosts of other things, though not of men and women'. What can he mean? 'Sounds', he tells Jasper. 'Cries'. Almost exactly a year earlier, on Christmas Eve, he says, he fell asleep in the crypt and was woken by something unearthly.

> 'And what woke me? The ghost of a cry. The ghost of one terrific shriek, which shriek was followed by the ghost of the howl of a dog: a long, dismal, woeful howl, such as a dog gives when a person's dead.'
>
> (Ch. XII)

The ghost of a cry – or the cry of a ghost? Perhaps Dickens planned eventually to provide a rational explanation of the cry and the howl. Or perhaps not. Jasper reacts with a 'fierce' retort: 'What do you mean?' Perhaps he hears a prophecy of his own murderous machinations. Dickens was quite prepared to admit the supernatural to his novels, to let us imagine ghostly warnings of what is to come. Yet there is flavouring of the absurd here too. Durdles is a drunkard, a confused witness to the schemes of others. Everyone – except Jasper, at this moment, in the gloom – laughs at his solemn, boozy mumblings.

It took Dickens to see that what is frightening is sometimes also what is funny. One of the grimmest of the inset narratives in *Pickwick Papers* is narrated in a public house by 'old Jack Bamber', expert in legends of the Inns of Court. As a prelude, he tells the nonplussed Pickwick a couple of ghostly tales of desperate denizens of the Inns. In one, the occupant of a set in Clifford's Inn finds himself constantly nervous. He prises open a closet to discover the previous tenant, 'with a little bottle clasped firmly in his hand, and his face livid with the hue of a painful death'. Such things are, the old man tells Pickwick, 'funny, but not uncommon'.

> 'Funny!' exclaimed Mr Pickwick, involuntarily.
>   'Yes, funny, are they not?' replied the little old man, with a diabolical leer.
>
> (Ch. XXI)

Funny-strange *and* funny-ha-ha. These comical hauntings are specimens of a special Dickensian incongruity. We are invited to laugh where we should not – or to laugh and then check ourselves. Nothing interested Dickens more than this inclination.

6

Laughing

... we all laughed more than we had ever laughed in our lives. I don't know why.
Letter to Mary Boyle, 28 December 1860[1]

Read the published letters of almost any twentieth-century novelist and you are likely to find him or her saying something disparaging about Dickens's novels, usually while confessing to enjoying them. Here is Iris Murdoch, writing to fellow novelist Brigid Brophy, her friend and sometime lover, in June 1961.

Having a great phase of read ng Dickens – gosh he is good – though *so* careless. But so beautifully funny – as well as other things. Oh to achieve the purely funny![2]

Few great novelists provoke such a mixture of admiration and condescension. Murdoch is typical of many writers in finding Dickens 'purely funny', as if this were a quality beyond critical analysis. For the same thought, we can go back to Henry James, deploring *Our Mutual Friend* as 'poor with the poverty not of momentary embarrassment, but of permanent exhaustion', yet opening his review by conceding that he does find the absurdly 'majestic' Mrs Wilfer, a clerk's wife with lofty ideas of herself, very funny.

> When, after conducting her daughter to Mrs Boffin's carriage, in sight of all the envious neighbors, she is described as enjoying her triumph during the next quarter of an hour by airing herself on the door-step 'in a kind of splendidly serene trance,' we laugh with as uncritical a laugh as could be desired of us.[3]

James has got it slightly wrong: Mrs Wilfer has impressed the neighbours by handing her daughter over to a 'male domestic' of the wealthy Boffins, with the announcement, 'Miss Wilfer. Coming out!' The lackey will conduct her to the carriage. But he is right about our delight in her triumph. James apparently laughed away at this, in an 'uncritical' state of mind, before settling down to pen his damning criticism. We might remember Dickens's rival and sometime friend, Thackeray, complaining that the character of Micawber 'is delightful and makes me laugh: but it is no more a real man than my friend Punch is: and in so far I protest against him'.[4] He does not imagine that his own laughter might be some indication that this character touches reality.

Dickens finds ways to make even those who have something against him laugh. He likes to do this unexpectedly. Take this exemplary moment from *David Copperfield*. David is at school and it is his birthday. He has been summoned from his classroom to the parlour, where he finds the headmaster, Mr Creakle, and his wife, the latter with an opened letter in her hand. David had been thinking that he might be getting a festive hamper, sent from home, but that letter means that he is about to be told of his mother's death.

> 'David Copperfield,' said Mrs Creakle, leading me to a sofa, and sitting down beside me. 'I want to speak to you very particularly. I have something to tell you, my child.'
>
> Mr Creakle, at whom of course I looked, shook his head without looking at me, and stopped up a sigh with a very large piece of buttered toast.
>
> (Ch. IX)

Mr Creakle, who normally issues commands and punishments, has withdrawn his authority and subcontracted this particular task to Mrs Creakle. Even as the child's dread of what is coming gathers, he watches that very large piece of toast going into Mr Creakle's mouth. The sentence behaves as if Mr Creakle is only eating it to suppress overwhelming feelings, but we know that it is tasty too. Life goes on. Or at least, breakfast goes on.

In manuscript, you can see Dickens minutely adjusting the wording to get the right effect. At first, the sentence was 'Mr Creakle shook his head and stopped up a sigh with a very large piece of buttered toast.'[5] The diversionary toast was always there. Then Dickens inserted those phrases about the child's look (why is Mr Creakle not speaking?) and the adult's evasion. So, that huge piece of toast gets noticed as part of the human drama, and is the funnier for it. Laughter unsettles the easy belief of critics that Dickens's fiction became better, through the course of his career, as it became darker; the entertainer became a serious novelist. From the first, in fact, Dickens liked to make humour out of the darkest materials. In the final instalment of *Pickwick Papers* the lawyer from the debtors' court, Solomon Nell, takes Sam Weller and his father, along with three of Mr Weller's coachman friends, to meet stockbroker Wilkins Flasher, Esquire in his rooms 'up a court behind the Bank of England'. Mr Weller needs to sell some stocks left to him by his recently deceased wife. They attend Wilkins Flasher, Esquire at the hour arranged but must wait while he finishes transacting business with 'a smart young gentleman' dressed more or less exactly like himself. The two men are discussing a fellow broker.

> 'I see there's a notice up this morning about Boffer,' observed Mr Simmery. 'Poor devil, he's expelled the house!'
>
> 'I'll bet you ten guineas to five, he cuts his throat,' said Wilkins Flasher, Esquire.
>
> 'Done,' replied Mr Simmery.
>
> 'Stop! I bar,' said Wilkins Flasher, Esquire, thoughtfully. 'Perhaps he may hang himself.'

Need the wager mention the actual means of self-annihilation? There is some give and take over the exact terms, before the contract is satisfactorily concluded.

> So it was entered down on the little books that Boffer was to kill himself within ten days, or Wilkins Flasher, Esquire, was to hand over to Frank Simmery, Esquire, the sum of ten guineas; and that if Boffer did kill himself

within that time, Frank Simmery, Esquire, would pay
to Wilkins Flasher, Esquire, five guineas, instead.

From the terms of the bet, it seems that Boffer's suicide is
thought to be twice as likely as not.

The two men do share some regrets about Boffer's
demise. ' "I'm very sorry he has failed," said Wilkins
Flasher, Esquire. "Capital dinners he gave." ' Mr Simmery
recalls Boffer's fine port and says that 'we are going to send
our butler' to the sale the next day to pick some up.

'The devil you are!' said Wilkins Flasher, Esquire.
'My man's going too. Five guineas my man outbids
your man.'
    'Done.'

(Ch. LV)

Everything is recorded in little books with gold pencil cases,
before Mr Simmery strolls off to the stock exchange 'to see
what was going forward' and Wilkins Flasher, Esquire turns
his attentions to Mr Weller's finances. It is a wonderfully
unnecessary episode. The brokers are buoyant gamblers
who relish their occupation enough to make a flutter
out of another man's catastrophe. They are dicing with a
prospect – suicide – elsewhere approached with horror in
Dickens's novels: Ralph Nickleby hanging himself, Merdle
slitting his wrists, Bradley Headstone drowning his enemy
along with himself. All these are memorable and terrible
incarnations of despair. But then, at least Boffer does still
live and maybe Simmery will win the bet.

We might think of *Pickwick Papers* as genially comical,
but its humour relies on collisions between the unworldly
Pickwickians and a cast of devious or ruthless operators.

These bit-part players often laugh at comic eventualities that pass the Pickwickians by. Pickwick's solicitor, Perker, takes him to meet Serjeant Snubbin, the barrister who will represent him in the breach of promise case brought against him by Mrs Bardell, and engages in some knowing joshing with Snubbin's elderly clerk, Mallard, about how to draw extra payment from their clients. The two men laugh together conspiratorially, but Mallard's is 'a silent, internal chuckle, which Mr Pickwick disliked to hear ... When a man bleeds inwardly, it is a dangerous thing for himself; but when he laughs inwardly, it bodes no good to other people' (Ch. XXX).

Different rogues laugh differently. The nefarious lawyers who specialise in breach of promise, Dodson and Fogg, habitually laugh loudly together ('Ha! ha! ha!' for Dodson and 'He! he! he!' for Fogg), 'pleasantly and cheerfully, as men who are going to receive money often do' (Ch. LII). Most of this laughter bemuses or outrages Mr Pickwick. The black humour of good people who nevertheless relish the farcical aspect of violent accident also passes him by. There is Mr Weller's tale of the man who was once master of a shop that he and Pickwick pass in a street near the Temple. He invented a steam-driven sausage machine 'as 'ud swaller up a pavin' stone if you put it too near, and grind it into sassages as easy as if it was a tender young babby' (Ch. XXX). He disappeared and was assumed by his wife to have 'run away' – until a customer turned up at the shop to complain that he had found buttons in his sausages. Or the medical students from St Bartholomew's Hospital with whom Pickwick dines, who love to tell tales of the senior surgeon Slasher's remarkable prowess with a blade.

'Took a boy's leg out of the socket last week—boy
ate five apples and a gingerbread cake—exactly two
minutes after it was all over, boy said he wouldn't lie
there to be made game of, and he'd tell his mother if
they didn't begin.'

(Ch. XXXII)

What makes us laugh often bemuses or shocks Mr
Pickwick. It is not clear that Pickwick, a stout person
himself, even notices how funny the fat boy is.

The fat boy filled Mr Pickwick's glass, and then retired
behind his master's chair, from whence he watched
the play of the knives and forks, and the progress of the
choice morsels from the dishes to the mouths of the
company, with a kind of dark and gloomy joy that was
most impressive.

(Ch. XXVIII)

The other characters call him by his name, Joe; it is
Dickens who calls him 'the fat boy'. The fat boy lives to
eat and sleep (Sam Weller addresses him as 'young boa
constructer'). Dickens is attentive to his painful stir of
emotions whenever he has to see food prepared for or
eaten by others:

the leaden eyes which twinkled behind his mountainous
cheeks leered horribly upon the food as he unpacked it
from the basket.
    'Now make haste,' said Mr Wardle; for the fat boy
was hanging fondly over a capon, which he seemed
wholly unable to part with. The boy sighed deeply,

and, bestowing an ardent gaze upon its plumpness, unwillingly consigned it to his master.

(Ch. IV)

Are we enjoying a horrid Victorian joke that no right-minded writer of today would think of perpetrating? No: the fat boy is a happy slave to indolence and appetite – those universal susceptibilities – who has successfully contrived a life that allows him to indulge both.

For the fat boy has more life and thought than those around him realise. Mr Tupman is canoodling with the spinster aunt, Rachael, in the arbour, when they notice the ubiquitous fat boy, who has come to call them for supper. Seeing 'the utter vacancy of the fat boy's countenance', Mr Tupman foolishly concludes that he has not witnessed their amours. Later, Rachael's 'timorous' elderly mother encounters the fat boy in the garden. Imagining that 'the bloated lad was about to do her some grievous bodily harm with the view of possessing himself of her loose coin', she tries to mollify him.

> 'Well, Joe,' said the trembling old lady. 'I'm sure I have been a good mistress to you, Joe. You have invariably been treated very kindly. You have never had too much to do; and you have always had enough to eat.'
>
> This last was an appeal to the fat boy's most sensitive feelings. He seemed touched, as he replied emphatically—
>
> 'I knows I has.'
>
> 'Then what can you want to do now?' said the old lady, gaining courage.
>
> 'I wants to make your flesh creep,' replied the boy.

It is not just food and sleep that motivate him. He tells the old lady that he has seen Tupman 'a-kissin' and huggin''. But whom? Her own daughter!

> 'And she suffered him!' exclaimed the old lady. A grin stole over the fat boy's features as he said—
>> 'I see her a-kissin' of him agin.'
>
> (Ch. VIII)

The fat boy's moment has come. All flesh himself, he is the perfect spy on others' fleshly pleasure. Dickens would surely have been delighted to find that it was thanks to 'the fat boy' that his first novel achieved a foothold in the literature of medical science. Obesity Hypoventilation Syndrome (OHS), a condition related to sleep apnea, was first called Pickwickian Syndrome.[6] 'A classic description of the signs and symptoms under discussion was written by Charles Dickens.' Though to find in the habits of the fat boy the symptoms of a medically verifiable syndrome, perhaps a certain po-faced-ness is necessary.

For almost a year, the writing of *Pickwick Papers* overlapped with the writing of his second novel, *Oliver Twist*. Usually Dickens would write an instalment of *Oliver Twist* first, then follow it with a considerably longer and more cheering instalment of *Pickwick Papers*. In *Oliver Twist*, Dickens likens the alternation of 'the tragic and the comic scenes' in 'all good murderous melodramas' to 'the layers of red and white in a side of streaky bacon' (Ch. XVII). It is evident that he is obstinately justifying the 'violent transitions' of his own fiction. Except that the characteristic effect of his own comic audacity comes from blending and not alternating incompatible materials. Early reviewers noticed this. An article published in the

Edinburgh Review in response to the early instalments of *Nicholas Nickleby*, but looking back at his earlier fiction, praised Dickens for 'that mastery in the pathetic which, though it seems opposed to the gift of humour, is often found in conjunction with it'.[7] 'Let him stick to his native vein of the *serio-comic*, and blend humour with pathos. He shines in this,' declared the *Quarterly Review* in 1839.[8]

The anonymous reviewer was right. The opening chapter of *Oliver Twist* is made of grim material: a baby boy is born in a workhouse; the young mother kisses her child with the last of her strength and then dies. Yet Dickens manages a tone of almost playful irony. The baby nearly dies; or rather, 'there was considerable difficulty in inducing Oliver to take upon himself the office of respiration'. Luckily, he is forced on his own resources, as he is attended only by 'a pauper old woman, who was rendered rather misty by an unwonted allowance of beer; and a parish surgeon who did such matters by contract'. 'Rather misty': Dickens chooses an amused euphemism for the nurse's drunkenness over any indignation. When the mother asks to see her baby before she dies, this boozy attendant encourages her to think more positively. When she has had thirteen children, like the nurse, 'and all on 'em dead except two, and them in the wurkus with me, she'll know better than to take on in that way, bless her dear heart!' The narrator cannot resist some incongruous wordiness. 'Apparently this consolatory perspective of a mother's prospects failed in producing its effect' (Ch. I). And a few moments later the unnamed mother is dead.

Dickens is the novelist who best enables us to laugh when we should not laugh. In a letter to his great friend, the actor William Macready, written in his late twenties, he described how well he knew that 'same perverse and unaccountable feeling which causes a heartbroken man at a dear friend's funeral to see something irresistibly comical in a red-nosed or one-eyed undertaker'.[9] So Mr Bumble, the parochial despot who superintends the system of deprivation from which Oliver and his fellow paupers suffer, is also the comic turn of *Oliver Twist* – not despite but because of his cruelty. He and Mrs Mann, with whom the younger orphans live, are a grotesque double act. Here he gives Mrs Mann her monthly stipend and asks for a receipt.

> 'It's very much blotted, sir,' said the farmer of infants; 'but it's formal enough, I dare say. Thank you, Mr Bumble, sir, I am very much obliged to you, I'm sure.'
>
> Mr Bumble nodded, blandly, in acknowledgment of Mrs Mann's curtsey; and inquired how the children were.
>
> 'Bless their dear little hearts!' said Mrs Mann with emotion, 'they're as well as can be, the dears! Of course, except the two that died last week.'
>
> (Ch. XVII)

Of course, except them. Most of these involved in parochial 'charity' are unwitting comedians. Here is the process by which Oliver is set to be sold, in effect, to the local chimney sweeper. He is being questioned by the local magistrate, who must authorise apprenticeships.

> 'And this man that's to be his master—you, sir—you'll treat him well, and feed him, and do all that sort of thing, will you?' said the old gentleman.
>
> 'When I says I will, I means I will,' replied Mr Gamfield doggedly.

'You're a rough speaker, my friend, but you look an honest, open-hearted man,' said the old gentleman: turning his spectacles in the direction of the candidate for Oliver's premium, whose villainous countenance was a regular stamped receipt for cruelty.

(Ch. III)

We can read this as an indictment of an enslaving system, which it is, but can laugh too. The old gentleman uses his spectacles and sees the salt of the earth where anybody without spectacles can see a brute. It is not as if it is not obvious.

The business by which the fate of the parentless or abandoned children of the poor gets decided is good material for indignation, but Dickens also finds something irresistibly comic in it. How could such random and incompetent shaping of a person's life not be funny? More than twenty-five years after completing *Oliver Twist*, he gave his readers a different example in *Our Mutual Friend*. Mr and Mrs Boffin, a childless and benevolent couple who have suddenly come into money, are visiting the impecunious young clergyman, Mr Milvey, and his wife in order to find a little boy to adopt. What ensues is an inadvertently comical double act, as Mr Milvey suggests particular local orphans and Mrs Milvey thinks of the obvious reason why each will not do. Perhaps, suggests Mrs Boffin, they should not have come. Not at all, the Milveys assure them. They will find someone suitable. '"We have orphans, I know," pursued Mr Milvey, quite with the air as if he might have added, "in stock"' (I Ch. IX).

As John Carey wonderfully says, 'once Dickens starts laughing nothing is safe, from Christianity to dead babies'.[10] As is clear enough in Dickens's third novel, *Nicholas Nickleby*, cruelty to children is certainly included. We first encounter the brutal schoolmaster Mr Squeers at the Saracen's Head inn in London, where he is hoping to collect some unfortunate pupils for transportation back to Yorkshire. So far, only one 'diminutive boy' has been deposited; he makes the mistake of sneezing. 'What's that, sir?' growls Mr Squeers. 'Nothing, please sir,' says the boy, before admitting that he sneezed.

> 'Oh! Sneezed, did you?' retorted Mr Squeers. 'Then what did you say "nothing" for, sir?'
> In default of a better answer to this question, the little boy screwed a couple of knuckles into each of his eyes and began to cry, wherefore Mr Squeers knocked him off the trunk with a blow on one side of the face, and knocked him on again with a blow on the other.
>
> (Ch. IV)

This schoolmaster from Hell is a clumsy ruffian, yet his violence to tiny victims is so habitual as to have a kind of aplomb. As Malcolm Andrews puts it, 'casual violence mutates into a slapstick routine' – a performance with a certain skill to it.[11]

Squeers is peculiarly comical in his tireless attempts to recruit pupils. This is a monomania that requires him to utter falsehoods with brazen directness. A Mr Snawley arrives at the inn to offload his two recently acquired stepsons and offers Squeers the opportunity of a little hypocritical to-and-fro.

> 'I should wish their morals to be particularly attended to,' said Mr Snawley.

'I am glad of that, sir,' replied the schoolmaster, drawing himself up. 'They have come to the right shop for morals, sir.'

'You are a moral man yourself,' said Mr Snawley.

'I rather believe I am, sir,' replied Squeers.

'I have the satisfaction to know you are, sir,' said Mr Snawley. 'I asked one of your references, and he said you were pious.'

'Well, sir, I hope I am a little in that line,' replied Squeers.

'I hope I am also,' rejoined the other.

(Ch. IV)

'A little in that line' is a deliciously inept attempt at proper modesty. This exchange is one step on – in both logic and absurdity – from that between the dim-witted magistrate and the chimney sweep in *Oliver Twist*. Squeers and Snawley 'understand each other'.

Critics have often paused on Squeers, knowing that they find him hilarious and wondering (or worrying?) why they do so. In his 1898 essay on Dickens as a satirist, George Gissing admired the depiction of Squeers and of Dotheboys Hall in *Nicholas Nickleby* for its 'inextricable blending of horrors and jocosity'.[12] 'We can hardly help an amiable feeling towards the Squeers family, seeing the hearty gusto with which they pursue their monstrous business.' Dickens gives them some of his own energy, allowing them to parade their vices.

Dickens, who surely was tender enough, had so irresistible a comic genius that it carried him beyond the gentle humour which most Englishmen possess to the absolute grotesque reality. Squeers, for instance, when he sips the wretched dilution which he has prepared for his starved and shivering little pupils, smacks his lips and cries: 'Here's richness!' It is savage comedy ...[13]

Violence is in the air they breathe. Fanny Squeers, disappointed in her amorous attentions to Nicholas, pens an illiterate letter to Ralph Nickleby, in which she attempts to blacken Nicholas's character. Having described how her father is 'one mask of brooses both blue and green' she brilliantly takes her dishonesty a step too far in complaining of the injuries supposedly done to her mother by Nicholas, who supposedly 'drove her comb several inches into her head'. 'A very little more and it must have entered her skull. We have a medical certifikit that if it had, the tortershell would have affected the brain' (Ch. XV). She could not resist that last detail of narrowly avoided tortoiseshell poisoning.

Gissing was right that Dickens had combined his fictionalised indictment of a real social evil – the Yorkshire Schools where unwanted children were despatched to suffer and even perish – with a kind of violent slapstick. The combination is something no other writer dared. Violence could be comic, as popular culture demonstrated. In 1849 Dickens had replied to a letter from Mary Elizabeth Tayler, expressing her horror at the influence of 'the street Punch' on young spectators and asking if he might write a new and morally improving Punch and Judy show for the modern age. Dickens put her right.

In my opinion the Street Punch is one of those extravagant reliefs from the realities of life which would lose its hold upon the people if it were made

moral and instructive. I regard it as quite harmless in
its influence, and as an outrageous joke which no one
in existence would think of regarding as an incentive
to any course of action, or a model for any kind of
conduct.[14]

Even the saintly Little Nell in *The Old Curiosity Shop*
finds Punch funny. She and her grandfather are travelling
in the caravan of Mrs Jarley, who proudly describes her
waxworks show to her.

> 'Never go into the company of a filthy Punch any
> more,' said Mrs Jarley, 'after this.'
>   'Is it funnier than Punch?'
>   'Funnier!' said Mrs Jarley in a shrill voice. 'It is not
> funny at all.'
>   'Oh!' said Nell, with all possible humility.
>   'It isn't funny at all,' repeated Mrs Jarley. 'It's calm
> and—what's that word again—critical?—no—classical,
> that's it—it's calm and classical. No low beatings and
> knockings about, no jokings and squeakings like your
> precious Punches …
>
> (Ch. XXVII)

Mrs Jarley is comical in her disapproval of Punch-inspired
laughter. *The Old Curiosity Shop* features two 'itinerant
showmen—exhibitors of the freaks of Punch'. For a
while, Nell and her grandfather join Mr Short (who does
the performing and is 'merry-faced') and Mr Codlin (who
takes the money and is 'surly').

> Short beguiled the time with songs and jests, and made
> the best of everything that happened. Mr Codlin on the

other hand, cursed his fate, and all the hollow things
of earth (but Punch especially), and limped along
with the theatre on his back, a prey to the bitterest
chagrin.

(Ch. XVI)

Poor Codlin! A misanthrope permanently chained to this
violent amuser of the people.

Mrs Jarley tells us that we should all know better than
to keep company with Punch, 'a low, practical, wulgar
wretch, that people should scorn to look at' (Ch. XXVI).
Part of what makes him funny is the thought that we
should not be laughing. In the same novel, Dickens
provides a Punch in human guise, the grotesque and
ebullient Daniel Quilp, a demonic mischief-maker. He is
so tickled by his wife's presumed 'anxiety and grief' at his
unexplained absence, that

he laughed as he went along until the tears ran down
his cheeks; and more than once, when he found
himself in a bye-street, vented his delight in a shrill
scream, which greatly terrifying any lonely passenger,
who happened to be walking on before him expecting
nothing so little, increased his mirth, and made him
remarkably cheerful and light-hearted.

(Ch. XLIX)

Quilp is often laughing, though always to himself. When
his cowed wife begs him to return home, he tells her he
will do as he please. Her frightened departure sends him
into 'an immoderate fit of laughter' (Ch. L). It is a laughter
of satisfaction – but also of amusement at the absurdity of
those he knows all too well. When Kit, framed for theft by

Sampson Brass, is being taken away in a hackney-coach, he spies Quilp at a tavern window, 'swollen with suppressed laughter' (Ch. LX). After gloating, 'he burst into a yell of laughter, manifestly to the great terror of the coachman'. Once they are gone, he rolls around on the ground 'in an ecstasy of enjoyment'. When Sampson Brass visits he finds Quilp shrieking with laughter at the possible words of the magistrate to the falsely accused Kit (Ch. LXII). His Punch-like humorous malice is active. He keeps turning up with some new trick, even if it is only to hang upside down from the top of a coach and make horrible faces at Kit's mother, travelling inside. 'Such an amazing power of taking people by surprise!' (Ch. XLIX). He enjoys a world where, as he tells his henchman who is stumbling through the timber yard, 'all the rusty nails are upwards' (Ch. LXII)

Knowing the inappropriateness (as we nowadays say) of much laughter, Dickens used it to fend off his own inclination for pathos. In *Nicholas Nickleby*, he sends Mrs Nickleby to save us, and perhaps to save himself, from gloom and sentimentality. As Nicholas, Kate and Miss La Creevy, 'profoundly silent', ponder the unspoken fact of Smike's despairing love for Kate, Mrs Nickleby rescues us with comparison of his 'unaccountable conduct' with legendary figures, who lead her to some bizarre familial reminiscence.

> One of them had some connection with our family. I forget, without looking back to some old letters I have upstairs, whether it was my great-grandfather who went to school with the Cock-lane Ghost, or the Thirsty Woman of Tutbury who went to school with my grandmother.
>
> (Ch. XLIX)

It is easy to get confused. In other early novels, bit-part
players arrive to divert us from distress. Having put Nell
and her grandfather through something like Hell in *The
Old Curiosity Shop*, Dickens has the girl's rescue heralded
by a deliciously self-important doctor, who appears for a
few moments, recommends everything that she has already
been given, and then exits, never to be encountered again.

> 'And a toast, Sir?' suggested the landlady.
> 'Ay,' said the doctor, in the tone of a man who makes
> a dignified concession. 'And a toast—of bread. But
> be very particular to make it of bread, if you please,
> ma'am.'
> With which parting injunction, slowly and
> portentously delivered, the doctor departed, leaving
> the whole house in admiration of that wisdom which
> tallied so closely with their own.
>
> (Ch. XLVI)

This is Dickens's better instinct. In an otherwise lachrymose
scene later in the same novel, when Kit's mother and
infant children visit Kit in prison, Dickens provides a
turnkey who reads his newspaper 'with a waggish look (he
had evidently got among the facetious paragraphs)'. He is
not inhumane, but when Kit's mother addresses him, he
requires her to wait a moment as he is 'in the very crisis
and passion of a joke' (Ch. LXI).

In his brilliant essay celebrating Dickens, George
Santayana argued that his improvisational method was
essential to his comedy.

> He is not thinking of us; he is obeying the impulse of
> the passion, the person, or the story he is enacting. This

faculty, which renders him a consummate comedian, is just what alienated from him a later generation in which people of taste were aesthetes and virtuous people were higher snobs; they wanted a mincing art, and he gave them copious improvization, they wanted analysis and development, and he gave them absolute comedy.[15]

So, even in the course of telling us something horrifying, he finds something funny. A man has been trained in covetousness by his money-obsessed father and has now grown up to wish that father dead, so that he might inherit his wealth. Such a character might well exist in the fiction of George Eliot or Emile Zola or Dostoevsky, but only in Dickens would the presentation of the case be funny.

The education of Mr Jonas had been conducted from his cradle on the strictest principles of the main chance. The very first word he learnt to spell was 'gain,' and the second (when he got into two syllables), 'money.' But for two results, which were not clearly foreseen perhaps by his watchful parent in the beginning, his training may be said to have been unexceptionable. One of these flaws was, that having been long taught by his father to over-reach everybody, he had imperceptibly acquired a love of over-reaching that venerable monitor himself. The other, that from his early habits of considering everything as a question of property, he had gradually come to look, with impatience, on his parent as a certain amount of personal estate, which had no right whatever to be going at large, but ought to be secured in that particular description of iron

safe which is commonly called a coffin, and banked
in the grave.

(Martin Chuzzlewit, Ch. VIII)

Jonas's wish for his father to die is terrible – and will be
shown in the novel to have terrible consequences – but
here it is dealt with facetiously. The mismatch of tone and
content is just what Dickens is after.

By the time of *Dombey and Son*, Dickens had fully
learned to contrive laughter at the oddest moments –
because they are the oddest moments. Plunge into
the novel's first chapter and you soon discover this.
The opening events are sad and grim. A baby has been
born, but not into a happy family. Mr Dombey, a man
preoccupied apparently only with the prosperity and
power of his firm (after which the novel is named), broods
on the future that he has mapped out for his new son. His
wife is dying, but he hardly seems to have any love for her.
His daughter, Florence, evidently scorned by her father, is
distraught and clings to her mother as her life ebbs. It is,
you might think, one of those solemn, emotion-wringing
Victorian deathbed episodes (Dickens had already given
his readers several of these in his preceding novels).

But this first chapter is also funny. In the very first
sentence the baby who is the much wished-for 'Son' of the
firm 'Dombey and Son' has been put in his basket close
to the fire 'as if his constitution were analogous to that of
a muffin, and it was essential to toast him brown while
he was very new'. The joke comparison has a point: this
child, Paul Dombey, will get a parody of care from the
father with whom he shares his name. Those who minister
to the dying Mrs Dombey, meanwhile, also make you
laugh just when they shouldn't. There is the nurse, who,

when addressed by Mr Dombey ('Mrs—'), is so servile as
to supply her own name with a question mark – 'Blockitt,
Sir?' – as if she 'did not presume to state her name as a fact,
but merely offered it as a mild suggestion'. There is the
society physician Doctor Parker Peps, attending because
Mr Dombey believes that whoever is most expensive is
best, but is so habituated to an aristocratic clientele that he
keeps mistaking the name of his patient. 'It would appear
that the system of Lady Cankaby—excuse me: I should
say of Mrs Dombey: I confuse the names of cases—'. Poor
man, he cannot get used to employers who are merely
very wealthy. Even as he tries to break the news of his
patient's desperate condition, he blunderingly dubs her
'the Countess of Dombey', before correcting himself with
a rapid 'I *beg* your pardon; Mrs Dombey'. Mr Dombey's
sister, Mrs Chick, meanwhile insists on speaking as if Mrs
Dombey's dangerous condition arose from a lamentable
unwillingness to exert herself. 'An effort is necessary.
That's all. If dear Fanny were a Dombey!—'

Mrs Dombey dies amidst all this folly and blunder.
Incongruous comedy is Dickens's way, when he is at
his best. Much later in the same novel there is another
inappropriately hilarious scene of getting names wrong
that strikes again at Mr Dombey's much prized dignity.
The ghastly Mrs Skewton has successfully pimped her
beautiful widowed daughter, Edith, to be Mr Dombey's
second wife. Now she has had a stroke, and gets confused
between her daughter's first husband, Colonel Granger,
and her second (both of them lovelessly married for
money). 'She fell into the habit of confounding the names
of her two sons-in-law, the living and the deceased.'
Mr Dombey – who *is*, after all, on the deathly side –
has to tolerate being called 'Grangeby' or 'Domber', 'or

indifferently, both' (Ch. XL). Her name errors are like inadvertent yet inevitable satire; nothing matters more to Mr Dombey than his name.

Dombey and Son has serious concerns – it is a novel about power and its abuse – but it lets us laugh at the ways in which important people take themselves seriously. The chilling Mr Dombey is absurd as well as life-denying. When Dickens began writing the novel in June 1846, it was with a strong interest and pleasure in the ridiculous. It had been two years since he finished writing *Martin Chuzzlewit*. In the interim he had been travelling in Europe with his family and had published an account of his trip to Italy. He felt he had a store of invention, much of it comic, to unlock. As he told his closest friend, John Forster, while he was working on the second instalment,

> Invention, thank God, seems the easiest thing in the world; and I seem to have such a preposterous sense of the ridiculous, after this long rest, as to be constantly requiring to restrain myself from launching into extravagances in the height of my enjoyment.[16]

Dombey and Son is rich in 'the ridiculous' and in comic superfluities whose very existence is a kind of admonishment to Mr Dombey. We may be concerned about Paul Dombey's fate at Doctor Blimber's academy in Brighton, but we get distracted by the boy's account of Glubb, the old man smelling 'like a weedy sea-beach when the tide is out', who pulls his invalid carriage and tells very tall tales of sea creatures he has seen. We are watching the ball at Doctor Blimber's that is Paul Dombey's touching farewell to the school, but instead find ourselves listening to the know-all dancing master Mr Baps, who is managing to convince the self-important Barnet Skettles that he is an expert on foreign trade.

Dickens also exploits the opposite of comic relief: humour that sets the reader up for shock or sadness. In his 'mem' for the tenth number of *David Copperfield* (containing Emily's elopement) he writes 'First chapter funny. Then on to [?the] Em'ly' (the last two words underlined).[17] The first chapter of this instalment is duly taken up with a dinner that David hosts for Mr and Mrs Micawber and Traddles, though interrupted first by the sinister Littimer, who is looking for his master Steerforth (but stays to grill the mutton for them), then by Steerforth himself, who invites David to visit him the next day at his mother's Highgate home. 'Who knows when we may meet again, else?' At the end of the chapter, Mr Micawber, who has departed in fine spirits, has sent one of his verbally expansive notes reporting that his possessions (and those of Traddles) have been seized because of unpaid rent. 'It is expedient that I should inform you that the undersigned is Crushed' (Ch. XXVIII). The comedy of manic-depressive Micawber-ism – from eloquent high spirits over the punch to equally eloquent dejection in that letter – might almost prevent us noticing (as it certainly prevents David noticing) what is really going on. Steerforth and his man are preparing to travel to Yarmouth for a rendezvous with Emily and her elopement. This will not come for another three chapters, at the very end of the instalment, but we should have sensed the impending disaster in that 'funny' chapter.

Dickens relishes the laughter that is close to disaster. In *Little Dorrit*, Amy Dorrit's mother goes into labour in the Marshalsea Prison, under the care (if that is the word) of Mrs Bangham, 'charwoman and messenger' at the debtors' jail.

The walls and ceiling were blackened with flies. Mrs Bangham, expert in sudden device, with one hand fanned the patient with a cabbage leaf, and with the other set traps of vinegar and sugar in gallipots; at the same time enunciating sentiments of an encouraging and congratulatory nature, adapted to the occasion.

She muses aloud on the size of the flies that are dropping into the traps all around them. 'What between the buryin ground, the grocer's, the waggon-stables, and the paunch trade, the Marshalsea flies gets very large.' Then she has an inspired notion. 'P'raps they're sent as a consolation, if we only know'd it' (I Ch. VI). There are often these minor characters who are genially habituated to other people's tribulations. In *Little Dorrit* Arthur Clennam finds himself ruined by the collapse of Merdle's bank and consults the Pentonville debt retriever Mr Rugg. Clennam is distraught that he has lost Daniel Doyce's money too and sighs that if he had only sacrificed his own money he should have 'cared far less'.

'Indeed, sir?' said Mr Rugg, rubbing his hands with a cheerful air. 'You surprise me. That's singular, sir. I have generally found, in my experience, that it's their own money people are most particular about. I have seen people get rid of a good deal of other people's money, and bear it very well: very well indeed.'

(II Ch. XXVI)

Of course, Clennam is sincere, yet for a moment Mr Rugg returns him to the world we all live in. Mr Rugg 'recovers' debts for a living and knows about people losing money – and the fortitude they show when it was never theirs in the first place.

Mr Rugg and his daughter, Miss Rugg, are two more who have been sent by Dickens to save us from gloom. We first encounter them when we find that Mr Pancks, the rent collector who secretly plots against his hypocritical employer, Mr Casby, lodges at the premises of Mr Rugg in Pentonville. Miss Rugg appears with a deliciously superfluous back story that declares her a chip off her father's block.

> Miss Rugg was a lady of a little property which she had acquired, together with much distinction in the neighbourhood, by having her heart severely lacerated and her feelings mangled by a middle-aged baker resident in the vicinity, against whom she had, by the agency of Mr Rugg, found it necessary to proceed at law to recover damages for a breach of promise of marriage.
>
> (I Ch. XXV)

She has won her case. The baker has had to pay up forty guineas and suffer the mockery of the local youth. 'But Miss Rugg, environed by the majesty of the law, and having her damages invested in the public securities, was regarded with consideration.' Pancks has taken the risk of bringing John Chivery, who pines over Little Dorrit, to dinner, and thus 'within range of the dangerous (because expensive) fascinations of Miss Rugg'. She begins the meal heaving the sighs of a cruelly deceived woman, but Chivery is so doleful that she ends up leaving the room 'to sit upon the stairs until she had had her laugh out'.

Dickens is sometimes found guilty of expecting us to laugh at unalluring women who insist on being flirtatious. In the case of Flora Finching in *Little Dorrit*, the indictment is persuasive because Dickens seems to have been fictionalising a real woman. In 1855 he had eagerly arranged a reunion with the former Maria Beadnell, whom he had unsuccessfully courted more than twenty years earlier. Now she was Mrs Henry Winter, wife of a London sawmill manager. After writing her some throbbingly emotional letters, he met her – and was appalled to find her, now in her mid-forties, stout and silly.[18] A decade later he turned her into Flora Finching, who rejected Arthur Clennam when both were young. Arthur returns to England after two decades working for his father in China and revisits the woman whom he once loved.

> Flora, always tall, had grown to be very broad too, and short of breath; but that was not much. Flora, whom he had left a lily, had become a peony; but that was not much. Flora, who had seemed enchanting in all she said and thought, was diffuse and silly. That was much. Flora, who had been spoiled and artless long ago, was determined to be spoiled and artless now. That was a fatal blow.

Giggly and coquettish, the now widowed Flora is absurd. She looks like Dickens's act of vengeance.

She speaks in unpunctuated outpourings in which she weirdly tries to revive the past.

> 'No one could dispute, Arthur—Mr Clennam—that it's quite right you should be formally friendly to me under the altered circumstances and indeed you couldn't be anything else, at least I suppose not you

ought to know, but I can't help recalling that there *was* a time when things were very different.'

She is ridiculous, yet Arthur Clennam's feelings, 'wherein his sense of the sorrowful and his sense of the comical were curiously blended' are offered as a guide to the reader (I Ch. XIII). At the end of the novel, when she finds that Arthur is to marry Amy Dorrit, she meets her in a pie shop near the Marshalsea Prison to give her blessing. At least she has her words to console her.

'The withered chaplet my dear,' said Flora, with great enjoyment, 'is then perished the column is crumbled and the pyramid is standing upside down upon its what's-his-name call it not giddiness call it not weakness call it not folly I must now retire into privacy and look upon the ashes of departed joys no more but taking a further liberty of paying for the pastry which has formed the humble pretext of our interview will for ever say Adieu!'

(II Ch. XXXIV)

Flowers and pies, pyramids and ashes: in her defeated hopes she is as upside down and gushing as ever, comic exactly because those hopes were real.

7

Naming

AVAILABLE NAMES
        Heading from the Book of Memoranda[1]

Dickens is the English novel's greatest name-monger. The *Oxford English Dictionary* shows how his names have lodged in the imaginations of his readers and thence in the English language. Dickens supplies the *OED* with more eponyms – words derived from the names of characters – than any other novelist. This started happening almost immediately. The *OED* has entries for *Pickwickian*, to mean 'resembling Mr Pickwick', from the 1840s and then reaching to the 1990s. More significantly, five or six years after the instalments of the novel began appearing, the adjective was being used to refer to the habit of interpreting an expression 'in such a way as to avoid unpleasantness'. Pickwick had given his name to a widely recognised character trait. Meanwhile, after an enterprising London cigar manufacturer started selling his product in a box decorated with a picture of Mr Pickwick, a *Pickwick* became a now obsolete word for a cheap cigar or cheroot.[2]

In his second novel, *Oliver Twist*, Dickens invented more names that became eponyms: Bumble, for a self-important minor official, the Artful Dodger, used for a lovably ingenious rogue from the year after the novel's publication until now, and Fagin, for the leader of a gang of child thieves, perhaps becoming less frequent because of the implicit anti-semitism of Dickens's characterisation. Later novels provided more eponyms: Scrooge, Pecksniffian, Gamp, Micawber, Uriah Heep, Gradgrind, Podsnappery. The singular names became labels for species of character. As John Forster put it in an anonymous review of *Bleak House*, 'Mr Dickens's characters, as all the world knows, pass their names into our language, and become types.'[3] In each one of these cases, the outline of the character is made the sharper and more memorable by the name. Dickens knew this. He himself was the first person to use 'Pecksniffian' and 'Podsnappery'. The former adjective echoes through *Martin Chuzzlewit*, as if the narrator has pinned down some special bundle of characteristics inhering in the name. So, for instance, after the conversation in which Mr Pecksniff has tried to blackmail Mary Graham into marrying him,

> For a minute or two, in fact, he was hot, and pale, and mean, and shy, and slinking, and consequently not at all Pecksniffian. But after that, he recovered himself, and went home with as beneficent an air as if he had been the High Priest of the summer weather.
>
> (Ch. XXX)

Pecksniff's achievement is to be Pecksniffian.

It is true that some once common Dickensian eponyms have become obsolete. The *OED* has *Stiggins* (from the censorious, but in fact dipsomaniac, clergyman in *Pickwick Papers*) as 'a pious humbug', but the word would be difficult to use now without explanation. Likewise, *Wellerism*, for a proverbial expression that has been given a humorous twist, the verbal habit of Toby Weller in the same novel, even if the *OED* treats it as current. *Tapleyism*, to mean incorrigible optimism in the face of all adversity, after the name of Martin Chuzzlewit's indefatigably loyal companion, seems to have been used readily in the second half of the nineteenth century, but now would be obscure.[4] *Dolly Varden* (from the character in *Barnaby Rudge*) once referred to a dress with a flower pattern and with a skirt gathered in loops, but the usage disappeared by the end of the nineteenth century. A *gamp* is no longer widely understood as a word for an umbrella. Yet even these obsolete usages are evidence of readers' willingness to recognise Dickens's peculiar names as labels for people and things they could see in the world around them.

Naming was, for Dickens, essential. Often, he began planning a novel with the main characters' names. After trying out a series of sample title pages for what would become *David Copperfield*, but was still being called 'Mag's Diversions', he wrote out some columns of names on one of these pages. Trotfield, Trotbury, Spankle, Wellbury, Copperboy, Flowerbury, Topflower, Magbury. Copperstone, Copperfield, Copperfield.[5] The repetition of the final name meant that he had finally got it. Alongside these possibilities he scribbled some name fragments: Stone bury, Flower, Brook, Well, boy, field. You can see that he was thinking of his protagonist's name as a combination of parts, one of which might be pastoral or rural. As he tries out the names for his protagonist, Dickens is discovering some of the essential elements of his story. As with previous heroes – Nicholas Nickleby, Martin Chuzzlewit – he will combine an ordinary forename with a potentially comic surname. His protagonist's name was also significant in another way, spotted by his friend John Forster.

> It is singular that it should never have occurred to him, while the name was thus strangely as by accident bringing itself together, that the initials were but his own reversed; but he was much startled when I pointed this out, and protested it was just in keeping with the fates and chances which were always befalling him. 'Why else,' he said, 'should I so obstinately have kept to that name when once it turned up?'[6]

Copperfield is a name with gentlemanly pretensions (David's mother solemnly, sometimes tearfully, refers to her dead husband as 'Mr Copperfield'). The pretensions are comically undermined by David's landlady. 'Mrs Crupp always called me Mr Copperfull: firstly, no doubt, because it was not my name; and secondly, I am inclined to think, in some indistinct association with a washing-day' (Ch. XXVI). They are sarcastically mocked by Uriah Heep, who inserts 'Master Copperfield' into almost every sentence he speaks to the protagonist, as if acknowledging someone better – and with a better name – than himself.

In some of the rejected names among Dickens's notes are the fragments of ideas that did come to fruition. The 'Trot' in the first two trial names went into David's great-aunt Betsey Trotwood's name and thence became her name for him. She has announced before the protagonist's birth

that he will be a girl. 'I intend to be her godmother, and
I beg you'll call her Betsey Trotwood Copperfield. There
must be no mistakes in life with THIS Betsey Trotwood'
(Ch. I). It was conventional for a child to be named after
a godparent. With this name, the younger Betsey will
achieve the happiness that eluded her godmother, who
married very unwisely. When the baby turns out to be
a boy, Betsey Trotwood departs without another word.
Ten years later, when young David flees the blacking
factory and seeks refuge with the very same great-aunt
Betsey, she rechristens him, in honour of his non-existent
sister, 'Trotwood' – thence, 'Trot', for short. And while
'Flowerbury' and 'Topflower' perish, the thought behind
them survives in Steerforth's half-affectionate, half-
disparaging nickname for David: 'Daisy'.

On the next page but one of his notes, in his first
number plan, Dickens is sketching out the opening
chapters of the novel and working out the name for
David's stepfather-to-be. 'Mr Harden', 'Murdle', 'Murdstone', 'Murden'.[7] Hardness and deadliness come together,
for from the first Dickens knew that the name had to
epitomise the character. Once David's mother has
succumbed to Mr Murdstone, the narrative fills with that
harshly arrived-at name. In Chapter IV, where David
has returned home to find his mother remarried, the
Murdstone name sounds some eighty times. Murdstones
have taken over. If the novel were being read aloud to
you, you would really hear it. Are the implications of the
name too obvious? But the obviousness has a point. As if
knowing the track of associations down which Dickens
has already gone to fashion this name, Betsey Trotwood,
after the death of David's mother, comments thus on the
folly of her second marriage. 'And then, as if this was not

enough … she marries a second time—goes and marries
a Murderer—or a man with a name like it' (Ch. XIII).
And she is right; Murdstone's name, like everything else
about him, proclaims his nature. David's mother should
have known. Flattered by his sly attentions, she alone did
not see him and hear him for what he plainly was. Her
death has something to do with his bullying of her and
her pregnancy, so he *is* almost a murderer.[8]

In *David Copperfield*, the characters are peculiarly
conscious of the possible meanings of names and often
ready to transform each other's names.[9] David bumps into
Steerforth, now a university student, in London and is
taken by him on a tour of its sights. Impressed by how
much his friend appears to know about the exhibits in the
British Museum, David supposes that he will soon 'take
a high degree at college' (Ch. XX). Steerforth, too much
the trifling gentleman to submit to this, brushes the idea
away. 'Not I! my dear Daisy – will you mind my calling
you Daisy?' He confirms a name that he first dreamt up in
the previous chapter, the day before, in response to David's
innocently gushing praise of a play he has been to see at
Covent Garden. '"My dear young Davy," he said, clapping
me on the shoulder again, "you are a very Daisy. The daisy of
the field, at sunrise, is not fresher than you are"' (Ch. XIX).

His hero-worshipping companion naturally accepts the
name without demur. In this exchange about renaming,
we sense what is implicit. Steerforth wonders at David's
unworldly idealism, relishes it – and scorns it. Rosa Dartle
understands the buried sarcasm of the renaming.

While we were talking, he more than once called me
Daisy; which brought Miss Dartle out again.

'But really, Mr Copperfield,' she asked, 'is it a nickname? And why does he give it you? Is it—eh?—because he thinks you young and innocent? I am so stupid in these things.'

She is, we know, the opposite of stupid, discerning just the psychological pattern. 'He thinks you young and innocent; and so you are his friend. Well, that's quite delightful!' (Ch. XX). And yet the name is weirdly yearning too. On what will be their final parting, Steerforth grabs at the name he has given to his fool of a friend.

'Daisy,' he said, with a smile—'for though that's not the name your godfathers and godmothers gave you, it's the name I like best to call you by—and I wish, I wish, I wish, you could give it to me!'
'Why so I can, if I choose,' said I.

(Ch. XXIX)

David shows how little he understands how names are given – and what makes them stick.

The novel is full of name giving. When Mr Murdstone takes David to Yarmouth for the day to meet his louche friends Quinion and Passnidge (possessors themselves of unsettling names), he talks to them about 'Brooks of Sheffield' (Ch. II). As they joke about the 'pretty little widow' whom Mr Murdstone is evidently courting, he warns them, 'Somebody's sharp' – though David is not sharp enough to realise that 'Brooks' is himself. The name is used to mock him, the child being given sherry and encouraged to give the toast 'Confusion to Brooks of Sheffield!' amidst much adult laughter. As Quinion, who will employ him in a London warehouse, tells him after his mother's death,

'You are Brooks of Sheffield. That's your name' (Ch. X).
The name evidently came out of nowhere, but Dickens
subsequently received a gift of a case of cutlery from the real
firm of Brookes & Sons in Sheffield. He had inadvertently
conferred an honour, and perhaps a commercial benefit, on
the company. In his letter of thanks he wrote,

> The introduction of your name in the story, is one of
> those remarkable coincidences that defy all calculation
> … It came into my head as I wrote, just as any other
> name and address might have done if I had been
> diverting the attention of a real child.[10]

A month later he sent John Brookes a signed presentation
copy of the novel.[11] During the same visit to Yarmouth,
Murdstone and his friends descend into the cabin of a
yacht to look at some papers (they are up to some financial
skulduggery). David is left on deck in the care of a man
he calls 'Mr Skylark' because he has 'Skylark' written on
his shirt, 'but when I called him Mr Skylark, he said it
meant the vessel' (Ch. II). Several of the characters have
problems with names. Betsey Trotwood objects very much
to Peggotty's name.

> 'It's a most extraordinary world,' observed my aunt,
> rubbing her nose; 'how that woman ever got into it
> with that name, is unaccountable to me. It would be
> much more easy to be born a Jackson, or something of
> that sort, one would think.'
>
> (Ch. XXXV)

Mr Peggotty, as Ham laughingly points out, gets Steerforth's
name wrong, calling him 'Rudderford' (Ch. X). It is an

ominous mistake. (Dickens himself had only one guess in his number plan – 'Steerford' – before he alighted on the very name. The same with his valet: 'Lirrimer? Littimer'.) Steerforth himself makes no such mistakes. He takes possession of people by naming them, as when he first meets Mr Peggotty.

'I do my endeavours in my line of life, sir.'
   'The best of men can do no more, Mr Peggotty,' said Steerforth. He had got his name already.

(Ch. VII)

He always knows what he is up to.

David Copperfield is not the only Dickens novel that began with its author chasing after a name for its protagonist. He left a similar trace some six years earlier in his initial notes for the novel that was to become *Martin Chuzzlewit.* The surviving working notes comprise sketchy memos for just two numbers of the novel, some trial title pages and four sheets containing lists of possible names. On the first of these, Dickens has written 'Martin chubblewig' before alighting immediately on 'The Pecksniffs' – but then hazarding 'chuzzletoe' and 'chuzzlebog'. On another leaf he writes out the possibilities in a column: 'Martin chuzzlewig', 'Martin Sweezleden', 'Martin chuzzletoe', Martin Sweezlebach', 'Martin Sweezlewag'. And (triumphantly?), on its own on the reverse of the first sheet, 'Martin chuzzlewit'.[12] You can hear the kind of thing he is looking for from the beginning. The name must fit not only his youthful hero, but also the hero's rich, sour, misanthropic grandfather. It must sound serio-comic and something of a burden: Martin regrets his attachment to his money-obsessed family and thus regrets his name. When he first meets Tom Pinch, he tells him that he wishes Martin were his surname, 'for my own is not a very pretty one, and it takes a long time to sign. Chuzzlewit is my name' (Ch. V).

Dickens was name-chasing again on the very first page of his preparatory notes for his last novel, *The Mystery of Edwin Drood*. This begins with a list of slightly archaic English male forenames: Gilbert, Alfred, Edwin, Jasper, Edwyn, Michael, Oswald, Arthur, Selwyn, Edgar.[13] It goes on to 'Mr Honeythunder' and 'Mr Honeyblast' (the former eventually chosen for the novel's loud, bullying philanthropist). The rest of the page is given over to seventeen alternative titles, in which he varies both the first part ('The loss of …', 'The flight of …', 'The Disappearance of …') and the main name ('James Wakefield', 'Edwyn Brood', 'Edwin Brude', 'Edwyn Drood'). The penultimate title is the one that was eventually used. It is clear he wanted a Christian name that seemed peculiarly traditional, even ancient sounding (which must be why he toyed with the 'Edwyn' spelling). The rightness of the surname is harder to pin down. Perhaps it contains 'rood', an Old English word both for a crucifix and for a measurement of land. Perhaps 'Drood' echoes *dread*, which is certainly true to the apprehensiveness that the narrative encourages in the reader.

Name coining was at the heart of Dickens's inventiveness, yet it was invention fed by what he heard and found. *Fagin* had been the surname of a boy called Bob, who had worked with Dickens in Warren's blacking factory. 'Plorn', Dickens's nickname for his youngest son, Edward, gave rise to the name *Plornish* in *Little Dorrit*. The writer Arthur Locker, a contributor to *All the Year Round*, reported Dickens's comments about his characters' names.

Dickens told Miss Knight that he never invented a name for his characters – they were real. Whenever he saw a queer name he jotted it down, and he used to keep a series of small bags, filled with scraps of paper containing various memoranda of this sort, upon his writing table ... He used to ask Mrs Knight to tell him of queer names.[14]

This seems to be Dickens claiming that even the oddest names in his fiction were taken from life. In January 1855, as he was about to set out on the writing of *Little Dorrit*, he began to keep a notebook that he titled 'Memoranda'. Along with ideas for stories, he jotted down lists of possible titles and names for characters. Some of these names, he noted, were drawn 'from Privy-Council Education Lists'.[15] Amongst the unusual Christian names that he copied from there (Aramanda, Homer, Zerubbabel) is Bradley, which would be taken for the erotically obsessed Bradley Headstone in *Our Mutual Friend*. Also listed, between 'Balzina' and 'Gentilla', is the forename 'Pleasant'. The delight of this discovery is preserved in the naming of Pleasant Riderhood, the notably sour daughter of the villainous Rogue Riderhood, in *Our Mutual Friend*. 'Why christened Pleasant, the late Mrs Riderhood might possibly have been at some time able to explain, and possibly not. Her daughter had no information on that point' (I Ch. XII).

Pleasant is a misanthropic pawnbroker, battered by her violent father, who finds the world pretty unpleasant. Her name is a sardonic joke that she just has to accept. 'Pleasant she found herself, and she couldn't help it.' A character is helpless in the face of his or her name. When Mr Venus, who has a *tendresse* for Pleasant, tells Wegg that she has rejected him, Wegg cannot resist turning on her name.

Pleasant Riderhood. There's something moving in the name. Pleasant. Dear me! Seems to express what she might have been, if she hadn't made that unpleasant remark—and what she ain't, in consequence of having made it.

(III Ch. VII)

Other pages of the 'Memoranda' book have lists of names not apparently taken from the Education Lists. Dickens would draw on the names in the notebook for each of his last five novels, composed over the next fifteen years. He ticked them off as he used them. One page, for instance, has a list that includes Casby, Chivery, Dorrit, Maroon, Merdle, Nandy, Plornish (all in *Little Dorrit*), Carton (*A Tale of Two Cities*), Magwitch (*Great Expectations*), Rokesmith and Snigsworth (*Our Mutual Friend*). He kept going back to it. Dickens was not the only novelist to do this. Henry James is the other most notable novelist to have made lists of possible names to be used for characters in his fiction. They are to be found in surviving notebooks, which are also rich in ideas for stories and fictional situations. In James's earliest notebook, one of his first lists, made in 1880 as he was planning *The Portrait of a Lady*, goes like this:

Names. Osmond—Rosier—Mr and Mrs Match—Name for husband in *P. of L.*: Gilbert Osmond—Raymond Gyves—Mrs Gift—Name in *Times*: Lucky Da Costa—Name in Knightsbridge: Tagus Shout—Other names: Couch—Bonnycastle—Theory—Cridge—Arrant—Mrs Tippet—Noad.[16]

Here we have not only the malevolent man whom Isabel Archer foolishly marries, Gilbert Osmond, but the young man who falls in love with Osmond's daughter, Pansy (Edward Rosier). James notes that one name has come from *The Times*, which he would often use as a source for names, and another from a sign, probably on a shop, in a London street. James, wanting to avoid the appearance of contrivance, liked names that, however odd, did exist. In his preparatory notes for his novel *The Ivory Tower*, unfinished at his death, he pondered using the name Moyra Grabham for a fortune-seeking young woman, this 'excellent thing' having cropped up 'in the *Times* of two or three days ago'.[17] Its 'only fault' was 'a little too much meaning, but the sense here wouldn't be thrown into undue relief'. The name, after all, had really existed. 'Everything of the shade of the real,' James added, as if reminding himself of the main principle of naming in fiction. He did not use 'Moyra Grabham'.

It is difficult to believe that there were ever people with names like Theory or Arrant (though apparently there was a man called Shout), but then James left the odder names he collected behind in the pages of his notebooks. Dickens too resisted some peculiarities. On the page of names copied from the Privy Council Education Lists, he wrote down other names under the headings 'More boys' and 'More girls'. It is not clear whether these are also selected from the Lists, but if so, some of them are remarkable. Henry Ghost, Walter Ashes, William Why, Robert Gospel, Rosetta Dust, Miriam Denial, Sophia Doomsday, Ambrosina Events. He used none of these. Yet, amongst his minor characters, he could not resist giving us one or two whose names are as improbably suitable or unsuitable as they might be in life. In *Our Mutual Friend*, Mortimer Lightwood has a 'dismal' office boy, 'whose appropriate name was Blight' (I VIII). When

David Copperfield and Dora first marry, they have a grim
and incompetent servant. 'Her name was Paragon. Her
nature was represented to us, when we engaged her, as
being feebly expressed in her name' (Ch. XLIV). Her
references, in other words, are mendaciously laudatory.
Her name is a satire on David and Dora's naivety.

Dickens generally avoided so-called *cratylic* names,
which clearly label a character's leading qualities.[18] His
hero Henry Fielding had called a benevolent squire
Allworthy; a tutor who relished corporal punishment
was Thwackum; a savage magistrate was Justice Thrasher.
There are just a few of these in Dickens. The magistrate
in *Oliver Twist* is called Fang: no one seems to have
noticed the proclamation in the name, just as no one
seems to have noticed that he has none of the qualities
that would suit him for his responsibilities. The same
must go for the schoolmaster in *Hard Times*, assistant
to Mr Gradgrind, who is called M'Choakumchild.
His pedagogical practice is so obviously destructive
that Dickens could not resist it. There is a comedy in
characters' imperviousness to the connotations of a
name. In *Martin Chuzzlewit*, Montague Tigg presents
Pecksniff with a letter 'addressed to Chevy Slyme,
Esquire'. 'You know Chevy Slyme, Esquire, I believe?'
(Ch. IV). The vicarious self-importance of the question
is all the better for the name that shouts the repellent
nature of its bearer, though with a 'y' instead of an 'i', to
transform any dirty qualities. In *Little Dorrit*, the man
who is high in the Circumlocution Office is Mr Tite
Barnacle, his name as much an unacknowledged affront
to good sense as the title of the department for which he
works (I Ch. IX). Given these names and titles, someone
should object – but no one does.

Dickens allowed himself, as Henry James never would have done, to call the haughty, enervated aristocrat in *Bleak House* Sir Leicester Dedlock, and the wealthy social climbers in *Our Mutual Friend* the Veneerings. These two joke names belong together. The Dedlock family name is so old and grand that no one could possibly notice that it announces the atrophy of those who bear it. The Veneerings, in contrast, are dedicated to everything that is new and that shimmers with recently acquired wealth. It would be wrong if their name did not so shimmer too. In the same novel, the schoolmaster Bradley Headstone is doomed by his name as he is doomed by his nature: he is driven by his unrequited and increasingly maddening passion for Lizzie Hexam to murder and self-destruction. He increases his deathly disadvantage by declaring his passion to her in a London churchyard. Rogue Riderhood, who now knows that Bradley Headstone tried to frame him for the attempted murder of Eugene Wrayburn, is out to blackmail him and tracks him to his classroom. He makes him write his name on the blackboard in front of his class. When the pupils read it out in a 'shrill chorus', Riderhood enjoys the oddity of it. ' "No?" cried Riderhood. "You don't mean it? Headstone! Why, that's in a churchyard. Hooroar for another turn!" ' (IV Ch. XV). Riderhood can hear the fatality in Headstone's name.

These cratylic names, though, are relatively rare in Dickens. Usually his audacity with his names was more poetic and so explaining why one of his names is so resonant is often difficult. Michael Slater thinks that *Scrooge* is a combination of *screw* and *gouge*.[19] (Though it might also have something of the slang word *scrouge*, meaning *to crowd a person* or *to push or squeeze a thing*; it is used in *The Old Curiosity Shop*.) *Gradgrind* ends with a verb that expresses the effect of the character's pedagogic method, as he grinds his pupils hard enough, and the harsh internal alliteration grinds the syllables against each other. Some of his names consort with unsettling English words without quite reproducing them. Wackford Squeers may recall Fielding's Thwackum, but is something more 'queer' too: 'Mr Wackford Squeers is my name, and I'm very far from being ashamed of it' (Ch. V). Yet why should *Pecksniff* – two animal reflexes glued together – so perfectly catch this pious hypocrite? Once we have met Mr Pecksniff, bowled over by the wind, in the second chapter of *Martin Chuzzlewit*, the narrator uses the Pecksniff name over and over again for the rest of that chapter. Ninety-five times in the chapter do we hear that odd word *Pecksniff*. Equally, the absurdly complacent and pompous Podsnap in *Our Mutual Friend* has a name made even more ridiculous by his own fondness for it. 'Mr Podsnap was well to do, and stood very high in Mr Podsnap's opinion' (I Ch. XI).

Dickens loved the ways in which a name could undo the pretensions of a character. Uncle Pumblechook in *Great Expectations* is a well-to-do corn chandler in a provincial town, who gives himself great airs. Small-minded and dishonest, he is seen for what he is by the young Pip and by the narrative that names him – but not by the rest of the characters. Joe Gargery (his nephew) and Mrs Joe are both, in their different ways, in awe of him. Given his name, how could they be? 'That abject hypocrite ... that basest of swindlers ... that diabolical cornchandler,' Pip calls him in his thoughts (Ch. XIII). The reader notices the comic oddness of his name even as the characters who pander to him fail to do so. Dickens relies on the name's affront to our sense of what is likely. 'A name such as "Pumblechook" makes the reader think it could never occur in real life, even if in fact it did.'[20] His is not the only Dickensian name to invite ridicule on its bearer. Here is Cherry Pecksniff's despairing suitor in *Martin Chuzzlewit*.

> He often informed Mrs Todgers that the sun had set upon him; that the billows had rolled over him; that the car of Juggernaut had crushed him, and also that the deadly Upas tree of Java had blighted him. His name was Moddle.
>
> (Ch. XXXII)

You can sound as grandiose as you like, but your name will announce who you really are.

Dickens's most memorable names are not all comic. The dwarfish villain of *The Old Curiosity Shop*, his ill-will burning with incandescent energy, has a name as short and sharp as his malicious wit. 'Quilp is my name. You might remember. It's not a long one—Daniel Quilp' (Ch. III). No one uses the 'Daniel'. 'Quilp' he is: a singular monster. Rosa Dartle in *David Copperfield*, in contrast, has a name that might almost be ordinary (Henry James could have used it). Yet there is sharpness inside it and the faint intimation of violence (helped by the rhyme between the first syllable of 'Dartle' and the 'scar' that is her distinguishing feature). The bullying, cynical, all-seeing lawyer Jaggers in *Great Expectation* has a name that is not entirely unlikely, but hints that you might cut yourself on him. (He is one of those characters who never seems to have a first name.) In contrast, his fellow lawyer Tulkinghorn, in *Bleak House*, is no less sharp, in his intellect or his perceptiveness, but, being 'an oyster of the old school whom nobody can open', wraps up his true nature in this antique-sounding name (Ch. X). At the end of his career, in *The Mystery of Edwin Drood*, Dickens was fashioning another distinctively suggestive family of names. We have Jasper and Crisparkle – glinting darkly and lightly next to each other – and then the fools, Tope and Sapsea and Durdles. And the benevolent lawyer Grewgious (which sounds like a previously undiscovered adjective) with his loyal but disrespectful clerk Bazzard, who has literary pretensions to go with his rather special name.

Dickens's two historical novels, *Barnaby Rudge* and *A Tale of Two Cities*, have the highest proportion of what we might call probable names, as if the novelist felt he had to rein in his onomantic playfulness when dealing with the stuff of history. It is when comic relief is to be supplied that we encounter truly Dickensian names: Simon Tappertit and Miggs in *Barnaby Rudge*; Miss Pross and Jerry Cruncher in *A Tale of Two Cities*. Each of the rest of Dickens's novels has its own family of names, drawn together to populate a distinct world. It begins with *Pickwick Papers*. A list of the names of minor characters in Dickens's first novel is a poetic catalogue. Here are some in the order of their first appearance: Trundle, Dumkins, Slumkey, Nupkins, Muzzle, Grummer, Dubbley, Gunter, Humm, Mudge, Snubbin, Phunky, Buzfuz, Mrs Cluppins, Mrs Mudberry, Mrs Bunkin, Mrs Wugsby, Slurk, Pruffle. Is the letter 'u' particularly amusing or ridiculous? Well, here it is. There are other other names too. Some that sound like odd new verbs – Raddle, Smangle – or people known for doing odd things – Dr Slammer, Mr Perker, Wilkins Flasher. Some are just reliably absurd: Jingle, Fizkin, Pott, Jinks, Noddy,

Stiggins. Everyone here is a potential eccentric. Especially if a character appears only briefly, he or she will have a name to notice. 'Pickwick' was itself taken from the name of a coach operator in Bath, a fact made into a joke in the thirteenth monthly number of the novel, when Sam Weller complains that the coach that he and his master are boarding has the name 'in gilt letters of a goodly size' on its side (Ch. XXXIV). Dickens surely fancied it because it reminds us of those English words that come from facetiously coupled rhymes (titbit, oddbod, nitwit). Lovably ridiculous is just what our protagonist is.

Here, at the beginning of his career as a novelist, you can sense Dickens's sheer delight in absurd names, each one delicious because its bearer does not find it absurd at all. By his second novel, *Oliver Twist*, naming has taken on greater weight. Mrs Mann the baby farmer in *Oliver Twist* grasps that naming is a creative activity when Mr Bumble the beadle tells her that he 'inwented' Oliver Twist's name.

> 'We name our fondlins in alphabetical order. The last was a S,—Swubble, I named him. This was a T,—Twist, I named *him*. The next one comes will be Unwin, and the next Vilkins. I have got names ready made to the end of the alphabet, and all the way through it again, when we come to Z.'

Mrs Mann is impressed by his linguistic fertility, which is a match for all the pauper children that the parish produces.

> 'Why, you're quite a literary character, sir!' said Mrs Mann.

'Well, well,' said the beadle, evidently gratified with
the compliment; 'perhaps I may be. Perhaps I may be,
Mrs Mann.'

Characters take it into their heads to rename others. Mr
Dombey tells Polly Toodle, recruited to nurse his son
Paul, 'While you are here, I must stipulate that you are
always known as—say as Richards—an ordinary name,
and convenient. Have you any objection to be known
as Richards? You had better consult your husband' (Ch.
II). The renaming is so wonderfully unnecessary – such a
foolish assertion of power. (Polly replies that if she is to
be 'called out of her name' she might merit an increase in
her wages.)

Name is prestige: no one is prouder of his name than Mr
Dombey. At the other end of things, those without secure
social identity hardly even have names. In *Our Mutual
Friend*, Betty Higden looks after two infant orphans
called Toddles and Poddles, and tells the Secretary that
Sloppy, her helper, was a foundling and 'took his name
from being found on a sloppy night' (I Ch. XVI). In
Little Dorrit, Mr and Mrs Meagles exercise their power –
benevolently, they would think – by renaming the
foundling Harriet Beadle whom they take on as a maid
for their daughter. Harriet Beadle is 'an arbitrary name,
of course', so they call her Hatty, then Tatty, and Coram
after the founder of the Foundling Hospital, 'until we got
into a way of mixing the two names together, and now
she is always Tattycoram' (I Ch. II). When Tattycoram
runs away, Mr Meagles is forced to tell Arthur that she
resented 'the wretched name we gave her': 'who were we
that we should have the right to name her like a dog or
cat?' She rejects the patronage of the Meagles family: 'she

would fling us her name back again, and she would go.'
Miss Wade, whom she rebelliously joins, calls her Harriet,
mockingly telling her, when Arthur and Mr Meagles find
them, 'You can have your droll name again, playfully
pointing you out and setting you apart, as it is right that
you should be pointed out and set apart' (I Ch. XXVII).
As Mr Meagles concedes near the novel's end, visiting
Miss Wade for a final time, 'Perhaps, if I had thought
twice about it, I might never have given her the jingling
name.' (Even if she finally returns, imploring 'take me
back again, and give me back the dear old name!') (II
Ch. XXXIII).

Dickens's early novels revel in their freedom to name
their characters as ludicrously or as wittily as they wish.
In *Nicholas Nickleby*, the author's delight in peculiar
names for minor characters is shared by the garrulous
Mrs Nickleby. She offers us her own wonderful list of
the names of her past suitors. She begins by recalling
'young Lukin' and then embarks on her recollection of
others, 'beginning with her left thumb and checking
off the names on her fingers—"Mogley—Tipslark—
Cabbery—Smifser—"' (Ch. XLI). She is interrupted,
but evidently could have gone on listing any number of
implausible names. Perhaps no one called Smith or Jones
would ever have had the presumption to court her. The
names are specimens from the utterly odd world that
Mrs Nickleby mentally inhabits. She recalls attending
extravagant parties in her early married life. 'I don't think
that there ever were such people as those Peltiroguses. You
remember the Peltiroguses, Kate?' (Ch. XLV). Can there
ever have been such people? Only the specificity of Mrs
Nickleby's recollections makes the names seem possible.
She remembers Jane Dibabs who lived in a house with

a porch 'where the earwigs used to fall into one's tea on a summer evening ...' (Ch. LV). Who can gainsay such details?

In this novel Dickens himself sometimes seems drunk on the delight of coining names. A few are rather too clearly representative, like the sexually predatory Sir Mulberry Hawk and his aristocratic stooge Lord Frederick Verisopht. (Dickens tries to rescue Verisopht from life as a cipher by giving him a surprisingly poignant death.) Or the Cheeryble brothers, properly melancholy for a moment when they remember the anniversary of their mother's death, but otherwise cheery indeed, and apparently able to pursue a highly profitable business without that cheeriness ever having to falter. Elsewhere in the novel, Nicholas meets a theatrical connoisseur called Mrs Curdle and her husband, the theatre critic Mr Curdle, who believes that 'the drama is gone, perfectly gone' (Ch. XXIV). Or there is Newman Noggs's acquaintance Mr Crowl, 'whose harsh countenance was the very epitome of selfishness', and who can soon be heard to utter 'a low querulous growl'. He is fixed in his attitude, his name a contrast to the neighbours with whom Noggs is taking supper: the Kenwigses. The comic name is soon borne out by our introduction to this couple and their 'olive branches'. We discover that one of their daughters is called Morleena,

> regarding whose uncommon Christian name it may be here remarked that it had been invented and composed by Mrs Kenwigs previous to her first lying-in, for the special distinction of her eldest child, in case it should prove a daughter.
>
> (Ch. XIV)

Their rich uncle who (rapaciously, we infer) collects water rates is called Mr Lillyvick, an absurdity made all the more comically unacknowledgeable by the fact that his name is given to the Kenwigs's baby (and only male child) who therefore 'rejoiced in the names of Lillyvick Kenwigs' (Ch. XV). This naming, which Mr Kenwigs pronounces 'one of the greatest blessings and honours of my existence', is done for the sake of extracting an inheritance from the hard-faced Mr Lillyvick.

Sometimes characters play off each other's names. In *Nicholas Nickleby*, Pyke and Pluck are the stooges of Sir Mulberry Hawk and make for a sinister twosome, chiming all the time, here as they bamboozle Mrs Nickleby.

> 'The loss has been ours, Mrs Nickleby. Has the loss been ours, Pyke?'
> 'It has, Pluck,' answered the other gentleman.
> 'We have regretted it very often, I believe, Pyke?' said the first gentleman.
> 'Very often, Pluck,' answered the second.
> (Ch. XXVII)

They play matching parts, their almost-rhyming names bandied between them with the speed and confidence of a practised double-act, in cahoots and delighting in it. Their names go together, and they bounce them back and forth when performing their deceptions.

> 'Pyke,' said the watchful Mr Pluck, observing the effect which the praise of Miss Nickleby had produced.
> 'Well, Pluck,' said Pyke.
> (Ch. XXVIII)

They are talking to be heard, talking for deceitful effect; those names are their way of nodding aurally to each other as they go about their business.

Others with comic names do not recognise them as such. Nicholas witnesses an MP's constituent heading a deputation to complain to him and approaching 'in a violent heat', to be met by the politician's attempt to disarm him. ' "Do my eyes deceive me," said Mr Gregsbury, looking towards the speaker, "or is that my old friend Pugstyles?" ' (Ch. XVI). Mr Wititterly, Kate Nickleby's employer, is forever talking of Mrs Wititterly's refined sensitivities ('Mrs Wititterly is of a very excitable nature; very delicate, very fragile; a hothouse plant, an exotic') without a thought to the titter hidden inside the name (Ch. XXI). Mr Vincent Crummles insists on plastering his name and the names of his wife and children all over Portsmouth (Ch. XXIII). The rest of his troupe have suitably eccentric names – Henrietta Petowker, Mr Folair, Miss Snevellicci – with poor Mrs Grudden, who stands in for any other actor in an emergency, being renamed by Mr Crummles if she ever appears on the playbill. This fertile world of comic names threatens to swallow Nicholas's romantic hopes when he is told by Newman Noggs that young woman whom he has loved at first sight is called Bobster.

> 'Bobster!' repeated Nicholas, indignantly.
>
> 'That's the name,' said Newman. 'I remember it by lobster.'
>
> 'Bobster!' repeated Nicholas, more emphatically than before. 'That must be the servant's name.'
>
> 'No, it an't,' said Newman, shaking his head with great positiveness. 'Miss Cecilia Bobster.'

'Cecilia, eh?' returned Nicholas, muttering the two names together over and over again in every variety of tone, to try the effect. 'Well, Cecilia is a pretty name.'

(Ch. XL)

Nicholas is right to object: the beautiful and melancholy young lady he has spotted could not possibly have a name that rhymed with 'lobster' – though it is wonderful that he has to try to reconcile himself to it and console himself with the prefatory 'Cecilia'.

Dickens has started making his characters conscious of how names might declare character. A name thrusts onto a person a narrative fate that he or she cannot escape. In his next novel, *The Old Curiosity Shop*, Quilp's agent Sampson Brass, a shameless and hard-hearted lawyer, has a name whose appropriateness Dickens highlights, referring to him as Quilp's 'brazen friend' (Ch. XXXIII). More than one character is aware of the resonance of Brass's name. The mysterious 'single gentleman' who lodges with the Brasses (and turns out to be Nell's great-uncle) comments that 'it's a good name for a lawyer' (Ch. XXXIV). Quilp pretends to address Sally Brass amorously and to lament her name when she fobs him off. ' "Hard-hearted as the metal from which she takes her name," said Quilp. "Why don't she change it—melt down the brass, and take another name?" ' (Ch. XXXIII). He delights in the notion that her name might have limited her sympathies. Later we find Dick Swiveller, who has become Brass's clerk, 'passing through the street in the execution of some Brazen errand' (Ch. XXXVIII). When angry, Quilp calls him a 'brazen scarecrow' (Ch. LXII). Brass's name is brazen, just as the man is so openly without principle.

In Dickens's world, there is no dignity in a name, a lesson that Mr Dombey fails to learn in the opening chapter of *Dombey and Son*, where the society doctor keeps getting his wife's name wrong. When the insinuating Major Bagstock engineers a meeting in Brighton and has the honour of addressing him as Mr Dombey, he replies with lofty modesty, 'I am the present unworthy representative of that name, Major' (Ch. X). Mr Dombey's inflexible dignity is in his name, now made into absurdity again when Mrs Skewton has her stroke and keeps conflating his name with that of his wife's first husband. He is not the only one to be snobbish about names. When the six-year-old Paul Dombey finds himself sent to Doctor Blimber's academy in Brighton, he misses the 'weazen, old, crab-faced man' who used to pull him in his carriage to the beach. He is explaining why he knows no Latin grammar.

> 'I have been a weak child. I couldn't learn a Latin Grammar when I was out, every day, with old Glubb. I wish you'd tell old Glubb to come and see me, if you please.'

The Blimbers know nothing of this man, but the name is enough.

> 'What a dreadfully low name,' said Mrs Blimber. 'Unclassical to a degree! Who is the monster, child?'

Later Paul tells Miss Blimber that he would feel better if he could talk to Glubb.

> 'Nonsense, Dombey,' said Miss Blimber. 'I couldn't hear of it. This is not the place for Glubbs of any kind.'
>   (Ch. XII)

Foolish names are an affront to Miss Blimber, who seems not to realise how foolish her own name might sound.

Dickens, of course, is not above making foolish-sounding names into transparent code for the folly of their bearers. In *Bleak House*, the list of visitors to Chesney Wold begins with the former political potentate Lord Boodle (Ch. XII). The name is possible: there was (and is) a London club named Boodle's, after its former Head Waiter. But then Dickens's Boodle tells his host, Sir Leicester Dedlock, that the power to form a new government presently lies 'between Lord Coodle and Sir Thomas Doodle—supposing it to be impossible for the Duke of Foodle to act with Goodle'. Now these names are alphabetically generating each other, rhyming predictably because these absurd individuals are in fact indistinguishable. We run through more politicians from Hoodle to Moodle, before reaching the end of the list with the delicious rhetorical question, 'but what are you to do with Noodle?' '*Noodle: colloquial.* A stupid or silly person; a fool, an idiot' (*OED*). This was always where the list was heading. Across the table, meanwhile, is Right Honourable William Buffy, MP, who talks of his fellow politicians Cuffy and Duffy and Fuffy and so on, all different and all the same, a list ending with his lament at the influence of Puffy.

Boodle and Buffy are the alternatives, equal generators of absurdities. Sir Leicester and his fellow guests cannot hear the idiocy of all this, but some characters have a better ear for stupid names. When Mr Boffin in *Our Mutual Friend* visits the office of the dilettante solicitor Mortimer Lightwood, Blight the office boy pretends to review his employer's appointments for the day, running through a page of the Appointment Book murmuring, 'Mr Aggs, Mr Baggs, Mr Caggs, Mr Daggs, Mr Faggs, Mr Gaggs,

Mr Boffin. Yes, sir; quite right. You are a little before your time, sir.' He relishes Mr Boffin's gullibility. He tells him that he will enter him in the firm's Callers' Book for the day, running over previous entries as he writes, 'Mr Alley, Mr Balley, Mr Calley, Mr Dalley, Mr Falley, Mr Galley, Mr Halley, Mr Lalley, Mr Malley. And Mr Boffin' (I Ch. VIII). Mortimer Lightwood, of course, has no appointments and no callers. Boffin's name stands out amongst these flagrant inventions. Perhaps Blight hears that Mr Boffin has just such a ridiculous name. (The word *boffin* did not exist before the 1940s.) When Bella Wilfer goes to live with the Boffins, her mother and sister angrily scorn their surname. Mrs Wilfer emphasises the first, plosive consonant, 'as if she could have borne Doffin, Moffin, or Poffin much better'. Miss Lavinia begins by calling them 'your Whatshisnames', but later exclaims 'I hate the Boffins! … I WILL call 'em the Boffins. The Boffins, the Boffins, the Boffins' (II Ch. VIII). And so on, using the name 'Boffins' thirteen times in five sentences. The ridiculous name becomes ridiculously tormenting to the Wilfers.

Their agony is that Mr and Mrs Boffin, undeserving by virtue of their name, have been left a fortune by Harmon the dust-heap magnate. Money brings visits from mercenary social climbers with even more foolish names. There are all those Tapkins daughters whose names (including 'Miss Malvina Tapkins') embellish the card left *chez* Boffin by Mr and Mrs Tapkins. One daughter has, by marriage, earned her own card: 'Mrs Henry George Alfred Swoshle, née Tapkins'. In a Dickens novel, you escape a ridiculous name only for one that is even more ridiculous. In *Hard Times*, the marital genealogy of Mrs Sparsit is made sufficiently laughable by the revelation that her great aunt is called Lady Scadgers, while her (dead) husband had been, 'by the mother's side ... a Powler' (she is proud to say).

> Strangers of limited information and dull apprehension were sometimes observed not to know what a Powler was, and even to appear uncertain whether it might be a business, or a political party, or a profession of faith.
>
> (I Ch. VII)

Such silly names, their silliness not heard by those who announce them, allow Dickens a special kind of dramatic irony. In *David Copperfield*, Dora's two spinster aunts like to imagine that the younger one, Lavinia,

> was an authority in affairs of the heart, by reason of there having anciently existed a certain Mr Pidger, who played short whist, and was supposed to have been enamoured of her.
>
> (Ch. XLI)

The name of Pidger is enough on its own to undermine the fantasy.

Esther Summerson, narrator of half of *Bleak House*, is too good to laugh at people's names, but when she tells us that Richard Carstone is to study medicine with 'a Mr Bayham Badger' we know that – however melancholy Richard's predestined lack of application – this character will provide us with comic diversion. Dickens makes sure of this by having Esther repeat his name and that of his wife ('Mrs Bayham Badger') as often as possible – not hard, as Mr Badger always refers to his wife as 'Mrs Bayham Badger'. She is magnetically drawn to men with silly names. She has had two previous husbands, frequently mentioned with admiration by her third spouse.

> 'Captain Swosser of the Royal Navy, who was Mrs Badger's first husband, was a very distinguished officer indeed. The name of Professor Dingo, my immediate predecessor, is one of European reputation.'
>
> (Ch. XIII)

'Dingo' apparently echoes around the academies of Europe. The Badgers are cheerfully unconscious of their ludicrous names. A sadder comedy comes of knowing that you have a silly name. Poor Flora Finching in *Little Dorrit* senses that her flutteringly alliterative name mocks her. When asked by Arthur Clennam if Finching is her married name, she replies, more in a statement than a question, 'Finching oh yes isn't it a dreadful name'. The deceased 'Mr F.' (as she calls him) has left her with the name, but 'he wasn't answerable for it and couldn't help it could he' (I Ch. XIII).

Names are what family and fate foist on us. In *Hard Times*, we discover that Gradgrind has named his two younger sons Adam Smith and Malthus, in honour of political economists whom he admires. It is another way of subjugating his children to the economic utilitarianism that is his creed. Yet we should remember Dickens's own habit of naming his sons after favourite authors. All but one of them (but none of his daughters) was given the name of a writer whom he admired: Walter Landor Dickens, Francis Jeffrey Dickens, Alfred D'Orsay Tennyson Dickens, Sydney Smith Haldimand Dickens, Henry Fielding Dickens and Edward Bulwer Lytton Dickens. Dickens behaved rather like Walter Shandy in

Tristram Shandy, believing that a dignifying name might raise the destiny of the person to whom it was given. 'How many Cæsars and Pompeys, he would say, by mere inspiration of the names, have been rendered worthy of them?'[21] Dickens was not the first to do this. As he must have known, Samuel Taylor Coleridge treated name-choice, that special power of a parent, similarly when he named two of his children Hartley Coleridge and Berkeley Coleridge, after the philosophers David Hartley and Bishop George Berkeley.

If the wish to dignify with a name is doomed, the refusal to acknowledge another's name is contemptible. In *Little Dorrit*, Mrs Gowan superciliously mistakes the name of the woman her sophisticated, worthless son is courting, Minnie Meagles. 'If it is a point of honour that I should originate the name – Miss Mickles – Miggles' (I Ch. XXVI). Despite Arthur Clennam's correction, she keeps calling her family 'the Miggles people'. Comparably, in *Hard Times*, Bounderby's servant and former companion, Mrs Sparsit, relishes not being able to get his wife's name right:

> often as she had had the honour of making Mr Bounderby's breakfast, before Mrs Gradgrind—she begged pardon, she meant to say Miss Bounderby—she hoped to be excused, but she really could not get it right yet, though she trusted to become familiar with it by and by—had assumed her present position.
>
> (II Ch. IX)

This kind of mistake might be evasive or it might be scornful. In *Our Mutual Friend* Mortimer Lightwood – possessor of no very special name himself – tells the story

of 'the man from somewhere' to an assembled gathering
at the Lammles and shows himself careless about the
name of Mr Boffin's secretary. He is 'an individual of the
hermit-crab or oyster species, and whose name, I think,
is Chokesmith—but it doesn't in the least matter—
say Artichoke' (II Ch. XVI). His *hauteur* allows him
to make fun of Rokesmith's ridiculous name. It is a
telling carelessness, as Rokesmith is in fact hiding from
Mortimer, who would be able to recognise him as the
Julius Handford who identified John Harmon's body.
But mistaken names can be unexpectedly, comically
dignifying. In *Bleak House*, the impoverished, opium-
addicted law scrivener who dies early in the novel is
apparently called Nemo. 'Nemo is Latin for no one,' as
Mr Tulkinghorn says (Ch. X). His is a non-name. Mr
Snagsby, the stationer who has employed Nemo, tells
Mr Tulkinghorn that his usually baleful wife was 'rather
took by something about this person' and called him not
Nemo but Nimrod. 'My little woman hasn't a good ear
for names' (Ch. XI). Thus, the muddled Mrs Snagsby
rescues Nemo from onomantic oblivion.

One Dickens protagonist hardly has a proper name. Pip
in *Great Expectations* tells us in the novel's first sentence
that he was christened Philip Pirrip, but 'my infant tongue
could make of both names nothing longer or more explicit
than Pip. So, I called myself Pip, and came to be called Pip.'
Dickens is surely echoing the opening of *Robinson Crusoe*,
a novel that obsessed him, where Daniel Defoe's narrator
tells us that his German father was called Kreutznaer 'but,
by the usual Corruption of Words in *England*, we are now
called, nay we call ourselves, and write our name *Crusoe*,
and so my Companions always call'd me.'[22] A hero who
sets out to make his fortune needs to have a malleable

identity. No wonder that Herbert Pocket asks if Pip would mind being called 'Handel', in honour of his origins. 'There's a charming piece of music by Handel, called the Harmonious Blacksmith.' Pip immediately declares that he would like it very much. The re-christening matters to the plot: when Pip encounters on the stage-coach the convict who gave him money when he was a child, Herbert calls out 'Good-bye, Handel!' 'I thought what a blessed fortune it was, that he had found another name for me than Pip' (Ch. XXII).

With barely the secure identity of a proper name, Pip is confronted by an antagonist with perhaps the strangest name in the whole Dickens canon. Orlick, who begins as Joe Gargery's journeyman, then becomes Miss Havisham's gatekeeper, assaults Mrs Joe and only just fails to murder Pip. The strange name seems to have come to Dickens in a moment of inspiration at the last minute: in manuscript, a different name is heavily erased and 'Orlick' written above it.[23] The name has a special significance because Orlick is one of those characters who keeps naming himself. 'Old Orlick, *he*'s a going up town,' he says, when we first meet him (Ch. XV). 'You was always in Old Orlick's way since ever you was a child,' he tells Pip when he is about to kill him. 'Old Orlick knowed you was burnt, Old Orlick knowed you was smuggling your uncle Provis away, Old Orlick's a match for you' (Ch. LIII). There are other Dickens characters who do this, naming themselves when they speak: Major Bagstock in *Dombey and Son*, Josiah Bounderby in *Hard Times*, Durdles in *The Mystery of Edwin Drood*. The first two are self-dramatising frauds, the third is self-important and hazily alcoholic. Orlick talks of 'Old Orlick' when he is describing how, as he thinks, he has been balked or wronged by Pip. To match his threatening surname, he has acquired a slouching forename that is a kind of offence to the narrator.

> He pretended that his Christian name was Dolge,—a clear impossibility,—but he was a fellow of that obstinate disposition that I believe him to have been the prey of no delusion in this particular, but wilfully to have imposed that name upon the village as an affront to its understanding.
>
> (Ch. XV)

Dolge Orlick has decided his strange and unharmonious name for himself. The power of the name is that it is impossible. No one can ever have borne it except this monstrous, resentful, violent person. Only Dickens would have dared make the name's unbelievability its power.

8

Using coincidences

I have been away from here, or I should have thanked
you sooner for that capital coincidence, and still
more capital application.

Letter to Shirley Brooks, 17 June 1864[1]

Coincidences can be most satisfying when they are most
extraordinary. When David Copperfield meets and
instantly falls in love with Dora Spenlow ('I was gone,
headlong'), it is her 'confidential friend' who speaks
before she does. This 'friend' – a paid companion to the
motherless young Dora – observes that she has 'seen
Mr Copperfield before' (Ch. XXVI). Yes, she has. The
speaker is none other than Miss Murdstone, grim sister
of David's grim stepfather. Seven years after he last saw
her, there she is again, in the Norwood breakfast room of
Mr Spenlow, Dora's father and the lawyer to whom David
is articled. 'Miss Murdstone, her duenna', Dickens wrote
in his number plan.[2] He was determined to have her

there. Should David not be amazed at this extraordinary coincidence?

> I don't think I was much astonished. To the best of my judgement, no capacity of astonishment was left in me. There was nothing worth mentioning in the material world, but Dora Spenlow, to be astonished about.

He remembers not being much surprised and suggests that he was too much stunned by the first appearance of Dora to experience any other kind of astonishment. He is also accepting his narrative destiny: Miss Murdstone was simply bound to turn up again. When his Aunt Betsey sent her and her brother packing from her Deal home, informing them that she would thenceforth look after David herself, he should have known that he was not rid of her.

'Of course!' we might exclaim. As a barrier against all romantic approaches, who could be better than the steely Miss Murdstone? She subsequently manages to turn Dora's father against his young clerk, and only Mr Spenlow's sudden death frustrates her repressive schemes. Her reappearance in this new guise of paid 'friend' to the daughter of an affluent widower also has a narrative logic: from the sudden sale of David's former home and all its furniture, we infer that Mr Murdstone's business has collapsed. His sister needs to maintain herself somehow (though soon Mr Murdstone will have entrapped another gullible young woman 'with a very good little property, poor thing', as Mr Chillip, the doctor in David's hometown, remarks (Ch. LVII)). Naturally she will have found her way to Mr Spenlow, clueless as he is about what the role of 'protector' of his daughter should involve.

Miss Murdstone is a cruel prude whose nastiness parades itself as virtue. Dickens relished the coincidence of her reappearance because it exhibited the true persistence of a certain kind of hypocrite.

David Copperfield is rich in coincidences. They show David narrative patterns that he should have foreseen. When he visits his former schoolfriend Traddles at his shabby Camden Town lodgings, he finds something familiar about them. 'The general air of the place reminded me forcibly of the days when I lived with Mr and Mrs Micawber.' Dickens is preparing us for a non-surprise. The house's 'indescribable character of faded gentility … reminded me still more of Mr and Mrs Micawber.' Arriving at the door in the afternoon to find the milkman trying to extract a payment of his bill, 'I was reminded of Mr and Mrs Micawber more forcibly yet.' David is admitted and meets Traddles, who reveals the identity of the couple from whom he rents his single room. 'I board with the people downstairs, who are very agreeable people indeed. Both Mr and Mrs Micawber have seen a good deal of life, and are excellent company' (Ch. XXVII).

Is it grotesquely improbable that, in all London, Traddles should have found the same landlord and landlady that David once had, in a different, if equally down-at-heel, part of the metropolis? In one sense, not at all. Living with the Micawbers is the doom of the naïve and the impecunious. Traddles is a natural victim and will be fleeced of the little money he ever obtains by the amiable but ever indebted Micawber.

Each offence against probability shows David how the world works. Late in the novel our hero, now a successful writer, receives a letter from his former schoolmaster, Mr Creakle, now a Middlesex Magistrate, inviting him to visit the innovative prison that he manages. David accepts and arrives at the penitentiary with Traddles to witness Creakle's 'true system of prison discipline; the only unchallengeable way of making sincere and lasting converts and penitents.'

> I heard so repeatedly, in the course of our goings to and fro, of a certain Number Twenty Seven, who was the Favourite, and who really appeared to be a Model Prisoner, that I resolved to suspend my judgement until I should see Twenty Seven. Twenty Eight, I understood, was also a bright particular star; but it was his misfortune to have his glory a little dimmed by the extraordinary lustre of Twenty Seven. I heard so much of Twenty Seven, of his pious admonitions to everybody around him, and of the beautiful letters he constantly wrote to his mother (whom he seemed to consider in a very bad way), that I became quite impatient to see him.

They come to the cell, the door is unlocked and 'whom should Traddles and I then behold, to our amazement, in this converted Number Twenty Seven, but Uriah Heep!' Orders are given to let out Twenty Eight, who is none other than Steerforth's former valet, Littimer. So astonished has David already been, that this time 'I only felt a kind of resigned wonder'(Ch. LXI). That Dickensian oxymoron, 'resigned wonder', gives us David's acceptance that what seems amazing is somehow not. *Of course* it is Littimer. The novel's two greatest rogues and hypocrites – umble Heep and respectable Littimer – have naturally ended up in adjacent cells. And naturally too, they are fellow model prisoners, straight-faced in their competing shows of penitence. The prominence of the coincidence is peculiarly satisfying.

Forster remarked in his *Life*,

> On the coincidences, resemblances and surprises of life Dickens liked especially to dwell, and few things moved his fancy so pleasantly. The world, he would say, was so much smaller than we thought it; we were all so connected by fate without knowing it; people supposed to be far apart were so constantly elbowing each other; and tomorrow bore so close a resemblance to nothing half so much as to yesterday.[3]

Dickensian coincidences are calculated to move the fancy, asking us to imagine what makes the improbable somehow plausible. Dickens loved coincidences and expected his readers to notice them. It is his interest in highlighting coincidences, rather than smuggling them into the narrative, that singles him out from his contemporary novelists.

In *The Mystery of Edwin Drood*, at dusk on Christmas Eve, Edwin is walking in a small park near Cloisterham Cathedral when he sees an old woman 'crouching on the ground near a wicket gate in a corner'. We immediately know her to be the opium woman who supplies Edwin's uncle, John Jasper, with the drug and knows dark secrets about him, perhaps from his drugged ramblings. Edwin 'seems to know her', because her glazed look and palpitations remind him of the odd state in which he once saw his uncle, 'Jack'. At her request, he gives her money and she asks him his name. When he tells her that it is Edwin, her response tells us more than it tells him. 'You be thankful that your name ain't Ned ... it's a bad name to

have just now … A threatened name. A dangerous name.'
Dickens makes the character half-notice that he is being
told something significant.

> He makes for the better-lighted streets, and resolves
> as he walks on to say nothing of this to-night, but
> to mention it to Jack (who alone calls him Ned), as
> an odd coincidence, to-morrow; of course only as
> a coincidence, and not as anything better worth
> remembering.
>
> (Ch. XIV)

What is the 'coincidence'? That she mentions the name
'Ned' (which might have alerted him to the fact that his
dear 'Jack' is really his deadly rival for the delicious Rosa)?
Or that she reminds him of Jack (which should have led
him to guess that Jack too is an opium addict)?

The repetition of the word 'coincidence' in Edwin's
thoughts draws our attention to the plot. With the novel
unfinished, we cannot know for certain that Jasper is to
be Edwin's murderer, but we can know that the opium
woman is privy to Jasper's true schemes. Edwin should
not have conquered his surprise. Dickens similarly repeats
the word *coincidence* early in *A Tale of Two Cities*. Here
the false witness Roger Cly, acknowledging under cross-
examination in court that he is an associate of the other
chief witness against Charles Darnay, brushes away the
thought that this fact might be revealing. It is 'merely
a coincidence'. 'He didn't call it a particularly curious
coincidence; most coincidences were curious' (II Ch. III).
So they are. In this case the coincidence is evidence of
a plot: Cly and Barsad have conspired to try to destroy
Darnay. Cly would rather that the members of the jury

think nothing of this particular coincidence; in this respect, he seems not unlike some great Victorian novelists.

The competition for the most unlikely coincidence in Victorian fiction is a fierce one and involves some great novels. Take some leading examples. In Charlotte Brontë's *Jane Eyre*, the distraught heroine, having discovered the secret of Mr Rochester's previous marriage, leaves his house and travels blindly down unknown roads for two days, by coach and then on foot, to 'a north-midland shire' where she has never been before.[4] She begs unsuccessfully for food in a remote village, before wandering distractedly down a track over the moors to an isolated house. Close to collapse, she is admitted and given food and lodging by the two sisters who live there, Diana and Mary Rivers, and their brother, St John Rivers, the local parson. She has been saved. She becomes a schoolteacher in the village and a few months later finds out that she is in fact the Rivers's cousin and has inherited a large amount of money from their uncle, who is also her uncle. 'Glorious discovery to a lonely wretch!'[5] The exclamation hardly does justice to the fortuitousness of her singling out her relatives' house from every other dwelling in the north of England, though St John Rivers, who reveals the connection to her, expresses no surprise whatever.

Brontë has frequently been admonished for this coincidence down the years.[6] Less often ticked off is Wilkie Collins, though *The Woman in White* pivots on a comparably far-fetched, if more carefully concealed, coincidence. In its bravura opening instalment, Walter Hartright, walking from Hampstead into London at one in the morning, encounters on 'the lonely high road' a mysterious woman dressed entirely in white. The brilliant shock of the meeting has tended to distract readers from the later discovery that it is an extreme coincidence. Walter has just accepted the post of drawing master to two young women in a household in the remote north-west of England; when the woman in white stops him with 'the touch of a hand laid lightly and suddenly on my shoulder from behind me', he is 'idly wondering … what the Cumberland young ladies would look like.'[7] The mysterious woman who interrupts these thoughts will turn out to be Anne Catherick, the half-sister of one of these same young ladies, Laura Fairlie. (The uncanniness of the resemblance between the two women will be essential to the plot.) There is a reason for Anne being in London: the villain, Percival Glyde, and his co-conspirator, Count Fosco, have kept her incarcerated in a private asylum there. But the fact that Walter so strangely encounters her, in the middle of the night, is pure accident – contrived by Collins for the sheer electricity of it.

Even the greatest of Victorian 'realist' novels turns on a coincidence. In George Eliot's *Middlemarch*, there must be a means to reveal the dubious past of the pious banker, Nicholas Bulstrode. The agent of his downfall will be John Raffles, an ageing profligate, who arrives in the locality because he has heard that his stepson, Joshua Rigg, has inherited wealth and a property near Middlemarch from his real father, Peter Featherstone. Raffles is after money, of course. Rigg, whom he mistreated as a child, dismisses him with some brandy and a sovereign, telling him never to trouble him again. But before he leaves, Raffles has picked up 'a folded paper which had fallen within the fender' in order to wedge his brandy flask firmly into its leather case.[8] The piece of paper is a letter, which Raffles eventually reads. It is from Bulstrode to Featherstone, negotiating a property deal; its discovery by Raffles is 'what you may call a providential thing', as he gloatingly observes.[9] It allows him to locate Bulstrode, whose secret he knows. Many years earlier, Bulstrode fraudulently inherited the entire fortune of the wealthy widow he married, concealing from her the whereabouts of her estranged daughter. This fortune helped him establish his bank in Middlemarch. Alerted to Bulstrode's new life by that coincidentally discovered letter, Raffles will set about blackmailing him.

These novelists have different attitudes to the coincidences on which they rely. Brontë gives Jane Eyre's narrative a providential intensity that leads her narrator to be unsurprised by the most improbable events. And if she is not surprised, why should we be? Collins must make some sacrifices to achieve the sensational effect of introducing a disturbing mystery into an ordinary person's life. The beautiful convolutions of his plot, with its multiple narrators, will allow him to hide the initiating coincidence. Eliot, however, feels the strain of the chance connection on which she depends – so much so that she provides a kind of justification. She begins the chapter in which Raffles first appears by ruminating on the fate of a piece of writing, whether it be an engraving on a stone that, after ages, 'may come by curious little links of effect under the eyes of a scholar', or 'a bit of ink and paper', which has served as 'an innocent wrapping or stop-gap', and finally comes to be seen by someone who knows enough 'to turn it into the opening of a catastrophe'.[10] 'To Uriel' (the most far-seeing angel in *Paradise Lost*) ' … the one result would be as much of a coincidence as the other'. She needs coincidence to enact 'the stealthy convergence of human lots' that her novel minutely observes, yet coincidence causes a kind of ripple in the surface of her hard-won realism.[11] She has to give her excuses.

Initially, Dickens took as models the eighteenth-century novels that he loved and that he gave the young David Copperfield to sustain him.[12] Many of these used coincidence with bravado. One of Dickens's favourites was Fielding's *Tom Jones*, whose coincidences are as elaborately engineered as they are unlikely. In Books IX and X of the novel almost every one of its main characters happens to arrive at the same wayside inn at Upton, in Gloucestershire. With a comic dramatist's panache, Fielding has them variously bump into, misidentify or just miss each other, with only the reader able to appreciate the novelist's artful management of all the chance entrances and exits. As we follow Tom's travels through England and his misadventures in London, we and he find that the same characters keep turning up.

In Dickens's early fiction, coincidences are blithely sprung on us in the eighteenth-century manner. They usually take the form of what we might call re-encounters – meetings with those whom we have met before. In *Pickwick Papers*, where, as a contemporary reviewer put it, 'the characters come and go like the men and women we encounter in the real world', coincidence is a necessary principle.[13] We keep bumping into people. Mr Pott, the rabid political journalist from Suffolk whom Pickwick and his companions meet at the Eatanswill election, reappears in a wayside inn in Towcester, on his way to report on a ball to be held in Birmingham by the Buff party he abhors. By a natural further coincidence, Mr Slurk, editor of the rival Eatanswill newspaper, arrives at the same inn, and soon the two are fighting. Sam Weller wonders how he will find Arabella Allen, Mr Winkle's sweetheart, in

Bristol, and promptly bumps into Mary, the maidservant he has been courting, in the street. When he tells her his mission, Mary informs him that Miss Arabella Allen lives next door to her. The one-eyed bagman who tells a story at the Peacock in Eatanswill later turns up again at the Bush in Bristol, to tell another story. We meet Joe, the fat boy, in Dingley Dell early in Pickwick's peregrinations, and then again near the end of the novel. And Alfred Jingle, the strolling actor, raconteur and conman, who appears in the second chapter of the novel, is liable to reappear at any stage, with his servant and henchman, Job Trotter. When Pickwick is confined in the Fleet Prison, he sees Jingle and Trotter among the inmates. 'Mr Pickwick was affected; the two men looked so very miserable' (Ch. XLII). But he is not surprised.

Jingle might have been taken straight out of *Tom Jones*. In Fielding's novel characters return in new guises in just this manner. Jenny Jones is the clever servant girl who assists Partridge in teaching the local children and who, after being accused of being Tom's mother, flees the neighbourhood. Hundreds of pages, and many years, later we meet the middle-aged Mrs Walters, sexually knowing companion to a soldier called Northerton, who seduces Tom over supper at an inn. Jenny Jones and Mrs Walters are, of course, the same person. Meanwhile Partridge is also driven away by false rumours about his affair with Jenny. Much later, Tom has been expelled from his adoptive father's home and, travelling on foot, is shaved by a barber called Benjamin at a wayside inn. Benjamin turns out to be the very same Partridge, who subsequently becomes Tom's travelling companion. From Fielding's example Dickens took Bailey in *Martin Chuzzlewit*, who first appears as a waggish servant at Todgers' Boarding House, but later

turns up as a cab driver for fraudulent insurance salesman
Tigg Montague, a character who has transformed himself
from Chevy Slyme roguish companion Montague Tigg
earlier in the novel.

In *Oliver Twist*, Dickens deploys extraordinary
coincidences without the least attempt to conceal or
naturalise them. Oliver is made an accomplice in two
robberies, as Fagin attempts to corrupt him. In the first,
the Artful Dodger and Master Bates pick the pocket
of an old gentleman who is inspecting a bookstall on a
London street. After Oliver is saved from Mr Fang, the
fearsome police magistrate, by the last-minute testimony
of the bookstall owner, he faints and is taken home by the
benevolent Mr Brownlow. It takes him days to recover, but
when he does he is transfixed by a portrait of a beautiful but
sad-eyed woman hanging on the wall of the housekeeper's
sitting room. When Mr Brownlow enters the room, he
sees that Oliver is the portrait's 'living copy' (Ch. XII). The
woman will turn out to be Oliver's mother; we will find
out that Mr Brownlow was Oliver's father's best friend. In
the second robbery, Bill Sikes thrusts Oliver through the
tiny ground-floor window of a house at Chertsey, outside
London, with instructions to unlock the door to let him
in. Oliver is shot, and then nursed back to health by the
inhabitants, Rose and her guardian, Mrs Maylie. Rose
is revealed to be the long-lost sister of Oliver's mother.
Fagin's attempts to corrupt the boy bring him closer to his
lost family. The fable-like construction of the plot must be
sufficient reason for such coincidences.

'Where have I seen something like that look before?'
Mr Brownlow asks himself when he sees Oliver. 'I am
sure I have seen that fellow before', is the characteristic
statement of the protagonist of Dickens's next novel,

Nicholas Nickleby, when he sees a man in a London hostelry (Ch. XLIII). The new acquaintance to whom Nicholas makes the remark himself turns out to be the nephew of the Cheeryble brothers, his friends and patrons. In *Nicholas Nickleby*, London makes coincidences easy. Nicholas returns from Portsmouth to the metropolis and wanders on a whim into a Mayfair hotel. As he sits waiting to be served, he overhears 'a noisy party of four gentlemen' drinking in the box next to him, talking raffishly about his sister (Ch. XXXII). One of them is the villainous Sir Mulberry Hawk, with whom he eventually comes to blows. Nicholas sees and falls for a young woman at an employment register-office – and then a few chapters and months later finds her again in the Cheerybles' office (Ch. XL). Nicholas and Kate lose themselves while walking through Soho. Nicholas looks into a lit cellar to ask directions and hears his old acquaintance Mr Mantalini, fruitlessly professing his wounded affection for the virago who has replaced Madame Mantalini (Ch.LXIV).

The characters of Dickens's early fiction accept that London is like this. '"Why, I don't believe now," added Tim, taking off his spectacles, and smiling as with gentle pride, "that there's such a place in all the world for coincidences as London is!"' (*Nicholas Nickleby*, Ch. XLIII).

Young Martin Chuzzlewit arrives in London with very little money, takes his watch to the pawnbroker, and immediately knows the voice of the man in the next box, who is Montague Tigg, the plausible rogue and sponger whom he first met in Salisbury. Tigg is delighted: 'but this is one of the most tremendous meetings in Ancient or Modern History!' (Ch. XIII). As an inveterate walker of London's streets, Dickens knew it as a city of coincidental

encounters. In February 1855 he was writing to the former
Maria Beadnell, who had been the object of his affections
more than twenty years earlier. Now she was Mrs Henry
Winter, and he was keen to arrange a secret meeting with
her, without their respective spouses. Yet being with her
in London was risky: he knew well, he told her, 'what
odd coincidences take place in streets, when they are not
wanted to happen'.[14] In a city of millions, you are always
going to bump into someone you know.

In early Dickens, the whole world is like this. In *The
Old Curiosity Shop*, Nell and her grandfather are at the
very limits of their endurance. On their long journey
on foot from London, they have just tramped across a
hellish industrial wasteland somewhere in the Midlands.
Famished and exhausted, Nell approaches a fellow
traveller and faintly implores his help. He turns his head
and, 'The child clapped her hands together, uttered a wild
shriek, and fell senseless at his feet' (Ch. XLV). It is the
last sentence of the weekly instalment. At the beginning
of the next instalment, Dickens's first readers found that
this randomly encountered fellow traveller is 'the poor
schoolmaster', a sympathetic character whom Nell and
her father last saw in a distant village many days earlier
(Ch. XLVI). He will help care for her; there is goodness in
the world, after all. In *Martin Chuzzlewit*, the hero and his
friend Mark Tapley travel to America to seek their fortunes.
On the voyage from England they befriend a poor woman
travelling with her three children to meet her husband.
Many weeks and chapters later, Martin and Mark have
arrived in the remote and desolate swampland of Eden, in
some Southern state of America. Mark introduces himself
to a neighbouring family and (with a token expression of
disbelief) finds that it is the same woman (now with her

husband) and her children. Desperate and guileless, they too have been conned by the projectors who sell plots of land in this sarcastically named frontier Hell.

People turn up again. According to Forster, Dickens was much taken with this phenomenon. Narrating his time at Wellington Academy, Forster observed,

> to the fact of one of its tutors being afterwards engaged to teach a boy of Macready's, our common friend, Dickens used to point for one of the illustrations of his favourite theory as to the smallness of the world, and how things and persons apparently the most unlikely to meet were continually knocking up against each other.[15]

With *Dombey and Son*, he began to use this unlikeliness in new ways. It has often been observed that this is the first of his novels to be closely plotted (and the earliest for which detailed number plans survive). Now coincidences are signs of careful planning. In the second monthly number, in Chapter VI, Florence Dombey, aged six or seven, becomes detached from her companions, the maidservant Susan Nipper and her brother's nurse Polly Toodle, in an insalubrious London street between Camden Town and the City Road. She is suddenly seized by the wrist by 'a very ugly old woman, with red rims round her eyes', who announces herself as 'Good Mrs Brown'. This baleful character, promising to help her find her friends, leads her off to a shabby little house, where, in a back room containing only 'a heap of bones, and a heap of sifted dust or cinders', she first questions her about her identity and then strips her of her expensive clothes, clothing her in 'some wretched substitutes' from a pile of rags. She finally takes her through 'a labyrinth of narrow streets and lanes', before abandoning her on the main thoroughfare, telling her she must find her way to the premises of Dombey and Son in the City.

The episode has important narrative purposes. Florence eventually finds her way to a Thames-side wharf where Walter Gay has been overseeing the shipment of goods for her father's firm. He is able to rescue her, cementing a bond between them (and awakening her father's resentment). Meanwhile Florence's misadventure gives her father reason to dismiss Polly, so that Paul loses 'his second mother'. But what about 'Good Mrs Brown'? Who is she? Where does she come from? She does not appear again for another twenty-one chapters (or another five months for the first readers), when she turns up in Leamington Spa, where Edith Granger is being paraded to Mr Dombey as his future wife by her mother, Mrs Skewton. She accosts Edith one morning as she walks alone, offering to tell her fortune for 'a piece of silver', but is interrupted by Dombey's manager, Carker, who tosses her a shilling. 'I know!' she mysteriously tells him, before muttering words that indicate that she is a kind of spy on proceedings. 'One child dead, and one child living: one wife dead, and one wife coming. Go and meet her!' (Ch. XXVII). We infer that she has followed the Dombey party to this spa town. But why?

Mr Dombey and Edith marry – a heartless arrangement on his side, and a mercenary one on hers. As the wedding party returns from church for the reception, the narrator wonders why Carker finds himself thinking of the old woman whom he met 'in the grove that morning' – and why Florence thinks 'with a tremble, of her childhood, when she was lost, and of the visage of good Mrs Brown'

(Ch. XXXI). She is the ghost at the feast. She will reappear more frequently, now in the company of her fallen daughter, Alice, who returns 'from abroad'. Dickens arranges for Alice, walking the high road into London, to meet Harriet Carker, wholly by chance. She tells Harriet that she has been a transported convict. Harriet gives her food and money. When she meets her mother again, she realises with fury the force of the coincidence: Harriet is the sister of Carker the Manager, the man who seduced her, many years before. She walks all the way back to Harriet's home and scornfully throws the money back at her (Ch. XXXIII).

Alice is, we discover, Alice Marwood. 'Good Mrs Brown' is Mrs Marwood, the mother who originally pimped her to Carker in the hope of money. Bitterly together, the daughter hating the mother, they now haunt the novel, following Carker and Dombey, plotting their revenge. They are doubles for Edith and her mother – such doubles that, near the end of the novel, Alice's mother reveals that her dying daughter is in fact Edith's first cousin (Ch. LVIII). The fates of the two mother-and-daughter pairings were always entangled. All this might lead us to overlook the bizarre coincidence of that first meeting between Florence and 'Good Mrs Brown'. All the old woman's later entrances are evidence that she is dogging the footsteps of the main characters, but that frightening original encounter was chance. It was Dickens's sign of what was to come, the exploitation and cruelty that would have to erupt again into the novel.

By the time that he wrote *Bleak House*, Dickens was prepared to make coincidence – that embarrassing weakness of Victorian fiction – a governing principle of his novel. The coincidences of *Bleak House* make us feel that characters move within some kind of inescapable magnetic field. Once sucked into the plot of this novel, no character can escape. When the lawyer's clerk, Mr Guppy, meets the wife of the odious evangelical preacher, Mr Chadband, she volunteers the information that she was, in a former life, 'left in charge of a child named Esther Summerson' (Ch. XIX). Mrs Chadband is none other than Mrs Rachael, austere servant to Miss Barbary, Esther's aunt and guardian. So, when Esther later meets Mrs Chadband, we are primed for the encounter. Esther struggles with 'the first chill of the late unexpected recognition'.

> 'Well! I am glad to see you, and glad you are not too proud to know me.' But, indeed she seemed disappointed that I was not.
> 'Proud, Mrs Rachael!' I remonstrated.
> 'I am married, Esther,' she returned, coldly correcting me, 'and am Mrs Chadband. Well! I wish you good day, and I hope you'll do well.'
>
> (Ch. XXIV)

There is a satirical point: the gloomily virtuous Mrs Rachael has become the wife of a religious hypocrite and confidence trickster. But there is more than this. Her reappearance will alert Guppy to the connection between between Esther and Miss Barbary. 'Was Miss Barbary at all connected with your ladyship's family?' Mr Guppy asks Lady Dedlock, as he begins to puzzle out the hidden story of her past life (Ch. XXIX).

In *Bleak House*, there is hardly a more important word to Dickens than 'connect'. You find it as a kind of command or goad to himself in his notes and plans. 'Connect Esther

& Jo? Yes'.[16] When Mr Tulkinghorn finds Nemo's body, he asks Snagsby for information about him. 'I speak of affording some clue to his connexions, or to where he came from, or to anything concerning him' (Ch. XI). *Bleak House* is sometimes a whirr of coincidences because it imagines such a web of connections. In the chapter introducing the repulsive moneylenders, the Smallweeds, and the retired soldier Mr George, we find that the former were Captain Hawdon's creditors, and that the latter was his close friend (Ch. XXI). When we hear that Richard is having fencing training from 'a person who had formerly been a cavalry soldier', we know that it must be Mr George almost before, a couple of sentences later, we are told so. When we later find that he has had to borrow money somewhere in London, we should not be surprised that he has turned to Mr Smallweed, as the predatory creditor has delight in announcing (Ch. XXVI). There is no getting away from those Smallweeds. After his death, Krook, Nemo's landlord and possessor of the papers that reveal his relationship to Lady Dedlock, is discovered to be Mrs Smallweed's brother, and therefore Grandfather Smallweed is the 'unexpected heir' to his property (Ch. XXXIII). We should have expected it, in this book where no one can be unrelated.

The novel insists on its coincidences, most evidently in the involvement of its minor characters. Lawrence Boythorn was at school with John Jarndyce and is now his devoted friend. He is also the immediate neighbour in Lincolnshire of Sir Leicester and Lady Dedlock. John Jarndyce tells Esther that he was 'all but married once. Long ago' (Ch. IX). We eventually discover that, coincidentally, the woman he loved was Miss Barbary, Lady Dedlock's sister and Esther's guardian. Or take the

impoverished brickmaker's family. Esther visits them
with the self-righteously philanthropical Mrs Pardiggle
early in the novel, just as the woman, Jenny's, baby dies
(Ch. VIII). This is near St Albans, but later in London,
when Mr Bucket and Mr Snagsby go to Tom-all-
Alone's to search for Jo, they encounter two drunken,
sleeping men and their wives in a squalid room. It is
the brickmakers again, with Jenny and her friend Liz,
who also now has a baby (Ch. XXII). Later still, one
night after his return from India, the benevolent young
doctor Allan Woodcourt is walking the streets when he
finds and tends to a woman who has been beaten by her
husband. Inevitably, it is Jenny, the brickmaker's wife,
yet again. She keeps being involved. She has brought Jo
back to St Albans, where he infects Charley and Esther
with smallpox. She is later visited by Lady Dedlock, who
is enquiring after Esther and who, leaving some money,
takes the handkerchief with Esther's name on it, which
Esther had placed over Jenny's dead baby's face. Finally,
it is she whom Lady Dedlock pays with a gold watch to
swap clothes in order conceal her whereabouts from her
pursuers.

It is as if this woman and her angry husband represent a
whole brutalised class of human beings, from whom their
social betters cannot detach themselves. The coincidence-
generating narrative method is also the moral and political
heft of the novel – as it dares to make explicit.

> What connexion can there be between the place in
> Lincolnshire, the house in town, the Mercury in powder,
> and the whereabout of Jo the outlaw with the broom,
> who had that distant ray of light upon him when he
> swept the churchyard-step? What connexion can there

have been between many people in the innumerable histories of this world who from opposite sides of great gulfs have, nevertheless, been very curiously brought together!

Jo sweeps his crossing all day long, unconscious of the link, if any link there be.

(Ch. XVI)

'Connect' and 'connection', words used more often in *Bleak House* than in any other Dickens novel, can refer to highly desirable social acquaintances: 'work, be industrious, earn money, and extend the connexion as much as possible', the enervated snob Mr Turveydrop tells his son, who teaches dancing; 'I have made it my business to study my high connexion and to be able to wind it up like a clock, sir,' says Mr Sladdery, who sells prints and books to the upper classes. But Dickens's intricate plot connects the rich and the privileged to those whom they would like to ignore.

All Dickens's later novels flaunt their coincidences. One of these, *Great Expectations*, is 'built on the most outrageous of all the coincidences in Dickens.'[17] This is the fact that Estella, the ward of Miss Havisham with whom Pip becomes obsessed, is the daughter of Magwitch, the escaped convict whom Pip meets by chance in the extraordinary opening chapter of the novel. Yet the outrageousness of the coincidence is its power. In this narrative about the discovery of hidden relationships, the narrator records his own perturbation at the connections that are revealed. All his 'great expectations' are thwarted. Pip, chafing at his apprenticeship at the blacksmith's forge, tells the devoted Biddy, 'I want to be a gentleman.' Like an emissary from the gods, the lawyer Mr Jaggers arrives

to tell him that 'he will come into a handsome property ...
be immediately removed from his present sphere of
life ... and be brought up as a gentleman – in a word,
as a young fellow of great expectations.' Yet gentlemen
and criminals are intimately linked by Dickens's plotting,
and coincidence is often a name for a moment when Pip
becomes aware of this link.

Coincidences fill Pip with dread. When he travels back
to Kent for the first time since moving to London, he has
to share the stage coach with two convicts, who are being
carried down to the dockyards, as 'outside passengers'.
One of the two he recognises as the man who accosted
him years earlier in the Three Jolly Bargemen. 'His head
was all on one side, and one of his eyes was half shut up, as
if he were taking aim at something with an invisible gun.'
On that occasion the man gave Pip a shilling, wrapped in
'two fat sweltering one-pound notes' that are put away in
an ornamental teapot by his sister, where 'they remained,
a nightmare to me, many and many a night and day'(Ch.
X). Now the man, a convict again with a number on his
back, is sitting just behind him, not recognising Pip but
'with his breath on the hair of my head'. Soon, to make
it worse, the convicts are talking about those two pound
notes, and how the man whom Pip recognises was given
them by another convict to pass to 'that boy that had fed
him and kep his secret':

> the coincidence of our being together on the coach,
> was sufficiently strange to fill me with a dread that
> some other coincidence might at any moment connect
> me, in his hearing, with my name.
>
> (Ch. XXVIII)

It is indeed an extraordinary coincidence, and the uneasiness of it is transferred to the narrator. It activates the fear of an unwanted connection.

Another moment when coincidence makes Pip aware of concealed relationships comes at the end of Chapter XLII, in which Magwitch, illegally returned from Australia to England under the name Provis, tells his history to Pip and Herbert Pocket. He describes his involvement with Compeyson, his criminal accomplice, manipulator and eventual betrayer. Born to crime, Magwitch took over as Compeyson's partner from someone called Arthur. 'Him and Compeyson had been in a bad thing with a rich lady some years afore, and they'd made a pot of money by it', but 'Arthur was a dying, and a dying poor and with the horrors on him.' Pip asks if Compeyson is dead, and Magwitch says that he has heard no more of him.

> Herbert had been writing with his pencil in the cover of a book. He softly pushed the book over to me, as Provis stood smoking with his eyes on the fire, and I read in it:
> 'Young Havisham's name was Arthur. Compeyson is the man who professed to be Miss Havisham's lover.'
> I shut the book and nodded slightly to Herbert, and put the book by; but we neither of us said anything, and both looked at Provis as he stood smoking by the fire.

The shocked silence is all the more charged because this was originally not just the end of a chapter, but the end of a weekly instalment in Dickens's magazine *All the Year*

Round. The reader is invited to feel the force of a revelation in that space between instalments. The coincidence is an affront to expectations that tells us, as it tells Pip, of the connections that shape his life.

The next chapter begins with Pip pausing to ask, 'how much of my shrinking from Provis might be traced to Estella?' The coincidence recognised by Herbert will indeed connect Estella to Magwitch, will connect what Pip desires to what he loathes. Coincidences hint at the links between worlds that Pip would like to keep apart. His dumb shock as he experiences these coincidences is brilliantly – because comically – represented as Herbert changes his dressings, after he has been burnt trying to save Miss Havisham from her conflagration. As he tends to Pip, Herbert tells him of a conversation he has had with 'Provis' about 'some woman that he had had great trouble with'.

> 'It seems,' said Herbert, '—there's a bandage off most charmingly, and now comes the cool one,—makes you shrink at first, my poor dear fellow, don't it? but it will be comfortable presently,—it seems that the woman was a young woman, and a jealous woman, and a revengeful woman; revengeful, Handel, to the last degree.'
>
> 'To what last degree?'
>
> 'Murder.—Does it strike too cold on that sensitive place?'
>
> 'I don't feel it. How did she murder? Whom did she murder?'
>
> (Ch. L)

That 'shrinking' is Pip flinching from what he is discovering: that Molly, Jaggers's housekeeper, whom the masterful lawyer successfully defended from a murder charge, is Estella's mother. Pip is learning of the novel's ultimate coincidence: that Magwitch is Estella's father. Yet this truth from which he flinches is not quite a surprise. He has been thinking 'how strange it was that I should be encompassed by all this taint of prison and crime ... that it should ... pervade my fortune and advancement' (Ch. XXXII). Coincidence has become the confirmation of something dreaded.

Which is why *shrinking* – 'my shrinking from Provis', 'makes you shrink at first' – is such a good word. It is the word Pip uses for his discomfort at sharing the coach with the convict. 'I was conscious of growing high-shouldered on one side, in my shrinking endeavors to fend him off' (Ch. XXVIII). *Shrinking* had a special meaning for Dickens. It was the word he found when he wrote to John Forster comparing his unhappiness during the breakdown of his marriage to his unhappiness as a child, when consigned to work in the blacking factory.

> The never-to-be-forgotten misery of that old time bred a certain shrinking sensitiveness in a certain ill-clad, ill-fed child, that I have found come back in the never-to-be-forgotten misery of this later time.[18]

In *Great Expectations*, it is the word for Pip's recognition of an insufferable coincidence, revealing a hidden story.

If only coincidences were what they appeared to be: chance events. Pip visits Miss Havisham when he has found out that his true patron is not her but Magwitch,

and asks her why he was brought to her house as a boy to
meet Estella:

> 'Mr Jaggers,' said Miss Havisham, taking me up in
> a firm tone, 'had nothing to do with it, and knew
> nothing of it. His being my lawyer, and his being the
> lawyer of your patron, is a coincidence. He holds the
> same relation towards numbers of people, and it might
> easily arise. Be that as it may, it did arise, and was not
> brought about by anyone.'
>
> Anyone might have seen in her haggard face that
> there was no suppression or evasion so far.
>
> Ch. XLIV

She speaks truthfully – but what she says is not true. Miss
Havisham does not know of Estella's parentage, and will
die without knowing. The coincidence that she notes
does not, as she supposes, 'easily arise'. It tells us of a
world of buried connections. But she is right to say that
such coincidence is 'not brought about by anyone'. Miss
Havisham read of Jaggers in the newspapers and engaged
him. She told him that she wanted a girl to rear, and
one day he brought her one (XLIX). Jaggers binds the
stories of Magwitch and Estella together. Yet even he, the
man who commands so many lives, cannot command
coincidence. When Pip reveals the identity of Estella's
father ('his name is Provis – from New South Wales')
Jaggers's frightening equanimity is shaken for the only
time in the book.

> Even Mr Jaggers started when I said those words. It was
> the slightest start that could escape a man, the most
> carefully repressed and the soonest checked, but he did

start, though he made it a part of the action of taking
out his pocket-handkerchief.

Ch. LI

Jaggers too has to recognise a plot larger and more
elaborate than any that he can control.

Coincidence in a narrative makes us uneasy, and no
novelist has more imaginatively exploited this uneasiness.
In *Great Expectations*, Dickens dares make his hero the
very focus of coincidence. If Pip had not been in the
graveyard when the escaped convict stumbled there from
the marshes, if he had not also been the 'chance boy'
selected from the neighbourhood by Miss Havisham,
on the advice of Uncle Pumblechook, for her scheme
of revenge on the male sex, the stories of Magwitch and
Estella would never have been connected. He embodies
coincidence. So, appropriately, *Great Expectations* ends
with a flourish of coincidence. In Dickens's original
ending, Pip, accompanied by Joe and Biddy's young son,
'little Pip', meets Estella in the street in London. She is
now married to a 'Shropshire doctor'. She shakes Pip's
hand and asks to kiss the little boy. '(She supposed the
child, I think, to be my child.)'[19] Pip and Estella part on
a misunderstanding, in a melancholy parenthesis. She
can console herself with the thought that he is married
and has a son, when in fact he is on his own. Dickens's
friends, notably the popular novelist Bulwer Lytton,
persuaded him that his readers would be aghast at such
an unhappy conclusion.[20] So Dickens wrote the ending
that was actually published, recruiting coincidence to
help him. Now Pip returns to his former home on the
marshes after eleven years abroad. In the evening he walks
over to the place where Satis House, since demolished,

once stood. He enters what was once the garden, and he sees 'a solitary figure'. It is Estella. He approaches her and they speak affectionately. She is a widow, and though she says that they will 'continue friends apart', he takes her hand and sees 'the shadow of no parting from her'. Their meeting might seem inevitable, but Dickens wants us to notice that it is by chance. Pip asks her if she often comes back to this place of their first meeting.

'I have never been here since.'
    'Nor I.'

(Ch. LIX)

After all those years, the two characters return to the old place at just the same time. Coincidence alone, by the remotest chance, can allow them something close to a happy ending.

9

Enjoying clichés

> My meaning in observing gaily, in the Carol, that
> I don't know what there is particularly dead about
> a door-nail, is, that I don't know why a door-nail is
> more dead (if I may use the expression) than anything
> else that never had life
>
> Letter to the Rev P. Gale, 25 March 1844[1]

What writer would ever want to use clichés? Martin Amis
entitled a collection of his reviews and essays *The War
against Cliché*, explaining in his Foreword, 'To idealize: all
writing is a campaign against cliché. Not just clichés of
the pen but clichés of the mind and clichés of the heart.
When I dispraise, I am usually quoting clichés.'[2] We
expect our best writers to avoid these dead combinations
of words. It is hard to catch Jane Austen (as opposed to
one of her characters) in a cliché. It is part of her brilliance
to offer as 'a truth universally acknowledged' a form of
words that had never been used before. Gustave Flaubert
announced the hard task of the novelist as finding a prose

style that avoided archaisms and clichés: '*L'idéal de la prose est arrivé à un degré inouï de difficulté; il faut se dégager de l'archaïsme, du mot commun.*'[3]

In his review of Flaubert's *Letters*, Henry James commented with admiration on Flaubert's stylistic fastidiousness.

> The horror, in particular, that haunted all his years was the horror of the cliché, the stereotyped, the thing usually said and the way it was usually said, the current phrase that passed muster.[4]

If we share the literary values of these writers, the vigour with which Dickens opens *A Christmas Carol* is hard to explain.

> Marley was dead: to begin with. There is no doubt whatever about that. The register of his burial was signed by the clergyman, the clerk, the undertaker, and the chief mourner. Scrooge signed it: and Scrooge's name was good upon 'Change, for anything he chose to put his hand to. Old Marley was as dead as a door-nail.

The cliché-averse critic might forgive 'to begin with' in the first sentence, as having a mischievous double meaning: Marley is dead at the beginning of the story, but he will soon come alive again. 'There is no doubt whatever about that' – the narrator pedantically provides the documentary evidence of his demise. And then the paragraph ends with the shameless flourish of that cliché – a dead phrase about being dead.

Dickens delights in that phrase and is distracted by its weird logic from the story he is supposed to be telling. The moment after using the cliché, he notices how very odd it is. We all use this phrase, but why?

> Mind! I don't mean to say that I know, of my own knowledge, what there is particularly dead about a door-nail. I might have been inclined, myself, to regard a coffin-nail as the deadest piece of ironmongery in the trade. But the wisdom of our ancestors is in the simile; and my unhallowed hands shall not disturb it, or the Country's done for. You will therefore permit me to repeat, emphatically, that Marley was as dead as a door-nail.

'The wisdom of our ancestors' is right: the analogy is a very old one, cropping up in Langland's *Piers Plowman* in 1362. 'Fey withouten fait is febelore þen nouȝt, And ded as a dore-nayl' ('Faith without works is feebler than nothing, and dead as a door-nail').[5] The formula is as ancient as those medieval doors that are studded with nails; by the 1840s, it has become deliciously mysterious. Its exact meaning is itself dead. 'I don't mean to say that I know, of my own knowledge': in the manuscript of *A Christmas Carol*, you can see that Dickens first wrote 'I don't mean to say that I know, myself' and went on to the end of the sentence, before checking back to erase 'myself' and insert that redundant qualification, 'of my own knowledge'.[6] He relishes its expressive clumsiness. He has to acknowledge that there might be somebody somewhere who does know why a door-nail is 'particularly dead'. (The likeness may derive from the fact that nails used to strengthen doors had their ends bent back, and thus could never be used again.)[7] Only Dickens would have had the idea of quibbling about the best way to say that someone is absolutely dead – before bringing him back to life. The cliché looks like a talisman against the dread thought that someone dead might not be dead at all.

Dickens uses this cliché defiantly. Twice. We notice the phrase because he wants us to notice it. He himself did not have to fear the opprobrious use of the word *cliché* by critics, because it did not exist. According to the *OED*, the earliest use of this word to refer to 'A phrase or expression regarded as unoriginal or trite due to overuse' dates from the 1880s, over a decade after the novelist's death. Yet, reading Dickens, we know that the thing existed before the word for it came into use. We know because so often, as in the opening of *A Christmas Carol*, Dickens drew attention to it. It is an aspect of language little studied by linguists because of the value judgement involved. After all, there are many frequently occurring combinations of words that are not perceived as clichés. As one linguist points out, 'frequency of use does not directly correlate with impressions of triteness'.[8] Writers of guides to style and usage readily describe – and deplore – clichés, but without always acknowledging our reliance, in all speech and writing, on pre-formed phrases. In his *Dictionary of Clichés*, Eric Patrtridge defines a cliché as 'an outworn commonplace: a phrase, or short sentence, that has become so hackneyed that careful speakers and scrupulous writers shrink from it because they feel that its use is an insult to the intelligence of their audience.'[9] But why is 'insult to the intelligence' not a cliché too? It is impossible to write or speak without using what corpus linguists, less judgementally, like to call *fixed expressions* or *idioms*. In

Dickens's fiction, we recognise those that we might call clichés precisely by the novelist's revivification of them. Far from avoiding these alreadyformed, too-often-used phrases, Dickens likes to hunt them out and find what life there is in them. The more apparently worn-out they are, the more he likes to do something with them.

Dickens uses that 'dead as a door-nail' cliché once more in his fiction, in *Dombey and Son*, the novel that he wrote immediately after *A Christmas Carol*. It is when we are being told of the pride taken by the ridiculous, though amiable, Sir Barnet Skettles in his occupation of 'making people acquainted with people' (Ch. XXIV). Sir Barnet lives to make introductions. 'He liked the thing for its own sake, and it advanced his favourite object too.' His modus operandi is to invite some new acquaintance to stay at his villa in Fulham and to ask him on the morning after his arrival if there is any eminent person he wishes to meet. If his guest does name someone, Sir Barnet claims a friendship with the very person. In a prose that imitates his staccato self-assurance, we hear what follows:

> immediately called on the aforesaid somebody, left his card, wrote a short note,—'My dear Sir—penalty of your eminent position—friend at my house naturally desirous—Lady Skettles and myself participate—trust that genius being superior to ceremonies, you will do us the distinguished favour of giving us the pleasure,' etc, etc.—and so killed a brace of birds with one stone, dead as door-nails.
>
> (Ch. XXIV)

Two clichés, imitating Sir Barnet's fatuous bluffness, resonantly combine; appropriately so, for he is a man

given to repetition, using the method over and over again
to give the illusion that he has a rich social life.

Dickens's love of clichés flares when two hackneyed
phrases are comically combined like this. Mr Pecksniff in
Martin Chuzzlewit is another character who, for different
reasons, deserves two clichés rather than one. Certain
characters induce idiomatic fancy in the narrator and
Pecksniff, himself a pompous re-shaper of clichés, is one
such.[10] Here he is reacting to old Martin Chuzzlewit's
declaration that his riches bring him only unhappiness.

> It would be no description of Mr Pecksniff's gentleness
> of manner to adopt the common parlance, and say that
> he looked at this moment as if butter wouldn't melt
> in his mouth. He rather looked as if any quantity of
> butter might have been made out of him, by churning
> the milk of human kindness, as it spouted upwards
> from his heart.
>
>   (Ch. II)

Pecksniff has in mind only the thought that his cousin's
money might come to him. One cliché is not enough for
his oozing display of piety at the proposition that wealth
might in fact be a curse. One cliché suggests another.
'Common parlance' has to be stretched a little, with
wonderful absurdity, as the imaginary butter in his mouth
gets muddled up with the non-existent milk of human
kindness from which it might be supposed to be churned.
Out of these commonplaces something truly fantastic –
milk spouting from the heartless Pecksniff's heart – is
conjured. We see that some clichés are fossils of verbal
inventiveness. Once upon a time, someone must have
written or said, for the first time, that 'butter would not

melt in his (or her) mouth'. (The turn of phrase goes back to at least the sixteenth century.) Dickens is rediscovering its figurative wit.

He was amused by the way that one cliché could reach out to another. In *Dombey and Son*, we hear that one of Dickens's many dubious pedagogues, Doctor Blimber, will, by command of Mr Dombey, 'take ... in hand' the six-year-old Paul Dombey. The boy's educational fate is immediately intimated, as Dickens hears the cliché *take in hand* for the euphemism that it is and turns it into something else. 'Whenever a young gentleman was taken in hand by Doctor Blimber, he might consider himself sure of a pretty tight squeeze' (Ch. XI). A second cliché makes comically literal the first one. In the chapter in *Little Dorrit* where we first become acquainted with the Circumlocution Office – that Kafka-esque bureaucracy *avant la lettre* – Arthur Clennam hears from Mr Meagles how the inventor Daniel Doyce has been punished for his publicly useful ingenuity. After a board of 'ancient members' of the House of Lords had failed to comprehend his invention, the Circumlocution Office 'took up the business ... muddled the business, addled the business, tossed the business in a wet blanket' (Ch. X). It makes a mockery of his hopes and puts a damper on them: the blanket of cliché is dual purpose. Those who wield influence in this novel are as ridiculous as they are complacent, so the well-worn metaphors applied to them mix absurdly. When we hear of the snobbery of Mrs Gowan and her supercilious friends, who like to think themselves superior to the parvenu financier Merdle while adoring his wealth, one cliché undoes another.

> True, the Hampton Court Bohemians, without exception, turned up their noses at Merdle as an

upstart; but they turned them down again, by falling
flat on their faces to worship his wealth. In which
compensating adjustment of their noses, they were
pretty much like Treasury, Bar, and Bishop, and all the
rest of them.

(Ch. XXXIII)

Upturned noses are pressed to the ground as superiority
and sycophancy combine. Language's commonplaces
come to life to ridicule them.

Dickens tapped the energy of ordinary language. He
knew that speech is cemented together by phrases that we
take for granted and metaphors dimmed by familiarity.
One of his tricks is take one of these with a sudden
literalness. In *Dombey and Son*, he tells us that the malign
Major Bagstock is selfish, so selfish that it requires some
Dickensian hyperbole to give us the right idea. 'It may
be doubted whether there ever was a more entirely selfish
person at heart' – then Dickens pauses at the sound of the
well-worn formula he has just used and gives it a twist –
'or at stomach is perhaps a better expression, seeing that
he was more decidedly endowed with that latter organ
than with the former' (Ch. VII). The normal phrases will
mislead you about the Major, who is indeed absolutely
heartless. Keen on his food and his drink, purple in
the face, avaricious: a man who lives off others, he is
all stomach. Dickens had an ear for the clichés people
like to use about their 'hearts' (in *Dombey and Son*, the
character who endlessly talks in praise of those who have
'Heart' is Mrs Skewton, the mother who eagerly presides
over the sale of her daughter in a loveless marriage to
Mr Dombey). In *Little Dorrit*, the recently enriched

William Dorrit, conversing with Mrs Merdle about the engagement between his daughter Fanny and her stepson, the empty-headed Edmund Sparkler, tells her that he will write to Mr Merdle to seek his approval. 'Mrs Merdle concurred with all her heart—or with all her art, which was exactly the same thing' (II Ch. XV). The narrator, having had enough of the platitudes and circumlocutions that these two have been exchanging, turns the cliché into the rhyming truth. Deeper feelings has she none.

We should listen to the exact meaning of hackneyed expressions. At the opening of the second chapter of *Bleak House*, we leave the High Court of Chancery for another world. 'It is but a glimpse of the world of fashion that we want on this same miry afternoon. It is not so unlike the Court of Chancery but that we may pass from the one scene to the other, as the crow flies' (Ch. II).

We pass from Lincoln's Inn Hall, where the Lord Chancellor presides, to the Dedlock London mansion: a short distance 'as the crow flies'. Dickens's use of the cliché (so unnecessary!) draws attention to the narrative move that he is making, with the implication that there will be a connection between the events and characters in the two separate chapters. Then, in Chapter X, the crow becomes literal. At the opening of the chapter we are introduced to Mr Snagsby, the law stationer, and his wife, the suspicious virago, Mrs Snagsby.

> The day is closing in and the gas is lighted, but is not yet fully effective, for it is not quite dark. Mr Snagsby standing at his shop-door looking up at the clouds sees a crow who is out late skim westward over the slice of sky belonging to Cook's Court. The crow flies straight

across Chancery Lane and Lincoln's Inn Garden into
Lincoln's Inn Fields.

(Ch. X)

We are being taken somewhere, another short distance,
from Mr Snagsby's premises off Chancery Lane to
Mr Tulkinghorn's chambers. We have already met Mr
Tulkinghorn in that second chapter, where he witnessed
Lady Dedlock's faintness when she saw the handwriting
on a legal document. Now we see Mr Tulkinghorn,
secretive and scheming, lawyer to 'the great ones of the
earth', in his home. No sooner have we seen him than he
is leaving his rooms.

> Mr Tulkinghorn goes, as the crow came—not quite so
> straight, but nearly—to Cook's Court, Cursitor Street.
> To Snagsby's, Law-Stationer's, Deeds engrossed and
> copied, Law-Writing executed in all its branches, &c.,
> &c., &c.

The crow again. The cliché was there to let us see
that physical movement is narrative movement. Mr
Tulkinghorn must be up to something, his sense of
purpose ('not quite so straight, but nearly') as undeviating,
corvine as can be.

Dickens let his readers see that a cliché might express
the truth that finer words belie. In *Our Mutual Friend*,
as the scheming Lammles force Georgiana Podsnap and
Fascination Fledgeby together, they must exhaustingly
supply all the conversation that these two limited people
fail to make. Mr Lammle reaches for every rhetorical
flourish he can manage, but while his 'teeth, studs, eyes,
and buttons' all sparkle, he secretly bends a 'dark frown'

on them, 'expressive of an intense desire to bring them
together by knocking their heads together' (II Ch. IV).
The cliché is a comical release of his real resentment at
all the effort he is having to make. That knocking of
heads together is supposed to be metaphorical, but Alfred
Lammle is not thinking metaphorically. He strokes and
encourages them, but really he would like to do them
violence.

In *Hard Times*, Louisa Bounderby is summoned by
Bitzer, the 'light porter' at Bounderby's bank, with the
news that her mother, Mrs Gradgrind, is dying. Louisa
must catch the train to Coketown, accompanied by
Bitzer, 'fit colourless servitor at Death's door when Mrs
Gradgrind knocked' (II Ch. IX). The cliché is wrested
to an unexpected use by Bitzer's presence – and death's
door becomes an opening at which he is the gruesome
attendant. Bitzer, once Gradgrind's most obedient pupil,
has been reared to be a lackey, serving the purposes of
Bounderby and Mrs Sparsit. There are other death's doors
in Dickens. In *Nicholas Nickleby*, our hero arrives in bitter
weather at Dotheboys Hall with some new recruits to Mr
and Mrs Squeers's appalling school.

> Supper being over, and removed by a small servant girl
> with a hungry eye, Mrs Squeers retired to lock it up,
> and also to take into safe custody the clothes of the five
> boys who had just arrived, and who were half-way up
> the troublesome flight of steps which leads to death's
> door, in consequence of exposure to the cold.
>
> (Ch. VII)

The jokey use of the cliché fits this world of farcical
brutality, presided over by that hilarious monster Mr

Squeers. Nicholas Nickleby is woken on his first morning at Dotheboys Hall not by Mr Squeers's voice (as would have been the case in a novel by any other writer) but by 'a voice he has no difficulty in recognising as part and parcel of Mr Squeers', which 'admonished him that it was time to rise' (Ch. VIII). This could not work without the cliché, a phrase used so often now jolted into unexpected life. Squeers's voice – peremptory, loutish, threatening – is inescapably, as we might say, part of the Squeers package, though it seems, to the half-awake Nicholas, early on this very cold morning, to have a horrible life of its own.

In *Bleak House*, Dickens uses the same cliché in an equally odd way. Guppy, the lawyer's clerk who is curious about what he senses is Lady Dedlock's secret, gains admission to Chesney Wold by announcing that he is acquainted with the Dedlock family lawyer, Mr Tulkinghorn. The housekeeper, Mrs Rouncewell, is disarmed. 'Now, Mr Tulkinghorn is, in a manner, part and parcel of the place and besides, is supposed to have made Mrs Rouncewell's will' (Ch. VII). We might think that the cliché is taken from Mrs Rouncewell's thoughts and is her habitual phrase for what she regards as a time-honoured association. Yet the peculiarity of using this idiom for a person is a sly alarm: she takes Mr Tulkinghorn for granted as a traditional functionary, when really he is a powerful manipulator. Clichés alert us to thoughts that come too easily. Later in the same novel, Dickens lets the reader inhabit Mrs Snagsby's groundless conviction that Jo, the boy summoned to listen to the pious Mr Chadband's evangelical admonitions, must be her husband's son.

> Why does he look at Mr Snagsby? Mr Snagsby looks at him. Why should he do that, but that Mrs Snagsby sees

it all? Why else should that look pass between them,
why else should Mr Snagsby be confused and cough
a signal cough behind his hand? It is as clear as crystal
that Mr Snagsby is that boy's father.

(Ch. XXV)

'Clear as crystal' makes it true.

Yet there *is* truth in clichés, especially the truth that
what a person thinks unique to them is, in fact, common
and therefore comical. Mr Dombey is ridiculous in his
haughty condescension to Mr and Mrs Toodle, when he
employs Mrs Toodle, after the death of his wife, to nurse
his baby son. He flinches from the fact of their involvement
in his life. When Mr Toodle tells him that he used to
work 'underground' (he was a miner), but now is going
to work 'on one of these here railroads', it is all too much.
'As the last straw breaks the laden camel's back, this piece
of underground information crushed the sinking spirits
of Mr Dombey' (Ch. II). 'Underground information' is
Dickens's own phrasing, but the camel's back, even with the
extra 'laden', is something we all recognise. The proverbial
analogy makes Mr Dombey's dismay ordinary – which is
just what he can never admit to being.

In his introduction to an index to proverbs in Dickens's
works, one of its compilers, Wolfgang Mieder, quotes the
narrator of *David Copperfield*: 'conventional phrases are a
sort of fireworks, easily let off, and liable to take a great
variety of shapes and colours not at all suggested by their
original form' (Ch. XLI). Dickens, Mieder says, is 'always
creating innovative variations' of 'traditional proverbs'.[11]
Certainly, he is apt to quote a wise old saying only in
order to ring changes upon it. In *Martin Chuzzlewit*,
Pecksniff, in pursuit of the Chuzzlewit fortune, travels to

London with his two daughters. 'Time and tide will wait
for no man, saith the adage. But all men have to wait for
time and tide.' Pecksniff's moment has come, and so the
idiom is playfully pursued.

> That tide which, taken at the flood, would lead Seth
> Pecksniff on to fortune, was marked down in the table,
> and about to flow. No idle Pecksniff lingered far inland,
> unmindful of the changes of the stream; but there,
> upon the water's edge, over his shoes already, stood the
> worthy creature, prepared to wallow in the very mud,
> so that it slid towards the quarter of his hope.
>
> (Ch. X)

The self-interested Pecksniff, as laughable as he is ruthless,
is so keen to seize his opportunity that the 'tide' of the
saying slops over his shoes as he wades into the mud. We
hear the villainous Jonas Chuzzlewit citing the biblical
adage that a man's life span should be three score and
ten (a span that his father has already exceeded), and the
narrator wonders if we are surprised to hear him 'making
such a reference to such a book for such a purpose'.

> Does any one doubt the old saw, that the Devil (being
> a layman) quotes Scripture for his own ends? If he
> will take the trouble to look about him, he may find
> a greater number of confirmations of the fact in the
> occurrences of any single day, than the steam-gun can
> discharge balls in a minute.

Jonas is the Devil, more or less, and Dickens enjoys
replying to his twisted Scriptural saying with his own
old saying. A little later in the same chapter, Jonas drags

Mercy and Charity Pecksniff (he is intent on marrying one of them) along to the premises that he shares with his father and legal partner, old Anthony Chuzzlewit.

> An ancient proverb warns us that we should not expect to find old heads upon young shoulders; to which it may be added that we seldom meet with that unnatural combination, but we feel a strong desire to knock them off; merely from an inherent love we have of seeing things in their right places. It is not improbable that many men, in no wise choleric by nature, felt this impulse rising up within them, when they first made the acquaintance of Mr Jonas; but if they had known him more intimately in his own house, and had sat with him at his own board, it would assuredly have been paramount to all other considerations.
>
> (Ch. XI)

Jonas, a young miser who wishes for his own father's death, is 'unnatural', certainly, but Dickens's wresting of that proverb invites the reader to laugh at him as well as despise him.

Dickens invokes the claim to wisdom of an 'old saw' with mock-respect. In *Oliver Twist*, the brutish and brutal Bill Sikes is assaulting his dog with a poker and a clasp-knife in a public house, when Fagin opens the door and the dog darts out. 'There must always be two parties to a quarrel, says the old adage. Mr Sikes, being disappointed of the dog's participation, at once transferred his share in the quarrel to the new comer.' Sikes needs some target for his fury and we can laugh at the predictable way he redirects it, licensed by the incongruously polite explanation, 'being disappointed of the dog's participation'. The truths of common sayings tinge any event with bathetic comedy. A saying is offered in mock-defence of Serjeant Snubbin's ineffectual defence of Mr Pickwick from the charge of breach of promise.

> It is sufficient to add in general terms, that he did the best he could for Mr Pickwick; and the best, as everybody knows, on the infallible authority of the old adage, could do no more.
>
> (*Pickwick Papers*, Ch. XXXIV)

So that (for all the farcical injustice of it) is that. Offering an explanation for the sheer stamina of the rioters in *Barnaby Rudge*, Dickens observes that they 'comforted themselves with the homely proverb, that, being hanged at all, they might as well be hanged for a sheep as a lamb' (Ch. LIII). The proverb works for any excess, from the trivial to the murderous. The intrusion of an overused platitude can even lend comedy to what we have learned to call domestic violence, as when we learn of the unlucky marriage of David Copperfield's aunt, Betsey Trotwood, who had had:

> a husband younger than herself, who was very handsome, except in the sense of the homely adage, 'handsome is, that handsome does'—for he was strongly suspected of having beaten Miss Betsey, and even of having once, on a disputed question of supplies, made some hasty but determined arrangements to throw her out of a two pair of stairs' window.
>
> (Ch. I)

If only she had thought of that adage before she walked down the aisle.

In Dickens's hands, clichés ask us to face truths we might prefer to avoid. In his later novels, he sometimes likes to use them as chapter or section titles, directing our attention to the ways in which the narrative will confirm or cheat expectations. Chapter titles in *Bleak House* include 'Quite at Home', 'Covering a Multitude of Sins', 'Our Dear Brother' and 'A Turn of the Screw'. Each one of these is taken up in the chapter that follows. In Chapter VI, Esther, the friendless orphan, finds herself 'at Home' for the first time, at John Jarndyce's Bleak House. In Chapter VIII, she hears from Jarndyce about the 'sins' that have followed from the interminable Chancery case. In Chapter XXXIV, Trooper George receives a letter from Smallweed ('a screw and a wice in his actions', as his companion Phil Squod rightly says) requiring instant repayment of a loan. Chapter XI, in which the dead, nameless law writer is interred, makes most sardonic use of its cliché title. The pauper undertaker

> bears off the body of our dear brother here departed to a hemmed-in churchyard, pestiferous and obscene, whence malignant diseases are communicated to the bodies of our dear brothers and sisters who have not departed.

Here 'they lower our dear brother down a foot or two'. The phrase is taken from the burial ceremony in the Book of Common Prayer; its repetition here in the novel is bitterly sarcastic. No one, except Jo the crossing sweeper, cares what happens to 'our dear brother'. The Christian sentiment that every single man and woman is our brother or sister is traduced in the state of the graveyard and the sicknesses it spawns.

Our Mutual Friend is divided into four Books, the first two of which ('The Cup and the Lip' and 'Birds of a Feather') take their titles from proverbial sayings. Each is one part of a rule about human nature that we are invited to complete. In his 'mem' for Chapter XIII of the novel, Dickens noted 'Kill Gaffer retributively – "Many a slip" for Mr Riderhood'.[12] Rogue Riderhood has falsely testified against Gaffer Hexam, accusing him of the murder of John Harmon in order to claim the large reward. Hexam's death snatches that cup from his lip. Dickens's use of the part-proverb as the title of a whole Book makes us see the larger drama of disappointed expectations. There is Bella Wilfer, expecting to marry a rich man, who is then declared dead. There are the Lammles, Alfred and Sophronia, who marry each other for money and find themselves mutually deceived. 'Birds of a Feather' directs our attention to the alliances that take shape in Book II: not just the 'Birds of Prey', Rogue Riderhood and his daughter, the ironically named 'Pleasant', but also Silas Wegg and his co-conspirator Mr Venus, plotting against the Boffins, and the Lammles and the repulsive Fascination Fledgeby, scheming to get their hands on Georgiana Podsnap's money. The plot is driven by these couplings. The truisms in titles give a wink to the reader about narrative patterns that are invisible to the characters.

The 'conventional phrases' to which Dickens sets light are not only proverbs: they run to every kind of pre-formulated platitude or dead metaphor. Dickens makes a stale idiom fresh again simply by extending its logic a little. In *Dombey and Son*, Miss Blimber, who teaches at her father's absurd little school, is as enraptured as

Dr Blimber by Latin and Greek, what even the Victorians were used to calling the 'dead languages'.

> She was dry and sandy with working in the graves of deceased languages. None of your live languages for Miss Blimber. They must be dead—stone dead—and then Miss Blimber dug them up like a Ghoul.
>
> (Ch. XI)

Helped by another cliché – the description of scholarly individuals as 'dry' – Dickens makes a comic graverobber of poor Miss Blimber, her enthusiasm a truly gruesome matter. We hear David Copperfield's inclination to delude himself when, impecunious but looking forward to marriage to Dora, he tells us that he was 'busily keeping red-hot all the irons I now had in the fire' (Ch. XXXVII). The phrase that might have been deployed to fend off another person's enquiries about his prospects ('I have got several irons in the fire') has become all his own. At the beginning of the next chapter – the next month's instalment – those proverbial irons are still hot. His scheme of recording Parliamentary Debates was 'one of the irons I began to heat immediately, and one of the irons I kept hot and hammered at' (Ch. XXXVIII). Clichés console. Thus, our introduction to Sir Leicester Dedlock in the second chapter of *Bleak House*. 'His family is as old as the hills and infinitely more respectable.' It would be amusing enough if it ended there, the narrator's analogy turning on the inadequate respectability of hills. But it goes on, handing the cliché over to the character. 'He has a general opinion that the world might get on without hills, but would be done up without Dedlocks.'

It is as if Sir Leicester's limited imagination has been possessed by the cliché and he really is willing to muse on the redundancy of hills.

A cliché can unsettle too. In *Little Dorrit* Arthur Clennam gets a capsule biography from Daniel Doyce of the louche Henry Gowan, his younger rival for the affections of Mr Meagles's daughter, Pet. He discovers that 'his genius, during his earlier manhood, was of that exclusively agricultural character which applies itself to the cultivation of wild oats' (I Ch. XVII). The euphemistic force of the cliché is brought out by being extrapolated like this. For a second, we might think that the elaborate wording betokens some worthwhile occupation, before we quickly understand that this is not so. It is the bitterly facetious expansion of a circumlocution that is usually used all too tolerantly. Similar wordiness accompanies Dickens's recourse to a cliché to characterise the breath-taking self-delusion of Silas Wegg in *Our Mutual Friend*, when, resenting Mr Rokesmith's advancement to the role of 'secretary' to Mr Boffin, he tells Mr Venus of his deceitfulness. Even Dickens, a connoisseur of hypocrisy, is amazed.

> See into what wonderful maudlin refuges, featherless ostriches plunge their heads! It is such unspeakable moral compensation to Wegg, to be overcome by the consideration that Mr Rokesmith has an underhanded mind!
>
> (II Ch. VII)

There is the ordinary thought of burying your head in the sand under all this, but Wegg's evasion of the truth merits a more elaborate phrasing.

Wegg is a bad-hearted rogue, a street vendor who is recruited by the uneducated, suddenly wealthy Mr Boffin as 'a literary man' to read to him (I Ch. V). The text will be Gibbon's monumental *Decline and Fall of the Roman Empire*, which the illiterate Mr Boffin has bought (in eight volumes) at a sale. Boffin discovers a relish for it. He has got into the habit of visiting Wegg, where he has been installed in Boffin's former home, the Bower, 'and would there, on the old settle, pursue the downward fortunes of those enervated and corrupted masters of the world who were by this time on their last legs' (II Ch. VII). The cliché comes in to cap the verbally inflated sentence that leads up to it, performing the incongruity that it describes. All the better as the reader, Wegg, himself has only one leg.

Wegg believes that he has discovered an alternate will, by which the dead Harmon has left his fortune not to Mr and Mrs Boffin but to the Crown. He will blackmail his patron with this discovery. The chapter detailing Wegg's scheme is headed 'Mr Wegg Prepares a Grindstone for Mr Boffin's Nose' (III Ch. XIV). The heading is taken from the cliché used with malicious relish by Wegg himself, as he unfolds his plan to Mr Venus, whom he believes to be his stooge. 'I consider his planting one of his menial tools in the yard, an act of sneaking and sniffing. And his nose shall be put to the grindstone for it.' He insists on the saying, 'his nose shall be put to the grindstone ... let it be fully understood that I shall not neglect bringing the grindstone to bear, nor yet bringing Dusty Boffin's nose to it.' Mr Boffin later asks Mr Venus if Wegg will 'turn to at the grindstone' and receives confirmation. 'Mr Boffin took his nose in his hand, as if it were already excoriated, and the sparks were beginning to fly out of that feature.'

It is the cliché that Wegg uses to torment Mr Boffin. 'Silas made no reply, but laboured with a will at turning an imaginary grindstone outside the keyhole, while Mr Boffin stooped at it within'(IV Ch. III). The narrative is as addicted to the cliché as Wegg himself, but his relish is hubristic. 'Of late, the grindstone did undoubtedly appear to have been whirling at his own nose rather than Boffin's' (IV Ch. XIV).

A rogue likes to cling to a cliché. In the mouth of Jonas Chuzzlewit, the well-worn phrase is a jocular transformation of shady practice into common parlance. He tells Mr Pecksniff that he and his father, having travelled to Salisbury for a family gathering, had tarried there 'watching the sale of certain eligible investments, which they had had in their copartnership eye when they came down ... It was their custom, Mr Jonas said, whenever such a thing was practicable, to kill two birds with one stone, and never to throw away sprats, but as bait for whales' (Ch. VIII). Mr Pecksniff, to whom he communicates 'these pithy scraps of intelligence', is enlightened not at all, the point of the clichés being to conceal villainous proceedings. In *Bleak House* the vampire lawyer Vholes seizes one particular cliché as the sign of his dedication to the cause of his client, Richard Carstone. 'Personally, or by letter, you will always find me here, sir, with my shoulder to the wheel' (Ch. XXXIX). In fact, he is encouraging Richard to pursue the futile suit in order to fleece him. The cliché is all too readily echoed by Richard.

> 'But it is some satisfaction, in the midst of my troubles and perplexities, to know that I am pressing Ada's interests in pressing my own. Vholes has his shoulder

to the wheel, and he cannot help urging it on as much
for her as for me, thank God!'

(Ch. XLV)

Vholes uses it again when speaking to Allan Woodcourt,
uniting it with a platitude about labour, as if he were a
simple man honestly exerting himself.

'I take every opportunity of openly stating to a friend
of Mr C. how Mr C. is situated. As to myself, sir, the
labourer is worthy of his hire. If I undertake to put my
shoulder to the wheel, I do it, and I earn what I get.
I am here for that purpose.'

(Ch. LI)

More knowing is *David Copperfield's* Uriah Heep, creator
of a kind of cliché with his 'very umble' refrain. He lets
us see, but also acknowledges, the origins of his hypocrisy
when he tells David how he first learnt to fake humility,
mimicking his deceit with the use of a cliché. ' "When
I was quite a young boy," said Uriah, "I got to know what
umbleness did, and I took to it. I ate umble pie with an
appetite" '(Ch. XXXIX).

Not only rogues rely on these tired turns of phrase.
What could be more tired than Lady Dedlock's self-
description in Chapter II of *Bleak House*, where she first
says she has been 'bored to death'. Yet even the first-time
reader of the first instalment in March 1852 would have
known from her impulsive question about the papers that
Mr Tulkinghorn has brought, from 'my Lady's animation
and her unusual tone', then from her sudden faintness,
that she is concealing something. At the chapter's
end, her husband repeats her complaint to explain her

unaccountable swoon: 'she really has been bored to death down at our place in Lincolnshire'. Now we know that 'bored to death' explains nothing. Dickens cannot shake off the formulaic phrase. Mr Tulkinghorn, we are told in Chapter X, is 'speechlessly at home in country-houses where the great ones of the earth are bored to death'. Speechless because he is watching for and storing up secrets, and will be the first to know when boredom is a screen.

The cliché is Lady Dedlock's occupation, her *hauteur*, but also her disguise. She leaves France to return to England with Sir Leicester and cannot escape that proclaimed boredom. 'Sooth to say, they cannot go away too fast, for even here my Lady Dedlock has been bored to death. Concert, assembly, opera, theatre, drive, nothing is new to my Lady under the worn-out heavens.' We infer that the cliché, incontrovertible because so easily repeated, is a disguise. 'Lady Dedlock is always the same exhausted deity, surrounded by worshippers, and terribly liable to be bored to death, even while presiding at her own shrine' (Ch. XII). A tired phrase for her display of tiredness: enervation is Lady Dedlock's way of hiding all her feelings and all her fears.

Dickens allows other characters to share his relish for clichés and his faith in their vigour. In the very first instalment of Dickens's first novel we encounter, outside a London coach-yard, a 'rather tall, thin young man in a green coat' who knows the art of spinning from one cliché to another. He intervenes to deal with a belligerent cab driver, who has accused Pickwick of being an 'informer':

'Here, No. 924, take your fare, and take yourself off—respectable gentleman—know him well—none of your nonsense—this way, sir—where's your friends?—all a mistake, I see—never mind—accidents will happen—best regulated families—never say die— down upon your luck—Pull him *up*—Put that in his pipe—like the flavour—damned rascals.'

The clichés brook no contradiction. The young man, who will turn out to be the resourceful charlatan Alfred Jingle, has any number of them he can string aptly together.

Incongruity is the thing. Jenny Wren in *Our Mutual Friend* looks for more words for her alcoholic father, and jars Shakespeare against a cliché. 'He'd be sharper than a serpent's tooth, if he wasn't as dull as ditch water.' King Lear's bitter words are too good for him, so she returns him to the dullness of that colourless old simile. The inventive use of clichés can earn our trust. In his final uncovering of Casby in *Little Dorrit*, his one-time operative, Pancks, uses cliché to sardonic effect to reveal the fraudulence of Casby's apparent benignity. Addressing the denizens of Bleeding Heart Yard, whose rents Casby employed him to extract, he announces,

> He is uncommonly improving to look at, and I am not at all so. He is as sweet as honey, and I am as dull as ditch-water. He provides the pitch, and I handle it, and it sticks to me.
>
> (II Ch. XXXII)

Sententious formulae throng the language, so it is hardly surprising that those who wish to sound worldly-wise should creatively mangle them. In *Martin Chuzzlewit*, the grotesque Mrs Gamp, alcoholic attendant equally on birth and death, concedes to Mr Mould that she wishes to take up a 'night-watching' job because she needs the money. 'Rich folks may ride on camels, but it an't so easy for 'em to see out of a needle's eye. That is my comfort, and I hope I knows it.' The second sentence triumphantly seals the comedy, as Mrs Gamp self-approvingly nods at the truthfulness of her bizarrely reconstituted biblical idiom. Her confidence in her expressiveness is complete. She wonderfully scrambles a bit of the Bible again in what Patrick McCarthy admires as 'the double-cliché zigzag she manages' with 'if I may make so bold as speak so plain of what is plain enough to them as needn't look through millstones, Mrs Todgers, to find out wot is wrote upon the wall behind.'[13]

It is almost beyond paraphrase. Her speech is replete with twisted biblical proverbs, from her 'Piljians Projiss of a mortal wale' to being 'led a Martha to the Stakes for it'. She seems to have a kind of power over the narrative voice, so that when it tackles her it comes up with a cliché that takes wing. 'She added daily so many strings to her bow, that she made a perfect harp of it; and upon that instrument she now began to perform an extemporaneous concerto' (Ch. XLVI).

Dickens's love of clichés seems to have been transfused into the speech of some of his characters. Such is surely the case with Sampson Brass in *The Old Curiosity Shop*, a rogue who turns to the poetry of hackneyed phrases when finally he gets his comeuppance. Once he abetted the villain of the novel, Quilp, but, now supposedly penitent, he displays his true humanity by stringing together some slightly adapted clichés.

'Now, gentlemen, I am not a man who does things by halves. Being in for a penny, I am ready, as the saying is, to be in for a pound. You must do with me what you please, and take me where you please. If you wish to have this in writing, we'll reduce it into manuscript immediately. You will be tender with me, I am sure. I am quite confident you will be tender with me. You are men of honour, and have feeling hearts. I yielded from necessity to Quilp, for though necessity has no law, she has her lawyers. I yield to you from necessity too; from policy besides; and because of feelings that have been a pretty long time working within me. Punish Quilp, gentlemen. Weigh heavily upon him. Grind him down. Tread him under foot. He has done as much by me, for many and many a day.'

(Ch. LXVI)

What more is there to say than what someone has often said before?

Speaking

Talk, Talk, Talk.

Note in collection of 'Memoranda'[1]

In *Bleak House*, a makeshift coroner's court convenes to pass judgement on the death of the impoverished law writer who called himself Nemo. It sits in an upstairs room of the Sol's Arms, the public house adjacent to the miserable lodgings where Nemo lived and died. It is the same room, the narrator tells us, where, twice a week, 'Harmonic Meetings' take place, featuring 'little Swills, the comic vocalist' (Ch. XI). What are these oddly named gatherings? Dickens describes a 'Harmonic Meeting' in a very early piece of journalism, 'The Streets – Night', published in a popular weekly paper.[2] Very late, after the theatre-goers and diners have gone home, up to a hundred guests gather in the upper room of a public house, where a master of ceremonies presides and singers entertain the boisterous crowd with glees and comic songs. Such alcohol-fuelled nocturnal entertainments in rooms in taverns were popular from the 1830s.

Little Swills, we hear, does songs, but specialises in impersonations. Living by vocal mockery, he is wise to the daytime drama taking place in his usual venue, realising that it is likely to present him with some rewarding new material. Once the court has convened,

> sensation is created by the entrance of a chubby little man in a large shirt-collar, with a moist eye and an inflamed nose, who modestly takes a position near the door as one of the general public, but seems familiar with the room too.

This is Little Swills in person. It is thought by the assembled locals that it is 'not unlikely that he will get up an imitation of the coroner' for the evening's performance. They know their man. Once the inquest is over ('Verdict accordingly. Accidental death'), Little Swills duly turns the recent proceedings into an act.

> In the zenith of the evening, Little Swills says, 'Gentlemen, if you'll permit me, I'll attempt a short description of a scene of real life that came off here to-day.' Is much applauded and encouraged; goes out of the room as Swills; comes in as the coroner (not the least in the world like him); describes the inquest, with recreative intervals of piano-forte accompaniment, to the refrain: With his (the coroner's) tippy tol li doll, tippy tol lo doll, tippy tol li doll, Dee!
>
> (Ch. XI)

The landlord of the Sol's Arms, hoping that more customers will be allured to his hostelry by this performer, vaunts his vocal adaptability, declaring that 'that man's character-wardrobe would fill a cart'. Little Swills, ready to take off the pompous accents of officialdom, is a rather less competent version of Dickens himself. Like the novelist, he finds comedy in the midst of the bleakest narrative. Into the dark pages of this novel he strolls to mimic the supposedly solemn legal proceedings surrounding a desperate man's premature death. He provides a facetious descant to the unfolding of a tragedy. Little Swills, the 'comic vocalist', like his creator, holds his audience's attention by adopting different voices.

Famously, T. S. Eliot once proposed taking for the title of the poem that became *The Waste Land*, an admiring comment from *Our Mutual Friend* about a reader's ability to perform the vocal variety implicit on the printed page. The semi-literate Betty Higden is wondering at the ability of her foundling assistant, Sloppy, to do dramatic justice to characters quoted in newspaper crime reports:

> 'For I aint, you must know,' said Betty, 'much of a hand at reading writing-hand, though I can read my Bible and most print. And I do love a newspaper. You mightn't think it, but Sloppy is a beautiful reader of a newspaper. He do the Police in different voices.'
>
> (I Ch. XVI)

'He do the Police in different voices' was to have been the title for Eliot's poem of many voices. Sloppy has the basic skill of a reader-aloud, a reader for whom Dickens scores his dialogue. He differentiates different characters through the ways in which they speak. This skill is essential to the plotting of the novel: at the behest of Mr Rokesmith, Sloppy becomes a spy on the scheming Silas Wegg, disguised as a dustman and aided by his vocal adaptability. 'He never thought as I used to give Mrs Higden the Police-news in different voices!' (IV Ch. XIV).

Dickens was fascinated by performers who could do different voices. As a young man he became addicted to the comic 'At Home' entertainments staged by Charles Mathews, who specialised in mini-dramas in which he took every part. Dickens was later to tell Forster that, when he was working as a shorthand writer at Doctor's Commons, he would go to the theatre almost every night, 'and always to see Mathews whenever he played'.[3] The one-man show, featuring a performer skilled in mimicry of well-known personalities or character types, was an established form of theatrical entertainment by the early nineteenth century.[4] Mathews was an actor who made his reputation as an imitator, first of all of other actors. In his forties, he developed a show in which anecdotes and songs culminated in a farcical drama in which he played all the roles. This was called a 'monopolylogue' (a word that he evidently coined). His 'At Home' was a huge success and new shows, following the same format, followed in subsequent years. The typical bill of entertainment for the show that opened in April 1830 ended with a monopolylogue entitled 'The Lone House' in which Mathews played a (female) deaf housekeeper, a butler and two visiting gentlemen. A contemporary wrote,

> The tip-top parts are capitally done—*Charles* does them;—the secondary parts are capitally done—*Charles* does them too;—the low parts are magnificently done—*Charles* does them too![5]

The reviewer gives us some idea of his characters. One of those on the bill is Mrs Neverend, who 'speaks in monotony, who despises colons and semi-colons and never in her life could be induced to make use of a full-stop'.[6] It is clear from the vignettes of some of Mathews's other characters that each has his or her special way of speaking. There is the energetic and omnivorous hypochondriac Squire Sadjolly, 'whose heart is wasted, whose lungs are worn out, whose liver is shrivelled'. Next comes 'the portly gourmand *Mr Dyspeps*' who 'soliloquises on pie-crust'. Or we might listen to the self-important Chairman of the Cork-cutters, whose discourse is distinguished by 'the expressive lapses, the magnificent *aposiopesis*, the Ciceronian "hems" and the Demosthenian "hahs"'. Like a certain kind of modern TV comic, Mathews created and inhabited a cast of representative yet singular characters. He had to distinguish them mostly by voice and facial expression (though he also used props and quick changes of costume). What one reviewer, admiring his range of idiolects, called his 'Proteus mouth' was his greatest power.[7]

'Mathews always scorned to be called a mimic, and, in fact, the name was below him. He was a mimetic genius, an imitative original.'[8] His powers fascinated the young Dickens. Years later, Dickens told Forster that Mathews had made him yearn for a career on the stage.

When I was about twenty, and knew three or four successive years of Mathews's At Homes from sitting in the pit to hear them, I wrote to Bartley who was stage manager at Covent-garden, and told him how young I was, and exactly what I thought I could do; and that I believed I had a strong perception of character and oddity, and a natural power of reproducing in my own person what I observed in others.

Bartley invited him to an audition. 'Punctual to the time, another letter came: with an appointment to do anything of Mathews's I pleased, before him and Charles Kemble, on a certain day at the theatre.'[9] As a test of his skills, the stage-hungry young Dickens was to mimic Mathews's mimicry. In the event, a heavy cold and facial inflammation prevented him from keeping the appointment. He would, it was agreed, try again the next season – by which time he had achieved such success as a parliamentary reporter that he no longer thought of the stage.

Some contemporaries recognised that Dickens's creation of voices was like that of the famous monopolyloguist. A review of *Bleak House* in the *Spectator* in 1853 deplored the author's habit of finding his own characters 'excessively funny', observing that 'Skimpole must be constructed with an especial eye to the genius of Mr Charles Matthews'.[10] Though meant disparagingly, the analogy was discerning. Just as Mathews had to use mainly speech habits to distinguish his characters, Dickens needed unique voices – idiolects, as linguists call them – to make each of his characters singular.[11] The serial form of his novels required it. In the third monthly instalment of *Pickwick Papers*, Mr Pickwick and his companions are to witness the cricket match between All-Muggleton and Dingley Dell. Mr Pickwick steps into a marquee at the side of the cricket field and hears someone speaking. ' "Capital game—smart sport—fine exercise—very," were the words which fell upon Mr Pickwick's ear as he entered the tent' (Ch. VII).

He and we know the voice: 'there was no mistaking him'. We met him in the very first instalment of the novel, speaking a staccato idiolect that brooks no interruption. The Pickwickians find that he is travelling on the same coach to Rochester as them and he is soon warning them of the dangers of the low archway as they exit the coach yard.

> 'Terrible place—dangerous work—other day—five children—mother—tall lady, eating sandwiches—forgot the arch—crash—knock—children look round—mother's head off—sandwich in her hand—no mouth to put it in—head of a family off—shocking, shocking.'

'Shocking': just what someone says when he relishes the story he is telling. No voice could be more distinctive.[12] No sooner heard than recognised.

Some considerable time later, during the foray to Kent, the stranger finally announces his name to Pickwick. 'Jingle—Alfred Jingle, Esq., of No Hall, Nowhere' (Ch. VII). He is, it turns out, a kind of con man. Now that we have his voice, we keep meeting him. During Mr Pickwick's trip to Eatanswill in Suffolk, he is invited to Mrs Leo Hunter's fancy dress *fête champêtre* where he encounters a notable guest, a certain Mr Charles Fitz-Marshall, who arrives late. ' "Coming, my dear Ma'am," cried a voice, "as quick as I can—crowds of people—full room—hard work—very" ' (Ch. XV). Here he is again! That comically abbreviated, staccato idiolect. 'Mr Pickwick's knife and fork fell from his hand.' Jingle, seeing Pickwick, makes a swift exit. Later, on a trip to Ipswich, Pickwick and Sam Weller confront Jingle, who has won the admiration of the local magistrate, Mr Nupkins, and his readily deceived wife and daughter. What stops Nupkins detaining him and his roguish sidekick, Job Trotter? Jingle has his answer.

> Wouldn't do—no go—caught a captain, eh?—ha! ha! very good—husband for daughter—biter bit—make it public—not for worlds—look stupid—very!
>
> (Ch. XXV)

We might guess where Pickwick and he are destined to meet for the last time: the Fleet Prison. Pickwick has been incarcerated for refusing to pay compensation to Mrs Bardell for supposed breach of promise; Jingle (with Job Trotter) is in prison for debt. When he first sees Pickwick, Jingle is muted but still aurally distinctive. 'Mr——! So it is—queer place—strange thing—serves me right—very' (Ch. XLII).

Dickens forges an idiolect to thrust a character before us. As his fellow novelist George Gissing observed, with a mixture of deprecation and admiration, 'for twenty months did these characters of favourite fiction make a periodical appearance, and not the most stupid man in England forgot them between one month and the next'.[13] The constraints of serial fiction obliged him to think about an experience that is familiar to all of us: meeting a person you have met before and finding them to be just the same. In the penultimate chapter of *Nicholas Nickleby*, Nicholas and his sister Kate are walking near Seven Dials, talking with happy complacency of their respective fiancés. In a side street they pause to ask their way when they hear the sound of 'a noise of scolding in a woman's voice' from a nearby cellar. It is an interesting marital dispute.

'You nasty, idle, vicious, good-for-nothing brute,' cried the woman, stamping on the ground, 'why don't you turn the mangle?'

'So I am, my life and soul!' replied the man's voice. 'I am always turning. I am perpetually turning, like a demd old horse in a demnition mill. My life is one demd horrid grind!'

Listening with Nicholas and Kate, we recognise as well as they do the doggedly amorous endearment and the insistent mispronunciation of 'damned' and 'damnation', rising from beneath the London pavement. One more interchange confirms it.

'Then why don't you go and list for a soldier?' retorted the woman; 'you're welcome to.'

'For a soldier!' cried the man. 'For a soldier! Would his joy and gladness see him in a coarse red coat with a little tail? Would she hear of his being slapped and beat by drummers demnebly? Would she have him fire off real guns, and have his hair cut, and his whiskers shaved, and his eyes turned right and left, and his trousers pipeclayed?'

(Ch. LXIV)

Kate is rightly confident that it is Mr Mantalini, foppish and feckless husband of the milliner Madame Mantalini, for whom she once worked. When we last saw him, he had just been disowned by his long-suffering and now property-less wife, despite appealing to her softer nature with a fake suicide bid. We should have known that he was destined to attach himself to another woman.

When the reader met Mr Mantalini for the first time in the third monthly instalment of the novel, Kate Nickleby had been taken by her uncle, Ralph Nickleby, to Madame Mantalini's premises. On being admitted, they are greeted by Mr Mantalini, with his first words, 'uttered in a mincing tone'. 'Demmit. What, Nickleby! oh, demit!' (Ch. X). There he is. Two instalments later, Kate arrives for her first day working for Madame Mantalini and it is the husband's voice that we recognise through a partition wall. 'If you will be odiously, demnebly, outrigeously jealous, my soul,' said Mr Mantalini, 'you will be very miserable—horrid miserable—demnition miserable' (Ch. XVII). He has been caught flirting with other women, again. Affecting devotion to Madame Mantalini, he is forever wheedling and flattering his way back into her favour after some amorous escapade or pecuniary outrage (his lavish spending eventually ruins her business). His older wife has been taken in by his elaborately maintained appearance of raffish allure. 'He had married on his whiskers; upon which property he had previously subsisted, in a genteel manner, for some years' (Ch. X).

His voice goes before him. The eleventh monthly instalment of the novel begins with the chapter heading 'Wherein Mr Ralph Nickleby is visited by Persons with whom the Reader has been already made acquainted'; it opens directly with one of them speaking. 'What a demnition long time you have kept me ringing at this confounded old cracked tea-kettle of a bell, every tinkle of which is enough to throw a strong man into blue convulsions, upon my life and soul, oh demmit' (Ch. XXXIV). The novel's first readers last encountered Mr Mantalini and heard him speak in the opening chapter of the eighth instalment, some five months of real time earlier. But, like us, they will have recognised him immediately. His way of speaking – exclamatory, *faux* indignant, extravagantly affectionate to his wife when he has offended her – is an occupational necessity for this dedicated scrounger. It is also his doom. When we last see him in that cellar, wedded to a woman considerably more formidable than the wronged Madame Mantalini, he has just caught sight of Kate and is hiding in his bed, giving the novel his appropriate final words. 'Shut the door, put out the candle, turn me up in the bedstead! Oh, dem, dem, dem!' As the Nicklebys leave that voice behind them, Mr Mantalini is being battered some more by his ferocious new paramour.

This recognition of voices is a binding principle of Dickens's fiction. In his book *Idiolects in Dickens*, Robert Golding rightly singles out the opening chapter of the second part ('Riches') of *Little Dorrit* as a virtuoso demonstration of this. Three parties of travellers have arrived for the night at the convent of the Great Saint Bernard in the Alps. With one exception, none of them is named by the narrator. The exception is a character whom we have not met before called 'Mrs General', an 'elderly lady, who was a model of accurate dressing, and whose manner was perfect, considered as a piece of machinery'. She is evidently an officious companion to two young ladies in one of the parties. As the other characters gather around the fire, they speak to each other and we begin to hear familiar voices. One gentleman makes an effort to converse, opening with some polite enquiries directed to the 'Chief' of the family group on which Mrs General attends.

'New to mountains, perhaps?' said the insinuating
traveller.

'New to—ha—to mountains,' said the Chief.

The second speaker's voice snags on something. We listen
for more.

'But you are familiar with them, sir?' the insinuating
traveller assumed.

'I am—hum—tolerably familiar. Not of late years.
Not of late years,' replied the Chief, with a flourish of
his hand.

We know this voice.

It can be none other than William Dorrit, whose odd
mid-sentence noises we first heard when Arthur Clennam
encountered him in the Marshalsea debtors' prison and was
told how visitors of any status would give him a 'Testimonial'.

'Sometimes,' he went on in a low, soft voice,
agitated, and clearing his throat every now and
then; 'sometimes—hem—it takes one shape and
sometimes another; but it is generally—ha—
Money. And it is, I cannot but confess it, it is too
often—hem—acceptable.'

(I Ch. VIII)

His little self-interruptions are his pretence of delicacy or
thoughtfulness. He speaks as if he is considerate of his
auditor's sensitivities. In fact, he is a practised sponger.
He imparts some false impression of thoughtfulness to his
banal responses with the same checks to his sentences that

we have heard before. In this chapter of this novel, Dickens is testing the reader's ear. As each one of the travellers speaks, we know the character. Who is the rather reserved and haughty young lady, who tells the same 'insinuating traveller' that 'the impossibility of bringing anything that one wants to this inaccessible place, and the necessity of leaving every comfort behind, is not convenient?' It has to be Fanny Dorrit, with her irritability and her pretentiously impersonal syntax. The young gentleman drawling that 'These fellows are an immense time with supper' must be her brother Tip (though now you must call him Edward). Sudden wealth has transformed the Dorrits from prison inmates to international travellers, but we know from their voices that their characters remain the same. The other young lady, silent until she offers water to a woman who has fainted, must be Amy Dorrit. The husband of this woman, who speaks with a kind of 'mocking inconsistency', must be the refined, shallow Henry Gowan; his 'insinuating' friend, who has a smooth word for everybody, can only be the novel's villain, call him what you will: Blandois, Lagnier, Rigaud. At the very end of the chapter, where we see the actual names of the characters recorded in the convent's visitors' book, we do not need the information. We have heard who they are.

Dickens made the invention of voices his business. His very breakthrough as a commercially successful writer came with the invention of a voice. It was the entrance of Sam Weller in the fourth monthly number of *Pickwick Papers* that turned Dickens's first novel into a bestseller and set his career going. As he cleans boots in the yard of the White Hart inn, Sam banters with a chambermaid, teases the landlady and tells Mr Jingle, a guest at the inn, how his widower father was gulled into a second marriage ('vhen

I gets on this here grievance, I runs on like a new barrow with the vheel greased') (Ch. X). Dickens's fellow clerk George Lear remembered, 'He could imitate, in a manner that I have never heard equalled, the low population of the streets of London in all their varieties, whether mere loafers or sellers of fruit, vegetables, or anything else'.[14] Sam Weller was the first of his verbally resourceful characters from 'the low population of London'. Sam's distinctive pronunciations might sound odd to the modern ear, but there is good evidence that the transposition of 'v' and 'w' ('Vy, that's just the wery point') was indeed a feature of contemporary working-class London dialect. Elocution teacher and former actor John Walker had deplored 'the peculiarities of my countrymen, the Cockneys' in his *A Critical Pronouncing Dictionary of the English Language* of 1791.[15] The second habitual fault in his list of the four major faults of Londoners is 'The pronunciation of *v* for *w*, and more frequently of *w* for *v*'. This is 'a blemish of the first magnitude'.[16] Henry Mayhew records the same peculiarity in his interview with a London dustman.[17]

The key word, which Sam shares with his father, is 'wery'. Dickens would later give this mispronunciation to a series of 'low' characters, from Dennis the hangman in *Barnaby Rudge* to Captain Cuttle in *Dombey and Son* to Jo the crossing sweeper in *Bleak House*. But no one uses it as frequently as the Wallers, *père et fils*. It was a supposedly cockney pronunciation that Dickens would sometimes adopt in bantering letters to friends. Writing to Forster in March 1839, about a visit to the actor Charles Kean, he wrote, 'Charles Kean is gone, and I have moved into his sitting room. I am sitting at this instant in his wery chair!!!'[18] Complimenting illustrator George Cruikshank in 1840 on his recently published *Omnibus* periodical, he joked about its title. 'It is wery light, wery easy on the springs, well horsed, driv in a slap up style, and altogether an uncommon spicy con-sarn.'[19] He carried on with it through the years. His letters to friends like *Punch* editor Mark Lemon are in the habit of adopting a cockney voice. 'I am wery sorry you have been and gone and asked those two men.'[20] He expected the recipients of these letters to recognise the accent.

This was not exactly a matter of being true to a particular dialect, as novelists like Emily Brontë and George Eliot would attempt. Dickens did occasionally dabble in dialect. In *Nicholas Nickleby* a Yorkshire coachman is given dialect almost as demanding as Joseph in *Wuthering Heights*. 'Hoold 'em toight ... while ar coot treaces. Dang 'em, they'll gang whoam fast eneaf' (Ch. VI). The effort to transcribe a Yorkshire dialect is pursued further with the appearances of John Browdie in that novel (Ch. IX). Before writing the Yarmouth chapters of *David Copperfield*, Dickens conscientiously read Edward Moor's *Suffolk Words and Phrases* (1823) in order to help with the voices of the Peggottys.[21] But his triumph with Sam Weller was to combine a small number of cockney pronunciations with certain rhythms of phrasing that are distinctive of the character. Sam Weller's most expressive idiosyncrasy is the 'wellerism', where the application of a phrase is given a new zest by being incongruously attributed to some imagined speaker. (The idea of a 'wellerism' is recorded by the *OED* from the late 1830s.) When we first meet Sam cleaning those boots, we find that he has arranged them by room number and intends to get through them in 'reg'lar rotation, as Jack Ketch said, ven he tied the men up' (Ch. X). The reference to England's most famous executioner, dealing with his victims in their proper order, is characteristic: there is always incongruity and often black humour in Sam's attributions.

> 'It's over, and can't be helped, and that's one consolation, as they always says in Turkey, ven they cuts the wrong man's head off.'
>
> (Ch. XXIII)

A tired idiom is jolted into comic life. 'Business first, pleasure arterwards, as King Richard the Third said when he stabbed the t'other king in the Tower, afore he smothered the babbies' (Ch. XXV). Dickens's contemporaries seemed ready to accept that these were examples of what one reviewer called the 'unadulterated vernacular idioms of the lower classes'.[22] Yet if Sam gets his worldly wisdom from the streets, it includes an odd seasoning of erudition. When he tells Pickwick that a man wishes to see him, he cannot resist a literary flourish. 'He wants you partickler; and no one else 'll do, as the devil's private secretary said ven he fetched avay Doctor Faustus' (Ch. XV). When the Pickwick party stops to change horses at Coventry on a gloomy wet day, Bob Sawyer marvels at Sam's good spirits and gets a just reply.

> 'Wotever is, is right, as the young nobleman sweetly remarked wen they put him down in the pension list 'cos his mother's uncle's vife's grandfather vunce lit the king's pipe with a portable tinder-box.'
>
> (Ch. L)

The socially subversive analogy almost prevents you hearing that Sam is quoting Alexander Pope's *Essay on*

Man at the beginning of the sentence. But then he is cleverer than anyone else in the company.

Everyone who appears in *Pickwick Papers* has his or her singular habits of speech, from Mr Peter Magnus ('Pickwick; very good. I like to know a man's name, it saves so much trouble. That's my card, sir. Magnus, you will perceive, sir—Magnus is my name. It's rather a good name, I think, sir') to Angelo Bantam ('Welcome to Ba— ath, Sir. This is indeed an acquisition. Most welcome to Ba—ath, sir. It is long—very long, Mr Pickwick, since you drank the waters. It appears an age, Mr Pickwick. Re-markable!') to the 'fierce gentleman' encountered at a coaching inn ('I withdraw my expressions. I tender an apology. There's my card. Give me your acquaintance'). You can hear Dickens trying out his gift for idiolect, like the comic vocalist he once aspired to be. He gave his attention to the ways in which a character dramatises him- or herself. Of course, this includes actual actors. As George Lear recalled, more than fifty years later, Dickens could 'give us Shakespeare by the ten minutes, and imitate all the leading actors of the time'.[23] Yet he did not only learn from the stage. As a young reporter at Doctor's Commons and then a reporter on debates in Parliament, Dickens was used to hearing not just people speaking but also people making speeches. This is what some of the characters in *Pickwick Papers* like to do. Mr Pott, the political journalist from Suffolk, is a dedicated speechifier, who shrivels into domestic obsequiousness in the presence of his wife. Encountered unexpectedly in an inn in Towcester, he sets off on the oral equivalent of his most recent leader article (Ch. L).

In other cases, we actually get speeches. Mr Anthony Humm, president of the Brick Lane Branch of the

United Grand Junction Ebenezer Temperance Association, addresses the ladies at the monthly meeting with a
descriptive catalogue of some recent 'converts to
Temperance'.

> Henry Beller was for many years toast-master at various
> corporation dinners, during which time he drank a
> great deal of foreign wine; may sometimes have carried
> a bottle or two home with him; is not quite certain of
> that, but is sure if he did, that he drank the contents.
> Feels very low and melancholy, is very feverish, and has
> a constant thirst upon him; thinks it must be the wine
> he used to drink (cheers). Is out of employ now; and
> never touches a drop of foreign wine by any chance
> (tremendous plaudits).
>
> (Ch. XXXIII)

When Pickwich is tried for breach of promise, the opening
speech for the plaintiff is made by Sergeant Buzfuz in a
spirit of shameless theatricality, aping high-mindedness.

> But Pickwick, gentlemen, Pickwick, the ruthless
> destroyer of this domestic oasis in the desert of Goswell
> Street—Pickwick who has choked up the well, and
> thrown ashes on the sward—Pickwick, who comes
> before you to-day with his heartless tomato sauce and
> warming-pans—Pickwick still rears his head with
> unblushing effrontery, and gazes without a sigh on
> the ruin he has made. Damages, gentlemen—heavy
> damages is the only punishment with which you can
> visit him …
>
> (Ch. XXXIV)

More than any other novelist, Dickens was fascinated by speakers who love speaking, speakers for whom speech provides the purest form of self-assertion. A character's manner of speech is less a way of communicating than of unleashing the self.

George Henry Lewes recalled in an article written shortly after the novelist's death, 'Dickens once declared to me that every word said by his characters was distinctly *heard* by him.'[24] To catch the speech habits of some of the characters we are required to hear them too – and to hear their pretensions and follies as they trip over words. In *Pickwick Papers*, Dickens was already delighting in the selective mispronunciations of self-important characters, who get wrong the very words to which they attach most significance. The ridiculous Ipswich magistrate Mr Nupkins has an even more ridiculous subordinate called Grummer who, when first addressed, replies 'Your wash-up' (Ch. XXIV). Obsequious to a fault, Grummer repeatedly addresses his superior as 'your wash-up'; only the reader notices the unintended mockery. Dickens is rehearsing for Mr Bumble, the officious beadle in *Oliver Twist*, who announces himself through one or two favoured mispronunciations. Here are his very first words in the novel, when he arrives at the house of the baby farmer, Mrs Mann, and finds himself unable to open her garden gate.

'Do you think this respectful or proper conduct, Mrs Mann,' inquired Mr Bumble, grasping his cane, 'to keep the parish officers a waiting at your garden-gate, when they come here upon porochial business with the porochial orphans? Are you aweer, Mrs Mann,

that you are, as I may say, a porochial delegate, and a
stipendiary?'

(Ch. II)

'Aweer' is a passing peculiarity, but, as we might infer
from its use three times in his first utterance, 'porochial'
is habitual and beloved. The mispronunciation speaks
Bumble's self-importance and love of his own voice.
He uses the word so often that it has become his alone.
It rings in his pronouncements through the rest of the
novel. Bumble's idiolect has other little mispronunciations
('fondlings' for 'foundlings' is deliciously inappropriate),
but 'porochial', the word for the supposed dignity of his
office, is his only consistent error. Asked by Mr Grimwig
if he is a beadle, he replies 'proudly', 'I am a porochial
beadle, gentlemen' (Ch. XVII). His status is nothing
without that Bumble-ised adjective. He clings to it at the
end of the novel, when Mr Brownlow and Mr Grimwig
confront him with the evidence of his nefariousness. 'I
hope that this unfortunate little circumstance will not
deprive me of my porochial office?' (Ch. LI)

A single mis-spoken word can do it. In *Bleak House*,
the evangelical fraud Mr Chadband, preaching at the
uncomprehending Jo, seems to have just one small
mispronunciation, which we hear when he declares, 'you
are delivered over untoe me'. He announces to his small
group of believers that the boy is a 'precious instrument',
which he will employ 'toe your advantage, toe your profit,
toe your gain, toe your welfare, toe your enrichment!'
Everyone should be able to hear that there is something
wrong with what Chadband is saying. It is a bit of grit in
the machinery of his well-greased eloquence. Chadband's
peroration mounts up and up to its climax, which is

another common word made strange, as he announces that
Jo has been deprived of 'the light of Terewth' (Ch. XXV).
And 'Terewth', the end point of each following paragraph,
is what he goes on to celebrate – a value made almost
unrecognisable by this oily hypocrite. Mispronunciation is
always comic in Dickens, but not necessarily contemptible.
Mr Sleary the circus master in *Hard Times*, with 'a voice (if
it can be called so) like the efforts of a broken old pair of
bellows', turns mispronunciation into a rebellion against
utilitarian conformity. When he first appears and addresses
Mr Gradgrind, his lisp is like language let loose in a world
of grim constraints.

> 'Thquire!' said Mr Sleary, who was troubled with
> asthma, and whose breath came far too thick and heavy
> for the letters, 'Your thervant! Thith ith a bad piethe of
> bithnith, thith ith. You've heard of my Clown and hith
> dog being thuppothed to have morrithed?'

He is respectful enough, but 'Thquire!' and 'your thervant!'
will always sound like a joke against submissiveness. The
motto of Sleary's philosophy, dispensed to the unheeding
Gradgrind at the chapter's end, is memorable because
so subversively mis-spoken. 'People must be amuthed,
Thquire, thomehow' (I Ch. VI).

Dickens can do the trick of characterisation with one
aural glitch. In *Nicholas Nickleby* we meet Miss Knag,
'marvellously loquacious and marvellously deferential to
Madame Mantalini' (Ch. XVII). She has a vocal tic:

> you have so much taste in all those matters, that really,
> as I often say to the young ladies, I do not know how,
> when, or where, you possibly could have acquired all

you know—hem—Miss Nickleby and I are quite a pair, Madame Mantalini, only I am a little darker than Miss Nickleby, and—hem—I think my foot may be a little smaller.

Her speech is distinguished by her signature self-interruption, 'a loud, shrill, clear "hem!" the import and meaning of which, was variously interpreted by her acquaintance'. Perhaps each 'hem!' is the herald of one of her inventive exaggerations? Perhaps it is what she throws into a sentence when she runs out of words, 'to gain time, and prevent anybody else from striking into the conversation'? Who knows? Dickens himself seems hardly sure. Miss Knag's non-verbal interjection is a precursor to the ludicrous, painful hesitations of William Dorritt, truly expressive of his moral evasiveness. They enable him to talk as if he were a thoughtful person rather than a self-deceiving one. Most painful are his manoeuvres to suborn his daughter Amy, the one person selflessly devoted to him, when he works out that she has not accepted the advances of the turnkey, John Chivery.

> Something, I—hem!—I don't know what, has gone wrong with Chivery. He is not—ha!—not nearly so obliging and attentive as usual to-night. It—hem!—it's a little thing, but it puts me out, my love.
>
> (I Ch. XIX)

The horrible truth is that he would have her marry Chivery so that he gets an easier time in prison. 'I—hem!—I can't think, Amy, what has given Chivery offence.' He is a liar, of course.

Perhaps those noises are signs that his deeply buried conscience is troubled? They certainly come thickest when he is admonishing his loving younger daughter. Suddenly made wealthy, he is dissatisfied by her failure to take pleasure in their new affluence.

> I have always made you a—hum—a friend and companion; in return, I beg—I—ha—I *do* beg, that you accommodate yourself better to—hum—circumstances, and dutifully do what becomes your—your station.
>
> (II Ch. V)

He becomes 'even a little more fragmentary than usual; being excited on the subject'. Contrariwise, only Mrs Merdle, the capitalist's wife, with her verbal parade of regard for his social status, can encourage him to lose his tic. Her unctuous assurances of her plutocratic husband's respect for the Dorrit clan act as 'a sedative on Mr Dorrit's cough' (II Ch. XV).

Dickens knew that the powers of speech are not exercised merely by words and sentences; he asks us to hear how speech is performed. In *Bleak House*, Mr Snagsby has not only his own idiolect, but also his versatile cough. 'Mr Snagsby, as a timid man, is accustomed to cough with a variety of expressions, and so to save words' (Ch. X). There is his 'deferential cough' (for Mr Tulkinghorn), his 'cough of mildness' (for Mrs Snagsby), his 'cough of sympathy' (when talking to Jo). He has any number of other coughs for different purposes. Speech is more than words. In *Martin Chuzzlewit*, Mrs Gamp, fraud of sentiment, gives a special intonation to one of the best-known interjections in English: 'Ah!' is her favourite exclamation in the face of the deaths that bring her employment.

> 'Ah!' repeated Mrs Gamp; for it was always a safe sentiment in cases of mourning. 'Ah dear! When Gamp was summoned to his long home, and I see him a-lying in Guy's Hospital with a penny-piece on each eye, and his wooden leg under his left arm, I thought I should have fainted away. But I bore up.'

'Ah' is the sound with which she pretends to experience a wave of feeling. In *Bleak House*, the baleful rag-and-bottle merchant Krook peppers his speech with his favourite exclamation: 'Hi!' 'Hi! Here's lovely hair!' he exclaims when he sees Ada, who has called at his shop with Esther and Richard. 'I have got three sacks of ladies' hair below, but none so beautiful and fine as this.' Esther describes his excitement when his cat jumps onto his shoulder. 'Hi! Show 'em how you scratch. Hi! Tear, my lady!' She leaps down and rips at a bundle of rags with her 'tigerish claws'(Ch. V). Krook's habitual 'Hi!' is emphatic and aggressive, a flourishing of the malign intent that does not quite find its way into the words that he uses.

To make speaking display character, Dickens alighted on elements of speech unconsidered in polite English. He saw that even when people used connected words, they were sometimes clinging to verbal formulae. In his 'At Homes', Charles Mathews usually featured one character who was distinguished by the repetition of a tell-tale phrase.[25] It may from this that Dickens learnt to distinguish a character by a talismanic phrase. We remember Fagin's 'my dear', insinuating and predatory, Uriah Heep's 'very 'umble' and 'too umble' and 'umbleness', like irritants upon the ear, or the 'portable property' that is Wemmick's motto in *Great Expectations*, his security in a dangerous world. Characters are distinguished by the words and phrases without which they would be lost. In *Little Dorrit*, Arthur Clennam arrives at Bleeding Heart Yard to find Plornish, the impoverished plasterer who knows the man to whom Amy Dorrit's brother is in debt.

> Was Mr Plornish at home? 'Well, sir,' said Mrs Plornish, a civil woman, 'not to deceive you, he's gone to look for a job.'
>   'Not to deceive you', was a method of speech with Mrs Plornish.
>
> (I Ch. XII)

Mrs Plornish never has the luxury of pretending things are better than they are, but 'not to deceive you' makes what she says seem a moment of candour. Dickens's most devoted reader, John Forster, knew that idiolect was Dickens's key to characterisation.

> There never was any one who had less need to talk about his characters, because never were characters so surely revealed by themselves; and it was thus their reality made itself felt at once. They talked so well that everybody took to repeating what they said … and the sayings being the constituent elements of the characters, these also of themselves became part of the public.[26]

Dickens wrote for the voice. He became a public performer of episodes from his novels, but he also used his voice while writing. His daughter Mamie famously remembered her father working on a new novel, making 'facial contortions' in a mirror and 'talking rapidly in a low voice' as 'with his natural intensity he had thrown himself completely into the character that he was creating' and become 'the creature of his pen'.[27] George Wooley recalled in an interview in 1938 (aged eighty-six) how he had, aged thirteen, worked for Dickens as a junior gardener.

> Opposite the house was a sort of wood the master called the Wilderness. He used to go over there to write … I used to hear what sounded like someone making a speech. I wondered what it was at first, and then I found out it was Mr Dickens composing his writing out loud. He was working on *The Mystery of Edwin Drood* then …[28]

When Dickens has to introduce a new character, he does so by introducing a new voice. But more than this: the character speaks him- or herself into being. Characters enjoy their own ways of speaking. In *The Old Curiosity Shop*, for instance, Daniel Quilp's speech patterns are thrillingly characteristic because they are elaborated with relish. When not employing the sarcastic politeness in which violence is always implicit, Quilp releases himself in delicious threats. With 'the boy' who is his *alter ego*, it is almost a sign of fellow feeling. 'I'll beat you with an iron rod, I'll scratch you with a rusty nail, I'll pinch your eyes, if you talk to me—I will' (Ch. V). When Kit and the boy fight, the sight inspires an ecstasy of threats.

> 'I'll beat you to a pulp, you dogs,' said Quilp, vainly endeavoring to get near either of them for a parting

blow. 'I'll bruise you until you're copper-coloured, I'll
break your faces till you haven't a profile between you,
I will.'

(Ch. VI)

Such pleasure does Quilp take in the making of threats
that he even threatens babies.

'Don't be frightened, mistress,' said Quilp, after a pause.
'Your son knows me; I don't eat babies; I don't like 'em.
It will be as well to stop that young screamer though, in
case I should be tempted to do him a mischief. Holloa,
sir! Will you be quiet?'

(Ch. XXI)

Dickens gives us some characters who enjoy speaking in
solitude, while we overhear. Major Bagstock in *Dombey
and Son* bursts into malign or triumphant 'ejaculations',
but only in the privacy of his own apartment (Ch. X).
' "But you won't catch Joe, Ma'am," said the Major. "He's
tough, Ma'am, tough, is J.B. Tough, and de-vilish sly!" '
(Ch. VII). He rejoices to know and describe himself in
his favourite phrase, 'Sly, Sir – sly, Sir – de-vil-ish sly!'
Whether in soliloquy or company, he always speaks of
himself in the third person. In the company of others, he
puts on a show of bluffness that is entirely disingenuous.

'Dombey,' said the Major, 'I'm glad to see you. I'm
proud to see you. There are not many men in Europe
to whom J. Bagstock would say that—for Josh is blunt.
Sir: it's his nature—but Joey B. is proud to see you,
Dombey.'

(Ch. XX)

As soon as he gets into his own company he can 'muse' out loud. When he recognises that Miss Tox hopes to marry the widower Mr Dombey, he congratulates himself on his perceptiveness. 'She's deep, Sir, deep, but Josh is deeper. Wide awake is old Joe—broad awake, and staring, Sir!' (Ch. X). One of the other leading frauds in Dickens's fiction, Harold Skimpole in *Bleak House*, similarly speaks of himself in the third person, with a kind of delight. Here he is as he is about to be arrested for debt.

> 'Now, my dear Miss Summerson, and my dear Mr Richard,' said Mr Skimpole gaily, innocently, and confidingly as he looked at his drawing with his head on one side, 'here you see me utterly incapable of helping myself, and entirely in your hands! I only ask to be free. The butterflies are free. Mankind will surely not deny to Harold Skimpole what it concedes to the butterflies!'
>
> (Ch. VI)

Dickens made us hear how people are enraptured by their own ways with words. From his father he learned the verbal pomposity that, in the character of Wilkins Micawber in *David Copperfield*, becomes a kind of buoyancy in the face of life's vicissitudes. Intermittently in his letters to Forster, Dickens will add to something he has written, 'or, as my father would say …' Thus, to Forster on 28 May 1844, 'Investigation below stairs renders it, as my father would say, "manifest to any person of ordinary intelligence, if the term may be considered allowable", that the Saturday's dinner cannot come off here with safety.'[29] Or, from Genoa in 1844 (telling Forster about the departure of an English physician):

> We are sorry to lose the benefit of his advice—or, as my
> father would say, to be deprived, to a certain extent,
> of the concomitant advantages, whatever they may
> be, resulting from his medical skill, such as it is, and
> his professional attendance, in so far as it may be so
> considered.[30]

Forster gave further examples of John Dickens's
orotundity in his *Life*, when discussing the background
to *David Copperfield*. Dickens was apparently delighted
when his father wrote of an acquaintance, 'And I must
express my tendency to believe that his longevity is (to say
the least of it) extremely problematical.'[31] This goes into
Micawber: you cannot beat him, when even the explanation
of a circumlocution ('our old and tried friend Copperfield
will, I am sure, forgive the momentary laceration of a
wounded spirit, made sensitive by a recent collision with
the Minion of Power') is another circumlocution '—in
other words, with a ribald Turncock attached to the water-
works' (Ch. XXVIII). As with Dickens's own father – a
man who failed socially and financially but could at least
confidently unroll his Latinate sentences – Micawber's
verbosity is the essence of his resilience.

Dickens loves characters who love speaking. When
Dick Swiveller in *The Old Curiosity Shop* asks his friend
Fred to pass the gin, it is with a swirl of words that goes
unappreciated by his companion: 'fan the sinking flame
of hilarity with the wing of friendship; and pass the rosy
wine' (Ch. VII). Dick lards his speech with fragments
from poetry and popular song, making the world a
little better than it is. He is another character for whom
eloquence is an addiction. For some it can be a kind of
madness. The elderly neighbour who woos Mrs Nickleby

with vegetables thrown over the garden fence assails her with a fantastic rhetoric. Why is beauty 'always obdurate'? he asks.

> 'Is it owing to the bees, who, when the honey season is over, and they are supposed to have been killed with brimstone, in reality fly to Barbary and lull the captive Moors to sleep with their drowsy songs? Or is it,' he added, dropping his voice almost to a whisper, 'in consequence of the statue at Charing Cross having been lately seen, on the Stock Exchange at midnight, walking arm-in-arm with the Pump from Aldgate, in a riding-habit?'
>
> (Ch. XLI)

Mrs Nickleby is sure that there is 'a quotation from the poets' here somewhere. Perhaps there are echoes of *Othello* and *A Midsummer Night's Dream*, transmuted into something weirder and brilliantly redundant. (The man is a madman who will eventually be dragged away by his 'keeper').

Some characters can hardly stop speaking. The strangest example is surely Mrs Clennam's manipulative servant Flintwinch in *Little Dorrit*. For almost the whole novel he speaks with brutal terseness. Near the end, however, he suddenly becomes loquacious. He reveals to Mrs Clennam how he has tricked her by appearing to destroy the codicil to Gilbert Clennam's will leaving a thousand guineas to Amy Dorrit but in fact conveying it to his own twin brother. Flintwinch speaks with relish of his revenge for all the years of being 'rasped' by her and delights in explaining to his mistress just how he has outmanoeuvred her. As he does so, we get the longest single paragraph in all Dickens's fiction, probably in all nineteenth-century fiction. In a paragraph that covered nearly five pages in the original opening chapter of the final double number of the serial version of the novel, he reveals what he really thinks of her ('you are the most Bumptious of your sex') and how he has tricked her ('I ... make a little exchange like the conjuror') (II Ch. XXX). After all his costiveness and secrecy, he lets it all out. The overwhelming paragraph enacts his overwhelming mix of bitterness and pride.

Idiolects isolate. A truly achieved idiolect seals its user off from other ways of seeing the world. Dickens's earliest experiment in this is Mrs Nickleby, whose outpourings are unhindered chains of free association. The comic effect is that, while we relish her, the characters in the book stop listening. Reading the sixth monthly instalment of the novel, Forster thought that one of Jane Austen's characters must have inspired Mrs Nickleby's freely associative garrulousness.

> I told him, on reading the first dialogue of Mrs Nickleby and Miss Knag, that he had been lately reading Miss Bates in *Emma*, but I found that he had not at this time made the acquaintance of that fine writer.[32]

Miss Knag, visiting Mrs Nickleby's lodgings, makes a polite compliment on Kate's abilities and gets back more than she bargained for.

> 'She always was clever,' said poor Mrs Nickleby, brightening up, 'always, from a baby. I recollect when she was only two years and a half old, that a gentleman who used to visit very much at our house—Mr Watkins, you know, Kate, my dear, that your poor papa went bail

for, who afterwards ran away to the United States, and
sent us a pair of snow shoes, with such an affectionate
letter that it made your poor dear father cry for a week.
You remember the letter? In which he said that he was
very sorry he couldn't repay the fifty pounds just then,
because his capital was all out at interest, and he was
very busy making his fortune, but that he didn't forget
you were his god-daughter, and he should take it very
unkind if we didn't buy you a silver coral and put it
down to his old account? Dear me, yes, my dear, how
stupid you are! and spoke so affectionately of the old
port wine that he used to drink a bottle and a half of
every time he came. You must remember, Kate?'
                          (*Nicholas Nickleby*, Ch. XVIII)

She is so busy recalling the details that she does not notice
the truth behind what she is saying: her husband's friend
conned him and her desperate husband was weeping for
the lost money. Dickens told Forster that her wonderfully
associative manner of speaking was copied from his mother,
though without her recognising the fact. 'Being the thing
falls a long way short of believing it. Mrs Nickleby herself
once asked me, as you know, if I really believed there ever
was such a woman.'[33] Mrs Nickleby's speech is all about
remembering, or trying to remember, things (a habit she
shares with Austen's Miss Bates). Speech takes her into
the past, where her materials are limitless. This is also the
case for the most unstoppable of all Dickens's speakers,
Flora Finching in *Little Dorrit*. Flora does not converse,
but outpours, in a torrent of observations whose checks
and swoops reveal her thoughts and wishes, but offer no
possibility of exchange. Invariably she is speaking to Arthur

Clennam, who had loved and courted her more than twenty years earlier. Memories of her now dead husband 'Mr F' jostle against almost-intimacies with Arthur.

'One last remark,' proceeded Flora, rejecting commonplace life with a wave of her hand, 'I wish to make, one last explanation I wish to offer, there *was* a time ere Mr F. first paid attentions incapable of being mistaken, but that is past and was not to be, dear Mr Clennam you no longer wear a golden chain you are free I trust you may be happy, here is Papa who is always tiresome and putting in his nose everywhere where he is not wanted.'

(I Ch. XIII)

Flora 'never once came to a full stop', but the careful reader can follow each of her little jumps of association if he or she tries hard enough. Take this, when Arthur tells her that Amy Dorrit is in Italy.

'In Italy is she really?' said Flora, 'with the grapes growing everywhere and lava necklaces and bracelets too that land of poetry with burning mountains picturesque beyond belief though if the organ-boys come away from the neighbourhood not to be scorched nobody can wonder being so young and bringing their white mice with them most humane, and is she really in that favoured land with nothing but blue about her and dying gladiators and Belvederes though Mr F. himself did not believe for his objection when in spirits was that the images could not be true there being no medium between expensive quantities of linen badly

got up and all in creases and none whatever, which
certainly does not seem probable though perhaps in
consequence of the extremes of rich and poor which
may account for it.'

Like Miss Bates, Flora knows her verbal affliction,
powerless as she is to escape it. She continues to follow the
path of Italian associations, from the play *Venice Preserved*
to Maccaroni to Mantua: 'what *has* it got to do with
Mantua-making for I never have been able to conceive?'
Arthur confirms that there is indeed no connection.

'Upon your word no isn't there I never did but that's
like me I run away with an idea and having none to
spare I keep it, alas there was a time dear Arthur that
is to say decidedly not dear nor Arthur neither but you
understand me when one bright idea gilded the what's-
his-name horizon of et cetera but it is darkly clouded
now and all is over.'

(II Ch. IX)

Flora's romantic memories and hopes keep inserting
themselves as the words pour out. Flora is wonderfully
ridiculous – all the more so when we know that Dickens
based the character on Maria Beadnall, whom he had
courted as a young man and rediscovered as a plump
married woman decades later.[34] Yet, entangled in her own
garrulousness, she is also good-hearted and touching.
When she visits Arthur at his workshop, he tells her that
she is welcome.

'Very polite of you to say so Arthur—cannot remember
Mr Clennam until the word is out, such is the habit

of times for ever fled, and so true it is that oft in the
stilly night ere slumber's chain has bound people, fond
memory brings the light of other days around people—
very polite but more polite than true I am afraid, for
to go into the machinery business without so much as
sending a line or a card to papa—I don't say me though
there was a time but that is past and stern reality has
now my gracious never mind—does not look like it
you must confess.'

                                                              (I Ch. XXIII)

Even Flora's commas seem to have fled on this occasion;
she is much more disjointed and voluble than in the
preceding interview.

Dickens's achievement is to make a way of speaking
comically distinct without being merely laughable. There
is a good example in Dickens's last completed novel: Mr
Venus in *Our Mutual Friend*. This taxidermist and
articulator of bones tells Silas Wegg how he first met and
fell in love with Pleasant Riderhood.

'I was down at the water-side, looking for parrots
brought home by sailors, to buy for stuffing ... And
looking for a nice pair of rattlesnakes, to articulate for a
Museum—when I was doomed to fall in with her and
deal with her. It was just at the time of that discovery
in the river. Her father had seen the discovery being
towed in the river. I made the popularity of the subject
a reason for going back to improve the acquaintance,
and I have never since been the man I was. My very
bones is rendered flabby by brooding over it. If they
could be brought to me loose, to sort, I should hardly

have the face to claim 'em as mine. To such an extent
have I fallen off under it.'

(III Ch. VII)

The peculiar mix of elaborate syntax and pointed
mispronunciation is distinctive. When Mr Venus later
explains to Wegg that the baleful Pleasant is willing to
marry him, thanks to the intercession of two friends, his
locutions may be funny but, even though marriage to
Pleasant might not seem an enviable fate, are not to be
mocked:

> The pint was thrown out, sir, by those two friends
> when they did me the great service of waiting on the
> lady to try if a union betwixt the lady and me could not
> be brought to bear—the pint, I say, was thrown out by
> them, sir, whether if, after marriage, I confined myself
> to the articulation of men, children, and the lower
> animals, it might not relieve the lady's mind of her
> feeling respecting being as a lady—regarded in a bony
> light. It was a happy thought, sir, and it took root.
>
> (IV Ch. XIV)

The decorousness is as real as it is ridiculous. The laugh
is not really against Mr Venus, whose way of speaking
allows him to conceive a happy ending for himself, even
'regarded in a bony light'.

II

Foreseeing

I am at work, and see the story in a wonderful glass.
To W. H. Wills, 8 July 1859[1]

Of all Dickens's calculated offences against narrative convention, few are as jolting as this, in the first monthly instalment of his seventh novel, *Dombey and Son*, published in October 1846. We have just been introduced to Paul Dombey's wet nurse, Polly Toodle, and seen her comforting his sister, the neglected Florence Dombey, after the death of her mother. Polly may be short on 'artificial accomplishments', but she is natural in her affections.

> And, perhaps, unlearned as she was, she could have brought a dawning knowledge home to Mr Dombey at that early day, which would not then have struck him in the end like lightning.

(Ch. III)

'In the end': suddenly, even as the story is beginning, the narrator is leaping forward to its end. If only the unseeing Mr Dombey knew what Dickens knows! The character is fated to discover the value of true affection, but much too late. Dickens, it seems, cannot resist telling us not just that Polly offers Florence the warmth and consolation that her own father fails to give her, but that he will eventually be 'struck', violently, by his realisation of his failure. Dickens gives us a glimpse of what lies distantly ahead. He even draws attention to the impropriety of this narrative slippage, adding, as if correcting himself, 'But this is from the purpose'.

In the novels of the second half of his career Dickens made an art of leaping ahead of himself to tell us what is to come. This technique, first called *prolepsis* in rhetoric books of the Renaissance, is the anticipation of what the narrator knows will occur in the narrative future. When Florence comes to her father to console him after the death of her brother and to share her grief, she sees in him 'not one gleam of interest, parental recognition, or relenting'. In fact, she half-detects what the author diagnoses, Mr Dombey's bitter idea of her as 'the successful rival of his son, in health and life'. When he turns her away, she gives 'one low prolonged cry' and Dickens thinks of the distant future.

> Let him remember it in that room, years to come. It has faded from the air, before he breaks the silence. It may pass as quickly from his brain, as he believes, but it is there. Let him remember it in that room, years to come! ... Let him remember it in that room, years to come. The rain that falls upon the roof: the wind that mourns outside the door: may have foreknowledge in

their melancholy sound. Let him remember it in that
room, years to come!

(Ch. XVIII)

What Dickens wanted to resonate with his readers evidently
resonated with him. In his notes for this number (headed
'Mems' for the first time), he wrote and underlined 'Let
him remember it in that room, years to come'.[2] Forty-one
chapters later, we get the fulfilment of what the novelist
told himself and us in advance. Mr Dombey is financially
ruined, his wife has left him, he is alone. He has driven his
daughter away and now understands that she was the only
one truly to love him. 'Let him remember it in that room,
years to come! He did remember it. It was heavy on his
mind now; heavier than all the rest' (Ch. LIX).

By the time of *Dombey and Son*, many of Dickens's
readers had got used to their author being *there* in his
narrative, exclaiming at his characters as if he had chanced
upon them rather than invented them. Yet even those
who had followed Dickens through all his previous stories
might have found it surprising, when Florence approaches
her father's bedside after he has been thrown from his
horse and lies injured and sleeping, to hear the author
exclaiming, 'Awake, unkind father! Awake, now, sullen
man! The time is flitting by; the hour is coming with an
angry tread. Awake!' Though her father has always looked
on her with 'repelling harshness', she looks on him with
love and Dickens cannot help calling out to him. 'Awake,
doomed man, while she is near! The time is flitting by;
the hour is coming with an angry tread; its foot is in
the house. Awake!' (Ch. XLIII). Mr Dombey sleeps on,
literally unconscious of his daughter's devotion. Dickens's
first readers were invited to wonder what that 'angry

tread' might be and would know only that it would be just retribution for his stony refusal of his daughter's love.

Today's readers might hear coercive moralism in these authorial interventions, but Dickens was up to something stranger and more experimental. *Dombey and Son* was the first of his novels to be closely planned, with a sense from the earliest chapters of what was to come. At the end of July 1846, three months before the first instalment of the novel was published, he wrote to John Forster with a close account of the overall narrative.[3] This foresaw Paul Dombey's death, when he is 'about ten years old (in the fourth number)', and the subsequent changing of Mr Dombey's 'feeling of indifference and uneasiness towards his daughter' into 'a positive hatred'. In the end, her 'love for him, when discovered and understood, will be his bitterest reproach'. Dickens's plotting was particular as well as general. With this novel, 'for the first time he planned each instalment on paper before he began writing'.[4] As the author foresaw events, so he wanted his readers, who were consuming the novel in monthly instalments of three or four chapters at a time, to do so too. As he learned to make his serial fiction move to a plan, he encouraged his readers to find the clues to a narrative's overall development within its apparently separate parts. Slipping into the future would become one of his distinctive tricks, used with increasing audacity as his plotting developed through his career.

In the novel that followed *Dombey and Son*, *David Copperfield*, Dickens thoroughly disrupted the convention, well established by the mid-nineteenth century, which dictated that a first-person narrator should not divulge more information than he or she possesses at the given moment in the represented time. He was drawn into doing so in the very first monthly number of the novel. Unusually, when he received the galley proofs back from the printer, Dickens found that he had not filled the required thirty-two pages. He swiftly added two new passages to the third chapter of the novel.[5] The latter fills out the character and the idiolect of Mrs Gummidge. The former is a disconcerting adult intervention in David's account of his childhood friendship with Little Em'ly. The narrator has been reflecting on the image of Little Em'ly, by the sea at Yarmouth, running along 'a jagged timber which protruded from the place we stood upon, and overhung the deep water at some height, without the least defence'. He remembers it with complete clarity, the girl 'springing forward to her destruction (as it appeared to me), with a look that I have never forgotten, directed far out to sea'. David, like the Victorian reader, would presume that Em'ly cannot swim; there is the immediate risk of 'destruction'. But this is also a premonition of where the daring spirit of this shy child will lead her: to another kind of 'destruction'.

At this point, Dickens added an extraordinary passage that goes beyond mere foreshadowing and entirely breaks the spell of childhood recollection.[6] There have been 'times since, in my manhood, many times there have been', the narrator tells us, when he has wondered if there might have been a 'merciful attraction' of the child 'into danger', a 'tempting' of her towards 'her dead father', who was himself drowned. 'Merciful' is the strangest word here, implying the adult narrator's dread knowledge of the future.

There has been a time since when I have wondered whether, if the life before her could have been revealed to me at a glance, and so revealed as that a child could fully comprehend it, and if her preservation could have depended on a motion of my hand, I ought to have held it up to save her. There has been a time since — I do not say it lasted long, but it has been — when I have asked myself the question, would it have been better for little Em'ly to have had the waters close above her head that morning in my sight; and when I have answered Yes, it would have been.

This may be premature. I have set it down too soon, perhaps. But let it stand.

(Ch. III)

In manuscript, the passage is much worked over, with many deletions and insertions. 'I do not say it lasted long, but it has been' and 'in my sight' were inserted afterthoughts. 'I have wondered' began as 'I thought'; 'This may be premature' was first 'This is premature'; 'perhaps' was inserted after 'too soon'. Dickens is emphasising the hesitancy of this strange confession. The narrator thinks of the girl's future fate and wonders if she might not have been better off drowning. More than this, he confesses that he has sometimes thought it would indeed have been better if she had died while still a child. The first readers would not know exactly what this 'life before her' was to be. Her destiny is to be seduced by Steerforth, whom we will not encounter until Chapter VI, near the end of the second monthly instalment. No doubt those readers might have surmised the fate most likely to await this girl, given that it is worse than death, as it seems to be.

It is the kind of thought for which Dickens is often arraigned (for a woman, better death than a sexual fall), yet here it is turned brilliantly into an expressive narrative lapse. 'I have set it down too soon': the narrator's knowledge of what happens later shapes his recollection. Often this is the case in *David Copperfield*. Look at the effect of the interpolated exclamation in his account of how he first introduces Steerforth to Mr Peggotty and Ham, when they visit him at his school. Steerforth is leaving the school dining-room, where David is meeting his visitors.

> I am not sure whether it was in the pride of having such a friend as Steerforth, or in the desire to explain to him how I came to have such a friend as Mr Peggotty, that I called to him as he was going away. But I said, modestly—Good Heaven, how it all comes back to me this long time afterwards!—
>
> 'Don't go, Steerforth, if you please. These are two Yarmouth boatmen—very kind, good people—who are relations of my nurse, and have come from Gravesend to see me.'
>
> (Ch. VII)

The narration interrupts itself to make us aware of that 'afterwards', for a precise reason. This will prove a fateful introduction: Steerforth will use his entrée into the Peggotty family to seduce Emily. With all that the narrator knows of what follows, no wonder that this episode 'comes back' to him with such force.

This novel's narration is haunted by its 'afterwards' (the word appears more often in *David Copperfield* than any other Dickens novel). When David describes his parting from his mother and her baby – his half-brother – to go back to school at the end of the holidays, the episode is moulded by his knowledge of what is to follow. The final vision of her and the baby 'lives in my mind'.

I was in the carrier's cart when I heard her calling to me. I looked out, and she stood at the garden-gate alone, holding her baby up in her arms for me to see. It was cold still weather; and not a hair of her head, nor a fold of her dress, was stirred, as she looked intently at me, holding up her child.

So I lost her. So I saw her afterwards, in my sleep at school—a silent presence near my bed—looking at me with the same intent face—holding up her baby in her arms.

(Ch. VIII)

In manuscript, you can see the small, decisive changes by which Dickens sharpened this. What was at first 'with her baby in her arms' became 'holding her baby up in her arms' – that phrase 'holding up' then being repeated twice. David's mother is – memorably, mysteriously – showing him something. Then 'nor a fold of her dress' is inserted, emphasising the strange stillness of what he sees. And finally, that simple 'So I lost her' is substituted for some longer sentence, hardly legible, but perhaps 'So I was never to set my eyes on her again'. The next chapter narrates the young David's discovery of his mother's death, but this cannot surprise us. He has already 'lost her'. It was impossible for him to wait for the proper moment to surprise us with what happens. There is a brilliantly observed detail when David is called from the classroom to be told the terrible news. It is his birthday and he imagines that a hamper has arrived, so he gets out of his seat 'with great alacrity'. The usually absurd master, Mr Sharp (he sports an ill-fitting wig), says something surprising. 'Don't hurry, David … There's time enough, my boy, don't hurry.' He knows something. 'I might have been surprised by the feeling tone in which he spoke, if I had given it a thought; but I gave it none until afterwards' (Ch. IX). 'Afterwards' again.

David finds himself having to tell us of things whose significance he only later understands and cannot but wince. He recalls the evening when Jack Maldon, who has been carrying on something more than a flirtation with Mrs Strong, leaves for India clutching the ribbon from her dress, and the look on Mrs Strong's (guilty) face later in the evening, as she sits with her ignorant and trusting old husband. 'It made a great impression on me, and I remembered it a long time afterwards, as I shall have occasion to narrate when the time comes' (Ch. XVI). David cannot help looking forward to 'afterwards'. Dickens had planned the transformation of David's affections, after Dora's death and his eventual marriage to Agnes. 'Carry the thread of Agnes through it all,' he had written on his 'mem' for the twelfth number of the novel.[7] He has his narrator wonder at his own lack of understanding, as when he speaks to Agnes of his love for Dora. 'Oh, Agnes, sister of my boyhood, if I had known then, what I knew long afterwards—!' (Ch. XXXV). Agnes loves him, but magnanimously encourages his courtship of another woman. The narrator cannot escape knowing this.

With *David Copperfield*, Dickens made his narrator live in the 'afterwards' of the events he recalls, yet discover that episodes from the past come shockingly alive as he narrates them. When David remembers Mr Peggotty telling him and Aunt Betsey the story of Emily's flight after she has been cast off by Steerforth, it is the extraordinary vividness of his memory that is surprising, more than the events themselves. 'I can hardly believe, writing now long afterwards, but that I was actually present in these scenes; they are impressed upon me with such an astonishing air of fidelity' (Ch. LI). Like no novelist before him, Dickens dramatises a story-teller's confrontation with his memories. This is most striking when he talks of Steerforth. David allows himself both to know and to turn away from the truth of Steerforth's actions. Here he is on his friend's 'determination to please' when taken by David to Mr Peggotty's home for the first time.

> If anyone had told me, then, that all this was a brilliant game, played for the excitement of the moment, for the employment of high spirits, in the thoughtless love of superiority, in a mere wasteful careless course of winning what was worthless to him, and next minute thrown away—I say, if anyone had told me such a lie that night, I wonder in what manner of receiving it my indignation would have found a vent!
>
> (Ch. XXI)

Despite what he now knows, the narrator remains seduced by his friend. Later, at a time when Steerforth's plans for Emily must be well in train, David watches him sleeping and more than hints at what is to follow.

> The time came in its season, and that was very soon, when I almost wondered that nothing troubled his repose, as I looked at him. But he slept—let me think of him so again—as I had often seen him sleep at school; and thus, in this silent hour, I left him.
>
> (Ch. XXIX)

Even with his later understanding of Steerforth's deceitfulness, he clings to an innocent image of him.

Dickens's fiction is well populated with frauds, but Steerforth is not exactly one of these. He almost declares himself for what he is. In the plan for Chapter XXII, featuring David and Steerforth's fortnight's stay in Yarmouth, Dickens recorded 'Steerforth's misgivings' and 'Em'ly's misgivings'. David has been on a 'solitary pilgrimage' to his parents' graves and returns to Yarmouth one dark evening to find Steerforth alone at Mr Peggotty's, gazing distractedly into the fire. Something is wrong. 'I wish with all my soul I could guide myself better!' Steerforth suddenly exclaims. The two friends have a strange conversation, during which Steerforth says, 'I have been afraid of myself' (Ch. XXII). He recovers from his preoccupation with an ominous quotation from the play that is quoted in Dickens's novels more often than any other.[8] ' "Why, being gone, I am a man again," like Macbeth. And now for dinner! If I have not (Macbeth-like) broken up the feast with most admired disorder, Daisy' (Ch. XXII).

He quotes the words used by Macbeth when the ghost of Banquo, whose murder he has arranged, vanishes. Thus, Steerforth dismisses guilt. The narrator knows where the story is taking him and the knowledge is a burden, even a curse. When he tells us of his return to Suffolk for Barkis's death and funeral, he understands that he has to tell us something else.

A dread falls on me here. A cloud is lowering on the distant town, towards which I retraced my solitary steps. I fear to approach it. I cannot bear to think of what did come, upon that memorable night; of what must come again, if I go on.

Telling a story is like making something happen again. Knowing what lies ahead, he does not want to go on. But then, 'It would be no better, if I stopped my most unwilling hand'(Ch. XXXI).

What he does not want to tell us is this. After Barkis's funeral, he visits Mr Peggotty's home where he meets Ham, whom Emily is to marry. Ham, 'deadly pale', takes him outside and tells him that 'she's gone!' She has eloped with David's dear friend, whom he introduced to the Peggottys and to Emily. David sees the irresistible trajectory of his own narrative. Eventually it will take him to the chapter entitled 'Tempest', where Steerforth drowns in a storm off Yarmouth and Ham dies trying to save him.

> I now approach an event in my life, so indelible, so awful, so bound by an infinite variety of ties to all that has preceded it, in these pages, that, from the beginning of my narrative, I have seen it growing larger and larger as I advanced, like a great tower in a plain, and throwing its fore-cast shadow even on the incidents of my childish days.
>
> (Ch. LV)

Dickens's planning has become his narrator's dread. He disobeys the convention that he should not admit that he knows the outcome. A 'Personal History' (as the title page of the novel declared it to be) concedes that the narrator cannot escape his foreknowledge.

Prolepsis is an indiscretion. Knowledge of the future has forced its way into the narrative. Setting things down too soon was much later to become a distinctive trick of post-modern fiction. Here is a paragraph from a novel first published in 1970. The protagonist, Lise, who has walked out of her job, on impulse, and is travelling to somewhere abroad, has struck up a conversation with a woman she has met in an airport bookstall.

> The woman has large breasts, she is clothed in a pink summer coat and dress. She smiles and is amiable in this transient intimacy with Lise, and not even sensing in the least that very soon, after a day and a half of hesitancy, and after a long midnight call to her son, the lawyer in Johannesburg, who advises her against the action, she nevertheless will come forward and repeat all she remembers and all she does not remember, and all the details she imagines to be true and those that are true, in her conversation with Lise when she sees in the papers that the police are trying to trace who Lise is, and whom, if anyone, she met on her trip and what she had said. 'Very gay,' says this woman to Lise, indulgently, smiling all over Lise's vivid clothes.[9]

This is taken from Muriel Spark's *The Driver's Seat*. It features the technique that Spark herself called 'flash-forwards'.[10] Lise's fate is sealed. She will be murdered at the very end of the novel, and the narrative insistently foresees this. Narrative pattern, we are to recognise, is only made by what is to come.

In what gets called post-modern fiction, the story is about the making of the narrative. Ian McEwan's *Enduring Love* (1997) has a now famous opening sequence describing a ballooning accident. Its power is not just in the drama of the men, including the narrator, Joe Rose, trying to hold down the untethered balloon with a child in the basket, but also of the narrator's attempts to make a narrative out of his memories.

> Knowing what I now know, it's odd to evoke the figure of Jed Parry directly ahead of me, emerging from a line of beeches on the far side of the field a quarter of a mile away, running into the wind … The encounter that would unhinge us was minutes away[11]

'Knowing what I now know': it is a characteristic McEwan opening to a sentence. The outcome precedes the telling. We only reach experience through the business of constructing a narrative. In McEwan's 2001 novel *Atonement*, Bryony Tallis has travelled to south London to try to make amends to her sister, Cecilia, and her lover, Robbie, for the false testimony that she gave against him five years earlier. She has promised to make a legal deposition and they are about to part. It is July 1941. 'They stood outside Balham tube station, which in three months' time would achieve its terrible form of fame in the Blitz.'[12] Weirdly, the narrator slips forward to the night a German bomb killed at least sixty people sheltering in Balham underground station. It is a deliberate glitch, for the novel is being written – and re-written – by its central character, Bryony, and we are to detect the signs of her activity.

Dickens pioneered the narrative trick that such later novelists were to exploit, deploying it differently in different novels. In the novel that followed *David Copperfield*, *Bleak House*, it is used far more sparingly and only in Esther's strand of the narrative. Dickens does something strange with this. For the most part, he makes his heroine, in the conventional manner, keep information back until the moment in her narrative when she herself makes the discovery. So, for instance, the reader's suspicion that Lady Dedlock is Esther's mother may have been growing to a certainty, but Esther only reveals her knowledge at the point when she narrates the meeting with Lady Dedlock in the park of Chesney Wold, and her mother's confession of her secret. Occasionally, however, she does look ahead. When Charley, now her maid, tells her of the arrival of Jo at the brickmaker's cottage, she leaves Bleak House on 'a cold wild night' to find him.

> I had no thought that night—none, I am quite sure— of what was soon to happen to me. But I have always remembered since that when we had stopped at the garden-gate to look up at the sky, and when we went upon our way, I had for a moment an undefinable impression of myself as being something different from what I then was. I know it was then and there that I had it. I have ever since connected the feeling with that spot and time and with everything associated with that spot and time, to the distant voices in the town, the barking of a dog, and the sound of wheels coming down the miry hill.
>
> (Ch. XXXI)

It is an extraordinary paragraph – a spot in time vividly recalled, but somehow presaging what is to come. The meeting with Jo will lead to first Charley and then Esther being struck down with smallpox, and Esther thereby losing her beauty.

Dickens wrote in his 'mem' for the monthly instalment in which this appeared, 'Esther's love must be kept in

<u>view, to make the</u> coming trial the greater and the victory
the more meritorious.'[13] Dickens makes Esther struggle
to keep her love for the young doctor Allan Woodcourt
hidden, almost from herself. When Mrs Woodcourt
comes to stay at Bleak House while her son is in India,
she is 'watchful' when she talks to Esther and, we infer,
keen that her son should not marry her. She makes Esther
feel uncomfortable. 'I don't know what it was. Or at least
if I do now, I thought I did not then. Or at least—but it
don't matter.' Mrs Woodcourt does everything she can to
put her off the (never expressed) idea of marriage to her
son, their conversations reducing Esther to 'perplexities
and contradictions that I could not account for'. 'At least,
if I could—but I shall come to all that by and by, and it
is mere idleness to go on about it now'(Ch. XXX). She
keeps things back, but tells us that she is keeping things
back. The reader is encouraged to guess at what Esther
feels for Allan Woodcourt. We might not be told now, but
Esther knows that she will have to tell us eventually.

Esther's glances to the future are appropriately modest.
As she looks back, she sometimes needs to emphasise that
she did not see what was coming. Before she recounts Sir
Leicester Dedlock's visit to Bleak House, 'I could have
no anticipation, and I had none, that something very
startling to me at the moment, and ever memorable to me
in what ensued from it, was to happen before this day was
out' (Ch. XLIII). The visit pushes her to discover that the
woman Boythorn once loved was her own stern aunt and
to tell John Jarndyce that Lady Dedlock is her mother.
Once she has told her guardian everything, he returns
the confidence and writes his letter to her proposing
marriage. Yet the future that Dickens allows to intrude
into her narration is limited. Esther does not intimate

any knowledge of the real outcome for her: John Jarndyce
eventually freeing her from her engagement so that she
can marry Allan Woodcourt.

In one respect only, Esther allows her knowledge of
what is to come to shape her narrative. One evening, soon
after moving to Bleak House, Ada is playing the piano
and singing while Richard bends over her; Esther catches
Mr Jarndyce looking at them. 'His look was thoughtful,
but had a benignant expression in it which I often (how
often!) saw again, which has long been engraven on my
heart' (Ch. VI). In that look is Jarndyce's benevolent hope
that these two will marry; in Esther's glance to the future
is her knowledge that Richard will fall out with Jarndyce.
As Richard becomes obsessed with his imagined gain
from the Jarndyce and Jarndyce case and alienated from
his former guardian, Jarndyce's benignity will remain
constant. Even as she looks back to a time before all this
happens, Esther assures herself of Jarndyce's unwavering
goodwill. Later, after Richard has left Bleak House to
dedicate himself to the futile Chancery case, Esther
arranges a meeting between him and Ada, wondering, as
she watches, if Richard truly returns Ada's love. Jarndyce
and Jarndyce gets in his way even here. 'Ah me! what
Richard would have been without that blight, I never
shall know now!' (Ch. XXXVII). The reader is to see that
Richard's case is a hopeless one. Esther visits him at Deal,
where he is stationed with the Army, and finds him in a
wild state amidst 'a great confusion of clothes, tin cases,
books, boots, brushes, and portmanteaus'. He is writing
at a desk, taken up in Jarndyce and Jarndyce. But he
greets her warmly. 'Dear Richard! He was ever the same
to me. Down to – ah, poor fellow! – the end, he never
received me but with something of his old merry boyish

manner' (Ch. XLV). When she remembers Richard, she cannot keep that 'end' out of her narration. About her own end, she manages to be more reticent.

In *Little Dorrit*, Dickens again uses prolepsis to illuminate the hidden feelings of a self-denying heroine. They are feelings hidden from the man that Amy Dorrit loves, though not at all from the reader. 'First suggestions of her being in love with clennam', Dickens wrote in his plan for Chapter XVIII of Book I, with Arthur still yearning after Minnie Meagles and Little Dorrit courted by the turnkey's son, Young John Chivery.[14] In his chapter plans for the next monthly number of the novel, he wrote 'Dawn of Little Dorrit's love for Arthur'.[15] Finally, in his chapter plan for the ninth number, he put,

> Little Dorrit and clennam – He putting before her his condition as that 'much older man who has done with that part of life,' and unconsciously stabbing her to the heart. Oh! If he had but known, if he had but known![16]

Then he wrote, and strongly underlined, '<u>Prepare for the time to come</u>', before adding 'in that room, long afterwards'. In the chapter itself, Arthur tells Little Dorrit, 'I fancied I loved some one', but says that he is too old to have such feelings. He does not understand that the woman whom he insists on addressing as a 'child' loves him. He implores her to accept money from him so that she can live 'in a more suitable place', given that she might have 'an interest in some one else'. She becomes 'very, very pale'.

> 'No. No. No.' She shook her head, after each slow repetition of the word, with an air of quiet desolation

that he remembered long afterwards. The time came
when he remembered it well, long afterwards, within
those prison walls; within that very room.

(I Ch. XXXII)

How things are later to be remembered is made part of
the telling. It will be the absurd, then suddenly not-so-
absurd, John Chivery, himself smitten by Little Dorrit,
who, nine monthly instalments later, tells Arthur that she
loves him.

When he turned to historical fiction in *A Tale of
Two Cities*, Dickens exploited his readers' knowledge
of the destination to which public events were leading,
against the grain of his main source, Thomas Carlyle's
The French Revolution (1837). Dickens had advertised
his reliance on 'Mr CARLYLE'S wonderful book' in his
1859 Preface to *A Tale of Two Cities*.[17] Carlyle's narrative
was an extraordinary stylistic experiment. Highly
unconventionally, it was narrated largely in the present
tense, restoring urgency and undecidedness to historical
events. Pausing in the chapter entitled 'Discrowned' to
explain the decisions leading up to the execution of Louis
XVI, Carlyle asked the reader to imagine how the question
of the King's fate 'looked then, in France, and struggling,
confused all round one!' In retrospect, we might wonder
that the revolutionaries showed no magnanimity, but
then 'it is a most lying thing that same past tense always'.
The past tense cannot do justice to 'the haggard element
of Fear!'

Not there does Fear dwell, nor Uncertainty, nor
Anxiety; but it dwells here; haunting us, tracking us;
running like an accursed ground-discord through all

the music-tones of our Existence;—making the Tense
a mere Present one! [18]

Very occasionally, an historical novelist has imitated
Carlyle's decision. When Hilary Mantel's *Wolf Hall* was
published in 2009, much attention was given to her
decision to narrate the events of Henry VIII's reign entirely
from the point of view of Thomas Cromwell, but little to
the fact that it was written entirely in the present tense.

Dickens takes the opposite tack. In the opening chapter
of *A Tale of Two Cities* it is 1775 and we are a decade and
a half away from what came to be called the French
Revolution, but our narrator thinks of the trees growing
'in the woods of France and Norway' that will make the
boards for 'a certain movable framework' (the guillotine),
and of the 'rude carts' inhabited by roosting poultry in
outhouses in the countryside outside Paris 'which the
Farmer, Death, had already set apart to be his tumbrels of
the Revolution'. The future is made inevitable. In order to
establish the oppressions and resentments that will burst
forth in the third of the novel's three Books, Dickens takes
his reader, at the beginning of the tale's second weekly
instalment, to the impoverished Paris suburb of Saint-
Antoine, where a large cask of wine has burst in the street.
The local poor cluster to dip in the wine puddles with
mugs, to scoop with their hands, even to suck on the wine-
sodden pieces of cask. The red wine stains hands and faces
and feet. Someone scrawls on a wall with a finger 'dipped
in muddy wine lees' a single word: BLOOD. It is all too
clear what this presages. 'The time was to come, when
that wine too would be spilled on the street-stones, and
when the stain of it would be red upon many there.' Later
in the same chapter, after surveying some of the misery

of those who live here, Dickens pauses on the system of
ropes and pulleys by which lamps are strung up over the
streets at night by the lamplighters. He sees the terrible
future in them.

> For, the time was to come, when the gaunt scarecrows
> of that region should have watched the lamplighter, in
> their idleness and hunger, so long, as to conceive the
> idea of improving on his method, and hauling up men
> by those ropes and pulleys, to flare upon the darkness
> of their condition. But, the time was not come yet;
> and every wind that blew over France shook the rags of
> the scarecrows in vain, for the birds, fine of song and
> feather, took no warning.
>
> (Ch. V)

In Dickens's imagination, a revolution is a narrative
whose advance signs are ignored. Only its composed and
terrifying agents, the Defarges, seem to know from the
beginning where the story is heading. We meet them early
in the novel in the wine shop that Defarge runs, where he
is already instructing his minions of the revolution, the
three Jacques, and where the frightening Madame Defarge
is already knitting away, practising for her place with the
citoyennes tricoteuses, knitting by the guillotine. When
Defarge takes Mr Lorry and Lucie Manette to her father,
reduced to haggard vacancy by his long imprisonment in
the Bastille, they note that Defarge has been exhibiting
Monsieur Manette to the three Jacques, presumably to
inflame their indignation. He knows very well what they
will be driven to. This novel is all prolepsis in the half that
precedes the Revolution. 'Another darkness was closing in
…' (II Ch. XVI). It is all evident and yet obscure. Darnay

travels back to post-Revolutionary France to try to rescue his uncle's servant, Gabelle, who has been imprisoned. He is soon imprisoned himself. Though worried, he is not as worried as he should be. 'Troubled as the future was, it was the unknown future, and in its obscurity there was ignorant hope.' Seen from our side of history, Darnay is an innocent, unable to dream of the horrors to come.

> The horrible massacre, days and nights long, which, within a few rounds of the clock, was to set a great mark of blood upon the blessed garnering time of harvest, was as far out of his knowledge as if it had been a hundred thousand years away. The 'sharp female newly-born, and called La Guillotine,' was hardly known to him, or to the generality of people, by name. The frightful deeds that were to be soon done, were probably unimagined at that time in the brains of the doers. How could they have a place in the shadowy conceptions of a gentle mind?
>
> (III Ch. I)

The unintelligibility of revolutionary violence to 'gentle minds' increases its horror.

Foreknowledge was at the heart of Dickens's next novel. The title of *Great Expectations* is itself a kind of mockery of its protagonist's ambitions. Pip believes in a certain narrative for himself (Miss Havisham will give him money, he will become a gentleman, he will gain the heart of Estella) and will find this is all folly and self-delusion. His glances at the future as he recalls his past are self-admonishing, even self-punishing. It is a novel that calls attention to the rueful or haunted latter knowledge of its narrator. *Afterwards* is still his special word. When wandering through the derelict brewery at Satis House, he remembers the vision he had as a child, in the same place, of Miss Havisham hanging from a beam. At the proof stage he inserted the sentence, 'I thought it a strange thing then, and I thought it a stranger thing long afterwards' (Ch. VIII). The vision has haunted him. The 'childish association' returns years later, on his last visit to Satis House, when he again thinks he sees Miss Havisham hanging from a beam (Ch. XLIX). In *David Copperfield*, hindsight gave the narrator melancholy wisdom about his childhood and youth. In *Great Expectations*, Dickens tries a new kind of first-person narration, where hindsight sometimes makes early experiences seem all the 'stranger'.

It happens again when Pip recalls the face of Jaggers's housekeeper, Molly, as she serves dinner at his house. It reminds him of the faces of the witches, bending over a cauldron in a production of *Macbeth* that he has seen a night or two earlier.

> Years afterwards, I made a dreadful likeness of that woman, by causing a face that had no other natural resemblance to it than it derived from flowing hair, to pass behind a bowl of flaming spirits in a dark room.
>
> (Ch. XXVI)

Why suddenly think of something he sees by a weird optical illusion 'years afterwards'? Later he is in a coach with Estella, who is asking him about this dinner.

> I should have gone on with the subject so far as to describe the dinner in Gerrard Street, if we had not then come into a sudden glare of gas. It seemed, while it lasted, to be all alight and alive with that

inexplicable feeling I had had before; and when we were out of it, I was as much dazed for a few moments as if I had been in lightning.

(Ch. XXXIII)

Finally, in Ch. XLVIII the connection gets made. Pip is back at Jaggers's house and seeing Molly again, with the same 'inexplicable feeling' as 'when I had passed in a carriage – not alone – through a sudden glare of light in a dark street'. In Molly's face he sees Estella's face. In between the two come the witches in *Macbeth*, their faces eerily illuminated. 'I thought how one link of association had helped that identification in the theatre.'

The known future mocks the unknowing past. Sometimes Pip seems to succumb helplessly to his knowledge of what is to come. On his second visit to Satis House, Estella slaps his face and asks him why he does not cry.

'Because I'll never cry for you again,' said I. Which was, I suppose, as false a declaration as ever was made; for I was inwardly crying for her then, and I know what I know of the pain she cost me afterwards.

(Ch. XI)

'I know what I know': reticent, but unable not to say it.

I reposed complete confidence in no one but Biddy; but I told poor Biddy everything. Why it came natural to me to do so, and why Biddy had a deep concern in everything I told her, I did not know then, though I think I know now.

(Ch. XII)

Her 'deep concern' for all that he tells her is her dawning love for him – just what he is unable to see. When young Pip wishes that he could get Orlick dismissed, the older Pip knows that Orlick perfectly understands his supposedly secret wishes. 'He quite understood and reciprocated my good intentions, as I had reason to know thereafter' (Ch. XVII). Pip watches himself failing to understand everything until too late. 'A great event in my life, the turning point of my life, now opens on my view' (Ch. XXXVII). The slight trip in that repetition of 'my life' betrays the narrator's emotion as he refers ahead (by a chapter) to the crushing of his 'expectations', with the reappearance of the convict from his childhood. *This* is what made him a 'gentleman'!

Pip narrates with the weight of what he now knows upon him. Chapters VIII and IX cover a single day on which he first visits Satis House, then returns home and tells Joe, Mrs Joe and the egregious Uncle Pumblechook a series of extravagant lies about the meeting with Miss Havisham and Estella. That evening, Pip confesses to Joe that he has lied and tells him that the lies have somehow come out of his misery at being called 'common' by Estella, 'and that I knew I was common, and that I wished I was not common'. In the chapter's final paragraph, the narrator cannot help knowing how important the visit – and the misery – will turn out to be.

> That was a memorable day to me, for it made great changes in me. But it is the same with any life. Imagine one selected day struck out of it, and think how different its course would have been. Pause you who read this, and think for a moment of the long chain of iron or gold, of thorns or flowers, that would never

have bound you, but for the formation of the first link on one memorable day.

(Ch. IX)

A life is only a narrative when the future is known. In his last novel, *The Mystery of Edwin Drood*, Dickens returned to this image of a narrative chain and of the small link forged at one moment, whose importance will only later be understood. Edwin and Rosa have met and agreed that they will not get married. Unknown to Rosa, Edwin carries the ring that was once his mother's and that he was to have offered her as her engagement ring. As they walk together, he decides not to show it to her. He will return it to Rosa's guardian, the lawyer Mr Grewgious, who gave it to Edwin in the first place.

> Among the mighty store of wonderful chains that are for ever forging, day and night, in the vast iron-works of time and circumstance, there was one chain forged in the moment of that small conclusion, riveted to the foundations of heaven and earth, and gifted with invincible force to hold and drag.
>
> Ch. XIII

Edwin's decision will be momentous. Clearly his continued possession of the ring will be significant in the novel's plot. Readers, noting John Jasper's interest in the power of quicklime to decompose a body, will guess that it will provide evidence of Jasper's crime.

Dickens knows what is coming and inserts that knowledge into his narrative. It is not his only such intervention in this novel. Just as he once called out to Mr

Dombey to warn him of what was to come, so he warns one of his characters here about future retribution. Helena Landless has been watching as John Jasper accompanies Rosa Bud on the piano as she sings, his eyes fixed on her lips. Helena has guessed from his attention that he loves her. After everyone else has left, Rosa tells Helena that she is terrified of him. Helena bends over Rosa, 'protectingly':

> There was a slumbering gleam of fire in the intense dark eyes, though they were then softened with compassion and admiration. Let whomsoever it most concerned look well to it!
>
> (Ch. VII)

The narrator cannot stop himself exclaiming. We presume that it is Jasper who is being warned and infer that Helena will, at a later stage in the narrative, fiercely defend Rosa from the man who is obsessed with her.

The mystery that Dickens left us with in his half-finished final novel has become a test of our narratological abilities, a sequence of clues evidently planted but never finally explained. The elaboration of the mystery looks forward to its solution. In one of the novel's past-tense chapters, Septimus Crisparkle visits John Jasper to try to broker a truce between Edwin Drood and Neville Landless, who have quarrelled violently. (We know, as Mr Crisparkle does not, that Jasper has fomented this quarrel.) Receiving no answer to his knock on the door, Mr Crisparkle turns the handle and looks in.

> Long afterwards he had cause to remember how Jasper sprang from the couch in a delirious state between

sleeping and waking, and crying out: 'What is the matter? Who did it?'

(Ch. X)

Is this yet another echo of *Macbeth*, whose amazed protagonist cries out on seeing Banquo's ghost, 'Which of you have done this?' Here we know, as Mr Crisparkle does not, that Jasper is an opium addict. He offers Mr Crisparkle the explanation that he has been 'dreaming at a great rate' and we suppose that his dreams have been shaped by opium. In any case, Jasper is haunted by his own fantasies. It is one of those moments in the novel, looking ahead at what is to come, that is used as evidence by those who foresee a plot device reminiscent of Wilkie Collins's *The Moonstone*, where a man steals a jewel under the influence of opium, and afterwards does not remember doing so. Perhaps, in a drugged state, Jasper will do something that his rational self does not remember? Or will believe that he has done something that his rational self falsely remembers? We know that Dickens is thinking of the future of his plot and wants his reader to do so too. Well in advance of those novelists of the late twentieth century, he has learnt to include within his narrative his reader's expectations about the designs of the novel. We can truly gauge the power of that Dickensian *afterwards* in this novel, which never reached it.

12

Drowning

Found Drowned. The descriptive bill upon the wall, by the waterside.

Note in collection of 'Memoranda'[1]

Could Dickens swim? Given the number of drownings – actual, supposed or feared – in his novels, it is worth asking this question. Throughout Dickens's novels, seas and rivers seem to be sucking his characters to their doom. Is this because the novelist was afraid of the water? Or was it his element? The answer is surprisingly difficult to find. Most leading biographers of Dickens do not even mention the subject.[2] They tell us about the novelist's manic physical vigour, but they do not follow him into the water. Yet his eldest daughter Mamie recalled, 'He was a firm believer in the hygiene of bathing, and cold baths, sea baths and shower baths were among his most constant practices.'[3] This does not necessarily imply swimming: many a nineteenth-century bather practised complete or partial immersion, often from a bathing machine, without ever going out of his or her depth. Perhaps there are clues in his letters? In June 1839, while living at Petersham, Dickens wrote to Daniel MacLise about the delights of plunging into the Thames, upstream from the filth of London:

> ... the leaves are all out and flowers too, swimming feats from Petersham to Richmond Bridge have been achieved before breakfast, I myself have risen at 6 and plunged head foremost into the water to the astonishment and admiration of all beholders.[4]

Was Dickens one of those performing the 'swimming feats'? Or did he stay in his depth for his submersion? When staying at Broadstairs on the Kent coast, he found a plunge in the sea irresistible. He told Forster how, on a warm September day in 1842, when he should have been writing his *American Notes*, he preferred a dip.

> To-day I had not written twenty lines before I rushed out (the weather being gorgeous) to bathe. And when I have done that, it is all up with me in the way of authorship until to-morrow.[5]

But did he just wade in and duck under, or did he actually float?

In September 1843, while he was writing *Martin Chuzzlewit* at the Kent resort, he described his regime to C. C. Felton, in the comical third person. After a morning spent writing, 'At one he disappears, and presently emerges from a bathing machine, and may be seen—a kind of salmon-coloured porpoise—splashing about in the ocean.'[6] This makes him sound like a swimmer; further clues in his correspondence suggest that when he made that porpoise comparison it was because, in his early thirties, he had indeed recently learned to swim. In a letter of 1842 to his great friend and former fellow reporter on the *Morning Chronicle* Thomas Beard, a keen and proficient swimmer, he wrote, 'If I don't swim, this Autumn, may I—but we will not anticipate.'[7] The next summer he tried to tempt Beard down to Broadstairs. 'The tide rushes in, demanding to be breasted.'[8] Look carefully through his letters and it becomes clear that by the early 1840s he was taking more than a douse in the shallows; at a time when this was still rare, he had become a swimmer. There is no doubting his delight in living next to the Mediterranean near Genoa in 1844.

> I turn out before 7 every morning, and plunge into the sea instantly. It is inexpressibly delicious—though the bottom is rocky; and I cut my knees to pieces when the waves are rough.[9]

It is now clear that he particularly relishes his swimming abilities.

> What do you think of my suddenly finding myself a Swimmer? But I have really made the discovery; and skim about a little blue bay just below the house here, like a fish in high spirits.[10]

He became keen that his sons in turn learned the 'noble art'. In 1850 he wrote to Beard ('you are amphibious') to ask him to introduce his son Charley to James Hedgman, proprietor of the National Baths on High Holborn, so that he could 'learn to swim at the Holborn Baths'.[11] In 1857 he was arranging for his sixteen-year-old son Walter to take swimming lessons.[12]

He was at the forefront of a manly fashion. It was in the 1850s and 1860s that Victorian England began to see the creation of swimming clubs and the spread of the activity amongst men of the middle classes.[13] The admirable Reverend Septimus Crisparkle in *The Mystery of Edwin Drood*, published in 1870, is a great swimmer and the representative of a new style of masculine vigour, his healthiness signified by the fact that he is 'fair and rosy, and perpetually pitching himself head-foremost into all the deep running water in the surrounding country' (Ch. II). The first chapter in the novel that is narrated from his point of view finds him before breakfast, already 'having broken the thin morning ice near Cloisterham Weir with his amiable head, much to the invigoration of his frame' (Ch. VI). Swimming signifies his vitality, moral as well as physical. When he travels to London he arrives before ten in the morning, having come 'at one plunge out of the river at Cloisterham' (Ch. XXI). His prowess in the water seems intended to be of some importance in the novel's plot. In Ch. XVI he plunges into the Weir to recover Edwin Drood's gold watch after his disappearance. This will be an important clue to Drood's fate. Later we discover that he became a good swimmer after being saved from drowning by Tartar, a sailor and his former fag at boarding school (Ch. XXI). We are surely being prepared for either man's swimming abilities to serve Dickens's narrative purposes.

Crisparkle was saved from the fate that awaits many in Dickens's world, and thereby taught to train himself to swim. No wonder that this kind of mastery was so important to Dickens: like no other novelist, he was drawn to drowning. Characters die in this way throughout his fiction: Quilp in *The Old Curiosity Shop*; Steerforth and

Ham Peggotty in *David Copperfield*; Compeyson in *Great Expectations*; George Radfoot, Gaffer Hexam, Rogue Riderhood and Bradley Headstone in *Our Mutual Friend*, a novel in which other characters (John Harmon, Rogue Riderhood, Eugene Wrayburn) are narrowly saved from drowning. In *The Old Curiosity Shop*, Nell's feckless and resentful brother Frederick Trent lives riotously abroad and dies young, his body being recognised by a stranger 'who chanced to visit that hospital in Paris where the drowned are laid out to be owned' (Ch. the Last). In *The Mystery of Edwin Drood*, the now parentless Rosa Bud has an abiding memory of her mother,

> who had been brought home in her father's arms, drowned. The fatal accident had happened at a party of pleasure. Every fold and colour in the pretty summer dress, and even the long wet hair, with scattered petals of ruined flowers still clinging to it, as the dead young figure, in its sad, sad beauty lay upon the bed, were fixed indelibly in Rosa's recollection.
>
> (Ch. IX)

In *Dombey and Son*, the passing mention of a drowning intimates grief that Dickens, rarely credited for his reticence, never directly represents in the novel. Mr Dombey and his manipulative adviser, Major Bagstock, have travelled to Leamington Spa where they meet – and size up – the beautiful, proud young widow, Edith Granger. After their first encounter, the Major briefs Dombey on the woman he is coldly considering as a potential wife. Edith was married at eighteen to the forty-one-year-old Colonel Granger, 'a de-vilish handsome fellow'. But he died in the second year of the marriage.

'Was there any family?' asked Mr Dombey presently.

'Yes, Sir,' said the Major. 'There was a boy.'

Mr Dombey's eyes sought the ground, and a shade came over his face.

'Who was drowned, Sir,' pursued the Major. 'When a child of four or five years old.'

'Indeed?' said Mr Dombey, raising his head.

'By the upsetting of a boat in which his nurse had no business to have put him,' said the Major. 'That's his history.'

(Ch. XXI)

The reader who has lived through the death of Mr Dombey's only son Paul a few chapters earlier will have no problems with the psychology of this. Mr Dombey wants to marry again to get himself another son. He does not want to give some stepson, another man's offspring, a claim upon his estate, or have him as a reminder of the loss of his own boy, his own heir.

There is something terrible in that raising of Mr Dombey's head. His first response is something between disappointment and despair, which turns into relief, we infer, when he hears that Edith's son drowned. The inference is numbing because Mr Dombey's feelings are so hidden. He thinks he gives nothing away. His relief is all the more terrible because we must imagine what this was like for Edith, the 'very handsome, very haughty, very wilful' woman whom we have only just encountered. The story snaps shut with the Major's summary, 'That's his history', leaving us to imagine all Edith's pain. We hear no more about that drowning, but in all her later performances of wounded pride and cold anger, we are expected to remember her unnamed drowned child. Like the road accident for a later generation, drowning is the most probable type of sudden, accidental death (all the more appallingly probable for the middle-class Victorian reader because it is the result of a servant's misjudgement). Drowning is the very realisation of vulnerability. It is the way that the hostile elements overwhelm us.

In Dickens's world, everyone could imagine drowning. The novelist's account of steaming across the Atlantic in a January storm on his first trip to America in 1842 would surely have discouraged any prospective traveller. 'What the agitation of a steam-vessel is, on a bad winter's night in the wild Atlantic, it is impossible for the most vivid imagination to conceive,' he tells us – but then duly conceives it on the page. With the sea swamping the skylights and forcing its way into cabins, Dickens tries to administer brandy and water to his wife, her maid and 'a little Scotch lady', who 'were all heaped together in one corner of a long sofa ... where they clung to each other in momentary expectation of being drowned'.[14] Being Dickens, he finds something 'exquisitely ridiculous' in the way they roll from one end of the sofa to another, while he staggers after them. He drew on this experience for his description of Martin Chuzzlewit and Mark Tapley's Atlantic voyage in *Martin Chuzzlewit*, where the ship full of sleeping passengers comes on

> as if no deadly element were peering in at every seam and chink, and no drowned seaman's grave, with but a plank to cover it, were yawning in the unfathomable depths below.
>
> (Ch. XV)

A sea voyage is a terrible thing and drowning at sea is always possible. The possibility is the material of Sissy's education in statistical probability in *Hard Times*. 'And I find (Mr M'Choakumchild said) that in a given time a hundred thousand persons went to sea on long voyages, and only five hundred of them were drowned or burnt to death. What is the percentage?' (Ch. IX)

In *Bleak House*, Mr George is convinced that his old friend Captain Hawdon must have drowned. 'He went over a ship's side. Whether intentionally or accidentally, I don't know' (Ch. XXI). Later he explains to Esther this was a transport ship 'in an Irish harbour' (Ch. LXIII). How was he to know that his friend was good enough at swimming to make the shore? In *Dombey and Son* the characters are allowed to think that Walter has drowned. We surely know otherwise, but get a glimpse of the true state of apprehension in which most live when Susan mentions to Florence that 'the captain's wife was at the office yesterday, and seemed a little put out about it' (Ch. XXIII).

Of course, there are deaths by drowning elsewhere in Victorian fiction. Maggie Tulliver and her brother drown at the end of George Eliot's *The Mill on the Floss*, as they are destined to do. They live in a water-bound world, by the banks of the Floss. From the second chapter, where the headstrong nine-year-old Maggie is warned by her mother, 'You'll tumble in and be drowned some day,' the portents are there to be seen. If a character is to be done away with in the nineteenth century, drowning is likely. Early in *Adam Bede*, Adam's father Mathias falls in a local river after a drinking bout and drowns. In Elizabeth Gaskell's *North and South*, Boucher drowns himself in a shallow stream rather than go home to face his querulous wife and eight hungry children. In George Eliot's *Daniel Deronda*, Gwendolen's sadistic husband Grandcourt conveniently falls from a boat in a sailing accident and drowns. At the terrible climax of Thomas Hardy's *The Return of the Native*, Eustacia Vye and Wildeve perish in Shadwater Weir. It seems that Eustacia has thrown herself into the water. Wildeve perishes attempting to save her.

Yet drowning in Dickens is not just a useful plot mechanism; it is a fate that lives in the imaginations of his characters. The fear of drowning is so visceral that, in *Oliver Twist*, even Bill Sikes's dog shares it, sensing, as they flee justice, his master's plan to drown him. 'When his master halted at the brink of a pool, and looked round to call him, he stopped outright' (*Oliver Twist*, Ch. XLVIII). He knows what the water means, and flees. Through Quilp, the vivid villain of *The Old Curiosity Shop*, it is imagined with relish. When he finds out that Sampson Brass has confessed, Quilp yearns to revenge himself by drowning him. He would take him to the river's brink and 'with a sudden push ... send him splashing down'.

> 'Drowning men come to the surface three times they say. Ah! To see him those three times, and mock him as his face came bobbing up,—oh, what a rich treat that would be!'
>
> (Ch. LXVII)

Quilp is confident that Brass, like most men at that time, cannot swim, but is doomed to drown himself, falling into the river in the gloom and then 'fighting with the cold, dark water' (Ch. LXVII). As he drowns, he knows that he is drowning.

Every Dickens novel has some reference to drowning in it, often unnecessarily. At the opening of Chapter V of that most jovial book, *Pickwick Papers*, on a beautiful morning in Rochester, Mr Pickwick is leaning over the balustrade of the bridge over the Medway. He is roused from his 'agreeable reverie' by 'the dismal man', who touches him on the shoulder and, after some sententious musings on the brevity and unhappiness of life, asks, 'Did it ever strike you, on such a morning as this, that drowning would be happiness and peace?' It is a comically incongruous question, yet the man has thought of the delight of drowning rather too much for the reader's comfort.

> 'The calm, cool water seems to me to murmur an invitation to repose and rest. A bound, a splash, a brief struggle; there is an eddy for an instant, it gradually subsides into a gentle ripple; the waters have closed above your head, and the world has closed upon your miseries and misfortunes for ever.'

Dickens's first novel cannot get away from drowning. In its eighth instalment, Pickwick and Sam Weller meet an old man in a London tavern, who tells them the story of the Queer Client, a man called Heyling. This man rightly blames his imprisonment for debt and the miserable deaths of his wife and son while he is in prison on his father-in-law. Some time after his release, he is walking by the sea when he hears the cries of a young man, struggling in the water. Heyling, a strong swimmer, is about to plunge in to save him when he realises that the young man's old father, 'wringing his hands in agony' on the shore, is his own father-in-law. As an act of revenge, he stands back and allows the son to drown:

… the last powerful struggle of the dying man agitated the rippling waves for a few seconds; and the spot where he had gone down into his early grave, was undistinguishable from the surrounding water.

(Ch. XXI)

Drowning gets in everywhere: Dickens was an epicure of fear, and this fear was the most primal. What could be more interesting than a drowning? Into the present-tense ennui of the second chapter of *Our Mutual Friend* – the Veneerings' utterly ghastly dinner party – erupts news of the very man the diners have been discussing. The clever, indolent lawyer Mortimer Lightwood has been telling the company the history of John Harmon, heir of a recently dead Dust Contractor, now returning from South Africa to claim his considerable fortune. A servant enters with a note, which he gives to Mortimer. It contains news of 'the identical man'. 'The story is completer and rather more exciting than I supposed. Man's drowned!' The note has been written and delivered by the son of Gaffer Hexam, who lives off the recovery of bodies from the Thames, and whom we have seen plying his trade in the opening chapter of the novel. Mortimer and his equally indolent friend Eugene Wrayburn exit the society gathering to travel down beyond Rotherhithe to see this drowned body. The two bored young men have something to divert them.

The fascination with drowning will prove disturbing. A little later, with another river scavenger, Rogue Riderhood, at the oars, Eugene and Mortimer accompany the Inspector down the Thames in search of Gaffer Hexam. The river seems to have 'a thirst for sucking them under'. Everything shows 'the spoiling influences of water' and speaks therefore of the consequences of being 'crushed, sucked under, and drawn down'. This is primal fear – for the two men and for the reader. 'Not a sluice gate, or a painted scale upon a post or wall, showing the depth of water, but seemed to hint, like the dreadfully facetious Wolf in bed in Grandmamma's cottage, "That's to drown *you* in, my dears!"' (I Ch. XIV). Dickens jestingly recasts the punchline from the tale of Red Riding Hood, for he knows that childish terrors are the strongest: deep down we fear not being eaten by the wolf but drowned by the river. Perhaps this was peculiarly so for earlier generations, when many fewer could swim (though deaths by drowning are still given a prominence in our news stories that is denied to other kinds of accidental death).

Like most piercing fears in Dickens, it can be turned into comedy. In *Great Expectations* Pip visits the Pockets' family home at Hammersmith, on the banks of the Thames. He finds the blithely negligent Mrs Pocket reading, with her feet up on a chair, while her children play in the garden next to the river. One of the two nursemaids casually invokes the fear of drowning.

> 'Master Alick and Miss Jane,' cried one of the nurses to two of the children, 'if you go a bouncing up against them bushes you'll fall over into the river and be drownded, and what'll your pa say then?'
>
> (Ch. XXII)

The possibility of death by drowning is treated as akin to all the other domestic mishaps that perplex the continually perplexed Mr Pocket. 'Drownded' is a repetition of the mispronunciation that members of the Peggotty family all use in *David Copperfield*. On his first visit to Yarmouth David hears from Mr Peggotty that his brother Joe, Ham's father, was 'Drowndead'. Then that Little Em'ly is not his daughter but his niece.

> 'My brother-in-law, Tom, was her father.'
>   I couldn't help it. '—Dead, Mr Peggotty?' I hinted, after another respectful silence.
>   'Drowndead,' said Mr Peggotty.
>
> (Ch.III)

Not just dead, but drowndead. Peggotty's solemn mispronunciation in the face of a child's polite curiosity is comic and melancholy at once, as if to be drowned were to be doubly dead. The young David's polite yet candid curiosity makes the exchange comic. Living from the sea, drowning is an occupational hazard for this family. So, *drowned* and *dead* are almost the same word. Em'ly, whose lover will drown as her father drowned, also says 'drownded'. The mispronunciation may be how Dickens heard working-class Victorians say the word. It first crops up in his novels in *Dombey and Son*, where Rob the Grinder, the train driver's son who has been ruined by Mr Dombey's scheme for his improvement, expresses his sense of his family's dismay at his character thus: 'I wonder … that I haven't been and drownded myself over and over again!' (Ch. XXII) Drowning yourself is so easy that it becomes common parlance. Rob later tells Mrs Brown that if Carker, his master, finds that he has been 'blabbing', a terrible fate awaits him. 'A cove had better drown himself. He says so' (Ch. XLVI).

Suicide by drowning has its comic aspect. In a letter to T. J. Thompson in 1840, Dickens joked about his own putative drowning in the Serpentine.[15] In *Martin Chuzzlewit* Mrs Gamp reveals the existence of a son, so

dutiful that, after squandering his parents' money, he
comes home to break the news, 'offering to drown himself
if that would be a satisfaction to his parents' (Ch. XXV).
It is a likely enough way to go. In *Nicholas Nickleby*, the
feckless Mr Mantalini, threatened by his wife with being
put on an allowance, comically offers his own threat in
return.

> 'I will fill my pockets with change for a sovereign in
> halfpence and drown myself in the Thames; but I will
> not be angry with her, even then, for I will put a note in
> the twopenny-post as I go along, to tell her where the
> body is. She will be a lovely widow. I shall be a body.'

Mrs Mantalini begins to relent and he presses on, a man
who 'for her sake will become a demd damp, moist,
unpleasant body!' (Ch. XXXIV). She can just imagine. In
Little Dorrit, Flora Finching, babbling to her former suitor
Arthur Clennam about her marriage to the now-dead
Mr Finching, justifies accepting his proposal thus: 'he
was so very unsettled and in such low spirits that he had
distractedly alluded to the river if not oil of something
from the chemist's and I did it for the best' (I Ch. XXIII).
Merely mentioning the river is enough to make a young
woman think of drowning and give in.

People did drown – and did drown themselves. The
Royal Humane Society, founded in 1776 to promote the
revival of those who appeared to have drowned, collected
statistics on the number of accidental drownings and
suicides by drowning taking place each year in England
and Wales.[16] According to the Society's figures, in the
mid-nineteenth century between 2,500 and 3,000
people were drowning each year in England and Wales,

approximately one in ten by suicide. This is nearly ten times as many deaths by drowning as in 2016; if we take into account the smaller population, it is proportionately at least twenty-five times as many deaths by drowning. The Society's figures are likely to underestimate the true number. Widespread provision of swimming lessons and the teaching of life-saving techniques date from the last decade of the century, after Dickens's death.[17] Dickens himself came across drownings. In August 1844 he wrote to John Forster from Albaro near Genoa, describing his pleasing surroundings, before mentioning, 'A monk was drowned here on Saturday evening. He was bathing with two other monks, who bolted when he cried out that he was sinking—in consequence, I suppose, of his certainty of going to Heaven.'[18] A month later it was less comic when Dickens's brother Fred very nearly drowned at the same place.[19] There was another drowning when the novelist was living in Switzerland and writing *Dombey and Son*. 'While we were sitting at dinner, one of the prettiest girls in Lausanne was drowned in the lake—in the most peaceful water, reflecting the steep mountains, and crimson with the setting sun.'[20] The picturesque detail is characteristic and unsettling. Dickens tells Forster that the woman was bathing and was 'an accomplished swimmer, as many of the girls are here'. She drifted out of her depth and became entangled in her skirts. Dickens went down to the lake and a boatman acted out the events to him.

Dickens knew what drowned bodies looked like. When he describes the Parisian jailer in *A Tale of Two Cities* as 'so unwholesomely bloated, both in face and person, as to look like a man who had been drowned and filled with water,' he knows what he is talking about (III Ch. II). On visits to Paris he frequented the city morgue, where corpses were displayed for identification. It was located at the Quai du Marché Neuf on the Ile de la Cité, by the edge of the Seine. Bodies recovered from the river were taken here. A corpse would be displayed behind plate-glass windows for up to three days, after which it would be sent for a pauper's burial (or for dissection in the anatomy schools). As Harry Stone notes, Dickens was not unusual in the visits he paid to the place: it 'came to be one of the celebrated sights of Paris ... and a place to which foreigners flocked every day of the week.'[21] Dickens confesses the allure in one of the articles he published in *All the Year Round* as the Uncommercial Traveller: 'Whenever I am at Paris, I am dragged by invisible force into the Morgue. I never want to go there, but am always pulled there.'[22] He goes for a dip in the Seine after visiting the morgue and is possessed by the idea that a 'large dark body was floating straight at me'.[23] It is a body that he has seen earlier in the day,

> a large dark man whose disfigurement by water was in a frightful manner comic, and whose expression was that of a prize-fighter who had closed his eyelids under a heavy blow, but was going immediately to open them, shake his head, and 'come up smiling.' Oh what this large dark man cost me in that bright city![24]

The shape keeps appearing to him during his stay in Paris.

In an article in *Household Words*, he describes his fascination with 'the clothes of the dead', which hang in the morgue for a certain time after the bodies have been removed for burial.[25]

They mostly have been taken off people who were found in the water, and are swollen (as the people often are) out of shape and likeness. Such awful boots, with turned-up toes, and sand and gravel clinging to them, shall be seen in no other collection of dress; nor, such neckcloths, long and lank, still retaining the form of having been wrung out; nor, such slimy garments with puffed legs and arms; nor, such hats and caps that have been battered against pile and bridge; nor, such dreadful rags.

Describing a visit to Paris in *All the Year Round*, he calls the place 'the obscene little Morgue, slinking on the brink of the river ... looking mortally ashamed of itself, and supremely wicked.'[26] But a few sentences later there is 'a quick rush of Blouses past me', for a new body is being brought in to the morgue – and soon the Uncommercial Traveller is part of the curious crowd. 'Was it river, pistol, knife, love, gambling, robbery, hatred, how many stabs, how many bullets, fresh or decomposed, suicide or murder?' The experience leads our narrator to recall a winter dusk in 1861, when, walking on the northern edge of Regent's Park, he had come upon two men, one of them a policeman, recovering the body of a woman from Regent's Canal.

I saw, lying on the towing-path, with her face turned up towards us, a woman, dead a day or two, and under thirty, as I guessed, poorly dressed in black. The feet were lightly crossed at the ankles, and the dark hair, all pushed back from the face, as though that had been the last action of her desperate hands, streamed over the ground.[27]

Dickens describes the corpse like an expert, assuming that this drowning is a suicide: 'So dreadfully forlorn, so dreadfully sad, so dreadfully mysterious, this spectacle of our dear sister here departed!'

Read the Uncommercial Traveller and you might think Dickens's interest in the drowned was obsessive. The series opens (28 January 1860) with him travelling to Anglesey, where the *Royal Charter* has been wrecked with the loss of over 400 lives. He re-imagines some of the drownings and describes (from witness accounts) the appearance of some of the drowned bodies brought ashore. The next article in the series, three weeks later, describes a workhouse in Wapping. On his way there the narrator crosses a swing bridge over a lock called Mr Baker's Trap, apparently popular with suicides. Here he encounters a 'dirty and shiny and slimy' young man,

> who may have been the youngest son of his filthy old father, Thames, or the drowned man about whom there was a placard on the granite post like a large thimble, that stood between us.[28]

A poster advertises the discovery of a drowned body. As if he already knows, our traveller asks this 'creature' if this is 'a common place for suicide', and the young man replies with the names of the women who have thrown themselves in – though he suggests that they take care to have a witness, so that they might be pulled out and put in a hot bath.

Posters announcing drownings recur in the novels. In *Little Dorrit*, Arthur Clennam walks through the crooked Thameside streets that lead to his family home, passing 'here and there a narrow alley leading to the river, where a wretched little bill, FOUND DROWNED, was weeping on the wet wall' (Ch. III). The phrase was used as the title of George Frederic Watts's painting (c. 1849-50) *Found Drowned*, depicting the body of a drowned young woman near the arches of Waterloo Bridge. Watts needed do little beyond placing a heart-shaped locket in the woman's lifeless hand to allow the Victorian viewer to infer that this was a fallen woman, seduced and abandoned, and that she had drowned herself. The huge painting, now hanging in the gallery in Surrey that Watts established before his death, has the woman lying as if she has been crucified, a victim rather than a sinner. The phrase 'Found Drowned' haunted Dickens.[29] In the notebook that he began keeping in 1855, while he was gathering his ideas for *Little Dorrit*, he wrote, 'Found Drowned. The descriptive bill upon the wall, by the waterside'.[30] Some nine years later he wrote next to this 'Done in Our Mutual'. Another entry on the same page of the notebook mentions 'A "long shore" man—woman—child—or family' and queries whether he might 'connect the Found Drowned Bill with this?'[31]

Connect he did. In *Our Mutual Friend* Mortimer and Eugene visit Gaffer Hexam who shows them a bill on the wall, 'BODY FOUND' (I Ch. III). His home is decorated with bills 'respecting the drowned people'. Though he cannot read, he knows the odd details of each corpse from the bill's position on the wall and gives Mortimer and Eugene a résumé.

'I know 'em by their places on the wall. This one was a sailor, with two anchors and a flag and G. F. T. on his arm. Look and see if he warn't.'
  'Quite right.'

'This one was the young woman in grey boots, and her linen marked with a cross. Look and see if she warn't.'

'Quite right.'

'This is him as had a nasty cut over the eye. This is them two young sisters what tied themselves together with a handkecher. This the drunken old chap, in a pair of list slippers and a nightcap, wot had offered—it afterwards come out—to make a hole in the water for a quartern of rum stood aforehand, and kept to his word for the first and last time in his life. They pretty well papers the room, you see; but I know 'em all. I'm scholar enough!'

(I Ch. XIII)

Lizzie later reminds Charley of 'the bills upon the walls at home' – which he wants to forget (II Ch. I). She does so to explain a connection that comes through a drowned man: Jenny Wren is the granddaughter of the old drunk in slippers and nightcap, described on one of those bills and taken drowned from the river.

When Inspector Bucket in *Bleak House* is searching for Lady Dedlock, who has fled the Dedlock mansion, he gazes out at the winter night from 'a high tower in his mind'. Familiar with the habits of outcast men and women, he thinks of 'solitary figures' wandering through the night.

Other solitaries he perceives, in nooks of bridges, looking over; and in shadowed places down by the river's level; and a dark, dark, shapeless object drifting with the tide, more solitary than all, clings with a drowning hold on his attention.

(Ch. LVII)

It is the vision of a man who, by profession, knows all about desperation. He thinks of the river and those who are drawn to it. The vision clutches at him like drowning hands. Drowned bodies are always being recovered. Soon Esther is accompanying him to a 'dreadful spot' near the Thames, 'at the corner of a little slimy turning, which the wind from the river, rushing up it, did not purify'. While Bucket talks to some men 'who looked like a mixture of police and sailors', Esther sees something.

> Against the mouldering wall by which they stood, there was a bill, on which I could discern the words, 'FOUND DROWNED'; and this, and an inscription about Drags, possessed me with the awful suspicion shadowed forth in our visit to that place.
>
> (Ch. LVII)

The inscription advertises drags of the Thames; she knows that Bucket has come to see any bodies lately taken from the river. For Esther, 'it was like the horror of a dream'. A man in 'long swollen sodden boots' is called from his boat and takes Bucket down some 'slippery steps'. 'They came back, wiping their hands upon their coats, after turning over something wet; but thank God it was not what I feared!'

Facing disgrace, what would Lady Dedlock do but drown herself? 'Suicide by drowning, a common route for those women who did take their own lives, was the way most visual artists and many writers of the Victorian era imagined female suicide.'[32] As well as Watts's painting there were other pictorial representations of the fate of fallen women, notably Gustav Doré's *The Bridge of Sighs* and the third of Augustus Egg's *Past and Present* series

(1858), 'Despair', depicting an adulterous wife on the point of drowning herself. The most influential representation of a fallen woman drowning herself in the Thames was Thomas Hood's poem 'Bridge of Sighs' (1844), which may well have inspired Watts's painting.

In *Daniel Deronda*, Daniel, rowing on the Thames near Kew Bridge, sees the despairing Mirah, and knows immediately that she is on the brink of throwing herself into the water. Why else would a lone woman be standing on the banks of the river? In *Oliver Twist*, Nancy looks at the Thames and thinks of drowning herself ('I shall come to that at last'). When Dickens looked at the Thames he thought of those who drowned themselves. On one of his night walks, the Uncommercial Traveller finds that

> the river had an awful look, the buildings on the banks were muffled in black shrouds, and the reflected lights seemed to originate deep in the water, as if the spectres of suicides were holding them to show where they went down.[33]

In *David Copperfield* Mr Littimer coldly imagines Little Em'ly's likely fate after she has been cast off by Steerforth. 'She may have drowned herself' (Ch. XLIV). Later Martha, shamed by her life of prostitution, tells David that her mission to save Emily is 'the only certain thing that saves me from the river' (Ch. XLVII). The idea of drowning obsesses her. 'Oh the River Oh the river!' Dickens notes in his mem for Ch. XIVII. She repeats these words 'over and over again'. She knows that it is the only thing she is 'fit for'. 'Oh, the dreadful river!' In *Our Mutual Friend*, Betty Higden hears 'the tender river whispering to many like herself' (III Ch. VIII). The temptation is to suicide. 'Come

to me, come to me! When the cruel shame and terror you
have so long fled from, most beset you, come to me!' It is
a temptation that Dickens seems to endorse. Drowning
is for those who have suffered enough. In the opening
chapter of *The Old Curiosity Shop*, the narrator describes
how anyone might pause on one of London's bridges of
an evening, looking down on the water, 'remembering to
have heard or read in old time that drowning was not a
hard death, but of all means of suicide the easiest and best'
(Ch. I). Dickens's fascination is hauntingly transferred to
his narrative. Those with 'heavy loads' gaze at the river
and think of drowning. They fear and desire it.

The Thames seems a river of the drowned. The second
series of his early *Sketches by Boz* ends with an account of
the destructive, despairing life of an alcoholic who finally
throws himself into the river at Waterloo Bridge and
drowns 'in agonies of terror'.[34] After a week his 'swollen
and disfigured' corpse washes ashore, miles down river.
Years later, Dickens's Uncommercial Traveller floats in a
boat down the Thames, looking at 'the drags that were
hanging up at certain dirty stairs to hook the drowned
out.'[35] Everyone knows about the bodies found in the
Thames. In *The Old Curiosity Shop* Quilp finds out that
his wife, mother-in-law and stooge, Samson Brass, have
gathered with some appearance of celebration because
they think that he is dead. 'They think you're — you're
drowned', says the nameless boy who works for him. Quilp
is delighted. 'Drowned, eh, Mrs Quilp? Drowned!' (Ch.
XLIX). Mr Brass is speaking to two 'waterside men' who
have been dragging the river. One of them believes that
the body will 'come ashore somewhere about Grinidge
tomorrow, at ebb tide'. Some live off these bodies in the
river. In *Great Expectations*, Herbert and Startop row

Pip and Magwitch down the Thames into the estuary. There they put up at an isolated public house, where they encounter only the landlord and his wife and the 'Jack' of the causeway, 'who was as slimy and smeary as if he had been low-water mark too'. He evidently relies on the drowned, for he wears 'a bloated pair of shoes' that he exhibits 'as interesting relics that he had taken a few days ago from the feet of a drowned seaman washed ashore'. After the struggle between Magwitch and Compeyson, and Compeyson's drowning, it is he who undertakes 'to search for the body in the places where it was likeliest to come ashore'. Yet this liver-off-the-dead is, in Dickens, a comic addition.

> His interest in its recovery seemed to me to be much heightened when he heard that it had stockings on. Probably, it took about a dozen drowned men to fit him out completely; and that may have been the reason why the different articles of his dress were in various stages of decay.
>
> (Ch. LIV)

The Royal Humane Society, with its mission to promote the revival of those recovered from the water, embodied a powerful ideal. In a world where medical intervention rarely appeared 'life-saving', here was an opportunity to drag a human being back from death to life. The ideal was so well acknowledged that Dickens used it for a joke at the beginning of *Nicholas Nickleby*, where Nicholas Nickleby's great-uncle leaves his money to his grandfather because the Royal Humane Society, intended recipient of his estate, irritates him by saving the life of a poor relative to whom he is paying a weekly allowance. The experiences of the nearly drowned, returning to life, were proverbial. In *The Old Curiosity Shop*, the mysterious but evidently benign 'single gentleman' is accompanying Kit's mother on a journey across England to try to find Nell, and decides that she needs reviving.

> Immediately flying to the bell, and calling for mulled wine as impetuously as if it had been wanted for instant use in the recovery of some person apparently drowned, the single gentleman made Kit's mother swallow a bumper of it at such a high temperature that the tears ran down her face.
>
> (Ch. XLIX)

Recalling his extreme sea-sickness on his first voyage to America, Dickens described experiencing 'an amount of anguish only second to that which is said to be endured by the apparently drowned, in the process of restoration to life' (*American Notes*, Ch. XXIII).

It seems that this process of 'restoration' is something with which everyone is familiar. When news of John Harmon being drowned is conveyed to Mortimer Lightwood near the beginning of *Our Mutual Friend*, his question is immediate. 'Were any means taken, do you know, boy, to ascertain if it was possible to restore life?' (Ch. III). This drowned man is beyond reviving, unlike Rogue Riderhood, later in the same novel. After a steamer runs down his wherry he is 'grappled up' from the river and his apparently lifeless body is brought in to the riverside inn. In that intensifying present-tense narration, over the course of a whole chapter, a doctor hauls him back from somewhere on the 'dark road' to death. He is revived using new, scientifically verified techniques, in

which – Riderhood's luck – the doctor is skilled.[36] Four
customers help, obeying instructions to turn the body.

> See! A token of life! An indubitable token of life! The
> spark may smoulder and go out, or it may glow and
> expand, but see! The four rough fellows, seeing, shed
> tears. Neither Riderhood in this world, nor Riderhood
> in the other, could draw tears from them; but a striving
> human soul between the two can do it easily.
>
> (III Ch. III)

It is one episode in a novel in which, as Adrian Poole
says, 'Nothing seems certainly dead nor entirely alive.'[37]
It demonstrates the obduracy of Riderhood's evil: his
daughter thinks ('sweet delusion') that 'the old evil is
drowned out of him'. But he is not in the least altered.
All the spectators know this before he even regains
consciousness. He will not take his chance or heed the
warning: in the river, oblivion still awaits him.

By a lock on the Thames, Riderhood tells Bradley
Headstone that, having been once revived after nearly
drowning, 'I can't be drowned'. He sees Headstone stare
into the water with 'a very dark expression on his face' and
thinks that he would not have been surprised if he had
'taken a leap, and thrown himself in'. This is the primal
instinct, as the narrator admits. 'Perhaps his troubled
soul, set upon some violence, did hover for the moment
between that violence and another' (IV Ch. I). When
Headstone, goaded to self-destructive passion, seizes
him on the brink of the lock, Riderhood tells him again,
'You can't drown Me. Ain't I told you that the man as has
come through drowning can never be drowned? I can't be
drowned' (IV Ch. XV).

But, like Macbeth, he has missed the point. ' "I can be!" returned Bradley, in a desperate, clenched voice. "I am resolved to be. I'll hold you living, and I'll hold you dead. Come down!" ' It was always his destiny.

It is a nice touch that Riderhood, a cunning cynic who lives by his instinct for other men's weaknesses, should defend himself with this confidently declared superstition. If drowning awaits us, how we need the magic that might ward off this peril! When Nicholas Nickleby accompanies Mr and Mrs Crummles to their lodgings in Portsmouth, it is the house of a pilot called Bulph, who 'had the little finger of a drowned man on his parlour mantelshelf, with other maritime and natural curiosities' (Ch. XXIII). Nothing more is said about it, but we can infer that this is the seaman's prophylactic against drowning. We remember that David Copperfield felt it worth telling us that he was born in a caul, and that this was subsequently advertised for sale. Later it was offered as a prize in a raffle and won by an old lady. 'It is a fact which will be long remembered as remarkable down there, that she never drowned, but died triumphantly in bed, at ninety-two' (Ch. I). The old lady defeats her fear of drowning by never going on or near water; the comedy of her superstition relies on the universality of the fear.

Drowning represents the elemental pull of death, mostly fearful, sometimes desirable. Dickens became an enthusiast for swimming to master this danger. The mastery was suitable for a novelist, for the invention of the English novel required a protagonist who was a strong swimmer. The narrator of *Robinson Crusoe* – that favourite novel of Dickens – survives to tell his story because of his strength as a swimmer. His ship is wrecked in a terrible storm and he and his shipmates take to a lifeboat. When this is overturned in sight of land death seems inevitable. But 'I swam very well', Crusoe tells us. He finally struggles ashore, 'reflecting upon all my comrades that were drowned, and that there should not be one soul saved but myself'.[38] God has singled him out. The novel as a genre begins as a story of self-reliance; its hero's abilities as a swimmer demonstrate his resourcefulness. No wonder Dickens loved this story so much.

13

Knowing about sex

I am a common woman, fallen. Is it devilry in me—
is it a wicked comfort—what is it—that induces me
to be always tempting other women down, while
I hate myself!

Note in collection of 'Memoranda[1]

This book tries to do justice to Dickens's inventiveness,
his ingenuity, his experimentalism – above all, to show the
daring of his fiction. Here is a novelist unafraid to disobey
most of the conventions governing literary form and
stylistic propriety. Yet all is not fearlessness in Dickens's
novels: in one respect he seems positively timid. When
it comes to the relationships between men and women,
to imagining sexual passion, his fiction is, it is generally
agreed, evasive, euphemistic, prim. His novels cannot face
up to the truth of sexual desire and are distorted by the
author's Victorian propriety. John Carey sums up what
many other readers and critics have thought, when he says
that sex in Dickens's novels 'is not banished but driven

underground, to emerge in perverted and inhibited forms.'[2]

Yet the society in which he mixed was not so censorious. Whatever the stern sexual morality of some of his novels, he readily befriended many whose private lives were not in the least respectable. Literary success took him into bohemian company. He enjoyed, for instance, a warm friendship with Count D'Orsay, a dandy and compulsive gambler, and with his mistress, the Countess of Blessington, who presided over glittering salons that included the young author. He had many male associates who had sexual relationships outside marriage. Most famously, his close friend and collaborator Wilkie Collins lived for many years with a woman to whom he was not married, Caroline Graves, though their friendship was perhaps undermined by Dickens's disapproval of the relationship.[3] Collins would go on to have an affair with a Norfolk servant girl, Martha Rudd, by whom he eventually had three children. From 1870, the year of Dickens's death, Collins was maintaining two separate households with the two women.

There is even some tantalising evidence of possible extra-marital wanderings of his own. In 1841 he wrote to his friend, the painter Daniel Maclise, who was a frequent companion in his London night walks, attempting to entice him to join him on holiday in Broadstairs. He offered as bait the fact that 'there are convenences of all kinds at Margate (do you take me?) And I know where they live.'[4] (Maclise, a confirmed bachelor, had been notorious in the late 1830s for his affair with Lady Henrietta Sykes, a married woman and Disraeli's former mistress.) Perhaps Dickens never himself sampled the local prostitutes to whom he here seems to refer, but the man-to-worldly-man tone of the information shows how he was willing to be anything but prim in the right company. In July 1859 he told his doctor Frank Beard that he wanted to see him because 'My bachelor state has engendered a small malady.'[5] This sounds very much like a reference to a venereal infection.

And, for more than a decade, he had a mistress. Or rather, most critics and biographers now consider that his secret thirteen-year intimacy with Ellen Ternan, the young actress he met in 1857 when she performed in the play *The Frozen Deep*, was a sexual relationship. When they met, he was forty-five and she was eighteen. Thomas Wright first presented the evidence for Ellen having been Dickens's mistress in his *Life of Charles Dickens*, published in 1935. In his wake, all Dickens biographers have had to come up with explanations for Dickens's financial support for Ellen, his frequent visits to her and his obsessive secrecy about the relationship. Though there is no final proof that theirs was a sexual relationship, since the publication of Claire Tomalin's *The Invisible Woman* in 1990, this has been the consensus. For the last twelve years of his life, she was a kept woman and he was preoccupied with concealing an intimacy that, he believed, would destroy his standing as the nation's most uplifting entertainer.[6]

His long-running affair makes even more appalling his cruel public renunciation of his loyal wife, Catherine (Kate), from whom he separated in 1858, the year after he met Ellen. His conduct has come to seem worse and worse. Even as I was writing this book, it became a news item once more. Victorian scholar John Bowen found that a previously neglected collection of letters written by Edward Dutton Cook, a man of letters who was Catherine Dickens's next-door neighbour after her separation from Dickens, revealed that her husband had tried to have her confined in a lunatic asylum.[7] The evasiveness of his novels about sexuality appears a worse fault for his own hypocrisy. He wanted to remain the morally impeccable favourite of the reading classes, while pursuing his own, extra-marital sexual desires.

In one respect, Dickens was not a hypocrite when it came to the inviolability of marriage. The year in which he separated from his wife was also the year in which the Divorce and Matrimonial Causes Act came into force, establishing a Divorce Court and widening the availability of divorce. Dickens was a strong supporter of this liberalisation. In *Hard Times*, he traded on his reader's expected sympathy with Stephen Blackpool, the man who has married the wrong woman and is legally condemned to his match. Stephen's nameless wife is a gibbering alcoholic who has deserted him but returns intermittently, like a curse. He is not permitted to consummate – or even declare – his love for another woman. In the chapter entitled 'No Way Out', Stephen visits Bounderby, his employer, to ask if there is any way in which he can obtain a divorce and to lament the laws that keep him tethered to his wife. Not surprisingly, contemporaries took this sub-plot as Dickens's protest against what he saw as the inequities of divorce laws.[8]

Victorian novels often turn on the predicament of a person trapped in a failed, sometimes a hellish, marriage. We might remember *Jane Eyre*, where Mr Rochester, shackled to his mad wife, asks the heroine to live with him in France – but not to consummate their relationship.

You shall be Mrs Rochester—both virtually and nominally. I shall keep only to you so long as you and I live. You shall go to a place I have in the south of France: a whitewashed villa on the shores of the Mediterranean. There you shall live a happy, and guarded, and most innocent life. Never fear that I wish to lure you into error—to make you my mistress.[9]

Rochester has previously kept mistresses while living abroad, but in order to make his offer to Jane at all tempting, Brontë has to remove the sexual motive. In the novel that followed *Hard Times*, *Little Dorrit*, Dickens arguably took more risks with his reader's sympathies. The novel's plot is founded on Mrs Clennam's righteous horror at her husband's sexual sin, but we cannot share this horror. She is a puritan fanatic, devoted to a harsh and loveless religion. We are given every reason to think that her husband, finding himself in a sexless marriage, erred through true love of another woman, who turns out to be Arthur Clennam's real mother.

There certainly are examples in Dickens's novels of the author's apparent timidity about sex. Take the story of Edith Dombey in *Dombey and Son*. The mercenarily arranged marriage between this beautiful young widow who is 'not quite thirty' and the chilly Mr Dombey is depicted with memorable exactitude (Ch. XXI). He marries her for the prestige of having an impressive wife, but also because he wishes to have a son, to replace the dead Paul Dombey. She marries him because she and her mother have no money and need an 'establishment'. Edith is clear-eyed and bitterly resigned about her fate. 'He sees me at the auction, and he thinks it well to buy me.' She knows that she will have to have sex with this man. All this is horribly clear from the grim business of their courtship.

Accomplished to a fault, she plays the piano or harp, she sings or draws, just as Mr Dombey requests. 'Such frigid and constrained, yet prompt and pointed acquiescence with the wishes he imposed upon her, and on no one else' must seem to Mr Dombey, as it is intended to seem, a prelude to her behaviour once he has married her. She will comply. To the watching, ever-watchful Mr Carker, Mr Dombey's 'Manager', it is clear that 'Mr Dombey was evidently proud of his power, and liked to show it' (Ch. XXVII). Dickens encourages us to think, with some kind of horror, of her future sexual subjugation.

Dickens shows us that Edith thinks of it too. The day before her ghastly wedding, she quarrels with her mother, whom she has barred from any corrupting contact with Florence Dombey. 'What are you, pray? What are you?' shrieks Mrs Skewton. Edith knows the answer, saying that she has seen her own reflection 'more than once' when she has looked out of the window 'and something in the faded likeness of my sex has wandered past outside' (Ch. XXX). That 'something' is a prostitute; Edith is adopting the evasive wording of her day to say something not in the least evasive. She too is, in effect, a prostitute. When they return from their honeymoon in Paris, Mr Dombey seems satisfied – 'well enough pleased to see his handsome wife immovable and proud and cold' (Ch. XXXV). We are to presume that he has had his share of the bargain: the chapter is sarcastically titled 'The Happy Pair'.

Before long Mr and Mrs Dombey are combatants in a marital war, the husband demanding deference and obedience, the wife proudly and angrily refusing. Edith appeals to Mr Dombey to agree to a truce, in the hope of eventually arriving at some semblance of 'friendship' between them (Ch. XL). She is proposing, it seems, a polite and sexless marriage of convenience. He refuses to accept anything but her submission to him; henceforth, though living in the same house, they are utterly estranged from each other. Carker sees it all and sets himself to conquer Edith. Dickens shows him gaining some kind of confidence from her by explaining how her evident affection for Florence 'will not benefit its object'. Mr Dombey will feel the more vindictive if he sees it. Carker finds Edith's weak point by declaring that he will help her 'ward off evil' from Florence (Ch. XLV). In his chapter plan, Dickens wrote, 'Carker and Edith. The last view of them before the elopement. She relenting by force'.[10]

When it becomes clear to Edith that she cannot help Florence by remaining in the family home, she demands a separation from her husband (Ch. XLVII). Denied this, she elopes with Carker, on the very anniversary of her wedding. Forster records Dickens's original intention that Edith was to have had an adulterous relationship with the man who has been acting as Mr Dombey's 'Manager' but for whom she also feels hatred 'in the most deadly degree.'[11] 'I have relied on it very much for the effect of her death.' Dickens was evidently planning that her adultery would end in death-bed penitence, presumably with Florence in attendance.[12] But his friend Lord Jeffrey wrote to him after reading Number XIV, protesting against Edith's impending infidelity. 'Note from Jeffrey this morning, who won't believe (positively refuses) that Edith is Carker's mistress.'[13] Dickens was receptive to Jeffrey's protest. 'What do you think of a kind of inverted Maid's Tragedy, and a tremendous scene of her undeceiving Carker, and giving him to know that she never meant that?' (In Beaumont and Fletcher's *The Maid's Tragedy*, the main female character, Evadne, refuses to sleep with her

new husband because the marriage has been arranged by
the King who had forced her to be his mistress.) He duly
changed tack.

Edith and Carker travel separately to France, and when
they meet at a hotel in Dijon, Carker, addressing her as
'my love', clearly expects that they will sleep together
(Ch. LIV). In his number plan, Dickens wrote 'Edith
and Carker. Edith <u>not</u> his mistress', making it clear to
himself that he needed to make this clear to his readers.[14]
In the novel, she tells Carker, 'We meet to-night, and
part to-night.' She remembers that, when they agreed to
elope, she did allow Carker to kiss her, but now she finds
him 'loathesome'. She announces what Dickens wants
us to know. 'I have resolved to bear the shame that will
attach to me – resolved to know that it attaches falsely.'
Edith abandons Carker, who himself flees the vengeful
Mr Dombey, to his death. Dickens wanted to make it
absolutely clear that Edith did not have sex with him.
Later, she meets Florence for one last time to tell her that,
whatever she was guilty of, she was 'not guilty with that
dead man. Before God!', 'I am innocent of that'. And
because she is 'innocent of that', she can live and retire
to the south of Italy with her amiable if foolish Cousin
Feenix (Ch. LXI).

Was Dickens conquered by his own prudishness?
What he had written in earlier parts of the novel might
have made it particularly hard for him to allow Edith
Dombey, as she has become, to go to bed with the man
with whom she has fled her torturing marriage. *Dombey
and Son* contains, in its very first instalment, Dickens's
clearest statement of the view – which was evidently his
view – that women are at heart better than men. He
is describing the virtues of Paul Dombey's wet-nurse,

Polly Toodle, who has little in the way of 'artificial accomplishments', but is still

> a good plain sample of a nature that is ever, in the mass, better, truer, higher, nobler, quicker to feel, and much more constant to retain, all tenderness and pity, self-denial and devotion, than the nature of men.
>
> (Ch. III)

In that eve-of-marriage argument with her mother, Edith exclaims, 'if you had but left me to my natural heart when I too was a girl – a younger girl than Florence – how different I might have been!' (Ch. XXX). Edith too is a woman, however she has been bent from that better nature.

We might think that this brew of insinuation and repression in *Dombey and Son* is thoroughly 'Victorian'. The *Oxford English Dictionary* records, in one of its definitions of this word, a later age's view, which is still operative in our use of the adjective.

> **2.** *figurative.* Resembling or typified by the attitudes supposedly characteristic of the Victorian era; prudish, strict; old-fashioned, out-dated.

It gives as the earliest example of this usage a definition offered in *Webster's New International Dictionary of the English Language* in 1934. Yet Dickens himself sometimes bridled at Victorian primness. He did so when he responded to critics of his second novel, *Oliver Twist*. In the preface that he wrote for the third edition of the novel in 1841, he sarcastically scorned those who had objected to the 'very coarse and shocking circumstance' that some of

the book's characters 'are chosen from the most criminal
and degraded of London's population'.[15] Among these is
Nancy: 'the girl is a prostitute', he declared emphatically.
There might be readers who found it difficult to accept
the fact, but there it was.

The word 'prostitute' is all the more emphatic because
it is never used in any of Dickens's novels. Without this
assertion, a reader has to be highly discerning to recognise
Nancy's occupation. Here is Oliver's first encounter with
her and her friend Bet.

> They wore a good deal of hair, not very neatly turned
> up behind, and were rather untidy about the shoes
> and stockings. They were not exactly pretty, perhaps;
> but they had a great deal of colour in their faces, and
> looked quite stout and hearty. Being remarkably free
> and agreeable in their manners, Oliver thought them
> very nice girls indeed. As there is no doubt they were.
>
> (Ch. IX)

Is this enough to tell the nineteenth-century reader what
these girls do for a living? Elsewhere in the novel, the clues
are in the phrases used to avoid saying what this living is.
'Do you know who you are, and what you are?' Sikes asks
Nancy (Ch. XVI). 'What you are': even the brutish Sikes
finds it distasteful to be any more specific. In the chapter
where she meets virtuous Rose Maylie, Dickens stops using
Nancy's name and she becomes just 'the girl' – a person
singled out briefly from others like her on the streets.
'If you knew what I am sometimes, you would pity me,
indeed' she says to Rose. At the chapter's end, when Rose
offers her help, she repeats that evasive self-description. 'I
have felt more grief to think of what I am, to-night, than

I ever did before, and it would be something not to die in the hell in which I have lived' (Ch. XL). 'What I am'. We remember Mrs Skewton in *Dombey and Son* shrieking at her daughter, 'What are you?' In *David Copperfield*, when Martha tells David and Mr Peggotty that she is innocent of Little Em'ly's fall, she uses the same phrase, twice, for her own fate. 'She never spoke a word to me but what was pleasant and right. Is it likely I would try to make her what I am myself, knowing what I am myself, so well?' (Ch. XLVII). She knows, but she cannot exactly say. It is Martha, as Mr Peggotty tells David, who finds Emily in London and saves her when she stands 'upon the brink of more than I can say or think on' (Ch. LI). That is, when she is about to be lured into prostitution.

Not being able to say or even think things is the point. For the unmentionableness of sex, listen to Miss Flite in *Bleak House*. This benign, mad old woman, obsessed with the case of Jarndyce and Jarndyce, has just been asked by Esther what the Mace and Seal upon the table in the Court of Chancery can do. She answers 'Draw' – and then this one word generates a sentence – 'Draw people on, my dear' – which forms the pattern repeated in the following sentences.

'Draw peace out of them. Sense out of them. Good looks out of them. Good qualities out of them. I have felt them even drawing my rest away in the night. Cold and glittering devils!'

This one word for the irresistible power of the legal proceeding, with its promise of some final inheritance, becomes the key to all her family's misfortunes.

First, our father was drawn—slowly. Home was drawn
with him. In a few years he was a fierce, sour, angry
bankrupt without a kind word or a kind look for any
one. He had been so different, Fitz Jarndyce. He was
drawn to a debtors' prison. There he died. Then our
brother was drawn—swiftly—to drunkenness. And
rags. And death. Then my sister was drawn. Hush!
Never ask to what!

(Ch. XXXV)

'Hush!' Miss Flite's exclamation draws attention to what
cannot be said. No adult Victorian reader would have
been in doubt about her sister's fate. She must have been
'drawn' to prostitution, the last recourse of a woman
desperate for money.

Dickens makes us hear what is repressed. Even the
most fearless Victorian novelists were guarded or evasive
about sex, yet could make creative opportunities from the
very business of repression. George Eliot's first full-length
novel, *Adam Bede* (which Dickens hugely admired),
centres on the affair between Hetty Sorrel, a seventeen-
year-old milkmaid, and Arthur Donnithorne, grandson
and heir of the local squire.[16] We see their assignations
in the Chase, the woodland in the heart of which is the
Hermitage, a kind of summerhouse to which Arthur has
the key. We see their first kiss, rendered with the intensity
of the present tense.

His arm is stealing round the waist again; it is tightening
its clasp; he is bending his face nearer and nearer to
the round cheek; his lips are meeting those pouting
child-lips, and for a long moment time has vanished.
He may be a shepherd in Arcadia for aught he knows,

he may be the first youth kissing the first maiden, he
may be Eros himself, sipping the lips of Psyche—it is
all one.[17]

It is only a kiss, interrupting their walk for a few moments
and leading to they know not what.

There was no speaking for minutes after. They walked
along with beating hearts till they came within sight of
the gate at the end of the wood. Then they looked at
each other, not quite as they had looked before, for in
their eyes there was the memory of a kiss.[18]

We end the chapter with Arthur determined to confess
his flirtation to his friend the vicar and thus escape the
temptation of pursuing it. Yet we know that Hetty has
convinced herself that Arthur will marry her. Arthur does
not avoid temptation. At the village dance we hear him
telling Hetty 'in low hurried tones' when he will next be
in the wood, waiting for her.[19] Our clue as to what will
follow is the narrator's observation that Hetty, in her 'joys
and hopes', is 'unconscious of the real peril'.

Then the narrative leaps forward by three weeks and
Adam Bede, who loves Hetty, comes upon her and Arthur
in the Chase. They are 'standing opposite to each other,
with clasped hands, about to part'.[20] Hetty flees and
Adam angrily tells Arthur that he knows that this is not
their first assignation. 'Arthur felt a startled uncertainty
how far Adam was speaking from knowledge and how far
from mere inference.'[21] We too need to rely on 'inference'.
Eliot requires her reader to be worldly enough to work
out what has happened, because Adam himself is too
naïve to do so.

'What if you meant nothing by your kissing and your presents? Other folks won't believe as you've meant nothing; and don't tell me about her not deceiving herself. I tell you …'

Arthur had felt a sudden relief while Adam was speaking; he perceived that Adam had no positive knowledge of the past …

Adam, himself in love with Hetty, cannot allow himself to imagine the truth. The reader must see through the narrative's evasiveness, which Eliot exploits to let us escape her characters' illusions. Ironically, it is perhaps the modern reader, passing too easily over the exact implications of Hetty's 'real peril', who might be more likely to be surprised eventually to discover that Hetty is pregnant. The nearest that Eliot gets to specifying what has taken place between Hetty and Arthur is a reference to the 'short poisonous delights' that she recalls after Arthur has deserted her.[22]

Dickens, then, is hardly alone amongst Victorian novelists in his evasiveness about sex. Like Eliot, he is capable of making creative use of that evasiveness. In *David Copperfield*, he invents a narrator who can hardly bear to understand the evidence of human desires that he sees. David describes the evening on which he introduces Steerforth to the Peggotty household in Yarmouth and relives the innocence of that experience. He recalls how Steerforth, though the most charming and eloquent person in the room, 'set up no monopoly of the general attention, or the conversation.' While David renews shared memories with Little Em'ly,

he was silent and attentive, and observed us thoughtfully. She sat, at this time, and all the evening,

on the old locker in her old little corner by the fire—
Ham beside her, where I used to sit. I could not satisfy
myself whether it was in her own little tormenting way,
or in a maidenly reserve before us, that she kept quite
close to the wall, and away from him; but I observed
that she did so, all the evening.

(Ch. XXI)

Her engagement to Ham has just been announced; that
slight distance she keeps from him in Steerforth's presence
tells you something. Steerforth's silent observation of the
scene is not tactful but scheming. Even the most proper
Victorian reader – perhaps especially such a reader – is
already being nudged to acknowledge what must follow.
As Dickens told his friend William de Cerjat, Little Em'ly
'*must* fall—there is no hope for her'.[23]

We can hear that David's delight in Steerforth's ability to
charm the Peggottys, even after his friend's cold comment
about Ham being 'rather a chuckle-headed fellow for the
girl', is wilfully naïve.

> 'When I see how perfectly you understand them,
> how exquisitely you can enter into happiness like
> this plain fisherman's, or humour a love like my old
> nurse's, I know that there is not a joy or sorrow, not an
> emotion, of such people, that can be indifferent to you.
> And I admire and love you for it, Steerforth, twenty
> times the more!'
>
> He stopped, and, looking in my face, said, 'Daisy,
> I believe you are in earnest, and are good. I wish we all
> were!' Next moment he was gaily singing Mr Peggotty's
> song, as we walked at a round pace back to Yarmouth.

(Ch. XXI)

David is finally summoned by Rosa Dartle and made to hear of Emily's fate, after her elopement with Steerforth, from his repulsive valet, Littimer. He speaks of her travels around Europe 'under Mr James's protection' (Ch. XLVI). They have lived together as if a married couple, though, naturally, he has not married her. The sexual transaction is made even clearer by the fact that Steerforth, having tired of Emily, has offered to pass her on, as a wife, to Littimer. David does not want to think of Emily as a sexual being, but Dickens uses Rosa Dartle to force on him the discomfort of doing so. He cannot quite take the refuge of Ham, who, according to Peggotty, does sometimes talk to her about Emily, but always in a manner that might provide a motto for Dickens's own supposed flinching from female sexual desire: 'he mentioned Emily as a child. But, he never mentioned her as a woman' (LI). Her end destination is Australia. In this, she follows the same path as many of the reformed prostitutes who had come to live in Urania Cottage, the home for fallen women that Dickens had founded and overseen, and that his friend Angela Burdett-Coutts had financed.[24]

David Copperfield in fact dramatises the same fears of which Dickens so frequently stands accused. Dickens raises the spectre of an affair between old Doctor Strong's young wife, Annie, and her cousin, Jack Maldon, in order to have his narrator turn away from the dread possibility. David looks back on the tableau of Doctor Strong and his wife, the night of Jack Maldon's departure for India, and cannot see what the expression on the woman's face tells him.

The eyes were wide open, and her brown hair fell in two rich clusters on her shoulders, and on her white

dress, disordered by the want of the lost ribbon.
Distinctly as I recollect her look, I cannot say of
what it was expressive, I cannot even say of what it
is expressive to me now, rising again before my older
judgement. Penitence, humiliation, shame, pride, love,
and trustfulness—I see them all; and in them all, I see
that horror of I don't know what.

(Ch. XVI).

It is the face of a woman who has been tempted by
adulterous passion, but even in knowing retrospect the
narrator cannot name it.

Eventually, Jack Maldon returns from India (the climate
has not agreed with him) to attend on Mrs Strong, with
her husband's unsuspicious encouragement. Uriah Heep
sees it and dares David to admit that he sees it too. 'I
endeavoured to appear unconscious and not disquieted,
but, I saw in his face, with poor success.' David pretends
not to understand Heep's insinuations and Heep doubles
up with laughter. Soon he will punish David for his
dishonesty in front of Doctor Strong. Has he not noticed
Mrs Strong's behaviour?

'Oh! it's very kind of you, Copperfield,' returned Uriah,
undulating all over, 'and we all know what an amiable
character yours is; but you know that the moment
I spoke to you the other night, you knew what I meant.
You know you knew what I meant, Copperfield. Don't
deny it! You deny it with the best intentions; but don't
do it, Copperfield.'

I saw the mild eye of the good old Doctor turned
upon me for a moment, and I felt that the confession
of my old misgivings and remembrances was too

plainly written in my face to be overlooked. It was of
no use raging. I could not undo that. Say what I would,
I could not unsay it.

Heep renders David powerless by making him
acknowledge his 'misgivings': 'he forced his confidence
upon me, expressly to make me miserable'(Ch. XLII).

David cannot bear to think of these sexual liaisons.
Uriah Heep himself has his thoughts bent on Agnes
Wickfield and torments David with the idea of their
eventual coupling. Mr Wickfield, the lawyer at whose
Canterbury home David lodged while he was at school,
has been brought low by drink. Heep, his clerk, sees this
and works on his weakness, becoming his partner and
making his former employer dependent on him. Mr
Wickfield becomes convinced that only Heep can save his
firm from ruin. In his lucid moments, Mr Wickfield is
appalled at the thought of his daughter marrying Heep,
yet knows that this is the only way for him to escape.
As Heep displays his power ('I've an ambition to make
your Agnes my Agnes') in front of David, Mr Wickfield
raves in desperation. Agnes evidently braces herself for
the sacrifice. 'Say you have no such thought, dear Agnes!'
exclaims David. She cannot quite satisfy him. The chapter
ends with Heep asking David if he has 'sometimes plucked
a pear before it was ripe'. The pear he is thinking of will
'ripen yet ... I can wait!' As David leaves Canterbury on
the coach he sees Heep, his mouth moving, 'as if the pear
were ripe already, and he were smacking his lips over it'
(Ch. XXXIX). We can feel David's disgust.

Dickens arouses disgust like no other Victorian
novelist. In *Nicholas Nickleby* he stirs our revolted
knowledge of the motivation of leering old miser Arthur

Gride, who schemes for Madeline Bray to be pressured by her father into marrying him. She is eighteen; he is in his seventies. Madeline's father is encumbered by debts; Gride will release him from these if he gets the hand of his daughter. Gride has another motive: he has discovered that, unknown to her, Madeline stands to inherit a large amount of money from her grandfather. But the money is the least of it. He wants his hands on Madeline. He describes her to his fellow conspirator Ralph Nickleby.

'Dark eyes, long eyelashes, ripe and ruddy lips that to look at is to long to kiss, beautiful clustering hair that one's fingers itch to play with, such a waist as might make a man clasp the air involuntarily, thinking of twining his arm about it...'

(Ch. CLVII)

As sensual raptures go, this might seem mild stuff. Yet the evasion of anything more explicit is what makes it so effectively repellent. Its restrained relish signals the lecherousness underneath. Gride looks forward with the acutest anticipation to what will follow his projected wedding. This is grotesque – but also, we sense, a horror that is conjured in order to be allayed. The novel is comic. Nicholas loves Madeline and will surely snatch her from Gride's ineffectual grasp. Equally, though *David Copperfield* may be less reassuring than *Nicholas Nickleby* about the happiness of the endings that it will provide, the practised reader of Dickens's fiction surely foresees that Agnes must be saved from having to share a bed with Uriah Heep.

Dickens would arouse a deeper and more disturbing sexual disgust in *Hard Times*, in the arrangement of

the marriage of Louisa Gradgrind to the appalling
Bounderby, abetted by Louisa's father. This is a marriage
that does take place. Early in the novel we see Bounderby,
who is forty-seven or forty-eight, and looks older, fixing
his attentions on Louisa, who is 'a child now, of fifteen
or sixteen; but at no distant day would seem to become
a woman all at once' (I Ch. III). The skin crawls. The
nearest thing that Gradgrind has to a friend, Bounderby
is first encountered as a welcome guest *chez* Gradgrind,
where he may talk about one of the other children, but
always looks at Louisa. Appraisingly, we infer. After
softening the outrage of Louisa's father, who has found
her peeping into the circus tent, Bounderby begs a kiss
off her. 'Always my pet; an't you, Louisa?' Louisa rubs her
cheek where Bounderby has kissed it until it is 'burning
red'. Dickens might not have had the word 'grooming'
to hand, but he wanted his reader to see an example of
it – and recoil.

'You are quite another father to Louisa, sir,' remarks
Mrs Sparsit, a housekeeper with airs who 'presides' over
Bounderby's household (I Ch. IV). It is a remark full
of insinuation, alerting us to his thoroughly unpaternal
motives. Mrs Sparsit sees just what Bounderby is up
to, while pretending not to. A little later, listening to
Stephen Blackpool telling Bounderby about his miserable
marriage, she asks if it was 'unequal … in point of years'.
When Stephen says that it was not, she pretends to mild
surprise. 'I inferred from its being so miserable a marriage,
that it was probably an unequal one in point of years'
(I Ch. XI). It is another stab at her bamboozled master.
Cleverly, disconcertingly, Dickens makes this thoroughly
malign woman the perceptive monitor of Bounderby's
sexual motives and the reader's guide to them.

After Bounderby has invited him in for a private consultation, Louisa's father is more than willing, in a chapter titled 'Father and Daughter', to put his proposal of marriage to Louisa – and to ease her into accepting it (I Ch. XIV). One of the disturbing repeated cameos in Dickens is of the father who would sell or give his daughter to a repulsive, predatory man. Louisa's brother Tom encourages her to believe that she is helping him, for Bounderby has held out the prospect of his patronage. She agrees out of a mix of fatalism and sisterly affection to become Bounderby's wife. Even John Carey concedes that 'Louisa is something of a breakthrough for Dickens', a woman pushed into a marriage that certainly will involve sex with a man who disgusts her.[25] Dickens depends on our thinking about what can never be directly expressed. Thus, the notorious passage in which Louisa talks to her father about the Coketown chimneys, out of which during the day comes nothing but 'languid and monotonous smoke'.

> 'Yet when the night comes, Fire bursts out, father!'
> 'Of course I know that, Louisa. I do not see the application of the remark.' To do him justice he did not, at all.
>
> (Ch. XV)

That authorial comment ensures that the reader cannot share Gradgrind's innocenece.

When, a year into the marriage, one of Dickens's louche, lounging gentlemen, Mr James Harthouse, arrives in Coketown and shows some passing interest in Mrs Bounderby, we overhear Mrs Sparsit, alone at supper, exclaim 'O, you Fool!' She thinks that she knows what is

coming to Bounderby. She thinks with relish that she sees
Louisa going down 'a mighty Staircase, with a dark pit
of shame and ruin at the bottom' (II Ch. X). Like Edith
Dombey, Louisa is given good reason for adultery, but is
(just) saved from this ultimate sin. Dickens seems always
to have planned to save Louisa from consummating her
dalliance with Harthouse (he was not going to allow Mrs
Sparsit her triumph). It is, however, worth imagining what
Dickens had originally intended for Edith Dombey: that,
for all her hatred of Carker, she would become his sexual
partner; that her loathing for him was entirely compatible
with her sleeping with him. Carker was supposed to have
some hold over her, by dint of seeing her for what she was.
After only a short acquaintance, Edith tells her mother
that he 'knows us thoroughly, and reads us right'. She is,
she says, 'degraded by his knowledge of me' (Ch. XXVII).
Degraded into eloping with him. Dickens was interested
in this strange, twisted logic of sexual influence. In *The
Old Curiosity Shop*, Quilp is grotesque and monstrous,
yet has a power over women that his pallid wife describes
with frightening clarity. 'Quilp has such a way with him
when he likes, that the best looking woman here couldn't
refuse him if I was dead, and she was free, and he chose
to make love to her. Come!' (Ch. IV). He is an enslaving
sadist, but cannot be resisted, if he has a mind to exert his
influence.

Sometimes the force of sexual magnetism or power
is the greater because of the characteristic Dickensian
suppression of sexual knowedge. In one instance,
Dickens makes us infer the exertion of sexual power in
the relationship between a man and his servant. Sexual
relationships between employers and servants must have
been common, yet they are very uncommon in fiction.

Here is one. In *Great Expectations*, Jaggers invites Pip and his companions to dinner at his stately but gloomy house in Soho, where they are waited on by his housekeeper, his only servant, 'a woman of about forty, I supposed'. Pip notices that, when dinner is ready, she touches Jaggers 'quietly on the arm with a finger' to let him know (Ch. XXVI). The physical contact is worth noticing. Wemmick has already told Pip, 'When you go to dine with Mr Jaggers, look at his housekeeper' (Ch. XXIV). He will see 'a wild beast tamed'. 'It won't lower your opinion of Mr Jaggers's powers.' At the end of dinner, as Bentley Drummle boasts of his strength at rowing, Jaggers suddenly exercises his powers, seizing the housekeeper's hand as she clears the table. 'If you talk of strength ... I'll show you a wrist. Molly, let them see your wrist.' She begs not to be made a show.

'Master,' she said, in a low voice, with her eyes attentively and entreatingly fixed upon him. 'Don't.'

But he is determined. He holds out her two wrists, one of which is 'deeply seamed and scarred'. He traces out her sinews with his forefinger. 'There's power here', he says, but the power is his. He dismisses her: 'you have been admired, and can go' (Ch. XXVI).

It is an extraordinary episode. The forced intimacy tells us of an intense and unusual relationship between master and servant. When, much later, Pip dines again at Jaggers's house, he hears his way of talking to her. 'Now, Molly, Molly, Molly, Molly, how slow you are today!' No other master speaks to a servant like this in any other Victorian novel. When he does so, she is overhearing him talk about the fate of Estella, recently married to the brutish Drummle. As she nervously moves her fingers, Pip realises that she is Estella's mother. As he walks home with Wemmick after the dinner, he asks him about the housekeeper. How did Jaggers 'tame her'? Twenty or more years before, says Wemmick, when she was 'a very handsome young woman', she was tried for murdering another woman, by strangulation, in a fight over a man, and was acquitted entirely thanks to the energy and ingenuity of Jaggers, who represented her. 'She went into his service immediately after her acquittal, tamed as she is now.' Why did he strive so hard to save her? 'Mr Jaggers was altogether too many for the Jury, and they gave in' (Ch. XLVIII). How exactly has she repaid him? Any discerning reader is encouraged to ask these questions, and to answer them in only one way.

As is almost never acknowledged, Dickens could be daring in the ways in which he implied how sexual power was exercised. He returned to this in his last novel, *The Mystery of Edwin Drood*. Here sexual obsession is the very motor of the plot. John Jasper lusts after Rosa Bud. Knowing of her engagement to his nephew Edwin, he plots to kill him. Rosa is repelled by Jasper. And yet ... he wields a strange influence over her. We first see them together, in Jasper's drawing-room, in the company of others, as he plays the piano, watching her all the time while she sings: 'he followed her lips most attentively, with his eyes as well as hands; carefully and softly hinting the key-note from time to time'. His attention is too much; she breaks down in tears. 'I can't bear this! I am frightened! Take me away!' Once they are alone, Helena Landless asks Rosa whether she loves Jasper, and she exclaims 'Ugh!' Yet she cannot deny his power over her.

'He haunts my thoughts, like a dreadful ghost. I feel that I am never safe from him ... He has made a slave of me with his looks. He has forced me to understand him, without his saying a word...'

(Ch. VII)

After Edwin Drood's disappearance, Jasper visits Rosa at Miss Twinkleton's establishment for young ladies, trapping her into a rendezvous in the garden, where he talks to her while leaning casually on the sundial. 'I do not forget how many windows command a view of us.' He delights in the fact that no one who sees him but cannot hear him would think that anything untoward is being said. But it is. He tells Rosa that he knows that she has not really been attached to Edwin.

'I did love him!' she says.
'Yes; but not quite — not quite in the right way, shall I say?'

Jasper's euphemism invites us to imagine what the 'right way' might be. Jasper is telling Rosa that he loves her 'madly' (it is his word, repeated over and over). She is terrified of him and repulsed by him. But then he does not imagine winning her heart.

'I don't ask you for your love; give me yourself and your hatred; give me yourself and that pretty rage; give me yourself and that enchanting scorn; it will be enough for me.'

Unsuspected by anyone looking into the garden, he can blackmail and compel her. He claims to have the fortunes,

indeed the very lives, of Neville and Helena Landless in
his hands. He will destroy them if Rosa does not comply
with him. He talks as though his sexual passion gives him
power over her.

> 'I love you, love you, love you. If you were to cast me
> off now — but you will not — you would never be
> rid of me. No one should come between us. I would
> pursue you to the death.'
>
>   (Ch. XIX)

What Jasper calls 'love' we would surely call sexual
obsession. It may be doomed – we can be confident that,
thanks to Dickens's plotting, he will not have his way with
her – but its power is strange and undeniable and real.

14

Breaking the rules

May the Spirit of English Style be merciful to me!
Letter to Wilkie Collins, 27 January 1870[1]

Anthony Trollope was just one of those educated Victorians who deplored the way that Dickens wrote.

> Of Dickens's style it is impossible to speak in praise. It is jerky, ungrammatical, and created by himself in defiance of rules ... To readers who have taught themselves to regard language, it must therefore be unpleasant.[2]

Dickens's hold over readers was undeniable, Trollope conceded, but his influence on other writers could only be bad. 'No young novelist should ever dare to imitate the style of Dickens. If such a one wants a model for his language, let him take Thackeray.' Trollope wrote this in his posthumously published *Autobiography*, which appeared in 1883, long after Dickens's death. It was a judgment

that Trollope offered to the public in the expectation
that many would agree with it. 'Created by himself in
defiance of rules' is perfectly right. In his very style – his
very sentences – Dickens offends against propriety. Yet
you cannot catch his originality without doing justice
to the idiosyncracy of those sentences. Other novelists
might aim for eloquence, balance or wit; Dickens goes for
stranger powers: incantation, intensification, repetition.
He knew that his sentences were unusual. Marcus Stone
records him saying,

> I generally find when I write a line which I believe to
> be a fresh thought expressed in an original way that
> the passage is marked 'query' in the proof when it first
> comes from the printer.[3]

The print setters wondered if some of what he seemed to
have written was proper English.

It is not hard to find him being 'jerky' and
'ungrammatical'. In that painful exchange in *Hard
Times* between Mr Gradgrind and his daughter, Louisa,
summoned to his study to be told of Mr Bounderby's
proposal of marriage, the narrative is in the past tense,
conventionally enough, until Mr Gradgrind awkwardly
tells her of the offer. Then this. 'Silence between them.
The deadly statistical clock very hollow. The distant smoke
very black and heavy' (I Ch. XV). Something deadly is
indeed happening, so the sentences are pared down to
mere impressions, leaving everything implicit. No verbs.
Louisa is giving her father the chance to help her refuse
this offer, but he does not take it. Those simple *very*s tell
us all we need to know of the grim fate that closes in on
the girl, abetted by her father. Or here is the opening of

the chapter in *A Tale of Two Cities* describing Monsieur the Marquis's arrival at his rural chateau.

> A beautiful landscape, with the corn bright in it, but not abundant. Patches of poor rye where corn should have been, patches of poor peas and beans, patches of most coarse vegetable substitutes for wheat. On inanimate nature, as on the men and women who cultivated it, a prevalent tendency towards an appearance of vegetating unwillingly—a dejected disposition to give up, and wither away.
>
> (II Ch. VIII)

Facts are thrust at the hard-hearted aristocrat for him to ignore. It comes down to this. Yet even Dickens's grimly facetious analogy between blighted crops and blighted people will not make any difference to him.

The most famous example of this technique is the opening of *Bleak House*, where the first three paragraphs describing London – 'Implacable November weather ... Fog everywhere .... Gas looming through the fog in divers places in the streets ...' – contain not a single finite verb (Ch. I). These sentences are not so much describing London as plunging us into it. Other nineteenth-century novelists had to choose between the psychological drama of first-person narration and the analytical powers of third-person narration. Dickens refuses that choice and finds ways to turn his third-person narration into performance. The first two chapters of *Little Dorrit* are set in Marseilles, before we switch to London on a Sunday evening, 'gloomy, close and stale'. The church bells are tolling maddeningly and every building is 'bolted and barred'.

No pictures, no unfamiliar animals, no rare plants or flowers, no natural or artificial wonders of the ancient world—all *taboo* with that enlightened strictness, that the ugly South Sea gods in the British Museum might have supposed themselves at home again. Nothing to see but streets, streets, streets. Nothing to breathe but streets, streets, streets. Nothing to change the brooding mind, or raise it up. Nothing for the spent toiler to do, but to compare the monotony of his seventh day with the monotony of his six days, think what a weary life he led, and make the best of it—or the worst, according to the probabilities.

(I Ch. III)

Deprived of its verbs, the very prose is enervated. Dickens was much exercised by Sunday observance laws, which robbed working men and women of diversions on their one day of rest. Thus, his collection of all the curiosities that they will *not* see on this day in London and his comparison of Christian prohibition with the taboos of pagan religion. (Attempts by some politicians in the 1840s and 1850s to have the British Museum open on Sundays were frustrated by the influential Lord's Day Observance Society.)[4]

Dickens pushes against the bounds of proper English. Mr Micawber's creator shared his character's relish for stretching the diction that he had to hand. Sometimes his characters drive him to neologism, as if normal words will not do for their excesses. In *Oliver Twist* we see Mr Bumble is 'in the full bloom and pride of beadleism' (Ch. XVII). The *OED* gives this as the first and last recorded use of 'beadleism' (later editions of the novel substituted the equally singular 'beadledom' and 'beadlehood', as Dickens fiddled to get just the right self-important but deeply odd word). When we are introduced to the bullying evangelist Mr Honeythunder in *The Mystery of Edwin Drood*, we are told that 'his philanthropy was of that gunpowderous sort, that the difference between it and animosity was hard to determine' (Ch. VI). The *OED* gives this use of 'gunpowderous' as the first and only appearance of the word, as excessive and absurd as the man himself. The *Dictionary* says the same of 'platformally', another strange new word generated by Mr Honeythunder, whom we find bellowing at Mr Crisparkle before 'platformally pausing' (Ch. XVII). The right word might be 'formally' for any other speechifier, but Mr Honeythunder takes it that much further, always putting himself on the stage that he loves.

Dickens is the seventh most frequently quoted individual author in the *Oxford English Dictionary* and is credited with the earliest recorded use of over 400 words. The latter statistic is something of an optical illusion: with searchable databases, some of these first uses will be corrected. Yet he was a word-shaper; when he is truly re-shaping words we can always see (or hear) him doing it. Often a newly coined word will announce its newness as part of its meaning. Little Swills, the mimic and stand-up entertainer in *Bleak House*, entertains with speech and song, 'his strength lying in a slangular direction' (Ch. XI). No one before has ever used 'slangular', which enacts Little Swills's demotic way with words. In *Little Dorrit*, William Dorrit's son Tip becomes a prison go-between. 'His son began to supersede Mrs Bangham, and to execute commissions in a knowing manner, and to be of the prison prisonous, of the streets streety' (I Ch. VI). Prisonous? Streety? He is made by the place and its surroundings.

Dickens experimented with a kind of mock wordiness, a verbal delicacy calculated to draw attention to the indignity that the narrator pretends to avoid. In *Bleak House*, Sir Leicester Dedlock cannot allow himself to remember the word for Mr Rouncewell's occupation (he is an ironmaster), so he refers to him as 'the iron gentleman'. Picking up on Sir Leicester's lordly distaste for industrial occupations, the narrator duly introduces us to 'the ferruginous person' (Ch. XLVIII). How polite our resourceful English language can be! In *Our Mutual Friend*, Silas Wegg explains to Mr Venus that he needs his collaboration, because his own wooden leg makes it difficult for him to climb on the dust heaps, where he imagines all sorts of treasures are buried.

> Mr Wegg next modestly remarks on the want of adaptation in a wooden leg to ladders and such like airy perches, and also hints at an inherent tendency in that timber fiction, when called into action for the purposes of a promenade on an ashey slope, to stick itself into the yielding foothold, and peg its owner to one spot.
>
> (II Ch. VII)

The circumlocutory style is delicious because it is sarcastically incongruous: Wegg is a malign rogue who acts always from the basest of motives. Yet Dickens takes the word-spinning further than any good writer should dare. What more poetic periphrasis has there ever been than 'timber fiction' for 'wooden leg'?

In both Dickens's two novels narrated entirely in the first person, elevated diction is used to give a sense of a narrator reliving childhood experiences, yet ruefully distanced from them. In *Great Expectations*, Pip is recalling being scrubbed by Mrs Joe before being despatched for his first visit to Mrs Havisham, when we get an eloquent parenthesis.

> (I may here remark that I suppose myself to be better acquainted than any living authority, with the ridgy effect of a wedding-ring, passing unsympathetically over the human countenance.)
>
> (Ch. VII)

At the heart of this euphemistically wordy rendering of a painful experience is that peculiar word 'ridgy', sticking out like the metal that rubbed against his face. The narrator's diction frequently mingles the childish and Latinate: 'Mr Pumblechook's premises in the High Street of the market town, were of a peppercorny and farinaceous character' (Ch. VIII). The young Pip (he is about eight years old) might have coined the first unusual adjective but would never have understood the second one. Words mix in a similar way when Pip remembers his fight with 'the pale young gentleman' outside Satis House, seeing him 'on his back in various stages of puffy and incrimsoned countenance' (Ch. XII). Dickens even makes verbosity delicately expressive. Here is the end of the penultimate chapter of *Great Expectations*, where Pip tells us of the relative success of the firm in which he has been working with Herbert Pocket.

> We owed so much to Herbert's ever cheerful industry and readiness, that I often wondered how I had conceived that old idea of his inaptitude, until I was one day enlightened by the reflection, that perhaps

the inaptitude had never been in him at all, but had
been in me.

(Ch. LVIII)

The wordiness ('I ... was enlightened by the reflection')
is self-mocking, appearing to dignify an absurdly
belated recognition. The passive voice (instead of 'I
realised') mimics him finally being struck by a blindingly
obvious fact.

Dickens began his career with a taste for incongruous
circumlocution learned from the eighteenth-century
novelists, Fielding and Smollett, whom he, like David
Copperfield, so enjoyed. As a scarcely educated imposter,
it sometimes seems that he is parodying the propriety of
refined and educated English. The inclination was gratified
early, in *Sketches by Boz*. He makes elevated words collide
with reality – but as they do so, transfigure it. Here the
narrator sees a crowd on the corner of Bow Street and
asks one of their number, a cobbler, what they are waiting
for. 'Her Majesty's carriage', he replies. The narrator is
mystified until he sees a covered vehicle approaching.

It then occurred to us, for the first time, that Her
Majesty's carriage was merely another name for the
prisoners' van, conferred upon it, not only by reason
of the superior gentility of the term, but because
the aforesaid van is maintained at Her Majesty's
expense: having been originally started for the exclusive
accommodation of ladies and gentlemen under the
necessity of visiting the various houses of call known
by the general denomination of 'Her Majesty's Gaols.'

(Ch. XII)

Dickens loves that 'superior gentility' of terminology, knowing that the lexical pretensions of the polite classes are readily parodied by the lower classes.

Words apparently snatched from the street are jammed up against orotund sentences. In the first monthly number of *Pickwick Papers*, a cab driver becomes incensed when he sees Pickwick writing in his notebook and loudly accuses him and his companions of being 'informers' for the civic regulators of hackney cabs. As he assails them, a crowd gathers. '"Put 'em under the pump," suggested a hot-pieman.'

> The mob hitherto had been passive spectators of the scene, but as the intelligence of the Pickwickians being informers was spread among them, they began to canvass with considerable vivacity the propriety of enforcing the heated pastry-vendor's proposition.
>
> (Ch. II)

Dickens narrates as if obliged to turn demotic language into the polite phrasing that his readers might respect, yet invites us to imagine what members of the mob, thoroughly enjoying the altercation, might actually be saying. The alchemy of elevating diction is one of the delights of *Pickwick Papers*. When Mr Weller goes looking for his old friend George, once a fellow-coachman, in a public house opposite the Insolvency Court where he is due to appear, he looks to Mr Solomon Pell, one of the court's attorneys, for his friend's whereabouts.

> Mr Pell jerked his head in the direction of a back parlour, whither Mr Weller at once repairing, was immediately greeted in the warmest and most flattering manner

by some half-dozen of his professional brethren, in
token of their gratification at his arrival. The insolvent
gentleman, who had contracted a speculative but
imprudent passion for horsing long stages, which had
led to his present embarrassments, looked extremely
well, and was soothing the excitement of his feelings
with shrimps and porter.

(Ch XLII)

Food and drink frequently provide existential solace in
Dickens, so that final clause has a wordy nicety that does
justice to George's temporary pleasure.

Dickens lets us enjoy the way that educated English
makes reality seem a little better than it is. 'Charley
Bates exhibited some very loose notions concerning the
rights of property', he observes of the Artful Dodger's
companion in *Oliver Twist* (Ch. X). He especially likes
to attach circumlocutory phrasing to brutish inclinations.
In *Nicholas Nickleby*, Mr Squeers returns home for a juicy
steak, but is disconcerted for a moment by the thought
that his wife might have bought it for their pupils: 'possibly
he was apprehensive of having unintentionally devoured
some choice morsel intended for the young gentlemen'
(Ch. VII). But possibly not. Late in the novel we find
Squeers in miserable London lodgings and 'grotesquely
habited':

perhaps Mrs Squeers herself would have had some
difficulty in recognising her lord: quickened though
her natural sagacity doubtless would have been by the
affectionate yearnings and impulses of a tender wife.

(Ch. LVII)

Mr and Mrs Squeers become magnets for diction that attempts unavailingly to raise them from their brutish condition.

Other characters in *Nicholas Nickleby*, guilty of nothing worse than self-delusion, merit a verbosity that apes their pretensions. When Vincent Crummles, manager of the travelling theatre company that Nicholas has joined, finds out that he is leaving, the narrator takes on Crummles's own theatrical grandiloquence:

> he evinced many tokens of grief and consternation; and, in the extremity of his despair, even held out certain vague promises of a speedy improvement not only in the amount of his regular salary, but also in the contingent emoluments appertaining to his authorship.
>
> (Ch. XXX)

When Mrs Nickleby begins to dress herself up in order to encourage the amorous attentions of the gentleman in small-clothes next door, Dickens duly dresses up his prose.

> Mrs Nickleby had begun to display unusual care in the adornment of her person, gradually superadding to those staid and matronly habiliments, which had, up to that time, formed her ordinary attire, a variety of embellishments and decorations, slight perhaps in themselves, but, taken together, and considered with reference to the subject of her disclosure, of no mean importance.

As a widow, she is still wearing mourning, and, as she adorns herself with ornaments and adapts the style of her dress, the very style of the sentences mimics the contradiction.

> her mourning garments assumed quite a new character. From being the outward tokens of respect and sorrow for the dead, they became converted into signals of very slaughterous and killing designs upon the living.
>
> (Ch. XLI)

Elevated diction serves incongruity. In *A Tale of Two Cities*, when Dickens tells us the suitably expressive name of the brutish porter at Tellson's Bank (who is also, by night, an occasional grave robber), he cannot resist a flourish of phraseology.

> His surname was Cruncher, and on the youthful occasion of his renouncing by proxy the works of darkness, in the easterly parish church of Houndsditch, he had received the added appellation of Jerry.
>
> (II Ch. I)

Even Jerry Cruncher was baptised, and the rites of the Church of England would have required some godfather to renounce the devil on his behalf. Thinking of the ruthless occupations that he has invented for some of his characters, Dickens sometimes seems unable to resist incongruous diction. In *Our Mutual Friend*, we are told that Pleasant Riderhood runs a pawnbroking business.

> Her deceased mother had established the business, and on that parent's demise she had appropriated a secret capital of fifteen shillings to establishing

herself in it; the existence of such capital in a pillow being the last intelligible confidential communication made to her by the departed, before succumbing to dropsical conditions of snuff and gin, incompatible equally with coherence and existence.

(II Ch. XII)

Death from 'snuff and gin' might be a reason for circumlocutory language, but Mrs Riderhood's last communication seems more maternal than absurd. Dennis, the psychopathic hangman in *Barnaby Rudge*, has at least earned the mockery that he gets from the over-elaborate description of his terror when he finds that he is likely to suffer the fate that he once inflicted on others.

To say that Mr Dennis's modesty was not somewhat startled by these honours, or that he was altogether prepared for so flattering a reception, would be to claim for him a greater amount of stoical philosophy than even he possessed. Indeed this gentleman's stoicism was of that not uncommon kind, which enables a man to bear with exemplary fortitude the afflictions of his friends, but renders him, by way of counterpoise, rather selfish and sensitive in respect of any that happen to befall himself.

(Ch. LXXIV)

In his late fiction, the device of mixing diction has become deep-rooted. In *Our Mutual Friend*, the newly enriched Mr and Mrs Boffin have decided that they should adopt an orphan. But how will they find one?

> Mrs Boffin suggested advertisement in the newspapers, requesting orphans answering annexed description to apply at the Bower on a certain day; but Mr Boffin wisely apprehending obstruction of the neighbouring thoroughfares by orphan swarms, this course was negatived.
>
> (I Ch. IX)

Those 'orphan swarms' briefly and wonderfully appear before us, clogging the streets, before they are cancelled. Would any other novelist think of turning the everyday hyperbole of 'swarms' into this comically rhyming phrase (plenty of orphans out there in Victorian London)? But then Dickens always loved hyperbole. From the first, reviewers complained about his exaggerations.[5] He was highly conscious of the yen for superlatives, embodied in 'The Poetical Young Gentleman' in *Sketches by Boz*.

> When the poetical young gentleman makes use of adjectives, they are all superlatives. Everything is of the grandest, greatest, noblest, mightiest, loftiest; or the lowest, meanest, obscurest, vilest, and most pitiful. He knows no medium: for enthusiasm is the soul of poetry; and who so enthusiastic as a poetical young gentleman?[6]

Dickens gives the true relish of hyperbole to one of his characters, Lawrence Boythorn in *Bleak House*. As John Jarndyce puts it, 'His language is as sounding as his voice. He is always in extremes; perpetually in the superlative degree' (Ch. IX). His hyperbole is all indignant and vengeful, but many an outburst will end in laughter, as though he knows that you could never believe in the feelings he professes.

Oh, the satisfaction for Pip in *Great Expectations* of calling Pumblechook 'the basest of swindlers' (Ch. XIII)! Hyperbole is native to everyday speech, now as in the nineteenth century. Usually it is purged from literary discourse, but Dickens restores it to its proper place. In *Our Mutual Friend*, Fascination Fledgeby is 'the meanest cur existing, with a single pair of legs' (II Ch. V). We have already seen him in all his social awkwardness and might have judged him wrongly. The demotic exaggeration is there to express the force of the narrator's sudden candour. This is how we speak when we really mean what we say, so why should the writer not express himself thus? Major Bagstock in *Dombey and Son* is a monster of calculation and self-interest, one of whose tricks is to announce to all who care to listen that he is 'hard-hearted ... tough, Sir, tough, and de-vilish sly'. It is a double bluff, for he is indeed, as Dickens informs us, 'selfish'. More than this. 'It may be doubted whether there ever was a more entirely selfish person at heart' (Ch. VII).

It is quite a claim, but one paralleled elsewhere in Dickens's fiction. In the same novel, the contents of Sol Gills's shop in *Dombey and Son* are 'jammed into the tightest cases, fitted into the narrowest corners ... screwed into the acutest angles' (Ch. IV), while Miss Tox lives in 'the most inconvenient little house in England, and the crookedest'. As she says, 'what a situation!' (Ch. VII). Hyperbole in these descriptions reminds us of the ordinary drama of our first impressions of particular places. In *Pictures from Italy*, Dickens recalls arriving in Piacenza.

> The sleepiest and shabbiest of soldiery go wandering about, with the double curse of laziness and poverty, uncouthly wrinkling their misfitting regimentals; the dirtiest of children play with their impromptu toys (pigs and mud) in the feeblest of gutters; and the gauntest of dogs trot in and out of the dullest of archways, in perpetual search of something to eat, which they never seem to find.[7]

True to experience, the superlatives recreate his feelings about what he was seeing. Later, on the coast road out of Genoa he visits the town of Camoglia, which he finds 'a perfect miniature of a primitive seafaring town; the saltest, roughest, most piratical little place that ever was seen'.[8] Only the most pedantic reader would refuse to believe it. The most enjoyable exaggerations are the biggest. In *Bleak House* Dickens fastens on to the grim joke that the Smallweed twins, Bart and Judy, grandchildren and apprentices to a ruthless money-lender, though scarcely fifteen years old, act as if they have never been children. But Dickens wants to say more than that Judy acts beyond her years. Instead, when she is admonishing the Smallweeds' servant, Charley, he tells us that 'Judy Smallweed appears to attain a perfectly geological age, and to date from the remotest periods' (Ch. XXI). Dickens dares himself to remind us of those extreme formulae ('I've told you millions of times') native to speech but foreign to literature.

Dickens uses sentences not just to describe the world, but to be overwhelmed by it. Thus his love

of that offence against good syntax, the list. Taking
the description of a junk-shop window in *Sketches
by Boz* as an example, Alastair Fowler rightly calls
Dickens 'the master of listing'.⁹ A list can give us not
just copiousness, as in all the delectable foodstuffs on
display in the grocers' shops in *A Christmas Carol*, but
too-much-ness. In the Meagles's house in *Little Dorrit*
we find an extraordinary collection of geographically
miscellaneous items.

> There were antiquities from Central Italy, made by the
> best modern houses in that department of industry; bits
> of mummy from Egypt (and perhaps Birmingham);
> model gondolas from Venice; model villages from
> Switzerland; morsels of tesselated pavement from
> Herculaneum and Pompeii, like petrified minced veal;
> ashes out of tombs, and lava out of Vesuvius ...
>
> (I Ch. XVI)

And so on. Every item comes from some destination of
the Meagles, inveterate travellers with little education and
no eye for a fake. They are kindly as well as affluent, but
the list is evidence of their unworldliness, uncorrectable
by any amount of travel. Dickens's pile-ups are always
worth going through. The list of objects that Esther finds
in the Jellyby closets in *Bleak House* make for a rich and
poetic progress:

> bits of mouldy pie, sour bottles, Mrs Jellyby's caps,
> letters, tea, forks, odd boots and shoes of children,
> firewood, wafers, saucepan-lids, damp sugar in odds
> and ends of paper bags, footstools, blacklead brushes,
> bread, Mrs Jellyby's bonnets, books with butter sticking

to the binding, guttered candle ends put out by being
turned upside down in broken candlesticks, nutshells,
heads and tails of shrimps, dinner-mats, gloves, coffee-
grounds, umbrellas...

(Ch. XXX)

Of course – at the end – umbrellas!

Lists, generated by the futile complications of the Law,
are a peculiarly important feature of *Bleak House*. When
we are first taken to the premises of Mr Snagsby, the law
stationer, we are told, before we are told anything else,
that he deals in

all sorts of blank forms of legal process; in skins and
rolls of parchment; in paper—foolscap, brief, draft,
brown, white, whitey-brown, and blotting; in stamps;
in office-quills, pens, ink, India-rubber, pounce,
pins, pencils, sealing-wax, and wafers; in red tape
and green ferret; in pocket-books, almanacs, diaries,
and law lists; in string boxes, rulers, inkstands—glass
and leaden—pen-knives, scissors, bodkins, and other
small office-cutlery; in short, in articles too numerous
to mention...

(Ch. X)

– except that Dickens has mentioned many of them. What
sterile fecundity! When Esther visits Miss Flite's lodgings
with John Jarndyce, Krook is keen to tell them the names
of all her caged birds.

The old man, looking up at the cages after another look
at us, went through the list.

'Hope, Joy, Youth, Peace, Rest, Life, Dust, Ashes, Waste, Want, Ruin, Despair, Madness, Death, Cunning, Folly, Words, Wigs, Rags, Sheepskin, Plunder, Precedent, Jargon, Gammon, and Spinach. That's the whole collection,' said the old man, 'all cooped up together, by my noble and learned brother.'

(Ch. XIV)

His 'noble and learned brother' is the Lord Chancellor, who presides over the interminable case of Jarndyce and Jarndyce. With sour relish, the malign old man runs through the list of all that is lost or found in its course, from 'Hope' to 'Ashes' to 'Jargon', all the way to 'Gammon and Spinach', a proverbial phrase meaning 'nonsense'. He delights in the ways that Jarndyce and Jarndyce curses the litigants who are entangled in it.

Dickens knew that listing could be performative. In *Little Dorrit*, it enacts the hopeless shiftlessness of Tip, Amy Dorrit's brother.

With intervals of Marshalsea lounging, and Mrs Bangham succession, his small second mother, aided by her trusty friend, got him into a warehouse, into a market garden, into the hop trade, into the law again, into an auctioneers, into a brewery, into a stockbroker's, into the law again, into a coach office, into a waggon office, into the law again, into a general dealer's, into a distillery, into the law again, into a wool house, into a dry goods house, into the Billingsgate trade, into the foreign fruit trade, and into the docks. But whatever Tip went into, he came out of tired, announcing that he had cut it.

(Ch. VII)

'The law again' three times, punctuating those other aimless occupations, suggesting that Tip or his advisers keep believing, against all the evidence, that this is the right occupation for him. Tip's fecklessness demands this list, a testimony to his remarkable lack of persistence.

The technique of listing may seem elementary, but Dickens gives it subtle psychological powers. Here is Pip in *Great Expectations*, after Magwitch has returned to him, noticing how everything about him seems to announce that he is a convict.

> In all his ways of sitting and standing, and eating and drinking,—of brooding about in a high-shouldered reluctant style,—of taking out his great horn-handled jackknife and wiping it on his legs and cutting his food,—of lifting light glasses and cups to his lips, as if they were clumsy pannikins,—of chopping a wedge off his bread, and soaking up with it the last fragments of gravy round and round his plate, as if to make the most of an allowance, and then drying his finger-ends on it, and then swallowing it,—in these ways and a thousand other small nameless instances arising every minute in the day, there was Prisoner, Felon, Bondsman, plain as plain could be.
>
> (Ch. XL)

Pip's horror and disgust are expressed in the list. He cannot help observing and enumerating each horrible detail. *This* is the man to whom he owes his great expectations.

These lists are made to be performed, to be read aloud, to be intoned. Capturing the railway boom of the 1840s, *Dombey and Son* gives us not just physical descriptions of the transformation of particular areas of London, but an inventory of all that is produced by a nation's new obsession.

> There were railway patterns in its drapers' shops, and railway journals in the windows of its newsmen. There were railway hotels, office-houses, lodging-houses, boarding-houses; railway plans, maps, views, wrappers, bottles, sandwich-boxes, and time-tables; railway hackney-coach and stands; railway omnibuses, railway streets and buildings, railway hangers-on and parasites, and flatterers out of all calculation.
>
> (Ch. XV)

It is a sublime and ridiculous collection, including the surprising ('railway sandwich-boxes') and the downright perplexing ('railway hangers-on'). Once he has the word 'railway', everything else follows. Of all Dickens's offences against good style, repetition is his favourite. It might be a single word, as in the adjective that memorialises the true extent of Jacob Marley's human relationships in *A Christmas Carol*. 'Scrooge was his sole executor, his sole administrator, his sole assign, his sole residuary legatee, his sole friend, and sole mourner' (Stave 1). The word 'sole' tolls gloomily enough. Dickens will write as if a certain word cannot be kept away, insisting on pushing itself into every sentence. Here, in *A Tale of Two Cities*, he surveys the chateau that belongs to Monsieur the Marquis.

> It was a heavy mass of building, that chateau of Monsieur the Marquis, with a large stone courtyard before it, and two stone sweeps of staircase meeting in a stone terrace before the principal door. A stony business altogether, with heavy stone balustrades, and

stone urns, and stone flowers, and stone faces of men,
and stone heads of lions, in all directions. As if the
Gorgon's head had surveyed it, when it was finished,
two centuries ago.

(II Ch. IX)

All that stone! The fancy of the Gorgon's gaze is the
fantastic measure of its excess of stoniness. Aristocrat
privilege makes itself look adamantine and eternal, though
the stoniness is really only inhuman.

A word acquires a strange new resonance by its
unwonted repetition. When the narrator introduces us to
Steerforth's valet Littimer in *David Copperfield*, it is as a
man 'who was in appearance a pattern of respectability'
(Ch. XXI). In the first short paragraph describing him, the
word 'respectable' is used half a dozen times. Much later,
Rosa Dartle gets Littimer to narrate his role in Steerforth's
seduction of Emily. He explains that his master tired of
her and finally 'proposed that the young woman should
marry a very respectable person, who was fully prepared
to overlook the past' (Ch. XLVI). 'Respectable' here, of
course, is the word that he uses for himself. It is the word
that cloaks every low motive and cynical act. Its repetition
enforces the stunned recognition that a bad-hearted person
can keep up such an appearance of bland propriety.

Characters are hooked on particular words and
cannot get away from them. When we first meet Bradley
Headstone in *Our Mutual Friend*, we get his social history
but also his temperamental doom in the repetition of
two words. Everything about him is, in appearance,
'decent': seven *decent*s in a single sentence make him 'a
thoroughly decent young man', but make that adjective
signify a nervous attention to sober appearance – an

anxious endeavour to convince the onlooker that here is someone worth respect. Then we are told that he had acquired his 'store of teacher's knowledge' 'mechanically', with five repetitions of *mechanical* in the next sentence to re-enact his remorseless self-drilling.

Crazily repeated words are inflicted on characters because those characters deserve it, following stupid or obsessive patterns of behaviour, like Mr and Mrs Veneering, whom we first meet at the opening of the third chapter of *Our Mutual Friend*.

> Mr and Mrs Veneering were bran-new people in a bran-new house in a bran-new quarter of London. Everything about the Veneerings was spick and span new. All their furniture was new, all their friends were new, all their servants were new, their plate was new, their carriage was new, their harness was new, their horses were new, their pictures were new, they themselves were new, they were as newly married as was lawfully compatible with their having a bran-new baby, and if they had set up a great-grandfather, he would have come home in matting from the Pantechnicon, without a scratch upon him, French polished to the crown of his head.
>
> (I Ch. II)

All that newness, which makes babies and servants interchangeable with furniture and pictures, is of the Veneerings' making. The nouveau riche have nothing but recent purchases – of friends as well as of property – with which to dignify themselves.

Comparably, the repetition of the word 'unfeeling' when Little Dorrit first meets Mrs Merdle is a testimony

to the lady's sophisticated social skills, deployed without
the slightest tinge of human sympathy.

> The lady was not young and fresh from the hand of
> Nature, but was young and fresh from the hand of
> her maid. She had large unfeeling handsome eyes, and
> dark unfeeling handsome hair, and a broad unfeeling
> handsome bosom, and was made the most of in every
> particular. Either because she had a cold, or because
> it suited her face, she wore a rich white fillet tied over
> her head and under her chin. And if ever there were an
> unfeeling handsome chin that looked as if, for certain,
> it had never been, in familiar parlance, 'chucked' by
> the hand of man, it was the chin curbed up so tight
> and close by that laced bridle.
>
> (I Ch. XX)

Many a novelist might notice 'unfeeling eyes', but only
Dickensian sentences can include 'unfeeling hair', treated
as a kind of achievement on Mrs Merdle's part, so complete
is her carefully arranged appearance.

Here is an equally Dickensian sentence, depending
on a different kind of repetition, which announces the
appearance in *Martin Chuzzlewit* of (the as yet unnamed)
Montague Tigg.

> He was very dirty and very jaunty; very bold and very
> mean; very swaggering and very slinking; very much
> like a man who might have been something better,
> and unspeakably like a man who deserved to be
> something worse.
>
> (Ch. IV)

Why is this so good? Another writer might have glimpsed the possibility of some of these near opposites, but Dickens's inelegant repetitions of that least exact of intensifiers, 'very', makes the jumble of qualities all the stranger. The narrator almost gives up on the attempt to categorise him – to catch his weird mix of qualities – until he has to resort to a colloquial word, 'unspeakably', even stronger than 'very'.

Repetition can be a kind of madness, a frenzy of sentences trapped in one pattern. Dickens is entirely conscious of this. An early experiment comes with the mob burning down Newgate in *Barnaby Rudge*.

> At first they crowded round the blaze, and vented their exultation only in their looks: but when it grew hotter and fiercer—when it crackled, leaped, and roared, like a great furnace—when it shone upon the opposite houses ...

And then on, 'when through the deep red heat ... when it shone and gleamed ... when blackened stone ... when wall and tower ... when scores of objects ... then the mob began to join the whirl ...' A single intensifying sentence mounts, accompanying the mob's delighted delirium. In *Dombey and Son*, a kind of madness seizes Carker as he flees through France, believing himself pursued by Mr Dombey. His journey is 'like a vision, in which nothing was quite real but his own torment'. The next paragraph begins, 'It was a vision of long roads ...' – and then, for another ten paragraphs, every sentence, every phrase begins with 'Of ...' (Ch. LV). On and on. Everything is 'a vision of ...' something, until we get to '... of being at last again in England' (Ch. LXIV).

There are patterns that we cannot escape and Dickens
put them on the page. *Hard Times* opens with Gradgrind
lecturing his charges about facts. 'The emphasis was helped
by …. The emphasis was helped by … The emphasis was
helped by … The emphasis was helped by … all helped the
emphasis.' And by the end of this paragraph, the emphasis
is indeed inescapable. Equally, when we are introduced to
Mr Bounderby it is via a series of repetitions, appropriate
for someone who always claims (falsely) to be a self-made
man. 'A man made out of a coarse material … A man
with a great … A man with a great puffed head … A man
with a pervading appearance on him of being inflated
like a balloon … A man who could never … A man who
was always … A man who was the bully of humility'
(Ch. V). And by the end of this, we feel what it is to
have been bullied into accepting his presence, his grim
reality. Equally mimetic is the opening of *Little Dorrit*,
where the pathetic fallacy of a 'staring' place is introduced
in order to overwhelm the narration. 'Everything in
Marseilles, and about Marseilles, had stared at the fervid
sky, and been stared at in return, until a staring habit had
become universal there.' The universality is enacted in
the paragraphs that follow, as everything in the landscape
(except the people) is duly found to be 'staring'.

> Strangers were stared out of countenance by staring
> white houses, staring white walls, staring white streets,
> staring tracts of arid road, staring hills from which
> verdure was burnt away.

The unforgiving heat and blinding light produce this
unforgiving effect.

Repetition becomes stranger and stranger in his later fiction. After we are introduced to all the Veneerings' new things (including baby) in the second chapter of *Our Mutual Friend*, we are admitted to their 'banquet'. 'The great looking-glass above the sideboard, reflects the table and the company.' This opening to the paragraph is conventional enough, but then something odd happens. 'Reflects the new Veneering crest, in gold and eke in silver, frosted and also thawed, a camel of all work.' The Veneerings have paid someone at the Heralds' College to find an ancestor and fabricate a coat of arms for them. The supposed ancestor might have had a camel on his shield, so camels are the theme. Odder still, the sentence begins, subject-less, 'Reflects ...' – and so do ten sentences that follow. 'Reflects Veneering; forty, wavy-haired, dark, tending to corpulence, sly, mysterious, filmy ... Reflects Mrs Veneering ... Reflects Podsnap ... Reflects Mrs Podsnap ...' No sentence has a subject. Every person is held as one more item in the frame of the looking-glass, by which means they are robbed of agency, reduced to the collection of their attributes. And within this pattern of repetition are other repetitions, notably in the characteristics of one of the company, a 'mature young gentleman' (who is Lammle) with 'too much nose in his face, too much ginger in his whiskers, too much torso in his waistcoat, too much sparkle in his studs, his eyes, his buttons, his talk, and his teeth'. There is plenty wrong with him, you should be able to see, in all the incongruity of his excess.

Sometimes it seems that repetition is the very essence of Dickens's style. Here is the opening of Chapter XXXVIII of *Great Expectations*, where Pip recalls his addiction to

Estella when she is staying at Mrs Brandley's house in
Richmond.

> If that staid old house near the Green at Richmond
> should ever come to be haunted when I am dead, it
> will be haunted, surely, by my ghost. O the many,
> many nights and days through which the unquiet spirit
> within me haunted that house when Estella lived there!
> Let my body be where it would, my spirit was always
> wandering, wandering, wandering, about that house.
>
> (Ch. XXXVIII)

From the 'haunted ... haunted ... haunted' in the first
two sentences, to 'the many, many nights and days' he
remembers, to the thought of his spirit 'always wandering,
wandering, wandering', the narrative re-experiences his
torment via repetition. Repetition is supposed to be crude,
but it can enact the drama of an experience with rare
subtlety. Here is the narrator of *David Copperfield*, recalling
his parting with Peggotty after his mother's death, when he
knows that he must return to live with the Murdstones.

> I felt the truth and constancy of my dear old nurse,
> with all my heart, and thanked her as well as I could.
> That was not very well, for she spoke to me thus, with
> her arms round my neck, in the morning, and I was
> going home in the morning, and I went home in the
> morning, with herself and Mr Barkis in the cart.
>
> (Ch. X)

'In the morning ... in the morning ... in the morning'.
So vividly remembered is the episode that the sentence

can hardly get past that phrase, which is the child's recognition, reviving again in the memory, of a doom he cannot escape.

In *Great Expectations*, more than anywhere else in Dickens's fiction, you can find an audacious poetry of repetitiousness. Late in the novel, Pip and Herbert, with the help of Startop, are trying to smuggle Magwitch out of the country, rowing down the Thames estuary in order to intercept a packet ship bound for the Continent. As the river widens, the mud spreads – into the sentences too.

It was like my own marsh country, flat and monotonous, and with a dim horizon; while the winding river turned and turned, and the great floating buoys upon it turned and turned, and everything else seemed stranded and still. For now the last of the fleet of ships was round the last low point we had headed; and the last green barge, straw-laden, with a brown sail, had followed; and some ballast-lighters, shaped like a child's first rude imitation of a boat, lay low in the mud; and a little squat shoal-lighthouse on open piles stood crippled in the mud on stilts and crutches; and slimy stakes stuck out of the mud, and slimy stones stuck out of the mud, and red landmarks and tidemarks stuck out of the mud, and an old landing-stage and an old roofless building slipped into the mud, and all about us was stagnation and mud.

(Ch. LIV)

We are back in the landscape of the novel's opening and of Pip's childhood. So those ballast-lighters are indeed like a child's representation of boats. And childlike, we might say, are the repetitions that run through these sentences. 'Turned and turned ... turned and turned'; 'last ... last ... last'. And all that mud: 'lay low in the mud ... stood crippled in the mud ... stuck out of the mud ... stuck out of the mud ... stuck out of the mud ... slipped into the mud ... all about us was stagnation and mud'. In that second, long sentence, with its eleven *and*s, the narration is both a primitive list and an extraordinary reverie. As the tide seeps out, the mud stretches away and the past claims the narrator back in the very rhythm of his narration. Such rhythm, realised best in reading aloud, was Dickens's invention, the simplest and the best of his tricks.

Acknowledgements

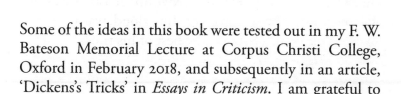

Some of the ideas in this book were tested out in my F. W. Bateson Memorial Lecture at Corpus Christi College, Oxford in February 2018, and subsequently in an article, 'Dickens's Tricks' in *Essays in Criticism*. I am grateful to Seamus Perry and Freya Johnston for advising me on this.

I would like to thank my colleagues at UCL who gave me suggestions and information that I used in writing this book: Bas Aarts, Kathryn Allan, Juliet Atkinson, Scarlett Baron and Philip Horne.

I also received generous and scholarly advice from Charlotte Brewer, David Crystal, Michael Slater and Garrett Stewart.

I am grateful to Philip Errington and David Goldthorpe of Sotheby's for giving me access to items in the sale of the extraordinary Charles Dickens: Lawrence Drizen Collection, and to Cindy Sughrue and Louisa Price at the Dickens House Museum in London, where I consulted manuscripts and collections of nineteenth-century responses to Dickens.

As indicated in my Introduction, anyone who wants to see Dickens in the fever of invention needs to examine the surviving manuscripts of his novels. (What is hard to decipher in the originals often becomes impossible in digitised versions of these.) Thanks to the trustees of the Wisbech & Fenland Museum, I was able to study the manuscript of *Great Expectations*. The Museum's curator, Robert Bell, was unfailingly helpful and hospitable. I spent absorbing days with Dickens manuscripts from the National Art Library Forster Collection of the Victoria and Albert Museum and am grateful to those at the V&A who helped me find my way to them: Elaine Tierney, Vicky Worsfold, Kati Price and Doug Dodds. I would particularly like to thank Catherine Yvard of the V&A's National Art Library for responding to my many enquiries and ensuring my access to those manuscripts.

I am grateful to Lauren Whybrow, managing editor at my publishers, Bloomsbury, and to my scrupulous and thoughtful copyeditor, Marigold Atkey. My editor, Michael Fishwick gave me great encouragement and showed great patience, as did my agent, Anna Webber. My wife, Harriet, and my children, Maud, Allegra and William, supplied me with the best of encouragement and scepticism.

This book is dedicated to John Sutherland, on whose matchless knowledge of Victorian fiction and the Victorian fiction industry I have often relied.

Notes

1

1 *Letters*, 4.3.
2 Anthony Trollope, *The Warden*, ed. David Skilton (Oxford: World's Classics, 1980), 206.
3 Ibid. 208.
4 G. H. Lewes, 'Dickens in Relation to Criticism', *Fortnightly Review*, XVII Feb. 1872, 143.
5 *Charles Dickens' Book of Memoranda*, ed. Fred Kaplan (New York: New York Public Library, 1981), entry 79.
6 Robert Douglas-Fairhurst, *Becoming Dickens: The Invention of a Novelist* (Cambridge, MA: Harvard University Press, 2011), 4.
7 For the startlingly good sales of *Bleak House* when first published in monthly instalments, see Robert L. Patten, *Charles Dickens and his Publishers* (Oxford: Oxford University Press, 1978), 224–7.
8 John Sutherland, *Victorian Novelists and Publishers* (Chicago: University of Chicago Press, 1976; rpt. 1978), 80.
9 *The Speeches of Charles Dickens*, ed. K. J. Fielding (Oxford: Clarendon Press, 1960), 240.
10 An invaluable 'Catalogue of Dickens's references to Shakespeare' is supplied by Valerie L. Gager in her *Shakespeare*

and Dickens: The Dynamics of Influence (Cambridge: Cambridge University Press, 1996), 251–369.

11 See Gager, 47–55.

12 *Robinson Crusoe* is explicitly invoked in *Pickwick Papers, The Old Curiosity Shop, Martin Chuzzlewit, A Christmas Carol, Dombey and Son, David Copperfield, Bleak House, Hard Times, Little Dorrit* and *Our Mutual Friend.*

13 *Journalism,* IV.171.

14 Ibid. 369–74.

15 The best guide to this is Ian Keable, *Charles Dickens Magician,* (privately published, 2014).

16 Ibid. 56.

17 Harry Stone, ed., *Dickens' Working Notes for His Novels* (Chicago and London: University of Chicago Press, 1987), xiv.

18 Helen Small, 'Dispensing with style', in Daniel Tyler, ed., *Dickens's Style* (Cambridge: Cambridge University Press, 2013), 268.

19 See John Butt and Kathleen Tillotson, *Dickens at Work* (London: Methuen & Co, 1957), 20–1.

20 In Philip Collins, ed., *Dickens: Interviews and Recollections,* 2 vols (London: Macmillan, 1981), II.188

21 Ibid. I.120.

22 See Patten, *Charles Dickens and his Publishers,* 323.

23 *Speeches of Charles Dickens,* 324–5.

24 So tantalising that Doug Dodds, Senior Curator at the Victoria and Albert Museum, working with Professor John Bowen of the University of York, has been leading a research project, 'Deciphering Dickens', aimed at developing crowdsourced transcriptions of Dickens's manuscripts. See www.vam.ac.uk/research/projects/deciphering-dickens

25 Forster Collection, National Art Library, MSL/1876/Forster/162

26 See Alan C. Dooley, *Author and Printer in Victorian England* (Charlottesville, VA: University Press of Virginia, 1992), 23.

27 Forster Collection, National Art Library, MSL/1876/Forster/162

2

1 *Letters*, 11.113.

2 *Household Words*, Vol. III, No. 74, 16 August 1851, 494.

3 Forster Collection, National Art Library, MSL/1876/ Forster/162.

4 *The Nation*, 21 December 1865, in Philip Collins, ed., *Dickens: The Critical Heritage* (London: Routledge and Kegan Paul, 1971), 469.

5 Letter to Bulwer Lytton, 28 November 1865, in *Letters*, 11.113.

6 London Hackney Carriage Act 1831, Sect. XXXI.

7 *Journalism*, I.85.

8 See, for instance, J. Hillis Miller, *Charles Dickens: The World of His Novels* (Cambridge, Mass.: Harvard University Press, 1965), 152 and Philip Horne, 'Style and the Making of Character in Dickens' in Daniel Tyler, ed., *Dickens's Style* (Cambridge: Cambridge University Press, 2013), 160.

9 George Eliot, *Middlemarch*, ed. Rosemary Ashton (London: Penguin, 1994), 9.

10 Ibid. 18.

11 Henry James, *The Portrait of a Lady* (1881), ed. Michael Anesko (Cambridge: CUP, 2016), 148.

12 *Great Expectations* MS, Wisbech and Fenland Museum.

13 In 1840 he attended the execution of the Swiss valet Francois Courvoisier, who had cut his master's throat; see Michael Slater, *Charles Dickens* (London: Yale University Press, 2009), 153. In November 1849 he wrote a letter to the *Times* describing the hanging of Frederick and Maria Manning outside Horsemonger Lane Gaol and the degrading effect on the spectators. See *Letters*, 5.644–5.

14 Such totalling is made reliable by Birmingham University's CLiC Dickens website, which allows for complex searches through the corpus of Dickens's fiction: clic.bham.ac.uk/

15 Harry Stone, *The Night Side of Dickens: Cannibalism, Passion, Necessity* (Columbus, OH: Ohio State University Press, 1994), 137.

16 See Keable, 223–4.

17 *American Notes*, ed. Patricia Ingram (London: Penguin, 2000), 194.

3

1   *Letters*, 8.86.
2   Collins, ed., *Dickens: Interviews and Recollections*, II.194–5.
3   *Pictures from Italy*, ed. Kate Flint (London: Penguin, 1998), 42.
4   Letter of 13 April 1856, in *Letters*, 8.86.
5   *Great Expectations*, ed. David Trotter and Charlotte Mitchell (London: Penguin, 1996), 498.
6   Forster, I.28.
7   Ibid. 33.
8   *The Uncommercial Traveller*, Ch. XII, in *Dickens' Journalism*.
9   Forster, I.11.
10 *Journalism*, IV. 231.
11 *Household Words*, Vol. XIX, No. 458, 1 Jan. 1859, 98.
12 See Gordon S. Haight, 'Dickens and Lewes on Spontaneous Combustion', in *Nineteenth-Century Fiction* Vol. 10, No. 1 (June 1955), 53–63.
13 See Rosemary Ashton, *One Hot Summer: Dickens, Darwin, Disraeli and the Great Stink of 1858* (London: Yale University Press, 2017), 15–16.
14 *The Speeches of Charles Dickens*, 129.
15 *The Examiner*, 14 July 1849.
16 Review in *The Rambler*, Jan. 1854, in Michael Hollington, ed., *Charles Dickens: Critical Assessments*, 4 vols (Mountfield, E. Sussex: Helm Information, 1995), I.357.
17 John Sutherland, *Orwell's Nose: A Pathological Biography* (London: Reaktion Books, 2016), 20.
18 Tobias Smollett, *Roderick Random*, ed. Paul-Gabriel Boucé (Oxford: Oxford University Press, 1979; repr. 1981), 144.
19 Ibid. 259.
20 Tobias Smollett, *The Expedition of Humphry Clinker*, eds Louis M. Knapp and Paul-Gabriel Boucé (Oxford: World's Classics, 1984; repr. 2009), 66.
21 Liza Picard, *Victorian London* (London: Weidenfeld & Nicolson, 2005), 1.
22 Jerry White, *London in the Nineteenth Century* (London: Jonathan Cape, 2007), 49.
23 Letter to John Forster, in *Letters*, 5.620; *Morning Chronicle*, 3 Sept. 1849.

24 Ashton, 121–130; Stephen Halliday, *The Great Stink of London: Sir Joseph Bazalgette and the Cleansing of the Victorian Metropolis* (Stroud, Gloucs: Sutton Publishing, 1999), 71–6.
25 Letter to W. J. Cerjat, 7 July 1858, in *Letters*, 8.598.
26 Letter to Thomas Mitton, 4 Nov. 1839, *Letters*, 1.597.
27 See *Journalism*, I.106–11.
28 Letter to Clarkson Stanfield, 24 Aug. 1844, in *Letters*, 4.185.
29 Letter to W. C. Macready, 3 Jan. 1744, in *Letters*, 4.9.
30 Letter to Georgina Hogarth, 16 Feb. 1855, in *Letters*, 7.541.
31 *Household Words*, Vol.II, No. 27, 28 Sept. 1850, 1.
32 Letter to W. H. Wills, 24 July 1869, *Letters*, 12.372.
33 *Journalism*, IV.110.
34 Ibid. 115.

4

1 27 July 1851, in *Letters*, 6.446.
2 See Sylvere Monod, ' "When the Battle's Lost and Won ...": Dickens *v.* the Compositors of *Bleak House*', *The Dickensian*, vol. 69 (1 Jan. 1973).
3 See for instance *Dickens: The Critical Heritage*, 273–99.
4 Dickens, *American Notes*, 90.
5 Ibid. 128.
6 Dickens would use the present tense again to recreate the experience of speed during a train journey in an article entitled 'A Flight' in in *Household Words*, Vol. III, No. 75, 30 August 1851, 529–33.
7 Clare Pettitt, 'Dickens and the Historical Present', in *Dickens's Style*, 125.
8 Charlotte Brontë, *Jane Eyre*, ed. Margaret Smith, rev. Sally Shuttleworth (Oxford: World's Classics, 2000; repr. 2008), 93.
9 Ibid. 248.
10 See Randolph Quirk, *Charles Dickens and Appropriate Language* (Durham: University of Durham, 1959).
11 John Harvey, 'Fiction in the Present Tense', *Textual Practice*, Vol. 20, No. 1 (2006), 75.
12 James Joyce, *Ulysses* (London: Penguin, 1960; rpr. 1984), 105.
13 Don DeLillo, *Underworld* (London: Picador, 1997; rpr. 2015), 829.

14 See Michael Cotsell, *The Companion to Our Mutual Friend* (London: Allen & Unwin, 1986), 65.

5

1 *Letters*, 4.622.
2 Stone, ed., *Dickens' Working Notes*, 208–9.
3 Emily Brontë, *Wuthering Heights*, ed. Ian Jack, rev. Helen Small (Oxford: World's Classics, 2009), 20–1.
4 Ibid. 299.
5 Charlotte Brontë, *Villette*, ed. Margaret Smith and Herbert Rosengarten (Oxford: World's Classics, 1990), 131.
6 Ibid., 306.
7 Ibid., 592.
8 *Letters*, 3.181.
9 Forster, II. 401.
10 Letter of 6 Nov. 1852, in *Letters*, 6.799–800.
11 Letter of 9 November 1852, in *Letters*, 6.800–1.
12 It began appearing in *All the Year Round*, 47, 23 Oct. 1869 and ran for four consecutive weeks, concluding on 13 Nov. 1869. Each week it was the final item in the magazine.
13 See Louise Henson, 'Investigations and fictions: Charles Dickens and ghosts', in Nicola Brown, Carolyn Burdett and Pamela Thurschwell, eds, *The Victorian Supernatural* (Cambridge: Cambridge University Press, 2004), 45–7.
14 See Slater, *Charles Dickens*, 232–3.
15 Letter to Emile de la Rue, 10 Feb. 1845, in *Letters*, 4.263.
16 Letter of 24 Nov. 1869, in *Letters*, 12.443.
17 Letter of 6 Jan. 1866, in *Letters*, 11.133.
18 *All the Year Round*, Christmas 1865, 605-10.
19 Letter of 8 March 1855, in *Letters*, 7.558.
20 It appeared as 'A Ghost Story', in *Household Words*, Vol. 11, No. 261, 24 March 1855.
21 George Augustus Sala, *Things I Have Seen and People I Have Known* (1894), in Collins, ed., *Dickens: Interviews and Recollections* II.201.
22 Letter of 12 Sept. 1867, in *Letters*, 1.425.

23 Letter of 25 Nov. 1851, in *Letters*, 6.546.
24 Forster, II.401.
25 See N. C. Peyrouton, 'Rapping the Rappers. More Grist for
    the Biographers' Mill', in *The Dickensian*, Vol. LV, No. 327,
    January 1959, 75–89.
26 *Household Words*, Vol. VI, No. 139, 20 November 1852, 217–23.
27 Letter to W. H. Wills, 5 Nov. 1852, in *Letters*, 6.799.
28 *Household Words*, Vol. VI, No. 147, 15 Jan. 1853, 420.
29 Letter of 7 March 1854 in *Letters*, 7.285–6.
30 Catherine Crowe, *The Night-Side of Nature* (1848), Preface.
31 *Journalism*, II.82.
32 *Household Words*, Vol. VI, No. 163, 7 May 1853, 218.
33 Ibid. 220.
34 *Journalism*, III.475–83.
35 Letter of 6 Sept. 1859, in *Letters*, 9.116.
36 Letter of 17 Dec. 1859, in *Letters*, 9.178–9.
37 *Journalism*, IV.207.
38 Ibid. 208.
39 See Alan Gauld's entry in the *Oxford Dictionary of National
    Biography*: https://doi.org/10.1093/ref:odnb/13638 and Ruth
    Brandon, *The Spiritualists: The Passion for the Occult in the
    Nineteenth and Twentieth Centuries* (London: Weidenfeld and
    Nicolson, 1983), 57–64.
40 *All the Year Round*, Vol. IX, No. 206, 4 April 1863, 135.
41 *All the Year Round*, Christmas 1859, 2.

6

1 *Letters*, 9.354.
2 *Living on Paper: Letters from Iris Murdoch 1934–1995*, ed. Avril
   Horner and Anne Rowe (London: Chatto & Windus, 2015), 217.
3 Henry James, *The Nation*, 21 Dec. 1865, in *Dickens: The
   Critical Heritage*, 469.
4 Letter to David Masson, 6 May 1851, ibid., 260.
5 Forster Collection, National Art Library, MSL/1876/Forster/161.
6 See A. G. Bickelmann, C. S. Burwell, E. D. Robin and
   R. D. Whaley, 'Extreme obesity associated with alveolar

hypoventilation; a Pickwickian syndrome', in *The American Journal of Medicine*, 21(5) Nov. 1956: 811–8.

7 *Edinburgh Review*, October 1838, 76.

8 *Quarterly Review*, June 1839, 93.

9 Letter of 7 April 1839, in *Letters*, 1.539.

10 John Carey, *The Violent Effigy. A Study of Dickens' Imagination* (London: Faber and Faber, 1973), 7.

11 Malcolm Andrews, *Dickensian Laughter: Essays on Dickens and Humour* (Oxford: Oxford University Press, 2013), 48.

12 In George Ford and Lauriat Lane, eds, *The Dickens Critics* (1961; rpt. Ithaca, NY: Cornell University Press, 1966), 80.

13 George Santayana, 'Dickens', in Ford and Lane, eds, 147.

14 Letter of 6 Nov. 1849, in *Letters*, 5.640.

15 Santayana, in Ford and Lane, eds, 145.

16 Letter of 30 Aug. 1846, in *Letters*, 4.612.

17 Stone, ed., *Dickens' Working Notes*, 160–1.

18 Slater, *Charles Dickens*, 387–8.

7

1 *Book of Memoranda*, entry 22.

2 These were amongst many products named after Dickens's comic protagonist: see Frederic George Kitton, *The Life of Charles Dickens* (London, 1902), 44.

3 *The Examiner*, 8 Oct. 1853, in *Dickens: The Critical Heritage*, 292.

4 See Ernest L. Abel, 'Dickensian Eponyms', in *Names: A Journal of Onomastics*, Vol. 61 No. 2, June 2013, 76–7.

5 Stone, ed., *Working Notes*, 138–9.

6 Forster, II.78.

7 Stone, ed., *Working Notes*, 142–3.

8 A name in one novel sometimes seems to suggest names in others. Harry Stone analyses how Dickens moves from Murdstone to Merdle to Headstone to Durdles. Harry Stone, 'What's in a Name: Fantasy and Calculation in Dickens', *Dickens Studies Annual*, 14 (1985): 191–204.

9 See Joseph Bottum, 'The Gentleman's True Name: *David Copperfield* and the Philosophy of Naming', *Nineteenth-Century Literature*, Vol. 49, No. 4 (March 1995).
10 Letter of 25 April 1851 in *Letters*, 6.362.
11 Sold at auction by Sotheby's on 24 Sept. 2019.
12 Stone, ed., *Working Notes*, 26–31.
13 Ibid. 380–1.
14 Collins, ed., *Dickens: Interviews and Recollections*, 2 vols, 1.124.
15 *Book of Memoranda*, entry 110.
16 *The Complete Notebooks of Henry James*, ed. Leon Edel and Lyall H. Powers (Oxford: Oxford University Press, 1987), 13. See Glenda Leeming, *Who's Who in Henry James* (London: Elm Tree Books, 1976).
17 Ibid. 467.
18 For the derivation of this term, see Anne Barton, *The Names of Comedy* (Toronto: Toronto University Press, 1990), 7-15.
19 See Michael Slater, introd., *A Christmas Carol and Other Christmas Writings* (London: Penguin, 2003), xix.
20 Alastair Fowler, *Literary Names: Personal Names in English Literature* (Oxford: Oxford University Press, 2012), 189.
21 Laurence Sterne, *Tristram Shandy*, ed. Melvyn New (London: Penguin, 2003), 43.
22 Daniel Defoe, *Robinson Crusoe*, ed. J. Donald Crowley (Oxford: World's Classics, 1983; repr. 1990), 3.
23 *Great Expectations* ms, Wisbech and Fenland Museum.

8

1 *Letters*, 10.405.
2 Stone, ed., *Dickens' Working Notes*, 159.
3 Forster, I.59.
4 Charlotte Brontë, *Jane Eyre*, 322.
5 Ibid., Ch. VII, 385.
6 See for instance David Goldknopf, 'Coincidence in the Victorian Novel, The Trajectory of a Narrative-Device',

College English, 31, No. 1 (Oct., 1969), 41-2 and W.A. Craik, *The Brontë Novels* (London: Methuen, 1968), 86-7.

7   Wilkie Collins, *The Woman in White*, ed. John Sutherland (Oxford: World's Classics, 1996; repr. 2008), 20.

8   George Eliot, *Middlemarch*, ed. Rosemary Ashton (London: Penguin, 1994), 415.

9   Ibid. 522.

10 Ibid. 412.

11 Ibid. 94.

12 'Roderick Random, Peregrine Pickle, Humphrey Clinker, Tom Jones, the Vicar of Wakefield, Don Quixote, Gil Blas, and Robinson Crusoe, came out, a glorious host, to keep me company. They kept alive my fancy, and my hope of something beyond that place and time,' *David Copperfield*, Ch. IV.

13 *Fraser's Magazine*, XXI, cxxiv, April 1840, 382.

14 Letter of 22 February 1855, in *Letters*, 7, 545.

15 Forster, I.42-3.

16 Stone, ed., *Dickens' Working Notes*, 224-5.

17 Neil Forsyth, 'Wonderful Chains: Dickens and Coincidence', *Modern Philology* 83, no. 2 (Nov. 1985), 163.

18 Letter of June 1862, in *Letters*, 10.98.

19 See *Great Expectations*, ed. Trotter and Mitchell, 508-9. It was first printed in 1870 in Forster's *Life*.

20 See Slater, *Charles Dickens*, 494-5.

9

1   *Letters*, 4.84-5.

2   Martin Amis, *The War Against Cliché: Essays and Reviews 1971-2000* (2001; rpt. London: Vintage, 2002), xv.

3   Letter to Louise Colet, 13 June 1852, in *The Letters of Gustave Flaubert*, ed. and trans. Francis Steegmuller (London: Harvard University Press, 1980), 160.

4   Henry James, *Literary Criticism: French Writers, Other European Writers, The Prefaces to the New York Edition*, ed. Leon Edel and Mark Wilson (New York: Library of America, 1984), 311.

5 *Piers Plowman*, A 1. 161. The *OED* gives this as the first recorded use, but Langland used the phrase in 1350 in his translation of the French poem 'Guillaume de Palerne'.

6 *A Christmas Carol: A facsimile of the manuscript in the Pierpont Morgan Library* (New York: Pierpont Morgan Library, 1967).

7 An unknown clergyman wrote to Dickens pointing out that the eighteenth-century Shakespeare editor George Steevens had offered an explanation: the door-nail was where the knocker struck and therefore dead from repeated blows. In a letter from which the quotation at the head of this chapter is taken, Dickens replied that he was 'perfectly aware of Steevens's note'.

8 George L. Dillon, 'Corpus, creativity, cliché: Where statistics meet aesthetics', *Journal of Literary Semantics*, 35, No. 2 (Oct. 2017), 98.

9 Eric Partridge, *A Dictionary of Clichés* (London: Routledge & Kegan Paul, 1950), 2.

10 See Patrick J. McCarthy, 'The Language of Martin Chuzzlewit', in *Studies in English Literature, 1500–1900*, Vol. 20, No. 4 (Autumn, 1980), 641–2.

11 George B. Bryan and Wolfgang Mieder, *The Proverbial Charles Dickens* (New York: Peter Lang, 1997), 30.

12 Stone, ed., *Dickens' Working Notes*, 341.

13 McCarthy, 643.

10

1 *Book of Memoranda*, entry 45.

2 One such is described in Dickens's 'The Streets – Night', first published in *Bell's Life in London* in January 1836, in *Journalism*, I.59.

3 Forster, I.373.

4 See Richard L. Klepac, *Mr Mathews at Home* (London: The Society for Theatre Research, 1979), 9–11.

5 *Memoirs of Charles Mathews, Comedian*, 4 vols (London, 1838–9), IV, 49.

6 Ibid. 50.

7 Klepac, *Mathews*, 62.

8 'Mathews the Comedian', *Blackwood's Magazine*, Vol. 45 (1839), 243.

9 Letter of 30–31 December 1844 and 1 January 1845, in *Letters*, 4.244–5.

10 The anonymous review was by a scholarly young essayist, George Brimley. See Hollington, ed., *Charles Dickens. Critical Assessments*, I.351.

11 The first recorded use of 'idiolect' is from 1948 in an academic linguistic journal. Only in recent decades has it escaped such specialist publications and entered literary critical usage.

12 Robert Douglas-Fairhurst suggests Jingle's idiolect might have been borrowed from one of Charles Mathews's favourite characters, Major Longbow. Douglas-Fairhurst, 194. Robert Golding finds a source in a play by Thomas Holcroft in which Mathews acted, *Idiolects in Dickens: The Major Techniques and Chronological Development* (Basingstoke: Macmillan, 1985), 19.

13 In Ford and Lane, eds, 89.

14 In Philip Collins, ed., *Dickens: Interviews and Recollections*, 2 vols (London: Macmillan, 1981), 11.

15 John Walker, *A Critical Pronouncing Dictionary of the English Language* (1791), source details? xii.

16 Ibid., xiii.

17 See Henry Mayhew, *London Labour and the London Poor*, 4 vols (London: 1861; repr. New York: Dover Publications, 1968), II, 178. He also uses *v* for *w*: 'ven I gets home arter my vork'. Many of those whose speech Mayhew represents say 'wery'. See, for example, the street seller of fly papers (I, 435) or the coster-lad (I, 39).

18 Letter of 5 March 1839, in *Letters*, 1.521.

19 Letter of 2nd May 1841, in *Letters*, 2.276.

20 Letter of 22 April 1854, in *Letters*, 7.321.

21 Slater, *Charles Dickens*, 287.

22 *Quarterly Review*, 59 (1837), in Florence E. Baer, 'Wellerisms in *The Pickwick Papers*', *Folklore*, 94:2 (1983), 174.

23 Collins, ed., *Interviews and Recollections*, I.11.

24 Lewes, 'Dickens in Relation to Criticism', 149.

25 Klepac, *Mathews*, 42.

26 Forster, I.96.

27 Mamie Dickens, *My Father as I Recall Him* (1898), 48.
28 In Collins, ed., *Interviews and Recollections*, II.272.
29 *Letters*, 4.133.
30 *Letters*, 4.243–4.
31 Forster, II.104.
32 Forster, I.96
33 Letter of 27 Sept. 1842, *Letters*, 3.333.
34 See Slater, *Charles Dickens*, 402–3.

11

1 *Letters*, 9.90.
2 Stone, ed., *Dickens' Working Notes*, 68–9; Tony Laing, *Dickens's Working Notes for Dombey and Son* (Cambridge: Open Book Publishers, 2017), 64–5.
3 Letter of 25–26 July 1846, in *Letters*, 4.589–90.
4 Butt and Tillotson, 90. See also Laing, *Working Notes*, 11 and 135.
5 See Nina Burgis, Introduction, *David Copperfield* (Oxford: Oxford University Press, 1981), xxviii.
6 The additions and their affect are described with great precision by Philip Davis, 'Deep Reading in the Manuscripts: Dickens and the Manuscript of *David Copperfield*', in *Reading and the Victorians*, ed. Matthew Bradley and Juliet John (London: Routledge, 2015), 66–9.
7 Stone, ed., *Working Notes*, 164–5.
8 Dickens kept returning to *Macbeth*. See Gager, 116–33.
9 Muriel Spark, *The Driver's Seat* (London: Penguin, 1970; rpr. 1974), 23.
10 Alan Taylor, *Appointment in Arezzo. A Friendship with Muriel Spark* (Edinburgh: Polygon, 2017), 99.
11 Ian McEwan, *Enduring Love* (London: Vintage, 1997; rpr. 1998), 2.
12 Ian McEwan, *Atonement* (2001; London: Vintage, 2001; rpr. 2002), 348.
13 Stone, ed., *Working Notes*, 224–5.
14 Ibid. 278–9.
15 Ibid. 280–1.
16 Ibid. 286–7.

17 See *A Tale of Two Cities*, ed. Richard Maxwell (London: Penguin, 2000), 398, He was repeating an adjective he had used in a letter to John Forster in the summer of 1851, in which he said he was 'reading that wonderful book the *French Revolution* again, for the 500th time': *Letters*, 6.452.

18 Thomas Carlyle, *The French Revolution*, eds David R. Sorenson and Brent E. Kinser (Oxford: World's Classics, 2019) Vol. III, Bk. II, 534–5.

12

1 *Book of Memoranda*, entry 36. The note was made by mid-1855, at the latest. In 1864, or later, Dickens returned to the notebook and added to this entry, '[Done in Our Mutual]'.

2 An exception is Clare Tomalin, *Charles Dickens: A Life* (London: Viking, 2011), 102 and 155. However, I believe that she is wrong to suppose that Dickens was already a good swimmer in the 1830s.

3 In Collins, ed., *Dickens: Interviews and Recollections*, I.148.

4 Letter of 28 June 1839, in *Letters*, 1.557.

5 *Letters*, 3.325.

6 *Letters*, 3.548.

7 Letter of 21 July 1842, in *Letters*, 3.277.

8 *Letters*, 3.523–4.

9 Letter to Thomas Mitton, 12 Aug. 1844, *Letters*, 4.176.

10 Letter to Clarkson Stanfield, 24 Aug. 1844, *Letters*, 4.185.

11 Letter to Thomas Beard, 22 March 1850, *Letters*, 6.71.

12 See letter to Angela Burdett-Coutts, 9 Apr. 1857, in *Letters* 8. 311. Also a letter to George Beadnell, 5 June 1857, in *Letters* 8.342.

13 Christopher Love, *A Social History of Swimming in England, 1800–1918* (London: Routledge, 2008), 7.

14 *American Notes*, 23–4.

15 Letter of 13 Feb. 1840, in *Letters*, 2.26.

16 Love, 102–43.

17 Ibid. 104–12.

18 *Letters*, 4.174.

19 Ibid. 193.
20 Ibid. 587.
21 Stone, *The Night Side of Dickens:*, 565.
22 *Journalism*, IV.88.
23 Ibid. 90.
24 Ibid. 88.
25 *Household Words*, Vol. XIII, No. 320, 10 May 1856, 388.
26 *All the Year Round*, 16 May 1863, in *Dickens' Journalism*, IV.220.
27 Ibid. 224.
28 Ibid. 44.
29 See, for example, his speech on behalf of the Artists' Benevolent Fund, in *The Speeches of Charles Dickens*, 302.
30 *Book of Memoranda*, entry 36.
31 Ibid. entry 40.
32 Barbara T. Gates, *Victorian Suicide: Mad Crimes and Sad Histories* (Princeton, NJ: Princeton University Press, 1988), 135.
33 *Journalism*, IV.151.
34 Ibid., I.471–2.
35 *All the Year Round*, 20 June 1863, in *Journalism*, IV.239.
36 See David McAllister, 'Artificial Resuscitation in *Our Mutual Friend*', *The Dickensian*, Vol. 105: 2 (Summer 2009).
37 Adrian Poole, Introduction, *Our Mutual Friend* (London: Penguin, 1997), ix.
38 Defoe, *Robinson Crusoe*, 46.

13

1 *Book of Memoranda*, entry 52.
2 Carey, 154.
3 See Catherine Peters, *The King of Inventors: A Life of Wilkie Collins* (London: Secker & Warburg, 1991), 196 and 233.
4 Slater, *Charles Dickens*, 144.
5 Letter of 25 June 1859, in *Letters*, 9.84.
6 The efforts of Dickens and of those who guarded his reputation to keep his relationship with Ellen Ternan concealed are documented in Michael Slater, *The Great Charles Dickens Scandal* (London: Yale University Press, 2012).

7 The revelation first came in an article in the *Times Literary Supplement*, 19 Feb. 2019.

8 See Kelly Hager, *Dickens and the Rise of Divorce: The Failed-Marriage Plot and the Novel Tradition* (Farnham: Ashgate, 2010), 155–79.

9 Charlotte Brontë, *Jane Eyre*, Vol. III, Ch. I, 303–4.

10 Stone, ed., *Dickens' Working Notes*, 88–9.

11 Letter of 19 Nov. 1847, in *Letters*, 5.197.

12 See Butt and Tillotson, 106.

13 Letter of 21 Dec. 1847, in *Letters*, 5.211.

14 Stone, ed., *Working Notes*, 94–5.

15 *Oliver Twist*, ed. Kathleen Tillotson (Oxford: Oxford University Press, 1966), I.iii.

16 Dickens recorded his admiration in a letter to George Eliot, 10 July 1859, in Letters, 9.93. He wrote, 'The conception of Hetty's character is so extraordinarily subtle and true, that I laid the book down fifty times, to shut my eyes and think about it.'

17 George Eliot, *Adam Bede* (1859), ed. Valentine Cunningham (Oxford: Oxford University Press, 1996), 137.

18 Ibid. 138.

19 Ibid. 288.

20 Ibid. 296.

21 Ibid. 297–8.

22 Ibid. 334.

23 Letter of 29 Dec 1849, in *Letters*, 5.682.

24 See Jenny Hartley, *Charles Dickens and the House of Fallen Women* (London: Methuen, 2008), which points out that David Copperfield was 'the first novel which Dickens planned and wrote during the Urania years', 159.

25 Carey, 162.

14

1 *Letters*, 10.471.

2 Anthony Trollope, *Autobiography and Other Writings*, ed. Nicholas Shrimpton (Oxford: World's Classics, 2014; repr. 2016), 155.

3 MS in the Dickens House Museum. Listed in Michael Slater, ed., *The Catalogue of the Suzannet Charles Dickens Collection* (London: Sotheby Parke Benet Publications, 1975), as J. 60, 'Autograph notes concerning Dickens'.

4 See Alex Murray, '"The London Sunday Faded Slow": Time to Spend in the Victorian City', in Juliet John, ed., *The Oxford Handbook of Victorian Culture* (Oxford: Oxford University Press, 2016), 317–26.

5 See, for example, *Metropolitan Magazine*, 29 (December 1840), 111.

6 *Sketches of Young Gentlemen and Young Couples*, ed. Paul Schlicke (Oxford: Oxford University Press, 2012), 134.

7 *Pictures from Italy*, 65.

8 Ibid. 102.

9 Alastair Fowler, *How to Write* (Oxford: Oxford University Press, 2006), 46.

Bibliography

DICKENS'S WRITINGS

Charles Dickens' Book of Memoranda, ed. Fred Kaplan
(New York: New York Public Library, 1981)
The Dent Uniform Edition of Dickens' Journalism, ed. Michael
Slater and John Drew, 4 vols (London: J. M. Dent,
1994–2000)
The Letters of Charles Dickens, ed. Madeline House, Graham
Storey et al., 12 vols (Oxford: Clarendon Press, 1965–2002)
The Speeches of Charles Dickens, ed. K. J. Fielding (Oxford:
Clarendon Press, 1960)

American Notes, ed. Patricia Ingram (London: Penguin, 2000)
Barnaby Rudge, ed. John Bowen (London: Penguin, 2003)
Bleak House, ed. Nicola Bradbury (London: Penguin, 2003)
*A Christmas Carol, A Facsimile of the Manuscript in the Pierpont
Morgan Library* (New York: Pierpont Morgan Library, 1967)
A Christmas Carol and Other Christmas Writings, ed. Michael
Slater (London: Penguin, 2003)
David Copperfield, ed. Nina Burgis (Oxford: Oxford University
Press, 1981)
Dombey and Son, ed. Alan Horsman (Oxford: Oxford University
Press, 1974)

Great Expectations, ed. Margaret Cardwell (Oxford: Oxford
   University Press, 1993)
Great Expectations, ed. David Trotter and Charlotte Mitchell
   (London: Penguin, 1996)
Hard Times, ed. Kate Flint (London: Penguin, 1995)
Little Dorrit, ed. Harvey Peter Sucksmith (Oxford: Oxford
   University Press, 1979)
Martin Chuzzlewit, ed. Margaret Cardwell (Oxford: Oxford
   University Press, 1982)
The Mystery of Edwin Drood, ed. Margaret Cardwell (Oxford:
   Oxford University Press, 1972)
Nicholas Nickleby, ed. Paul Schlicke (Oxford: Oxford University
   Press, 1990)
The Old Curiosity Shop, ed. Elizabeth M. Brennan (Oxford:
   Oxford University Press, 1997)
The Pickwick Papers, ed. James Kinsley (Oxford: Oxford
   University Press, 1986)
Oliver Twist, ed. Kathleen Tillotsson (Oxford: Oxford University
   Press, 1966)
Our Mutual Friend, ed. Adrian Poole (London: Penguin, 1997)
Pictures from Italy, ed. Kate Flint (London: Penguin, 1998)
Sketches of Young Gentlemen and Young Couples, ed. Paul Schlicke
   (Oxford: Oxford University Press, 2012)
A Tale of Two Cities, ed. Richard Maxwell (London: Penguin,
   2000)

OTHER WORKS

Articles in *Household Words* and *All the Year Round* were
   consulted via Dickens Journals Online at http://www.djo.org.
   uk/household-words.html and http://www.djo.org.uk/all-the-
   year-round.html
Abel, Ernest L., 'Dickensian Eponyms', *Names, A Journal of
   Onomastics*, 61, No. 2 (June 2013), 75–91
Amis, Martin, *The War Against Cliché, Essays and Reviews 1971–
   2000* (London: Vintage, 2001; repr. 2002)

Andrews, Malcolm, *Dickensian Laughter, Essays on Dickens and Humour* (Oxford: Oxford University Press, 2013)

Baer, Florence E., 'Wellerisms in *The Pickwick Papers*', *Folklore*, 94, No. 2 (1983), 173–83

Barton, Anne, *The Names of Comedy* (Oxford: Oxford University Press, 1990)

Bickelmann, A. G. et al., 'Extreme Obesity Associated with Alveolar Hypoventilation, A Pickwickian Syndrome', *American Journal of Medicine*, 21, No. 5, Nov. 1956

Bodenheimer, Rosemary, *Knowing Dickens* (Ithaca, NY: Cornell University Press, 2007)

Bottum, Joseph, 'The Gentleman's True Name, *David Copperfield* and the Philosophy of Naming', *Nineteenth-Century Literature*, 49, No. 4 (March 1995), 435–55

Bradley, Matthew and Juliet John, eds, *Reading and the Victorians* (London: Routledge, 2015)

Brandon, Ruth, *The Spiritualists: The Passion for the Occult in the Nineteenth and Twentieth Centuries* (London: Weidenfeld and Nicolson, 1983)

Brontë, Charlotte, *Jane Eyre*, ed. Margaret Smith (Oxford: World's Classics, 1975; repr. 1982)

—— *Villette*, ed. Margaret Smith, rev. Tim Dolan (Oxford: World's Classics, 2000)

Brontë, Emily, *Wuthering Heights*, ed. Ian Jack, rev. Helen Small (Oxford: World's Classics, 2009)

Brown, Nicola, Carolyn Burdett and Pamela Thurschwell, eds, *The Victorian Supernatural* (Cambridge: Cambridge University Press, 2004)

Bryan, George B. and Wolfgang Mieder, *The Proverbial Charles Dickens* (New York: Peter Lang, 1997)

Butt, John, *Pope, Dickens and Others* (Edinburgh: Edinburgh University Press, 1969)

—— and Kathleen Tillotson, *Dickens at Work* (London: Methuen & Co, 1957)

Carey, John, *The Violent Effigy: A Study of Dickens' Imagination* (London: Faber and Faber, 1973)

Carlyle, Thomas, *The French Revolution*, eds David R. Sorenson and Brent E. Kinser (Oxford: World's Classics, 2019)

Collins, Philip, ed., *Dickens, Interviews and Recollections*, 2 vols (London: Macmillan, 1981)

—— ed., *Dickens, The Critical Heritage* (London: Routledge and Kegan Paul, 1971)

Collins, Wilkie, *The Woman in White*, ed. John Sutherland (Oxford: World's Classics, 1996; repr. 2008)

Coolidge, Archibald C., *Charles Dickens as Serial Novelist* (Ames, IA: Iowa State University Press, 1967)

Cotsell, Michael, *The Companion to Our Mutual Friend* (London: Allen & Unwin, 1986)

Craik, W.A., *The Brontë Novels* (London: Methuen, 1968)

Crowe, Catherine, *The Night-Side of Nature* (London: 1848)

DeLillo, Don, *Underworld* (London: Picador, 1997; repr. 2015)

Dickens, Mamie, *My Father as I Recall Him* (London: 1898)

Dillon, George L., 'Corpus, creativity, cliché: Where statistics meet aesthetics', *Journal of Literary Semantics*, 35, No. 2 (Oct. 2017), 97–104

Dooley, Alan C., *Author and Printer in Victorian England* (Charlottesville, VA: University Press of Virginia, 1992)

Douglas-Fairhurst, Robert, *Becoming Dickens, The Invention of a Novelist* (Cambridge, MA: Harvard University Press, 2011)

Eliot, George, *Adam Bede*, ed. Valentine Cunningham (Oxford: Oxford University Press, 1996)

—— *Middlemarch*, ed. Rosemary Ashton (London: Penguin, 1994)

Flaubert, Gustave, *The Letters of Gustave Flaubert*, ed. and trans. Francis Steegmuller (London: Harvard University Press, 1980)

Ford, George and Lauriat Lane, eds, *The Dickens Critics* (Ithaca, NY: Cornell University Press, 1961; repr. 1966)

Forster, John, *The Life of Charles Dickens*, ed. A. J. Hoppé, 2 vols (London: J. M. Dent, 1966)

Forsyth, Neil, 'Wonderful Chains, Dickens and Coincidence', *Modern Philology*, 83, No. 2 (Nov. 1985), 151–165

Fowler, Alastair, *How to Write* (Oxford: Oxford University
    Press, 2006)
—— *Literary Names, Personal Names in English Literature*
    (Oxford: Oxford University Press, 2012)
Gager, Valerie L., *Shakespeare and Dickens, The Dynamics of
    Influence* (Cambridge: Cambridge University Press, 1996)
Gates, Barbara T., *Victorian Suicide, Mad Crimes and Sad
    Histories* (Princeton, NJ: Princeton University Press, 1988)
Golding, Robert, *Idiolects in Dickens, The Major Techniques and
    Chronological Development* (Basingstoke: Macmillan, 1985)
Goldknopf, David, 'Coincidence in the Victorian Novel, The
    Trajectory of a Narrative-Device', *College English*, 31, No. 1
    (Oct. 1969), 41–50
Goodin, George, *Dickens's Dialogue, Margins of Conversation*
    (New York: AMS Press, 2013)
Hager, Kelly, *Dickens and the Rise of Divorce: The Failed-Marriage
    Plot and the Novel Tradition* (Farnham: Ashgate, 2010)
Haight, Gordon S., 'Dickens and Lewes on Spontaneous
    Combustion', *Nineteenth-Century Fiction*, 10, No. 1 (June
    1955), 53–63
Halliday, Stephen, *The Great Stink of London: Sir Joseph
    Bazalgette and the Cleansing of the Victorian Metropolis*
    (Stroud, Gloucs, Sutton Publishing, 1999)
Hardy, Barbara, *Dickens and Creativity* (London: Continuum,
    2008)
Hartley, Jenny, *Charles Dickens and the House of Fallen Women*
    (London: Methuen, 2008)
Harvey, John, 'Fiction in the present tense', *Textual Practice*, 20,
    No. 1 (2006), 71–98
Hollington, Michael, ed., *Charles Dickens, Critical Assessments*, 4
    vols (Mountfield, E. Sussex: Helm Information, 1995)
James, Henry, *The Complete Notebooks of Henry James*, eds
    Leon Edel and Lyall H. Powers (Oxford: Oxford University
    Press, 1987)

—— *Literary Criticism, French Writers; Other European Writers; The Prefaces to the New York Edition* (Cambridge: Cambridge University Press, 1984)

—— *The Portrait of a Lady* (1881), ed. Michael Anesko (Cambridge: Cambridge University Press, 2016)

John, Juliet, ed., *The Oxford Handbook of Victorian Culture* (Oxford: Oxford University Press, 2016)

Joyce, James, *Ulysses* (London: Penguin, 1960; repr. 1984)

Keable, Ian, *Charles Dickens Magician* (Privately published, 2014)

Kitton, Frederic George, *The Life of Charles Dickens* (London: 1902)

Klepac, Richard L., *Mr Mathews at Home* (London: The Society for Theatre Research, 1979)

Laing, Tony, *Dickens's Working Notes for Dombey and Son* (Cambridge: Open Book Publishers, 2017)

Leeming, Glenda, *Who's Who in Henry James* (London: Elm Tree Books, 1976)

Lewes, G. H., 'Dickens in Relation to Criticism', *Fortnightly Review*, XVII, Feb 1872

Love, Christopher, *A Social History of Swimming in England, 1800–1918* (London: Routledge, 2008)

McAllister, David, 'Artificial Resuscitation in *Our Mutual Friend*', *The Dickensian*, 105, No. 2 (Summer 2009), 101–8

McCarthy, Patrick J., 'The Language of Martin Chuzzlewit', *Studies in English Literature, 1500–1900*, 20, No. 4 (Autumn, 1980), 637–49

McEwan, Ian, *Enduring Love* (London: Vintage, 1997; repr. 1998)

——, *Atonement* (London: Vintage, 2001; repr. 2002)

Mathews, Anne Jackson, *Memoirs of Charles Mathews, Comedian*, 4 vols (London: 1838–9)

Mayhew, Henry, *London Labour and the London Poor*, 4 vols (London: 1861; repr. New York: Dover Publications, 1968)

Miller, J. Hillis, *Charles Dickens, The World of his Novels* (Cambridge, Mass.: Harvard University Press, 1965)

Monod, Sylvere, ' "When the Battle's Lost and Won ...", Dickens *v.* the Compositors of *Bleak House*', *The Dickensian*, 69 (1 Jan 1973), 3–12

Murdoch, Iris, *Living on Paper: Letters from Iris Murdoch 1934–1995*, eds Avril Horner and Anne Rowe (London: Chatto & Windus, 2015)

Partridge, Eric, *A Dictionary of Clichés* (London: Routledge and Kegan Paul, 1950)

Patten, Robert L., *Charles Dickens and his Publishers* (Oxford: Oxford University Press, 1978)

—— John O. Jordan and Catherine Waters, eds, *The Oxford Handbook of Charles Dickens* (Oxford: Oxford University Press, 2018)

Peters, Catherine, *The King of Inventors: A Life of Wilkie Collins* (London: Secker & Warburg, 1991)

Peyrouton, N. C., 'Rapping the Rappers, More Grist for the Biographers' Mill', *The Dickensian*, 55, No. 327 (January 1959), 75–89

Picard, Liza, *Victorian London* (London: Weidenfeld & Nicolson, 2005)

Quirk, Randolph, *Charles Dickens and Appropriate Language* (Durham: University of Durham, 1959)

Schwarzbach, F. S., *Dickens and the City* (London: Bloomsbury Academic, 1979, repr. 2013)

Slater, Michael, *Charles Dickens* (London: Yale University Press, 2009)

—— *The Great Charles Dickens Scandal* (London: Yale University Press, 2012)

—— ed., *The Catalogue of the Suzannet Charles Dickens Collection* (London: Sotheby Parke Benet Publications, 1975)

Smollett, Tobias, *Roderick Random*, ed. Paul-Gabriel Boucé (Oxford: Oxford University Press, 1979; repr. 1981)

——, *The Expedition of Humphry Clinker*, eds Louis M. Knapp and Paul-Gabriel Boucé (Oxford: World's Classics, 1984; repr. 2009)

Sørensen, Knud, *Charles Dickens, Linguistic Innovator* (Aarhus: Arkona, 1985)

Spark, Muriel, *The Driver's Seat* (London: Penguin, 1970; repr. 1974)

Sterne, Laurence, *Tristram Shandy*, ed. Melvyn New (London: Penguin, 2003)

Stewart, Garrett, *Death Sentence, Styles of Dying in British Fiction* (Cambridge, Mass: Harvard University Press, 1984)

Stone, Harry, ed., *Dickens' Working Notes for His Novels* (Chicago and London: University of Chicago Press, 1987)

—— 'Dickens and Interior Monologue', *Philological Quarterly*, 38 (1959), 52–60

—— *The Night Side of Dickens: Cannibalism, Passion, Necessity* (Columbus,OH: Ohio State University Press, 1994)

—— 'What's in a Name, Fantasy and Calculation in Dickens', *Dickens Studies Annual*, 14 (1985), 191–204

Sucksmith, H. P., 'Dickens at Work on *Bleak House*, A Critical Examination of His Memoranda and Number Plans', *Renaissance and Modern Studies*, 9, No. 1 (1965), 47–85

—— *The Narrative Art of Charles Dickens, The Rhetoric of Sympathy and Irony in His Novels* (Oxford: Oxford University Press, 1970)

Sutherland, John, *Victorian Novelists and Publishers* (Chicago, University of Chicago Press, 1976; repr. 1978)

—— *Orwell's Nose: A Pathological Biography* (London: Reaktion Books, 2016)

Taylor, Alan, *Appointment in Arezzo: A Friendship with Muriel Spark* (Edinburgh: Polygon, 2017)

Toker, Leona, *Eloquent Reticence: Withholding Information in Fictional Narrative* (Lexington, KY: University Press of Kentucky, 1993)

Tomalin, Claire, *The Invisible Woman: The Story of Nelly Ternan and Charles Dickens* (London: Viking, 1990)

—— *Charles Dickens, A Life* (London: Viking, 2011)

Trollope, Anthony, *An Autobiography and Other Writings*, ed. Nicholas Shrimpton (Oxford: World's Classics, 2014; repr. 2016)

—— *The Warden*, ed. David Skilton (Oxford: World's Classics, 1980)

Tyler, Daniel, ed., *Dickens's Style* (Cambridge: Cambridge
    University Press, 2013)
Vargish, Thomas, *The Providential Aesthetic in Victorian Fiction*
    (Charlottesville, VA: University Press of Virginia, 1985)
Walker, John, *A Critical Pronouncing Dictionary of the English
    Language* (London: 1791)
Wheeler, Burton M., 'The Text and Plan of *Oliver Twist*',
    Dickens Studies Annual, 12 (1984), 41–61
White, Jerry, *London in the Nineteenth Century* (London:
    Jonathan Cape, 2007)
Wood, Claire, *Dickens and the Business of Death* (Cambridge:
    Cambridge University Press, 2015)

Index

All the Year Round (and the Uncommercial Traveller), 4, 7, 42, 49–50, 68, 164, 211–12
  and drowning, 324–6, 330–1
  'The Ghost in Master B's Room', 121
  'The Martyr Medium', 120
  'Rather a Strong Dose', 119
  and the supernatural, 110, 112–14, 119–21
  'To Be Taken with a Grain of Salt', 112–13, 124
American Notes, 35, 78, 310, 333
Amis, Martin, 217
Andrews, Malcolm, 139
animals, 19, 31–2
  smells of, 48, 61–4
anticipation, *see* foreknowledge
'as if' constructions, 15–40
Astley's Amphitheatre, 65
Atkinson, Kate, 88
Atwood, Margaret
  The Blind Assassin, 88
  The Handmaid's Tale, 86–7
Austen, Jane, 217, 275–6

Barnaby Rudge, 19–20, 157, 172, 232, 258, 375, 387
  and the supernatural, 105–6
Bath, 59
Bazalgette, Joseph, 61
Beadnell, Maria, 153, 202, 278
Beard, Frank, 339
Beard, Thomas, 311
Beaumont and Fletcher, *The Maid's Tragedy*, 343–4
Beckett, Samuel, 85
Berkeley, Bishop George, 185
Bleak House, 4, 11–12, 156
  'as if' constructions, 15–18, 29, 33–4, 38–9
  chapter titles, 233
  and clichés, 225–6, 228–9, 233, 235–6, 238–40
  and coincidences, 205–9
  and different voices, 245–7, 250, 258, 264–5, 267–8, 272
  and drowning, 316, 328–9
  and foreknowledge, 294–8
  literary style, 365, 367–8, 376–81
  and names, 169, 171–2, 181, 183–4, 186

and sex, 347–8
and shifts of tense, 72–7, 85, 88
and smells, 54–8, 60, 63, 67–8
and the supernatural, 95–101,
   113, 124
Blessington, Countess of, 338
body, and character, 37–8
Book of Memoranda, 3, 155, 165–6,
   245, 309, 337
Booker Prize, 87
Bowen, John, 339
Boyle, Mary, 112, 127
British Museum, 366
Brontë, Charlotte
   Jane Eyre, 81–2, 195, 197, 340–1
   Villette, 103–4
Brontë, Emily, 101–3, 259
Brookes & Sons of Sheffield, 162
Brooks, Shirley, 189
Brophy, Brigid, 127
Browne, Hablot, 100
buildings, 34–5
Burdett-Coutts, Angela, 113
Burroughs, William, 86

cannibalism and vampirism, 28–30
Carey, John, 138, 337, 357
Carlyle, Jane, 9
Carlyle, Thomas, 299–300
characterisations, simplicity of, 1–3
Chatham, 49–50
childhood
   and elevated diction, 368–9
   and present tense, 82–3, 85–6
   and smells, 48–9, 51–3
children, cruelty to, 139–41
cholera, 56
Christmas Carol, A, 7, 34, 53,
   379, 383
   and clichés, 218–21

and the supernatural, 108–9
Church of England, 374
churches, smell of, 67–70
circuses, 65–6
Clare Market, 60
clichés, 217–43
cockney dialect, 258–9
coincidences, 189–216
   repetition of 'coincidence', 194
   in Victorian fiction, 195–8
Coleridge, Berkeley, 185
Coleridge, Hartley, 185
Coleridge, Samuel Taylor, 185
Collins, Wilkie, 41, 45, 55, 66, 119,
   121, 338, 363
   The Moonstone, 308
   The Woman in White, 195–7
compositors, 10
conjuring, 8–9
coughing, 267
Crowe, Catherine, 116
Cruikshank, George, 258
Crystal Palace, 16

David Copperfield, 6, 13
   'as if' constructions, 30–1, 33, 37
   and clichés, 229, 232, 235, 239
   and coincidences, 189–93
   and different voices, 259, 272–3
   and drowning, 312–13, 320–1,
      330, 335
   and foreknowledge, 284–92, 303
   and humour, 128–9, 150
   literary style, 384, 390–1
   and names, 157–63, 168, 171, 183
   and present tense, 82–6
   and sex, 347, 350–4
   and smells, 47–8, 51–2, 63
   and Smollett, 58–9, 370
de Cerjat, William, 351

De La Rue, Augusta, 111
Defoe, Daniel, *Robinson Crusoe*,
    6–7, 186, 335–6
DeLillo, Don, 88
Dickens, Alfred D'Orsay
    Tennyson, 184
Dickens, Catherine, 339–40
Dickens, Charles
    Atlantic crossings, 46, 315, 333
    childhood and marital
        breakdown, 213
    children's names, 184–5
    and coincidental
        encounters, 201–3
    comments on characters'
        names, 164–5
    and drownings, 323
    education, 5
    early reading, 5–6
    fascination with theatre, 248–50
    and father's speech, 272–3
    and ghost stories, 108, 110–14
    imitates actors, 261
    manuscripts, 9–12
    and mesmerism, 111–12
    opposition to
        spiritualism, 115–20
    as performer, 8–9
    self-sufficiency, 7–8
    separation from wife, 339–40
    and sex, 337–40
    and swimming, 309–12, 335
    talking while writing, 269–70
    vengeance on Maria
        Beadnell, 153
    works as reporter, 8, 248,
        250, 261
Dickens, Charley, 10, 311
Dickens, Edward Bulwer
    Lytton, 184

Dickens, Fanny, 51
Dickens, Francis Jeffrey, 184
Dickens, Fred, 323
Dickens, Henry Fielding, 184
Dickens, John, 6, 272–3
Dickens, Mamie, 269, 309
Dickens, Sydney Smith
    Haldimand, 184
Dickens, Walter Landor, 184, 311
dinosaurs, 15–17
Disraeli, Benjamin, 338
divorce laws, 340
Doctor's Commons, 248, 261
Dombey and Son, 323
    and clichés, 221–4, 229, 234–5
    and coincidences, 203–5
    and different voices, 258, 271–2
    and drowning, 313–16, 320
    and foreknowledge,
        281–4, 306–7
    and humour, 147–50
    literary style, 377, 382–3, 387
    and names, 174, 180–1, 187
    and present tense, 78–81
    and sex, 341–5, 347, 358
    and smells, 67
Doré, Gustave, 329
D'Orsay, Count, 338
Dostoevsky, Emile, 146
drowning, 309–36
    and fallen women, 329–30
    suicide by, 321–3, 326, 329–31
    and superstitions, 334–5
Drury Lane Theatre, 66
Dutton Cook, Edward, 339

Edinburgh Review, 136
Edrupt, William, 45
Egg, Augustus, 329
Eliot, George, 146, 259

Adam Bede, 316, 348–50
Daniel Deronda, 317, 330
Middlemarch, 20–1, 196–8, 259
The Mill on the Floss, 316
Eliot, T. S., *The Waste Land*, 247
Elliot, Frances, 114
Examiner, The, 57, 116
excrement, smell of, 60

Felton, C. C., 1, 310
Fielding, Henry, 168, 170, 370
  Tom Jones, 198–9
Flaubert, Gustave, 217–18
foreknowledge (prolepsis), 281–308
  and modern fiction, 293–4
Forster, John, 50, 61, 71, 95, 106,
    108, 114, 149, 156, 158, 193,
    203, 213, 284, 310, 323
  and Dickens's voices, 248–9,
    258, 269, 272–3, 275–6
Fowler, Alastair, 379
Frozen Deep, The, 339
funerals, 51–2, 84, 137

Gale, Rev. P., 217
Galileo, 120
Gaskell, Elizabeth, 114, 121
  North and South, 316–17
  'The Old Nurse's Story', 110
ghost stories, 108–14, 120–1
ghosts, *see* supernatural, the
Gibbon, Edward, 237
Gissing, George, 140–1, 252
Golding, Robert, 255
Gothic fiction, 104
Graves, Caroline, 338
Great Expectations, 2–3, 5
  'as if' constructions, 21–9, 35–7
  and coincidences, 209–16
  and different voices, 269

and drowning, 313, 320, 331–2
and foreknowledge, 302–6
literary style, 369–70, 377,
    382, 389–92
and names, 166, 170–1, 186–8
revised ending, 215–16
and sex, 359–60
and 'shrinking', 213
and smells, 41–7, 51–2, 63
and the supernatural, 121–4
'Great Stink, The', 60–1

Handel, George Frideric, 187
Hard Times, 4, 7
  and circus smells, 65–6
  and clichés, 227
  and different voices, 265
  and drowning, 316
  literary style, 364, 388
  and names, 168–70, 182–5, 187
  and sex, 340, 355–8
Hardy, Thomas, 317
'Harmonic Meetings', 245
Hartley, David, 185
Harvey, John, 85
hat-manufactories, 49
Hawkins, Benjamin, 16
Hayden, Mrs W. R., 115–16
Hedgman, James, 311
Holborn Baths, 311
Hollingshead, John, 119
Home, Daniel Dunglas, 120
Hood, Thomas, 330
horses and stables, smell of,
    48, 61–3
Household Words, 4, 15, 50, 67
  and drowning, 324–5
  'The Ghost of the Cock Lane
    Ghost', 115–16
  'Shadows' series, 72–3

and the supernatural, 110,
113–18
Howitt, William, 118–20
humour, 127–54

idiolects, *see* voices, different

James, Henry, 17, 20, 128, 166–7,
169, 171, 218
The Ivory Tower, 167
The Portrait of a Lady, 21, 166–7
Jeffrey, Lord, 343
Jones, William, 5
Joyce, James
Finnegans Wake, 85
Ulysses, 85–6

Kean, Charles, 258
Kemble, Charles, 250
Ketch, Jack, 259
King, Stephen, 29
Knight, Charles, 71–2

Langland, William, *Piers
Plowman*, 219
laudanum, 56
laughter, *see* humour
Le Fanu, Sheridan, 110–12
Lear, George, 258, 261
Lemon, Mark, 259
Lewes, G. H., 2, 5, 54–5, 263
literary style, 363–92
hyperbole, 16, 224, 376–7
listing, 379–83
neologisms, 366–7
repetitions, 383–92
Little Dorrit, 165
'as if' constructions, 24, 32,
35, 39–40
and clichés, 223–5, 236, 241

and different voices, 255–7,
266–7, 269, 274–9
and drowning, 322, 326–7
and foreknowledge, 298–9
and humour, 150–4
literary style, 365–7, 379, 381–2,
385–6, 388
and names, 164, 166, 168,
174–5, 184–5
and sex, 341
and smells, 53–4, 62–3
Lively, Penelope, 87
Locker, Arthur, 164
London Hackney Carriage Act, 18
Lord's Day Observance
Society, 366
Lovecraft, H. P., 29
Lytton, Edward Bulwer, 15, 17,
116, 215

McCarthy, Patrick, 242
McEwan, Ian, 293–4
Maclise, Daniel, 310, 338
Macready, William, 61, 66,
136, 203
Mantel, Hilary, 300
Martin Chuzzlewit, 149, 310
'as if' constructions, 17, 31–2, 38
and clichés, 222–3, 229–31,
238, 241–2
and coincidences, 199–203
and different voices, 267–8
and drowning, 315, 321–2
and humour, 146–7
literary style, 386–7
and names, 156–8, 163–4,
168, 170–1
and present tense, 77–8
and smells, 64–5
and the supernatural, 106–8

Mathews, Charles, 248–50, 268
Mayhew, Henry, 258
mesmerism, 111–12
Metropolitan Sanitary
    Association, 57
miasmas, 56–7
Mieder, Wolfgang, 229
Milton, John, 120
    Paradise Lost, 197
Mitchell, Charlotte, 47
Mitton, Thomas, 61
monopylologues, 248–9
Moor, Edward, 259
Morley, Henry, 16, 115
Morning Chronicle, 60, 311
Mulock, Dinah, 113
Murdoch, Iris, 127
mutton fat, used in candles, 58
Mystery of Edwin Drood, The,
    13, 270
    and coincidences, 193–4
    and foreknowledge, 306–8
    literary style, 367
    and names, 164, 172, 187
    and sex, 360–2
    and shifts of tense, 71–2,
        88, 92–4
    and smells, 69–70
    and the supernatural, 125
    and swimming and
        drowning, 312–13

names, 155–88
    cratylic, 168–9
    eponyms, 156
    probable, 172
    taken from life, 165
narration, first- and third-person,
    13, 73–4, 77, 87, 271–2, 284,
    303, 310, 365, 368

Nicholas Nickleby, 66, 136
    'as if' constructions, 19, 36–7
    and clichés, 227–8
    and coincidences, 200–1
    and different voices, 252–5, 259,
        265–6, 273–6
    and drowning, 322, 332, 335
    and humour, 139–41, 144
    literary style, 372–4
    and names, 158, 175–9
    and sex, 354–5

Obesity Hypoventilation
    Syndrome (OHS), 135
Old Curiosity Shop, The, 4, 12, 37
    and clichés, 242–3
    and coincidences, 202
    and different voices, 268,
        270–1, 273
    and drowning, 312–13, 317,
        331, 333
    and humour, 142–5
    and names, 169, 171, 179
    and present tense, 77
    and sex, 358
    and smells, 65
Oliver Twist, 8
    and clichés, 231
    and coincidences, 200
    and different voices, 263–4, 268
    and drowning, 317, 330
    and humour, 135–8, 140
    literary style, 366–7, 372
    and names, 156, 168, 173–4
    and sex, 345–7
Omnibus, 258
Ondaatje, Michael, 87
orphans and abandoned children,
    137–8, 375–6
Orwell George, 19, 58

Our Mutual Friend, 10, 128, 138
  'as if' constructions, 17, 30,
    32, 35, 38
  book titles, 234
  and clichés, 226–7, 234,
    236–8, 241
  and different voices,
    247–8, 279–80
  and drowning, 313, 319–20,
    327–8, 330–1, 333–5
  literary style, 368, 374–7,
    384–5, 389
  and names, 165–7, 169–70, 174,
    181–2, 185–6
  and shifts of tense, 72, 88–92
Owen, Robert, 117
Oxford English Dictionary (*OED*),
    6, 155, 157, 220, 259, 345, 367

Paris morgue, 323–5
Partridge, Eric, 220
Pickwick Papers, The, 4, 18
  and clichés, 232, 240–1
  and coincidences, 198–9
  and different voices,
    250–2, 257–63
  and drowning, 318–19
  and humour, 130–5
  literary style, 371–2
  and names, 155–7, 172–3
  and smells, 67, 70
  and the supernatural, 104–5,
    126
  wellerisms, 157, 259–61
Pictures from Italy, 45, 378
police news, 247–8
Poole, Adrian, 334
Pope, Alexander, *Essay on
    Man*, 260–1
Printers' Pension Society, 10

Privy Council Education
    Lists, 165–7
prolepsis, *see* foreknowledge
prostitution, 338, 346–8
proverbs, 157, 229, 231–2, 234–5,
    242, 333, 381
Punch and Judy shows, 141–2

Quarterly Review, 136

rabbits, smell of, 64
Radcliffe, Anne, 104
railway boom, 382–3
Rake's Progress, The, 69
Red Riding Hood, 320
Regent's Canal, 325
Rochester Cathedral, 67, 69–70
Royal Charter shipwreck, 326
Royal Humane Society, 322–3, 332
Rudd, Martha, 338

Sala, George Augustus, 113–14
Santayana, George, 145
Sartre, Jean-Paul, 85
Scott, Sir Walter, 104
serialisation, 4, 10, 284
sewers, 57, 61
sex, 337–62
  between masters and
    servants, 358–60
Shakespeare, William, 5–6, 261
  Hamlet, 96
  King Lear, 241
  Macbeth, 6, 37, 291, 303–4,
    308, 335
  *A Midsummer Night's
    Dream*, 274
  Othello, 274
Sketches by Boz, 18–19, 65, 331,
    370, 379

'The Poetical Young
     Gentleman', 376
Slater, Michael, 169
Small, Helen, 9
smells, 41–70
     and childhood, 48–9, 51–3
     in *Jane Eyre*, 82
Smollett, Tobias, 58–60, 370
soap, smell of, 42–5, 64
Socrates, 120
Spark, Muriel, 293
speaking, ways of, *see* voices
     different
spiritualism, 115–20
Spontaneous Combustion, 54–5
Stanfield, Clarkson, 65
Sterne, Laurence
     A Sentimental Journey, 59
     Tristram Shandy, 184–5
Stone, Harry, 9, 28–9, 324
Stone, Marcus, 10, 90, 364
street magicians, 33
'Streets, The – Night', 245
suicide, 130–1
     by drowning, 321–3, 326, 329–31
supernatural, the, 95–126
     'true' accounts of, 113–14
     Victorian novelists and, 101–4
     see also ghost stories;
          spiritualism
Sutherland, John, 58
Swift, Graham, 86
swimming, 309–12
Sykes, Lady Henrietta, 338

Tale of Two Cities, A, 112
     'as if' constructions, 32, 34–5
     and coincidences, 194–5
     and drowning, 323
     and foreknowledge, 299–302
     literary style, 365, 374, 383–4

and names, 166, 172
Tayler, Mary Elizabeth, 141
tenses, 12, 52, 71–94, 299–300
     in modern fiction, 85–8, 300
Ternan, Ellen, 339
Thackeray, William
     Makepeace, 128
Thompson, T. J., 321
Tomalin, Claire, 339
Trollope, Anthony, 1, 93, 363–4

umbrellas, 65, 157, 380
Uncommercial Traveller, the, *see*
     All the Year Round

'Victorian' (the word), 345
voices, different, 245–80
     defined as idiolects, 249–52, 406
     London dialect, 258–9
     tell-tale phrases, 268–9
vomit, smell of, 45–6

Walker, John, 258
Warren's blacking factory, 49, 164
Washington, DC, 78
Waterloo Bridge, 327, 331
Waters, Sarah, 88
Watts, George Frederic, 327, 329
Wellington House Academy, 5, 203
White, Rev. James, 116
Wiles, William, 5
Wills, W. H., 115, 119, 281
Winter, Henry, 153, 202
Wooley, George, 270
Woolf, Virginia, *The Waves*, 85–6
Wright, Thomas, 339

Yorkshire Schools, 141

Zola, Emile, 146

A Note on the Author

John Mullan is Lord Northcliffe Professor of Modern
English Literature at University College London. He has
published extensively on eighteenth- and nineteenth-
century literature. He is also a prolific broadcaster and
journalist, and writes on contemporary fiction for the
Guardian. In 2009 he was one of the judges for the Man
Booker Prize. His most recent book is *What Matters in
Jane Austen?*. He has lectured widely on both Austen
and Dickens in the UK and the US, and makes regular
appearances at UK literary festivals. He lives in London.

A Note on the Type

The text of this book is set Adobe Garamond. It is one of several versions of Garamond based on the designs of Claude Garamond. It is thought that Garamond based his font on Bembo, cut in 1495 by Francesco Griffo in collaboration with the Italian printer Aldus Manutius. Garamond types were first used in books printed in Paris around 1532. Many of the present-day versions of this type are based on the *Typi Academiae* of Jean Jannon cut in Sedan in 1615.

Claude Garamond was born in Paris in 1480. He learned how to cut type from his father and by the age of fifteen he was able to fashion steel punches the size of a pica with great precision. At the age of sixty he was commissioned by King Francis I to design a Greek alphabet, and for this he was given the honourable title of royal type founder. He died in 1561.